For Our CATHOLIC, ORTHODOX, *and* PROTESTANT *Friends*

For Our CATHOLIC, ORTHODOX, and PROTESTANT Friends

DAN KANE

Pleasant Word
A Division of WINEPRESS PUBLISHING

Pleasant Word (a division of WinePress Publishing, PO Box 428, Enumclaw, WA 98022) functions only as book publisher. As such, the ultimate design, content, editorial accuracy, and views expressed or implied in this work are those of the author.

All biblical quotes are from the "Holy Bible," Imprimatur, Rt. Rev. MSGR. Francis W. Byrne, Vicar General, Archdiocese of Chicago, May 6, 1969, 1969 edition (Douay-Challoner text), Catholic Bible Publishers, Chicago, Illinois, unless indicated otherwise. Words in italics enclosed within parenthesis within quotes are not part of the Bible text but are added for clarity. Words in italics not in parenthesis are for emphasis. In a relatively few instances, the King James Version (kjv) of the Holy Bible is cited because in those instances it is clearer in its translation than the Catholic Bible. Such citations are clearly identified as such by the letters kjv. In some instances, the New King James Version is cited for clarity, nkjv.

ISBN 13: 978-1-4141-1143-8
ISBN 10: 1-4141-1143-6
Library of Congress Catalog Card Number: 2007908746

To God be the glory
Great things He hath done,
So loved He the world that
He gave us His Son,
Who yielded His life
an atonement for sin
And opened the lifegate
That all may go in.
Praise the Lord!

CONTENTS

I noticed an unusually large book. Its immediate neighbor had been a gift, a book on wines for connoisseurs. I had never had inclination to open it. I had simply exiled it to the same location as its larger neighbor.

The Bible Is the Only Book Ever to Bring About Successful Heart Transplants

The spine on the behemoth looked like new, so new, in fact, I could read the two-word, gold-lettered title from where I sat. I got out of my recliner and reached for the green-bound book. It was heavier than any textbook. I turned on the reading light and sat back down.

Toward the top of the book was a well-done relief. It appeared to be a miniature reproduction of a classic painting. The colors, contrasts, and details were impressive. It portrayed a smooth-faced boy with dark, curly, shoulder-length hair who looked to be about twelve years old. He was dressed in a white robe with a golden girdle (wide belt). He seemed to be talking to several older, learned-looking men situated around him. One was seated. He held a large book in his hands. Another stood holding a scroll. The men wore pensive looks above their long beards. They appeared to be listening to what the lad was saying and checking his words to see if they were true. The two words under the picture read simply: Holy Bible.

I felt confident that I knew as much about what was in the Bible as I knew about what was in any of those textbooks. After all, I had attended Catholic grade school, high school, and college. We had studied the Bible often, or at least what the nuns and priests told us was in the Bible. I couldn't remember any classes where the Scriptures had been used as the text. I recalled that short pieces from the Old Testament, the Gospels, and epistles were read at Mass and I had attended countless times in years past. I felt confident I had nothing new to learn.

I glanced out the window. The snow was still coming down with no hint of a letup. I abandoned all hope and opened the book. "In the beginning God created the heavens and the earth..." it read. Yep, I thought, I remember that verse. I decided to skip over to the Gospels.

I started in Matthew, "Saint Matthew," it was titled. I read the litany of "begats." I was puzzled for a moment, though, at 1:25: "And he (*Joseph*) did not know her (*Mary*) till she brought forth her firstborn son." The nuns and priests had been adamant that Mary was a perpetual virgin. I wondered how those little words *till* and *firstborn son* fit into the perpetual virginity doctrine. It briefly crossed my mind that it might be a Protestant Bible. Continuing in St. Matthew, I read through the familiar Sermon on the Mount, Jesus' healing miracles, the feeding of the five thousand,

and about a king who gave a marriage feast for his son. The story had no particular relevance. However, something caught my eye in 23:9. Jesus was criticizing the traditions of the Scribes and Pharisees, the hierarchal religious establishment of His day. He warned the people, "And call no one on earth your father; for one is your Father, who is in heaven." Give no one on earth the title of Father, I thought! But that's what priests are called. I read on. In Acts 8:16, I was surprised to learn that some had been baptized, but the Holy Spirit had not come upon them. This too, I knew, was contrary to Catholic teaching. I hurriedly flipped to the front of the book. On the inner page was the Imprimatur, along with a color picture titled, "Pope Paul VI and the Vatican, 1969 edition (Douay-Challoner text), published by Catholic Bible Publishers, Chicago, Illinois." My interest was no longer in getting out of the house.

What compelled me that cold, blustery January day, at the age of 41, to pick up a book in which I had never before had an interest puzzled me. I didn't understand until some time later. God used one of His smallest and most delicate creations, the snowflake, to turn me around, and bring me face to face with the Jesus of the New Testament, the prophesied Messiah of the Old Testament. This Jesus was previously unknown to me. By the time the snows of winter ended, I had accepted the Jesus of the New Testament as my Lord and Savior and made a pretty good start reading the only book ever to bring about successful heart transplants. I discovered that despite my earned degrees, I had lived a life devoid of wisdom [see Proverbs 9:10], totally lacking in knowledge [see Proverbs 1:7].

God Wants to Speak to You, Too

My sincerest hope is that you will begin to read this work and at some point be prompted to pick up the only book that has ever changed lives and, most important, eternal destinies. *If you allow it,* God will use the Scriptures to speak to your heart through His Holy Spirit. He will regenerate your dead spirit, seal you with the Holy Spirit for the day of your redemption, renew your mind, reveal the good works He has already prepared for you to walk in, and give you life everlasting. He stands at the door and knocks [see Apocalypse 3:20]. It is up to you to answer. The will of the Father is clear, as proclaimed in that beautiful Catholic Bible:

"For God so loved the *world* that he gave his only-begotten Son, that those who believe in him may not perish, but may have life everlasting. For God did not send his Son into the world in order to judge the world, but *that the world might be saved through him.* He who believes in him is not

judged: but he who does not believe is already judged, because he does
not believe in the name (*Jesus*) of the only-begotten Son of God."
—St. John 3:16-18

If God sent His Son to save *the world*, then that includes you.

The Bible Presents the Word of God

How can one be sure the Word of God is true and not just the musings
of men? The Catholic Bible has the answer. St. Peter tells us:

> "And we have the word of prophecy, surer still, to which you do well to
> attend (*study*), as to a lamp shining in a dark place, until the day dawns
> and the morning star rises in your hearts. This, then, you must understand
> first of all, that no prophecy of Scripture is made by private interpretation.
> For not by the will of man was prophecy brought at any time; but holy
> men of God spoke as they were moved by the Holy Spirit."
> —2 St. Peter 1:19-21

St. Peter assures us that no man wrote down his own thoughts. Rather,
holy men of God, who could and would respond to the prompting of the
Holy Spirit, wrote those things the Holy Spirit moved them to write. This
is referred to as "inspired" writing. The literal Greek translation is "God-
breathed." Old Testament prophets did not literally walk with Jehovah-God.
Therefore, they used the literary form, "Thus says the LORD," to make clear
that the written words were from the LORD. Those who wrote the books
of the New Testament walked with the Lord, that is, with Jesus. They were
personal witnesses and His friends. Therefore, there was no need for them
to preface their writings with, "Thus says the Lord."

The present-day understanding of "prophet" can be problematic. It is
often misinterpreted to mean one who can predict the future. However, the
word prophet means simply one who tells the truth. That truth, spoken
or written, may, from the prophet's perspective, be "past truth," "present
truth," or "future truth." But true prophecy is always from the Lord!

At the times of the writing of the individual books that make up the
Bible, about twenty-five to thirty percent of their content was future-truth
prophecy. This characteristic is unique to the Holy Bible. There are no
future-truth prophecies in the Hindu Vedas, or in the sayings of Buddha,
Confucius, Muhammed, or Zoroaster. God tells us that one of His reasons
for including future-truth prophecy in Scripture is to authenticate that the
revelations are from Him:

Remember the former age, for I am God, and there is no God beside (*me*), neither is there the like to me (*neither is there anyone like me, god or man*), who show from the beginning the things that shall be at last (*the future*), and from the ancient of times the things that as yet are not done, saying: My counsel shall stand, and all my will shall be done.

—Isaias 46:9-10

God tells us in His Holy Word the endings of things even before their beginnings! Moreover, these prophecies have been fulfilled literally and exactly as described by the prophets. For example, the Old Testament contains numerous references to a people called Hittites (also spelled Hethites, sons of Heth). For centuries, unbelieving archaeologists and anthropologists had not only dismissed the notion of any such people, but used the lack of historical proof of their existence to denigrate those who accepted the Bible literally. That changed in 1906 when the royal archives of the Hittites were discovered in excavations at Bogazköy in central Turkey. Today, one can earn a college degree in Hittitology.

Jesus' coming to earth as the suffering servant, along with His death, manner of death, burial, and resurrection were prophesied in dozens of Old Testament verses, all of which were fulfilled in the minutest detail. Some New and Old Testament prophecies are yet to be fulfilled. Many of these relate to Jesus' Second Coming as King of kings and Lord of lords. Most of the book of Apocalypse is future-truth prophecy. All prophecy is "past truth" from God's perspective.

During the 6th century B.C. Babylonian captivity, the prophet Daniel foretold in chronological order the future world kingdoms that would rule over Jerusalem. These kingdoms included the Medes and Persians; Greeks; Romans; and, lastly, the earthly millennial (1,000 years) kingdom of Jesus. During His ministry, Jesus specifically referred to many Old Testament prophets by name, including Daniel [St. Matthew 24:15], thus affirming their validity.

Early believers considered the writings that would one day be assembled to form the New Testament to be the inspired Word of God. In 2 St. Peter 3:16, he refers to St. Paul's epistles as "Scriptures." In St. Peter's mind there was no distinction between the writings of the Hebrew Bible (Old Testament) and St. Paul's epistles. He considered both "God-breathed." Deuteronomy 13:1-6 commands us to test the words of the prophets and gives us criteria by which to evaluate their veracity. More will be said on this later.

The Relationship Between God's Word and Tradition

In attempting to defend the role of tradition against the infallible Word of God, when tradition clearly contradicts God's Word, some apologists argue that the Bible wasn't written until hundreds of years after the death and resurrection of Jesus. The implication is that tradition was in existence long before God's Word in the New Testament and, therefore, tradition must take precedence.[1] This is more than a little misleading. While the writings that one day would be assembled into the New Testament had not been put together in a single book at the time of St. Peter, St. Peter's words in 2 St. Peter 3:16 clearly demonstrate that St. Paul's writings were in existence and well circulated among Christian communities at that time. Moreover, if certain Christian traditions were being practiced prior to the writing of the New Testament, then one would logically expect to see such traditions endorsed in those books. On the other hand, if traditions practiced after the writing of the books are not sanctioned in them but, in fact, are contradicted by God's Word, then such traditions are the traditions of men. More will be said about this in later chapters.

How does the Roman Catholic Church view Scripture? According to the Catechism of the Catholic Church, the Scriptures are inspired by Almighty God and are free from error.[2] However, following the fiasco involving Galileo, the Catholic Church modified its position. It now stipulates that Scriptures are infallible with regard to faith and morals, but not with regard to the physical universe. The Church and Galileo controversy will be explored in chapter five.

What Is the Biblical Meaning of "Church"?

The New Testament uses two different Greek words for church. The first, *ekklesia*, is used to designate a local assembly of believers such as the church at Jerusalem or the church at Antioch. The second, *autos*, is used to designate an institution. God created three institutions: marriage, human government, and His church.

The Bible teaches that the *ekklesia* is the body of Christ on earth. Jesus' physical body is in heaven. Therefore, numerous local churches function as His body in countless communities worldwide. They spread the gospel and minister to the needs of the sheep. Jesus is the head of each local church. If one changes the head, then one also changes the body since the head is part of the body. If a man is the head of a church, then that church cannot be the body of Christ.

The English word "church" is used some 115 times in the New Testament. Some 92 times it refers to a local congregation, *ekklesia*. The other 23 references are to the institution. It is in this sense that the word "company" is used in, "And day by day the Lord added to their company (*autos*) such as were to be saved" [Acts 2:47]. On the other hand, when Jesus said, "... upon this rock I will build my church," He used *ekklesia* [St. Matthew 16:18].

As used in this work, the non-capitalized word "church" refers to an *ekklesia*. It functions under the direction of one or more pastors and several deacons and is autonomous. The capitalized word "Church" refers to a collection of churches (*ekklesia*) in a hierarchical relationship under the control of a denomination that considers itself to be "The Church." These generally speak of salvation in terms of "religion," "sacraments," and "process" and tend to think within the framework of Protestantism versus Catholicism. They also follow so-called "tradition" rather than the Scriptures. Examples include The Roman Catholic Church, The Old Catholic Church (denies papal infallibility), The Greek Orthodox Church, The Russian Orthodox Church, The Albanian Orthodox Church, The Syrian Orthodox Church, The Ukrainian Orthodox Church, The Bulgarian Orthodox Church, The Romanian Orthodox Church, The Serbian Orthodox Church, The Antiochian Orthodox Church, The Anglican Church, The Episcopal Church, some Lutheran Churches, The Methodist Church, some Presbyterian Churches, etc. Each believes to varying degrees that it, and it alone, controls the entrance to the kingdom of heaven and that apart from it there is no salvation. Each also subscribes to "replacement theology." More will be said on this in later chapters.

The Old Catholic Church separated from the Roman Catholic Church in 1871, following the First Vatican Council's 1870 declaration that the pope is infallible. While the Catholic Church claims that it has always taught papal infallibility, it was only after this teaching was incorporated as doctrine, something the faithful *must* accept, that the Old Catholics split. Today, there are more than 70,000 Old Catholics in the U.S.[3]

Some attach a unique and even mystical significance to the word "church." They mistakenly believe this idea to be unique to the New Testament. However, its Old Testament equivalent is "congregation," which appears many times. The word "congregation" is used once in the New Testament where its meaning is the same as "church," *ekklesia*. In either case, it refers to the same thing: a called out assembly to do the work of God on earth. Many who belong to the various Churches, which stress the role of "The Church" in salvation, mistakenly believe that Jesus spent much time preaching about His Church. They are surprised to learn that Jesus mentioned the word "church" only three times, all recorded in the Gospel of St. Matthew [once in 16:18 and twice in 18:17]. In all three instances, He referred to an *ekklesia*, never to an *autos*. On the other hand, Jesus referred to the written Word, that is, the Scriptures, the Law and the Prophets, many times, as recorded in all four Gospels [e.g., see St. Matthew 5:17-18; 7:12; 11:13; 22:40; St. Mark 15:28; St. Luke 4:21; 10:26; 16:16; 24:44; St. John 5:39; 7:38; 13:18; and 17:12]. Moreover, the Gospels record numerous instances of Jesus scolding the Scribes, Pharisees, Sadducees, and others for not knowing the Scriptures [e.g., see St. Matthew 12:3; 12:5; 19:4; 21:16; 21:42; 22:29; 22:31; St. Mark 12:10; 12:24-27; St. Luke 6:3; and St. John 7:19]. Some of these are addressed in later chapters.

With this brief background, let us now proceed to get a better understanding of how God's Holy Word came down to man. Most biblical citations are from the Roman Catholic Bible, Douay-Challoner text unless otherwise indicated. A few citations are from the King James Version (KJV) or the New King James Version (NKJV) where that version provides a clearer meaning. See the following note for details concerning citations and use of italics.[4]

Chapter 1

WHOSE BIBLE IS IT, ANYWAY?

THE BIBLE CONTINUES to be the best-selling book in the U.S. However, it never appears on the New York Times' best-seller list. It certainly is not the most widely read book. Someone remarked that "Bible" is really an acrostic for "Basic Instructions Before Leaving Earth."

Many admit they do not read the Bible because their denominations do not allow them to interpret what God's Word says. Jehovah's Witnesses is but one example. Also known as the Watchtower and Bible Tract Society, Jehovah's Witnesses conduct an aggressive door-to-door witnessing program across the U.S. and in other countries. The Society was founded by Charles T. Russell in 1884. Russell felt that the concept of the Trinity, among other teachings in Scripture, was too difficult to comprehend. Therefore, the Society does not believe in the divinity of either Jesus or the Holy Spirit. Thus, the Jesus of the Witnesses is not the Jesus of the New Testament. However, they *claim* the Scriptures are the inspired Word of God. Moreover, they maintain that there is no conflict between what their Society teaches and what the Scriptures teach. Many Churches and churches claim to believe in the Scriptures but then proceed to modify the Jesus and teachings described therein to support their particular doctrines. When asked to explain the meaning of verses such as,

... Let *us* make mankind in *our* image...

—Genesis 1:26

And he (*the Lord*) said, 'Indeed! The man has become like one of *us*, knowing good and evil...

—Genesis 3:22

1

"Let *us* go down, and there confuse their language so that they will not understand one another's speech..."

—Genesis 11:7

and

And I heard the voice of the Lord, saying: Whom shall I send, and who shall go for *us*?

—Isaias 6:8

the Witnesses reply that only the president of the Society is permitted to interpret Scripture.

No one reads a book written in a language he cannot understand. When a Church tells its members they can read the Bible, even encourages them to do so, but cautions that only the Church can interpret its meaning, the members are logically disinclined to read. Yet, this is exactly what many denominations do. Such a prohibition is the mark of a cult, as will be explored in chapter two.

A common but mistaken notion among those unfamiliar with the Bible is that there are numerous versions of "the Bible," Catholic, Protestant, Orthodox, Byzantine, Alexandrian, and others, each describing a different path to salvation. This is not true. However, before addressing this point, let's take a brief moment to get some idea of how we got that precious book known by simple titles such as "Holy Bible" and "The Book."

Who Wrote the Books of the Bible?

The writings that comprise the Bible were written by more than forty scribes over a period of more than fifteen-hundred years.[1] The writers lived on three continents—Africa, Asia, and Europe—and spoke three primary languages: Hebrew, Aramaic, and Greek. They had occupations spanning the full range of human endeavors and were most often called and used by God while simultaneously continuing to perform their day-to-day jobs. These included farmers, shepherds, fishermen, tent makers, tax collectors, rich men, poor men, a physician, and even a king.

Why Was God's Holy Word Written Down?

In the Old Testament, God commanded Moses to write down the things He would reveal to him and to take His commandments to the people. The prophets often included God's command to "write it in a book." God tells us why He wanted His Word written down:

Now therefore go in and write (*it*) for them upon (*a*) box (*clay tablet*), and note it diligently in a book (*scroll*), and it shall be in latter days (*the time after Jesus' ascension*) for a testimony for ever.

—Isaias 30:8

God tells us that His written Word is to be a testimony for ever! In St. Matthew 24:35, Jesus revealed, "Heaven and earth will pass away, but *my words* will not pass away." Words passed down orally through tradition do pass away. You probably participated in a school exercise where a short, simple story was started at the first desk and transmitted orally, whispered by one student to another and so on, until it reached the last student. The first and last versions were compared. The story changed in the span of a relatively few minutes among a relatively few transmitters. Even common sense tells us that in order to preserve what is said, it must be *written*. This has been standard practice in law, business, and virtually all human endeavors since recorded history began. The fact that Jesus promised that His words would not pass away is what allows St. Peter to conclude:

'... the word of the Lord endures forever.' Now this is the word of the gospel that was preached to you.

—1 St. Peter 1:25

There is no recording in the Gospels of Jesus directing His disciples to "write it in a book." However, Jesus told His disciples He was going away and that where He was going they could not follow at that time [St. John 13:31-36]. In chapter 14, He assured them that there were many mansions in His Father's house and that He would return for them. In verse 26 He revealed, "But the Advocate, the Holy Spirit, whom the Father will send in my name, he will teach you *all things*, and bring to your mind whatever (*the things*) I have said to you." Jesus' promise that they would be taught "all things" by the Holy Spirit and led into remembrance of all things He had said was necessary so they could faithfully record His words in the books of the New Testament. This will be discussed in more detail in chapter four. Following His resurrection, Jesus told St. John (around 95 A.D.): "... What thou seest write in a book..." [see Apocalypse 1:11].

All Books of the New Testament Were Completed by 95 A.D.

Some state sincerely, but nonetheless erroneously, that the Roman Catholic Church or Catholics wrote the Bible. That is what they have been taught. That is what I was taught. Most realize this is not true, certainly not for the Old Testament. The Old Testament was completed four hundred years before Jesus' birth and was written by Jews.

After the coming of the Holy Spirit at Pentecost, the followers of Jesus obeyed His command to be His witnesses [see St. Matthew 28:19-20]. As early as 95 A.D., there were established churches with large memberships in Jerusalem and Antioch [Acts 11:26], as well as in Ephesus, Smyrna, Pergamum, Thyatira, Sardis, Philadelphia, and Laodicea, as revealed in chapters 2 and 3 of the book of Apocalypse. There were also churches at Corinth, Philippi, Colosse, Thessalonica, and multiple churches at Galatia [see Galatians 1:2]. It is also generally agreed among most Catholic, Protestant, and Orthodox theologians that the book of Apocalypse (in the Catholic Bible, Revelation in the Orthodox Study Bible and King James Version) was the last book written. All the books that make up the New Testament were completed by 95 A.D. However, most were completed much earlier. Neither the gospels nor the epistles speak of Nero's persecutions which began around 64 A.D. Neither do they mention St. James' martyrdom in 62 A.D., the Jewish revolt in 66 A.D., nor the destruction of the Temple in 70 A.D. The reason is that these books were written, copied, and circulated among the early churches before these events occurred.

The churches were autonomous. The word "bishop" meant pastor. There were no bishops acting over several churches and no cardinals acting over the bishops. Neither was there a "Pope," nor a Bishop of Rome, acting over all. The Nicolaites established a clerical hierarchy over the laity at Pergamum during the first century. However, as recorded in Apocalypse 2:6 and 2:15, Jesus condemned this practice. More will be said about the Nicolaites in chapter five.

Many Catholics have been told that the Bible records Jesus saying, "My Church will be Catholic." However, this is not true. The word "catholic" comes from the Greek word *katholikos* which means "universal." St. Vincent of Lérins is credited with defining and applying the concept of a single, catholic or universal Church to the many disparate churches that accepted Roman Emperor Constantine's invitation to join him and form an Empire-wide *religion* early in the 4th century. According to St. Vincent's definition, the Catholic Church is the custodian of, "That which has been believed everywhere, always, and by all. This is what is truly and properly catholic."[2] As will be explored in chapter five, not all autonomous, persecution-wearied churches accepted Constantine's invitation. Thus, it is clear that neither Constantine's universal Church nor the Roman Catholic Church nor any of their members could be credited with having written any part of the New Testament. Moreover, many of the doctrines taught in the New Testament are in direct opposition to those taught by the Catholic Church. For example, Jesus told His followers not to give the title of "Father" to any spiritual leader because only The Father in heaven is their spiritual Father [St. Matthew 23:9]. The Bible also records that Mary did not remain a virgin after Jesus' birth, and that Jesus had brothers and sisters [St. Matthew 1:25, 13:55; St. Mark 3:31; St. Luke 8:19-21; and St. John 2:12, 7:3-10]. Like the Old Testament, the New Testament warned believers to stay away from graven images [Acts 15:20; 1 St. John 5:21]. These are just a few of the many divergent teachings between the New Testament recorded in the Roman Catholic Bible, and the manmade traditions of the Roman Catholic Church.

The Writings That Would One Day Comprise the New Testament Were Widely Circulated Among the Early Churches

Sometimes people remark, "If Jesus wanted a New Testament, then why didn't He write it instead of establishing His church?" Others note that Jesus never wrote so much as one line of Scripture.[3] The answer is that God chose to enter onto the human stage in a very personal way—as the Son of Man, God in human flesh. While some apologists contend that, "The Apostles were never reported to have circulated a single volume of the Holy Scriptures,"[4] this is misleading on several counts. First, what is meant by "volume"? Biblical terms generally include New Testament, Old Testament, Scriptures, books, and writings. The word Bible comes from the Greek, *biblion*, meaning book. However, the term volume is unknown in the area of biblical exegesis. Also, what is meant by "reported"? Certainly it is not *reported* in the New Testament that the apostles believed in the Trinity, because the word "Trinity" does not appear in the Bible! If these apologists are trying to mislead people into believing that the writings that would later be assembled into the New Testament were not in wide circulation among the early churches, then what are we to do with 2 St. Peter 3:16, discussed in the Introduction, wherein St. Peter referred to St. Paul's writings as "Scriptures"? St. Peter was certainly under the impression that St. Paul's epistles, like his own, were widely circulated. Even a casual reading of the epistles reveals that they were shared among the early churches:

> Timothy, my fellow-laborer, greets you, and Lucius, and Jason, and Sosipater, my kinsmen. I, Tertius, who have written (*a scribe*) this epistle, greet you in the Lord.
> —Romans 16:21-22

> I wrote to you in the letter not to associate with....
> —1 Corinthians 5:9

You are our letters, written on our hearts....

—2 Corinthians 3:2

Greetings to the brethren who are at Laodicea and to Nymphas and the church (*ekklesia*) that is in his house. And when this letter has been read among you, see that it be read in the church of the Laodiceans also; and that you yourselves read the letter from Laodicea.

—Colossians 4:15-16

I charge you by the Lord that this epistle be read to all the holy brethren (*believers*).

—1 Thessalonians 5:27

And if anyone does not obey our word by this letter, note that man and do not associate with him, that he may be put to shame.

—2 Thessalonians 3:14

This, beloved, is now the second epistle that I am writing to you....

—2 St. Peter 3:1

Moreover, in the Gospel that bears his name, St. John clearly states that testimonies were being written at that time:

There are, however, many other things that Jesus did; but if every one of these should be written, not even the world itself, I think, could hold *the books that would have to be written*. Amen.

—St. John 21:25

Finally, St. Paul prophesied that the Word of God would soon be made complete:

For we know in part and we prophesy in part; but when that which is perfect (*complete*) has come, that which is imperfect (*partial knowledge and partial prophecy*) will be done away with.

—1 Corinthians 13:9-10

New Testament Canon of Scripture Identified by Early Churches

The individual books were assembled into what we call the New Testament around 397 A.D., some three hundred years after the death of St. John, the last apostle to die. St. John, who died a natural death, wrote a number of books, including the last book, the Apocalypse, which he wrote while exiled on the Island of Patmos during the reign of Emperor

Domitian around 95 A.D. However, the collection of writings we call the New Testament was recognized by Christians long before 397. A heresy questioning the deity of Jesus was being promoted by certain factions that taught Jesus was only human until His baptism, at which time He became deity. The heretical Cerinthians were led by Paul of Samosata, the bishop (pastor) of the church at Antioch. In refuting this Gnostic heresy in 268 A.D., the Synod of Antioch (an assembly of members from that church) found such teaching to be "foreign to the ecclesiastical canon." Moreover, during the Great Persecution under Emperor Diocletian beginning in 303, the individual writings that would later be assembled into the New Testament were confiscated and destroyed. The fact that copies of these writings were preserved so that today we have them is an indication of how widespread those writings were among the early churches. Also, in 363, the Council of Laodicea decreed that only the canonized books, as opposed to the Apocrypha, were to be read from the pulpits. Thus, the Gospels and epistles of St. Paul, St. Peter, St. James, and others were widely held and identified as canon among early Christians. Gutenberg published the first Bible around 1450 A.D. It should be understood that churches and councils derive their authority from the Scriptures [see Acts 15:1-35]. The Scriptures do not derive their authority from any Church or Church Council.

Apocryphal Books of the Old Testament

The original canon contained forty-six books in the Old Testament and twenty-seven in the New. However, only certain books were considered inspired. These included all of the New Testament and thirty-nine books of the Old Testament. Books considered not to be inspired, but included for historical reasons, are called Apocrypha, which means "hidden." In the first publications of the canon, the seven apocryphal books were noted as such in the index and in the titles. This notation remained through the production of the Latin translation by Jerome, called the Vulgate, in the late 4th century. In 1546 A.D., the Council of Trent, in response to the Protestant Reformation, called the Vulgate the Church's only authentic version of the Bible and instructed that the books with previous apocryphal designations be inserted into the revised version without such designations.[5] This was in part a posthumous slap in the face to Martin Luther (1483-1546) and many other reformers inside the Roman Catholic Church who, in pursuing reforms from *within* their Church, advocated deletion of the non-inspired Apocrypha.

A Revised Vulgate Is Commissioned by Pope Sixtus V

Due to a number of disputes among Catholic theologians following the Reformation, a revised version of the Vulgate was commissioned by Pope Sixtus V (1585-1590). When presented with the revision in 1588, Sixtus opined that the work was "too scholarly" and decided to conduct the re-write himself. He wrote a papal Bull, *Aeternus Ille*, in which he declared his version to have been "… approved by the authority of the Lord," and warned it was to be held as "… unquestioned in all public and private discussions, preachings and explanations."[6] After Sixtus' death, a successor, Pope Gregory XIV (1590-1591), inherited Sixtus' papal Bull, complete with threats of excommunication and declaration that the revised Vulgate was the only true Bible approved by the Lord.

Pope Gregory recognized that the work contained numerous errors inserted by Sixtus himself. Roman Church theologians were unable to agree on how to address the problem. Prominent Catholics like Wycliff, Hus, Erasmus, and Luther had been pushing the Church toward reforms that would move Catholicism toward total reliance on Scripture, a position referred to as *Sola Scriptura*, and away from what reformers called "damnable traditions." The internal battle had gotten so vociferous that in 1546 the Council of Trent had no choice but to declare Church tradition on the same level of authority as Scripture, more or less. This will be discussed in more detail in chapter five. The Council also directed that the non-inspired Apocrypha be viewed on the same level of authority as the thirty-nine inspired books in the Old Testament.[7] At this point the reformers and their faithful followers had no choice but to separate themselves from what they believed to be an apostate Roman Catholic Church.

In order to limit the damage done by Sixtus' revised Vulgate, Father Robert Bellarmine cunningly advised Pope Gregory to halt further production, remove the errors inserted by Sixtus, and then resume issuance of a corrected Vulgate under Sixtus' name. Bellarmine was determined to protect the image of the papacy at all costs. With regard to errant copies already in circulation, courtesy of a new invention called the printing press, Bellarmine suggested that the Church buy them back and holders allow for same under penalty of excommunication and worse. In a short time the Inquisition in Venice and the Jesuit General (the worse) began to bring back copies of the error-riddled Sixtus Bible. Pope Clement VIII (1592-1605), Gregory's successor, released the largely corrected Vulgate under Pope Sixtus' name in 1592.[8] The indicator of apocryphal books was no longer included in the index or on book titles.

The People Petition the King for An English Version of the Bible

Shortly after Trent and the release of the "corrected" Sixtus Bible, the people petitioned King James I on several matters, including the need for a Bible in the English language.[9] Given the turmoil in the Roman world over the production of a new Latin Bible, it is little wonder that the people feared for what might be passed off as Scripture. However, the king's Anglican roots were buried deep in the soil of Catholic tradition. None of their petitions was granted except the production of an English Bible free from papal chicanery. The Authorized King James Version of the Holy Bible was printed and subsequently distributed free to the people in 1611.

The Catholic and King James New Testaments Are Virtually Identical

With all the machinations concerning the production, distribution, recall, redrafting, reformation, and free dissemination of "Bibles" during the late 1500s to early 1600s by Catholics and Protestants, one might expect that there would be significant differences between what has come to be known as the historical Catholic version of the Holy Bible and the Authorized King James Version. In fact, there is little difference. Whereas the Catholic version kept the apocryphal books and dropped the distinction between what is apocryphal and what is inspired in the Old Testament, the original King James Version included the apocryphal books for historical reference only and retained their apocryphal designations. Some of the inspired Old Testament books have different titles and contain minor differences in the spelling of the names of some of the prophets, people, and locations. For example, books 1 and 2 Samuel and 1 and 2 Kings in the King James Version are called 1-4 Kings in the Catholic Bible. 1 and 2 Paralipomenon in the Catholic Bible are called 1 and 2 Chronicles in the King James Version. The Catholic Bible's Canticle of Canticles is called the Song of Solomon in the King James Version.

Today's Catholic Bible includes the seven apocryphal books in its Old Testament: Tobias, Judith, Wisdom, Sirach, Baruch, 1 Machabees, and 2 Machabees. The King James Version no longer includes them. The older, authoritative Hebrew text, referred to as the Hebrew Bible (Old Testament), did not contain the Apocrypha.[10] It contained the same thirty-nine books as the King James Version, although the books are presented in a different order. Genesis is first and 2 Chronicles (same as 2 Paralipomenon in the Catholic Bible) is last. Jesus endorsed the makeup of the Hebrew Bible, and therefore the makeup of the Old Testament as found in King James

Version. As recorded in St. Matthew 23:35, Jesus accused the Scribes and Pharisees of killing the prophets from Able to Zacharias. Able appears in Genesis and Zacharias appears in 2 Paralipomenon 17:7. Jesus accused them of murdering the prophets from beginning to end. Moreover, Josephus, the noted Jewish historian, recorded the Jews' rejection of the Apocrypha and Jesus never quoted or even mentioned one of the books during His ministry. Neither did any writers of the books of the New Testament refer to the Apocrypha, although they often made references to many other Old Testament books. Since the apocryphal books taught things contrary to the Law and the prophets, the Jews considered the Apocrypha to be not only impure, but dangerous as well![11] The apocryphal books were written after prophecy and direct revelation had ceased.[12] There were about four hundred years between Malachias, the last Old Testament prophet, and John the Baptist (who was actually the last Old Testament-type prophet). This silent period is confirmed in the apocryphal book of 1 Machabees:

> ... And there was a great tribulation in Israel, such as was not since the day, that there was no prophet seen in Israel.
> —1 Machabees 9:27

There is little difference between the New Testament portions of the English Douay-Challoner translation of Jerome's Latin Vulgate and the King James Version and, most important, no difference between what the two teach with regard to soteriology, the doctrine of salvation. Moreover, the Douay-Challoner translation is based on old texts that predate the injection of Textual Criticism (also called "higher criticism") such as is found in many modern translations (see below). As a child in Catholic school, I was taught to believe that there were great differences between Catholic and all others' views on attaining salvation—differences so important that all but Catholics are condemned to hell![13] However, if there is no difference between what the two Bibles teach about salvation, then the differences must originate somewhere outside the Word of God, that is, outside the Bible. And, in fact, such is the case. This point will be explained more fully in chapter five.

The psalmist wrote in Psalms 118 (119):89 (119:89 in the King James):

> Your word, O Lord, endures forever.

Spiritual Discernment Is Necessary for Correct Interpretation of Scripture

Some allege that the reason there are so many denominations is because there are so many different interpretations of Scripture. However, God's Word is clear as to the reason behind differing interpretations:

> ... our gospel... is veiled only to those who are perishing. In their case, the god of this world (*Satan*) has blinded their unbelieving minds, that they should not see the light of the gospel of the glory of Christ, who is the image of God.
>
> —2 Corinthians 4:3-4

Those who cannot accept the truth of Scripture have had their minds blinded to the truth of the gospel. Because they have not believed in the Jesus of the New Testament, they do not have discernment [see St. John 16:9]. This is what causes various denominations. More will be said in chapters four and five on how to obtain spiritual discernment so that Scripture can be interpreted correctly.

Only the Scriptures Identify the One and Only Path to the Father

God the Father gave mankind His Word in the person of Jesus the Christ [St. John 1:14]. Jesus gave us His Word during His earthly ministry. His disciples documented His Word in the books of the New Testament. Jesus established His church not to change His teaching, but to spread the gospel, the Good News. He gave believers His written Word, the New Testament, so they could separate that which is from God from manmade traditions which the New Testament writers warned would come. In fact, the traditions of men were already in existence at the time of Jesus and before:

> Then the Scribes and Pharisees from Jerusalem came to him saying, "Why do thy disciples transgress the traditions of the ancients? For they do not wash their hands when they take food." But he answered and said to them, "And why do you transgress the commandment of God because of your tradition?"
>
> —St. Matthew 15:1-3

Moreover, the Scripture is a moral compass. It points the way—the only way. If one rejects the authority of Scripture, he may, as he stands in front of Jesus for judgment, ask why He gave mankind His written Word. The response he will hear is: "For you. So you could find Me." After explaining that He was going away, Jesus said to His disciples:

> "'And where I go you know, and the way you know.' Thomas said to him, 'we do not know where thou art going, and how can we know the way?' Jesus said to him, 'I am the way, and the truth, and the life. No one comes to the Father but through me.'"
>
> —St. John 14:4-6

While none of us knows the way on our own, some of us know the One who does know the way. Similarly, I may not know the way to Boston, but I trust that the airline pilot does. Therefore, my way to Boston is through the pilot.

Again, Jesus promises:

> Heaven and earth will pass away, but my words will not pass away.
>
> —St. Matthew 24:35

and St. Peter confirms:

> For, "All flesh is as grass, and all its glory as the flower of grass; the grass withered, and the flower has fallen-but the word of the Lord endures forever."
>
> —1 St. Peter 1:24-25

Modern Translations of the Bible Are Not Recommended

While the historical Douay-Challoner Catholic text and the King James Version of the New Testament present the same gospel, many modern translations are corrupted on other doctrines. Therefore, translations such as the New International Version, American Standard Version, New American Version, New Jerusalem Bible, and the Revised Standard Version cannot be recommended for Bible study. Some seventy "modern" Bibles were published in the 20th century. All have been corrupted to some degree by textual criticism which inculcated the philosophies of German rationalism, Darwinism, and French skepticism. The King James Version, which is based on the original Greek *Textus Receptus* (received text), is recommended for Bible study. Also, the Catholic Church's older English translation, the Douay-Rheims (1582 A.D.), cannot be recommended. Bishop Richard Challoner corrected many of the errors in the earlier Douay-Rheims translation, which had been inserted to support evolving Catholic doctrines. For example, Genesis 3:15 in the Douay-Challoner reads: "I will put enmity between you and the woman, between your seed and her seed: He shall crush your head, and you shall lie in wait for his heel." Even most not familiar with the Bible are somewhat familiar with this passage. Satan caused Adam and Eve to sin, but God promised a future Redeemer who will crush Satan's head. However, Satan will strike His heel, which he did at the cross. With the Catholic Church's increasing emphasis on Mary, the Douay-Rheims retranslates Genesis 3:15: "I will put enmities between thee and the woman, and thy seed and her seed: *she* shall crush thy head, and thou shall lie in wait for *her* heel." Thus, the Douay-Rheims translation gives glory to Mary for overcoming Satan, rather than to Jesus. Perhaps you've seen an image of Mary treading on the head of the serpent. Another example of Catholic doctrine foreign to the Douay-Challoner translation but contained in the older Douay-Rheims is revealed in St. Mark 1:4: "John was in the desert baptizing, and preaching the baptism of *penance*, unto remission of sins." There was no concept of penance in Judaism. The Douay-Chaollner text records St. Mark 1:4: "there came John in the desert, baptizing and preaching a baptism of repentance for the forgiveness of sins." John was telling the people to repent, that is, to change their minds about their need for a Savior, to turn away from their attitude of self-righteousness. Bishop Challoner produced the Douay-Challoner text around 1752 A.D.

Let us proceed now with a clear understanding that the Bibles under discussion, the Douay-Challoner Catholic text, and the Authorized King James Version are virtually identical, with differences confined largely to the Old Testament and on matters not related to salvation. Also, *The Orthodox Study Bible, New Testament and Psalms*, is sometimes quoted in later chapters. This study Bible, too, is based on the received text and is therefore in concert with the New Testament gospel presented in the Douay-Challoner Roman Catholic Bible cited in this work and the King James Version. It should be noted that the versions quoted in this work often do not capitalize personal pronouns when referring to deity (Father, Jesus, and the Holy Spirit).

Chapter 2

WHY READ THE BIBLE?

AFTER HE WAS baptized in the River Jordan by John the Baptist, Jesus was led by the Holy Spirit into the desert to be tempted (tested). He had been fasting for forty days and nights and was hungry. Satan appeared and said, "... If thou art the Son of God, command that these stones become loaves of bread" [St. Matthew 4:3]. Jesus could have answered in many ways. He could have told Satan that He could create loaves of bread without stones. Jesus later did so on at least two occasions. As Creator of the universe and the One having all authority over everything in it, Jesus could have simply ordered Satan to depart, something He did several times during His public ministry. Rather than answer in any other way, however, Jesus replied, "It is written, 'Not by bread alone does man live, but by every word that comes forth from the mouth of God'" [St. Matthew 4:4]. It is written in Deuteronomy 8:3.

In the second temptation, Satan took Jesus into the holy city of Jerusalem to the pinnacle of the Temple and said, "... If thou art the Son of God, throw thyself down; for it is written, 'He will give his angels charge concerning thee; And upon their hands they shall bear thee up, lest thou dash thy foot against a stone'" [St. Matthew 4:6]. Jesus again deferred to Scripture: "It is written further, 'Thou shalt not tempt the Lord thy God'" [St. Matthew 4:7]. It is written in Deuteronomy 6:16.

In the third and last temptation, Satan took Jesus to a high mountain and showed Him all the kingdoms of the world and their glory and said, "... All these things will I give thee, if thou wilt fall down and worship me" [St. Matthew 4:9]. Jesus replied: "Begone, Satan! For it is written, 'The Lord thy God shalt thou worship and him only shalt thou serve'" [St. Matthew 4:10]. It is written in Deuteronomy 6:13.

There are several revealing points in the three tests. First, Jesus deferred to the written Word of God, the Scripture, in each response. If Jesus believed the Scripture so important that He used the written Word to rebuke Satan, how can we conclude anything less? Moreover, He did not dilute His responses with the traditions of men. He quoted God's Word as it appears in Scripture. Second, Satan, in his pride, tries to imitate God. This is what led to Lucifer's fall [Isaias 14:13-14]. That is why he incorporated the words "it is written" in his second temptation. He wanted to show Jesus that he, too, could quote Scripture. Jesus' response was poignant. By using the words, "It is written further," Jesus revealed that Satan had no spiritual discernment. In the third temptation, Satan offered Jesus the world and the glory thereof. The revealing point is that Jesus did not argue with Satan that the world was his to give [2 Corinthians 4:4 and Ephesians 2:2].

St. John records in the opening verse of the Gospel that bears his name:

> In the beginning was the Word, and the Word was with God; and the Word was God.
>
> —St. John 1:1

God's Word came to earth in human form in the person of Jesus, the Christ prophesied in the Old Testament and fulfilled in the New. While walking this earth, He spoke His Word to men. Shortly before leaving this earth, He promised His Word would remain, that is, just as in the Old Testament, it would be a testimony forever [see St. Matthew 24:35]. Thus, through the Scriptures, the Jesus of the New Testament, along with His promises, remains with men even to this day.

God's Word Instructs Believers on How to Live

One reason to study Scripture is to know how to live. In Ephesians Chapter 4, St. Paul tells those who have been born again—believers—to put off the old man with regard to their former lives and put on the new man in Christ Jesus. He encourages new Christians to stop their sinful ways, to get away from lying, speaking evil of their neighbors, and letting their righteous anger against sin cause them to fall into the devil's snare. Ephesians 6:10-18 tells the believer to accomplish these things by putting on the whole armor of God. Romans 1:17 tells us, "He who is just lives by faith." In 2 Corinthians 5:7, God's Word instructs believers to "... walk by faith and not by sight." Hebrews 11:1 tells us, "... faith is the substance of things hoped for, the evidence of things that are not seen." God's Word tells believers in Romans 14:7-8, "For none of us lives to himself, and none dies to himself; for if we live, we live to the Lord, or if we die, we die to the Lord. Therefore, whether we live or die, we are the Lord's." St. Paul cautions believers in Ephesians 4:30, "And do not grieve the Holy Spirit of God, in whom you were sealed for the day of redemption." Believers grieve the Holy Spirit by lying, being angry, and the other sins discussed in Ephesians 4:25-29. Finally, in 1 Thessalonians 4:18, St. Paul tells believers to "comfort one another with these words." These instructions for righteous living are put in context in subsequent chapters.

God's Word Assures Believers of their Eternal Destiny

Another reason to study Scripture is to know how to face death and understand what lies beyond the grave. St. Paul tells us as he is awaiting death in a Roman prison:

> As for me, I am already being poured out in sacrifice, and the time of my deliverance is at hand. I have fought the good fight, I have finished the course, I have kept the faith. For the rest (*his eternal destiny*), there is laid up for me a crown of justice (*righteousness*), which the Lord, the just Judge, will give to me in that day; yet not to me only, but also to those who love his coming.
>
> —2 Timothy 4:6-9

His remark about being poured out as a sacrifice was a reference to the blood flow associated with the daily sacrifices at the Temple. St. Paul knew he was to be executed shortly. But in facing death, he was not the least depressed. His remark about this being the time of his deliverance was a well-understood euphemism. St. Paul was just as confident about his eternal destiny. He expressed no fear about where he would go after departing this world. He knew that he and many others would receive their crowns for Christian service [see Apocalypse 22:12]. It will be received at the Bema Judgment Seat where the *works* of the *saved* will be judged. The question, "Did you build upon that foundation, which is Christ Jesus, with gold, silver, and precious stones, or with worthless materials like wood, hay, and straw?" will be answered [1 Corinthians 3:11-15]. This is different from the Great White Throne Judgment, which is the judgment only of the lost [Apocalypse 20:11-15]. Not all who are saved will receive crowns, but only the saved can receive them. St. Paul was looking forward to going to his mansion to be with his Lord forevermore [St. John 14:2]. As he stated in Philippians 1:21, "For me to live is Christ and to die is gain." Eternal security and the Bema judgment are addressed more fully in subsequent chapters.

God's Word Reveals the One and Only Path to Eternal Life

The Bible has a message in it. The high-level message in the Old Testament is that there is only one God: Jehovah. All other gods are false. The high-level message in the New Testament is that there is only one path to salvation and that is through the Lord Jesus, the Christ of the New Testament. Most do not know this. Many times we hear people say, "There are many paths to God and it doesn't matter which one you take. We all end up at the same place." If this extraordinary claim were true, then one would have to wonder why Jesus, the Creator of the universe, came to earth as the Son of Man—God in human flesh—and willingly became sin for us, suffered humiliation at the hands of His creatures, died an agonizing death on the cross, and let His payment for our sins *separate* Him from the Father for the first time in eternity? [see St. Matthew 27:46] If you believe what the Catholic Bible teaches, then not only does the path you take make a difference, it makes a difference for all your eternity! Jesus reveals:

> I am the way, and the truth, and the life. No one comes to the Father but through me.
>
> —St. John 14:6

Jesus' words do not fit—even badly—with the supposition that all paths lead to the same place. In fact, Jesus' words clearly contradict this satanic lie. Moreover, there is no parenthetical to add or substitute any saint, preacher, work, Church, church, or denomination. In St. Matthew 7:13-14, Jesus tells us:

> Enter by the narrow gate. For wide is the gate and broad is the way that leads to destruction, and many there are who enter that way. How narrow and close the way that leads to life! And few there are that find it.

The above citation puts to rest any notion of multiple paths. Also, those who feel that they must be in God's Church because their denomination is large should examine Jesus' words carefully. He is saying just the opposite. The broad way, that is, the most populated path, leads to hell.

In addressing the Sanhedrin, St. Peter boldly proclaimed salvation through Jesus' death and resurrection:

> Neither is there salvation in any other. For there is no other name under heaven given to men by which we must be saved.
>
> —Acts 4:12

St. Paul tells us in 2 Timothy 3:15-17 that:

> For from thy infancy thou hast known the Sacred Writings (*Scriptures*), which are able to *instruct thee unto salvation* by the faith which is in Christ Jesus. All Scripture is inspired by God and useful for teaching, for reproving, for correcting, for instructing in justice; that the man of God may be perfect (*complete*), equipped for every good work.

The reason "all paths lead to the same destination" is called a satanic lie is because, like all Satan's lies, it is so *nearly* true and so universally appealing. There are only two destinations taught in Scripture: heaven and hell. Only one path leads to heaven. All remaining paths, and there are many, do lead to the same place: hell. Thus, while Satan, a liar and the father of lies, tells us that all paths lead to the same place, the truth is *all paths save (except) one* lead to hell [see St. John 8:44]. Notice, too, in the above citation, that God's Word tells us that the believer must know the Scriptures in order to be *equipped for every good work*. No good work can be performed without knowing the Scriptures. Moreover, as will be demonstrated later, apart from God's Holy Word, one cannot even tell what works are good or where "good works" come from.

God's Word Tells Us That The *Work* the Believer is to Perform is *to Believe*

Some ask, "What *work* are we supposed to do to be saved?" Jesus reveals the surprising answer:

> They said therefore to him, 'What are we to do that we may perform the works of God?' In answer Jesus said to them, 'This is the work of God, that you believe (*trust*) in him (*Jesus*) whom he (*God the Father*) has sent.'
> —St. John 6:28-29

Man has a natural tendency to add to God's Word. It is hard for us to accept that our *work* is to *believe on* or *trust in* Jesus. However, as recorded in St. John 16:9, Jesus tells us that the sin of the world is that "... they do not *believe* in me." It should be noted that the belief in Jesus discussed in Scripture is not an intellectual belief such as one might believe in Einstein, even though never having met him. Rather, we are to believe Jesus is who He said He was and is, based on and confined within Scripture. If we have such belief, we will keep His commands [St. John 15:10]. Most believe in a Jesus different from the Jesus of the New Testament, as will be demonstrated later.

It just doesn't seem credible to most that salvation could be totally independent of our works. The reason for this lack of faith is the human experience in a fallen world. As human beings, we constantly bargain with each other: husband with wife; wife with husband; both with kids; kids with parents; employees with employers; and even with God. "Oh, God, if you will just give me… I promise I will…." It is a universal prayer we've all prayed. Moreover, we use phrases like "quid pro quo"; "tit for tat"; "let's make a deal"; and "everything's negotiable" in our bargaining. It's the way of the world. Since, "There's no such thing as a free lunch," we ponder, "how could something so important as salvation be offered to us free?"

Because of pride, we add to what is required, thinking, in our hubris, that we can contribute to our salvation through our own "goodness." However, God tells us that He sees our *works of righteousness* as "the rag of a menstruous woman" [Isaias 64:6]. Moreover, adding our works to God's plan of salvation robs God of His glory and adds to our own [Ephesians 2:4-7]. God promises curses for those who do such things [Apocalypse 22:18-19]. The only way the believer can perform works that glorify God will be explained in chapter four.

Salvation is not free. It was purchased with a price, the greatest price that has or ever will be paid for anything. That price was the suffering and death of God's only-begotten Son on that cruel cross at Calvary. Jesus, our kinsman redeemer, suffered and died in our place. According to the Roman Catholic and all other Bibles, the debt owed to God for sin has been paid. God now offers each of us the gift His Son has already paid for. Therefore, it is free in the sense that *we* don't have to pay for it. That gift is eternal life, salvation. Proverbs 14:12 tells us, "Sometimes a way seems right to a man, but the end of it leads to death!" That is why we must turn to God's Word for direction and not rely on our feelings or common experience in a fallen world: "The heart is perverse (*deceitful*) above all things and unsearchable (*desperately wicked*)…" [Jeremias 17:9]. We must stand on the promises of God recorded in His Holy Word. Proverbs 9:10 tells us, "The beginning of wisdom is the fear (*respect*) of the LORD, and knowledge of the Holy One (*Jesus*) is understanding." St. Mark 1:24 reveals that the Holy One is Jesus.

The Serpent Enters the Garden

Lest you think man's tendency to add to God's Word and its consequences is a bit overstated, consider Genesis 3:2-3:

> The woman answered the serpent, "Of the fruit of all the trees in the garden we may eat; but of the fruit of the tree in the middle of the garden," God said, "you shall not eat, neither shall you touch it, lest you die."

As can be seen from Genesis 2:16-17, the woman added to God's Word. To add to God's Word is to speak a lie. God simply commanded they not eat of the tree. The woman's reply to Satan revealed that she did not have proper respect for the LORD or His Word. That was all the invitation Satan needed. And the rest, as they say, is history! Had Eve had a copy of Proverbs, she would have known that fear (*respect*) of the LORD is the beginning of wisdom rather than eating the forbidden fruit [Proverbs 9:10].

There Are Many Reasons to Read the Scriptures

You might ask why *you* should read the Bible. Most importantly, Jesus said the Scriptures are they which testify of Him [St. John 5:39]. There are also many other reasons. First, it is the vehicle through which God speaks to His creatures (unsaved mankind) and reveals things to His children (those who are saved). Moreover, it tells us how to become His child. The Bible is the only work that reveals a part of the heart and mind of God, who He is, how man came into existence and why, and that he will exist forever. Moreover, it tells us what God expects of us. The writer of Ecclesiastes describes the natural man, that is, a man with a still-dead (not reborn) spirit as he searches for meaning in his life. He quickly discovers the problem of vanity, "... vanity of vanities. All things are vanity!" [Ecclesiastes 1:2] The word vanity could be translated today as a "soap bubble." It is virtually nothing and is short lived. After considering all human achievements and possessions, the writer, king Solomon, whom God called the wisest man ever, concludes:

> The last word, when all is heard: Fear God and keep his commandments, for this is man's all; because God will bring to judgment every work, with all its hidden qualities, whether good or bad.
> —Ecclesiastes 12:13-14

It is only through God's Word that we learn that what separates God from His creatures is their iniquity, their will to sin. Only through God's Word do we learn that He has a plan for removing that barrier so that we can become His children:

> "Come now, and let us reason together," Says the LORD, "Though your sins are like scarlet, They shall be as white as snow; Though they are red like crimson, They shall be as wool (*white*). If you are willing and obedient, You shall eat the good of the land."
> —Isaias 1:18-19 NKJV

It is only through God's Word that we learn that God wants the best for His creatures and His children, desiring that all His creatures (lost) become His obedient children (saved). It is only through the Word of God that we learn that the only way we can be obedient and become children of God is by calling on the Jesus of the New Testament to be our Lord and Savior. This is explained more fully in chapters three and four.

God's Word Reveals Secrets of the Universe

One evening in July 2000, CNN interviewer Larry King had four guests on *Larry King Live*, two from "Christian" denominations and two Jewish. The subject of discussion was whether the Bible was God's Word or just the writings of men. Larry said he would believe it was God's Word if it contained some revelation that man could not possibly have known at the time of its writing, "like the earth is round, rather than flat." Unfortunately, none of the guests was able to tell him that the exact test he suggested for establishing scriptural authenticity is, in fact, stated plainly in Scripture. The "Christians" were not biblical scholars. In discussing ecumenicity within the framework of the "many paths to God," one of the guests, a Franciscan priest, agreed with Larry that there are many paths. To support his position, the priest quoted Jesus: "He who isn't against me, is with me." This makes it clear that Buddhists, Hindus, Muslims, and others who are not opposing Christ will find their way to heaven. The problem is that the priest misquoted Jesus [see 2 Timothy 2:15]. Jesus said just the opposite:

> He who is not with me is against me, and he who does not gather with me scatters.
>
> —St. Matthew 12:30

Had any of Larry's guests been well versed in Scripture, he could have told Larry there are many things revealed in the Bible that could not possibly have been known by man at the times of its writings. For example, Isaias 40:22 reveals, "It is he (*God*) that sittith upon the globe of the earth...." It was not until after the voyages of Columbus that men discovered the earth was round, a globe, not flat. Job 26:7 reveals, "He (*God*) stretches out the North over empty space, and suspends the earth over nothing at all...." Scientists have believed this only for the last few centuries. However, the veracity of this verse was first *seen* only in the last half of the 20th century. At about the same time the book of Job was written, over four-thousand years ago, some eastern religions taught that the world was supported on the back of a turtle floating in the sea. Many centuries later, the Greeks taught that Atlas bore the earth on his back. This is why a book containing maps is called an atlas. Plato later suggested that the earth was a living entity. Some Native American cultures today hold such views.

Hebrews 11:3 reveals "... things visible were made of things invisible." Atoms. Isaias 60:8 appears to predict that man will one day fly and Nahum 2:4 may well be a prediction of cars: "...the chariots jostle one against another in the streets: their looks are like torches (*headlights?*), like lightning running to and fro." Soap operas and television talk shows seem to have been prophesied by St. Paul:

> But know this, that in the last days dangerous times will come. Men will be lovers of self, covetous, haughty, proud, blasphemers, disobedient to parents, ungrateful, criminal, heartless, faithless, slanderers, incontinent, merciless, unkind, treacherous, stubborn, puffed up with pride, loving pleasure more than God, having a semblance indeed of piety, but disavowing its power (*having a form of godliness but denying its power*). Avoid these. For of such are they who make their way (*sneak*) into houses (*through the television?*) and captivate silly women (*not all women, but those who are gullible enough to get interested in the lives of such people*) who are sin-laden and led away by various lusts (*that come from watching and listening to such people*); ever learning (*believing there is something important to be learned from these people*) yet never attaining knowledge of the truth (*that Jesus is Lord*).
>
> —2 Timothy 3:1-7

Today, these reprobate characteristics can be seen in soap operas and on television talk shows.

Skeptics of biblical inspiration maintain that the scribes wrote their own words. However, such is contrary to man's nature. At the time of Isaias's writing, it was common knowledge and a "scientific fact" that the earth was flat. Anyone maintaining otherwise would have set himself up for ridicule. It was also known at the time of Job that the earth must be supported by something, because everyday experience confirmed that things not supported by something would fall. Moreover, St. Paul must have wanted to argue with the Holy Spirit when told to write that wicked men would sneak into houses and captivate some of their wives and daughters and lead them away in their lusts. He knew that houses were locked at night and that husbands slept in front of the only door to the house. How could wicked men sneak in and lead these women away? St. Paul must have wondered. Such revelations were antithetical to human experience.

God's Word Reveals Secrets for Man's Benefit

One of the most famous people to have died from having been bled too much was George Washington. It was not until some godly physicians understood the revelations in Leviticus 17:11 that they abandoned the practice of bleeding patients. Verse 11 says, "... the life of a living body is in its blood...." God's Word teaches and reiterates in numerous places that the "life of the flesh is in the blood." Science caught up to the Word of God in the late 18th century when physicians finally came to understand that if they removed some of the blood, then they removed some of the life. As a result, bleeding patients is no longer a part of medicine in most countries. However, it is still practiced by primitives in many areas. The cleanliness laws revealed in Leviticus became the foundation for many aspects of the practice of modern medicine. God told Moses and the Israelites how to fight germs, infections, and their spread more than two thousand years before Pasteur (1822-1895) and other scientists looked into their microscopes and "discovered" the little varmints! The "scientific" theory of Pasteur's day was "spontaneous generation." Leading scientists believed that if food was exposed to air for a critical period of time, it would spontaneously generate microbes.

God's Word Dispels Satan's Lies

The Catholic Bible addresses evolution, a centuries-old satanic lie that gained prominence near the end of the 19th century. In Genesis 2:7, God reveals:

> Then the LORD God formed man out of the dust of the ground and breathed into his nostrils the breath of life, and man became a living being.

The Holy Bible contains not a word on the "big bang" theory. Scientists announced on May 4, 2000 that the "other half of the universe had been found." Most of us didn't know it was missing! News accounts reported that astrophysicists had been concerned for some time that the total mass of material identified in the universe was too small to support the big bang theory of creation. According to these same scientists, the other half of the universe was there all along. But since it consisted of interplanetary gasses that could be detected only with a certain spectrum of light, it had been overlooked. Neither does the Bible suggest that our distant ancestors pulled themselves out of the primordial ooze onto dry land. St. Paul reveals:

All flesh is not the same flesh, but there is one flesh of men, another of beasts, another of birds, another of fishes.

—1 Corinthians 15:39

God's Word Reveals the Future

You have lived to see *how* the fulfillment of a biblical prophecy that was for centuries thought to be impossible and ridiculed by nonbelievers and numerous denominations has become not only possible, but routine. Those who took the Bible at its word confessed they could not imagine how it could be true, but they said they stood by the Word of God. Their position was summarized and denigrated by their critics as: "God said it, the prophets wrote it, I believe it, that settles it!" Can you guess what prophecy that might be? "Behold, he comes with the clouds, and *every eye* shall see him, and they also who pierced him..." [Apocalypse 1:7]. Prior not only to the development of television but also to worldwide, real-time news coverage, fulfillment of this prophecy was, humanly speaking, impossible.

We have yet to see another seemingly impossible prophecy be fulfilled. Jesus tells us in St. Matthew 24:15 that by the time the Antichrist rises to power, the Jews will have restored Temple worship and animal sacrifices. This will require the rebuilding of the Jewish Temple, which has been destroyed twice before, both times on August 9th. The first destruction was at the hands of the Babylonians in 586 B.C., and the second by the Romans in 70 A.D. However, the Muslim Dome of the Rock, one of the three most holy sites in Islam, presently stands near where the Jewish Temple twice stood before and where devout Jews intend to rebuild it. The Jews believe Messiah will come after worship and animal sacrifices have been restored. Rabbinic schools have identified male Jews with the last name of Cohen to become priests. Cohen is associated with the descendants of the tribe of Levi, Jacob's third son. Levites served as Temple priests. These priests would be a necessary part of the construction force for rebuilding the Holy of Holies [St. Matthew 27:51]. The Jews have been working for a number of years to breed a red heifer without blemish. The heifer's ashes are needed for the Temple rededication ceremony [Numbers 19]. It was reported by the Temple Mount Institute that such a red heifer was born in Israel in 2002. We can only speculate as to when this prophecy will be fulfilled.

Daniel 12:4 refers to another future prophecy: "But thou, O Daniel, shut up the words, and seal the book, even to the time appointed (*end times*): many shall pass over (*travel*) and knowledge shall be manifold (*greatly increased*)." We live in an ultra-mobile society. Until the beginning of the 20th century, few people traveled more than a few hundred miles from home and even fewer traveled overseas. Today, we all know people who have sojourned to other continents even if we have not. There was little increase in knowledge between the time man began using tools and the time Columbus discovered the Americas. Knowledge doubled between the time of Columbus and the industrial revolution. Now experts tell us our scientific knowledge base doubles every two years![1] Daniel may soon be ready to unseal the book.

God's Word Gives Us Eyes to See and Ears to Hear in a Lost World

Many world religions teach that only they can provide reliable interpretations of God's Word. Doesn't it seem strange that God would give us something to bring about His will (that all should come to salvation) and for our benefit that He knew we couldn't understand? Yet, we have many denominations claiming to be Christian and few seem to be able to agree on most matters. Some argue that the reason is due to the many interpretations of Scripture by different individuals. They argue that a single interpreter, such as a pope, is therefore necessary.[2] However, a closer examination reveals several things. First, not all have what the Bible calls an eye to see or an ear to hear [see Ezechiel 12:2]. Scripture reveals truths on several levels. The natural man can understand the truth revealed on natural matters. However, the Word of God speaks through the Holy Spirit to the reborn (regenerated) spirit of man. If one's spirit has not been reborn, then his or her spirit is dead to the Word of God and spiritual things cannot be discerned:

> But the sensual (*natural*) man does not perceive the things that are of the Spirit of God, for it is foolishness to him and he cannot understand, because it is examined spiritually (*spiritually discerned*).
> —1 Corinthians 2:14

Chapter 3 of St. John's gospel begins with Jesus telling Nicodemus that for one to see the kingdom of God, he must be born again. In verse 6, Jesus tells a bewildered Nicodemus, "That which is born of the flesh is flesh; and that which is born of the Spirit is spirit." In other words, one cannot understand things of the Holy Spirit of God with one's flesh [see Galatians 3:3]. Since we are born with a spirit that is dead to the things of God, our spirit must be reborn before our eyes and ears are open to the things of God. In chapter 2, verse 7 of the Apocalypse, Jesus says, "He who has an ear, let him hear what the Spirit says to the churches." God's Word makes it clear that not all standing at the pulpit and sitting in the pews on

Sunday morning have ears to hear. Jesus repeats this same admonition in each of His letters to the seven churches. Only those who have been reborn have ears to hear what the Spirit says [see Apocalypse 2 and 3]. In Psalms 118(119):125, King David prays, "I am your servant; give me discernment that I may know your decrees." As David makes clear, one must be His servant to have discernment. Spiritual rebirth will be addressed in chapter four.

Knowing God's Word Protects Us from the Teachings of Cults

Differing interpretations often are based on a desire to have the Scripture fit tradition or some other teachings of man. This is seen, too, in virtually all cults.[3] A cult is an organization claiming to believe in and follow the Scriptures, but which has isolated and so manipulated selected verses that their interpretations are not supported by the remainder of biblical text and, in fact, are contradicted by God's Word. Common characteristics of cults include: a claimed source of divine revelation outside of God's revealed Word in His Scriptures; a claim to be the only organization that can lead one to salvation; salvation based on works, which includes many denominations of so-called Christian Churches; a belief in an afterlife that includes places other than heaven and hell, the only two possibilities taught by Jesus and His disciples; no hell at all; and the belief that only the head of the organization can interpret Scripture.

As mentioned in chapter one, the Jehovah's Witnesses do not believe in the Trinity [see St. Matthew 28:19]. They do not believe in Jesus' resurrection. When a member of their Church is asked to comment on Apocalypse 1:18, wherein the speaker says, "... I am the First and the Last, and he who lives, *I was dead*, and behold, I am living forevermore," the Witness replies that only the president of the Society can interpret Scripture. The Witness is caught between a rock and a hard spot. Jehovah never died. Jesus did. Therefore, it is clear that the speaker in Apocalypse 1:18 is not Jehovah but none other than the resurrected Christ of the New Testament.

Remember Jim Jones? Over nine hundred of the "faithful," including nearly three hundred children and babies, committed murder and mass suicide at his "spiritual" encampment in Jonestown, Guyana on November 18, 1978. After Jones told his followers he was Christ returned, many of his 20,000 faithful followed him from his People's Temple in San Francisco to Guyana to help him establish a utopia on earth. Instead, Jones led them to a "poisoned well" from which they freely drank [compare with St. John 4:13-14]. The commander of the U.S. forces responsible for clean-up operations was a born-again Christian. Upon return to the states, he remarked: "The thing that interested me most about Jonestown is that when we cleaned the camp out, we did not find a single Bible in all of Jonestown."[4] Jim Jones had effectively substituted his own teachings for God's Word. His followers were not familiar with the Jesus Christ of the New Testament.

You may remember David Koresh and the Branch Davidians just outside Waco, Texas. Koresh, too, convinced his followers he was Christ returned. The "Reverend" Sun Myung Moon, founder of the Unification Church, also claims to be the second coming of Christ. While the secular world tells us there are many paths, the cults give us many "christs." Jesus said, "The sin of the world is that it does not *believe in Me*" [St. John 16:9]. To accept any of these other christs is to reject the Jesus of the New Testament.

You may recall the Heaven's Gate crowd. The cult was led by an older man named Marshall Applewhite, alias Do (pronounced Doe). Thirty-nine of the faithful followed Do in mass suicide in a rented, multi-million dollar mansion in the exclusive Rancho Sante Fe area of California. There were twenty-one women and eighteen men, ranging in age from twenty to seventy-two. The group believed that Heaven's Gate was an extraterrestrial world populated by aliens and that the Hale-Bopp comet would provide a window for members to pass through. The faithful packed their bags, ate poison, and laid down on beds to die in anticipation of a UFO transporting them to this advanced utopian society. Applewhite, like most cultic leaders, perverted God's Word. He taught that Christ was an alien who came to earth to take over the body of a man named Jesus. According to Do, the deity entered into the man Jesus' body at the time of His baptism. Sound familiar? It should. It is the same heresy put forward by Paul of Samosata, the bishop (pastor) of the church at Antioch, discussed briefly in chapter one. We will see it again in the doctrines of Mormonism, discussed later in this chapter, and again in heresies among mid-3rd century churches that caused the first schism in 251 A.D., as will be explored in chapter five. Applewhite taught that humans were planted on this earth by extraterrestrials:[5]

> ... For they have not received the love of truth that they might be saved. Therefore God sends them a misleading influence that they may believe falsehood, that all may be judged who have not believed the truth, but have preferred wickedness (*a lie*).
>
>   —2 Thessalonians 2:10-12

Does it surprise you that some claim to be Christ returned to earth? In His Olivet Discourse, recorded in chapters 24 and 25 of St. Matthew's Gospel, Jesus responded to His disciples' questions on His return: "Take care that no one leads you astray. For many will come in my name, saying,

'I am the Christ,' and they will lead many astray" [St. Matthew 24:5]. Jones, Koresh, Moon, and others have done exactly this. What would *you* do if someone claiming to be a preacher, an angel, or even the Virgin Mary appeared to you, performed a great sign, and told you that Jesus was at a certain place waiting for you?

> ... if anyone say to you, "Behold here is the Christ," or, "There he is," do not believe it. For false christs and false prophets will arise, and will show great signs and wonders, so as to lead astray, if possible, even the elect (*His followers*). Behold, I have told it to you beforehand. If therefore they say to you, "Behold, he is in the desert," do not go forth; "Behold, he is in the inner chambers," do not believe it. For as the lightning comes forth from the east and shines even to the west, so will the coming of the Son of Man be.
>
> —St. Matthew 24:23-27

When Jesus entered onto the human stage the first time as an infant in a stable, the world took little note. Not so with the hosts of heaven [St. Luke 2:8-15]. Jesus' first earthly visit was prophesied in Isaias 53:2-9:

> ... there is no beauty in him (*Jesus*), nor comeliness; and we have seen him, and there was no sightliness, that we should be desiring of him. Despised, and the most abject of men, a man of sorrows and acquainted with infirmity: and his look was as it were hidden and despised, whereupon we esteemed him not. Surely he hath borne our infirmities and carried our sorrows: and we have thought him as it were a leper, and as one struck by God and afflicted. But he was wounded for our iniquities, he was bruised for our sins: the chastisement of our peace was upon him, and by his bruises (*stripes*) we are healed. All we like sheep have gone astray, every one hath turned aside into his own way: and the LORD hath laid on him the iniquity (*sins*) of us all. He was offered because it was his own will, and he opened not his mouth: he shall be led as a sheep to the slaughter, and shall be dumb as a lamb before his shearer, and he shall not open his mouth.

Jesus promises in His Olivet discourse that His next coming will be much different. His second coming will be proclaimed to all mankind from the heavens and as easily identifiable as lightning in the sky. When He returns, "Behold, he comes with the clouds, and every eye shall see him, and they also who pierced him. And all the tribes of the earth shall wail (*weep and mourn*) over him..." [Apocalypse 1:7]. When Jesus returns, He will do so not as the suffering servant of Isaias 53, but as King of kings and Lord of lords. Sitting upon a white horse with a regal crown upon His head, He will lead forth from heaven an army of saints arrayed in white linen and riding white horses [Apocalypse 19:11-16]. This Second Coming is referred to as His "glorious appearing" [Titus 2:13] and is distinct from His coming in the clouds to catch away His bride (His church), referred to as the "Rapture" [1 Thessalonians 4:16-18]. His glorious appearing will provide a visual answer to that part of the Lord's Prayer "... your kingdom come, your will be done, on earth as it is in heaven...." The meaning of the Rapture is more fully developed in later chapters.

The appearance of false christs is not limited to what might be considered fringe groups. Consider one of the largest denominations whose members are among some of the most Christlike-acting people in the world, the Church of Jesus Christ of Latter-Day Saints (LDS), also known as Mormons. I have friends who are Mormon and I can tell you that they are as sincere in their belief as they are wrong. Their missionary programs dwarf most Christian efforts. Perhaps you have seen one of their brief promotional adds on television. It shows a bearded, companionate-looking man wearing a prayer shawl walking among the people. The man is easily identifiable as Jesus. A voice over says, "... you can know the Savior through his revealed Word, the Holy Bible, which we will send to you for free." All looks and sounds New Testament Christian. But then the voice adds, "We will also include a free copy of Another Testament of Jesus Christ, the Book of Mormon." A phone number appears on the bottom of the screen. You may think, "It doesn't sound bad—a Church with Jesus' name in its title offering a free Bible and an additional revelation of Jesus Christ. What could be wrong with that?" The answer is: plenty!

While Latter-Day Saints claim to believe the Old and New Testaments, they don't confine their beliefs to them. Like many Churches, they have added non-biblical revelations to the doctrines contained in the Old and New Testaments. Also, like many Churches, they believe these non-scriptural revelations are from God. They are recorded in the Book of Mormon and other LDS books. While one could go on and on about what is at odds between the Holy Bible and the teachings of the Church of Latter-Day Saints, it is sufficient to note only a few. Latter-Day Saints teach that Jesus was a created being, as was the Father; only one of many gods and the half-brother of Lucifer; that the man Jesus *ascended* to godhood; and that we can do the same. However, the Scriptures teach that neither Jesus nor the Father are created beings [St. John 10:30; Genesis 1:1]; that Jesus created all things that were created [Colossians 1:16]; that Lucifer, a created being, is a fallen angel [Ezechiel 28:11-15] and the enemy of man [Isaias 14:12-16 and 1 St. Peter 5:8]; and that Jesus is God who took on human flesh [St. John 1:1-14], not flesh who achieved godhood through baptism! The problem is not confined to the Church of Latter-Day Saints. The problem is going outside the Bible, non-scriptural or post-scriptural, for additional revelations about Jesus Christ. God's Word warns against adding to or deleting from the Scriptures [see Apocalypse 22:18-19]. The moment one adds to or subtracts from the Jesus described in the Scriptures, one has a different Jesus than the Christ prophesied in the Old Testament and fulfilled in the New. Most understand that to believe that He did not rise bodily from the grave gives a different Christ. What is not so immediately obvious to the same people is that to believe that He did not pay the sin debt of the entire world in full, as prophesied in Isaias 53:4-6 (cited above) and confirmed in St. John 19:30, is to believe in a different Christ! Any Jesus other than the all-powerful Christ revealed in the New Testament cannot save you.

The idea that man could ascend to godhood was a staple in eastern mystery religions for many centuries before Jesus' birth. Today the same teaching is prevalent in many "New Age" cults. Satan recycles this damnable lie from generation to generation. It is puzzling that two canonized by the Roman Catholic Church, namely, Saints Athanasius and Aquinas, held positions similar to those taught by Paul of Samosata; Do and Heaven's Gate; Latter-Day Saints; and New Age cults. Saint Athanasius' and Saint Aquinas' anti-scriptural teachings are endorsed in paragraph 460 of the Catechism of the Catholic Church: "For the Son of God became man so that *we might become God*" [St. Athanasius]. The paragraph continues, "The only-begotten Son of God, wanting to make us sharers in his *divinity*, assumed our nature, so that he, made man, *might make men gods*" [St. Aquinas]. As evidenced by its inclusion in the Catechism, this teaching on man's *divinity* is still part of Roman Catholic doctrine. However, it is not preached from the pulpits. This erroneous teaching results in the Catholic Church mistakenly holding man in high regard, even crediting him with some innate good. This will be discussed further in chapter six.

However, this teaching is not found in the Roman Catholic or any other Bible. Rather, it is a teaching found among heathens, as documented in the Old Testament. This teaching is also found among today's New Agers. The Roman Catholic Bible teaches that there is none who is good, none who ascend to godhood [see Romans 3:10-12]. Moreover, the Roman Catholic Bible condemns any teaching that man can ascend to godhood. As recorded in Jeremias 7:18 and 44:19, certain women forsook their husbands (disobeyed) and made little wafer cakes for the goddess Semiramis. Jeremias recorded that they ate the cakes as offerings to the "queen of heaven." These early feminists believed that when they ate the cakes, they shared in the *divinity* of the goddess. Today, witches practice this same thing. By eating the wafer at the beginning of the ritual, the witch believes she becomes a goddess for the remainder of the ceremony.[6]

Latter-Day Saints is not the only Church that uses New Testament terms to promote concepts contrary to the Bible and the Jesus of the New Testament. For example, if you were to go into a Christian Science Reading Room and ask for information on the Trinity, you would be given pamphlets on the three ethical principles: life, truth, and love.[7] As will be discussed in the following chapters, The Roman Catholic Church, The Orthodox Churches, The Anglican Church, and virtually all Protestant denominations have incorporated into their theology non-biblical teachings that are contrary to those taught by Jesus and His disciples. One of the most widespread errors is that baptism regenerates a dead spirit and is thus necessary for salvation. As will be shown in later chapters, there is no scriptural support for this widespread heretical teaching.

God's Word Warns Us to Beware of Wolves in Sheep's Clothing

Many cults and false religions are seeking our attention and commitment. However, the Catholic Bible comes to the believer's rescue. Jesus warns:

> Beware of false prophets, who come to you in sheep's clothing, but inwardly are ravenous wolves.
>
> —St. Matthew 7:15

A prophet is someone who speaks the truth. Therefore, a false prophet is one who speaks lies. And a partial truth is a lie. Jesus *is* the Lamb of God, but He warns nonbelievers to beware of imposters who put on *sheep's clothing* but inside are hungry wolves ready to devour their very souls. Beware of those who put on a partial, Christlike appearance or title to deceive. How can you know? Fortunately, the Catholic Bible has that answer, too. St. John exhorts believers:

> Beloved, do not believe every spirit, but test the spirits to see whether they are of God; because many false prophets have gone forth into the world. By this is the spirit of God known: every spirit that confesses that Jesus Christ has come in the flesh, is of God. And every spirit that severs Jesus (*presents a Jesus different from the totality of the Jesus preached by His disciples and presented in the New Testament*), is not of God, but is of Antichrist, of whom you have heard that he is coming, and now is already in the world.
>
> —1 St. John 4:1-3

St. Peter, St. Paul, St. Jude, and St. John all warned that false prophets and false christs were already in the world and that more would come. How should believers respond to a prophet who preaches a false gospel, be he a preacher, an angel, or any other apparition? St. Paul gives us the answer:

> But even if we or an angel from heaven should preach a gospel to you other than that which we have preached to you, let him be anathema! As we have said before, so now I say again: If anyone preach a gospel to you other than that which you have received, let him be anathema!
> —Galatians 1:8-9

The word anathema, as used today, means an ecclesiastical ban. St. Paul's meaning was much stronger. He meant that the offender not only should be cut off from God for all eternity but also become the primary target of His wrath and destruction. He and the other apostles would be accused of being mean-spirited, intolerant, and divisive in today's politically correct climate. The disciples would not celebrate the "diversity of paths." They would not embrace so-called self-help doctrines teaching self-realization, karma, enlightenment, out of body experiences, reincarnation, and the "power" of crystals. They would condemn the New Age belief that the True Self in man is God and that ignorance of this fact, not sin, is all that keeps man from realizing that True Self and becoming a god.[8] The reason for St. Paul's attitude toward those who pervert the gospel of Jesus Christ is understandable. What is at stake is no less than one's eternal destiny. Anyone who tells another that there are many paths to God is a liar and a wolf in sheep's clothing.

God's Word Warns Against Following the Doctrines of Demons

While you may never run into a Jim Jones or David Koresh or consider converting to Mormonism, you are bombarded every day by what St. Paul called the doctrine of demons [see 1 Timothy 4:1-2]. Major daily newspapers and most magazines for men, women, and even some for teens, carry horoscopes. Nancy Reagan relied on the services of astrologer, Ms. Joan Quigley, during President Reagan's years in office. Psychic Hotlines are being used by many. Any number of television talk-show hosts interview witches, mediums, and channelers who "communicate with the dead." Contacting the spirit world is known as necromancy and God's Word, as recorded in the Catholic and all other Bibles, strongly condemns the practice, as well as the practitioners [Leviticus 20:27]. Many New Age religious practices are dismissed casually by most as just so much harmless hocus-pocus. However, much of it is anything but harmless. If one believes in the power of an activity, an object, or a person, Satan can use that to gain an individual's trust and establish a foundation of the occult in his or her life.[9] Any attempt to contact or communicate with the dead is strictly prohibited by the Roman Catholic and all other Bibles:

> And when they shall say to you: "Seek the pythons (*familiar spirits*) and diviners, who mutter in their enchantments:" should not the people seek of their God, for the living of the dead?
>
> —Isaias 8:19

God is asking rhetorically, should the living not seek their God? Why should the living seek help from the dead? Saul, the first king of Israel, banished all witches and soothsayers in accordance with God's Word. However, fearing the outcome of a battle with the Philistines, Saul went to the Witch of Endor and asked her to summon the spirit of the dead Samuel, a prophet whom Saul had trusted. What materialized was the spirit of a demon. Such a spirit is known as a "familiar" because it imitates the one being sought. The event is recorded in chapter 28 of 1 Kings (1 Samuel in the KJV). The LORD had warned the people against attempting to contact the dead. Such practices were prevalent among the heathens the Israelites were to dispossess of their lands:

> When you come into the land which the LORD, your God, is giving you, you shall not learn to imitate the abominations of the peoples there. Let there not be found among you anyone who immolates his son or daughter in the fire (*sacrifices his firstborn child to the gods*), nor a fortuneteller, soothsayer, charmer, diviner, or caster of spells, nor one who consults ghosts and spirits or seeks oracles from the dead (*prays to the dead*). Anyone who does such things is an abomination to the LORD, and *because of such abominations* the LORD, your God, is driving these nations out of your way.
>
> —Deuteronomy 18:9-12

While such activities might seem intriguing to a lost world, God's people are commanded to stay away from such because they are abominations to the LORD. Jesus confirms in St. Luke 16:19-31 that there can be no communication between the living and the dead. When the deceased rich man, who was in torment from the flames, found there would be no relief, he called across the great chasm to Abraham (in Paradise) and asked him to send a messenger from the dead to warn his five brothers about "... this place of torments." Abraham refused and told him that even if someone were to rise from the dead (a foreshadowing of Jesus' resurrection), his brothers still would not believe.

Failure to follow God's Word leads to a life less than what He desires for His children (believers) and His creatures (nonbelievers). *The Exorcist,* the book and multimillion dollar box office hit by the same title, was based on the true story of a boy, not girl, who was introduced to the occult by his favorite aunt. She taught him how to "communicate with the dead" via a Ouija board. The boy continued this activity after her death. This provided a pathway for demons, not the deceased spirit of a loved one, to enter the boy's life. Demons use a person's belief in the occult to manipulate his or her future. Maybe you've heard someone exclaim, "That's exactly what her psychic said would happen!" Why are psychics and fortunetellers so often right? Do they know the future? Are they in league with demons who know the future? No. God alone knows the future. However, demons can have significant influence over unsaved people.

When a demon knows a person believes the things the psychic or fortuneteller tells him, that demon can enter his life through the use of another over which that same or another demon exerts some control. For example, if a psychic tells a female client she will meet a tall, dark, handsome man and that she should pursue him and a demon exerts strong control over a tall, dark, handsome man, then the demon works circumstances to bring the two together. The demon wants the woman to place increasing reliance on the psychic because this will result in the demon getting a foothold in the woman's life and the client not perceiving the need to turn to God. [10] This explains how demons use so-called psychics in the realm of the living. But how are some psychics able to tell the living specific details about deceased loved ones?

A well-known psychic and author appeared on CNN's *Larry King Live* on August 31, 2000. Her then-current book had been on the New York Times' best-seller list for over a month. Larry allowed some twenty or so people to call in. Callers asked her questions about deceased loved ones. She assured them that their departed relatives were all doing quite well "on the other side," where there is no suffering, no pain. Moreover, she identified the departed by specific physical features, causes of death, and other details one would not expect a stranger to know. She discussed one's scar and another's peculiar tic. None of the callers had to correct her. How did she know these details? Was she really looking through the veil of death to the other side, as she claimed, or in league with the devil, or was it something else? There are some alive today who were intimately familiar with the looks, habits, and peculiarities of the deceased. Demons. They have been around since before the creation of man. Thus, when a client asks a psychic about a deceased loved one, the demon associated with the psychic gets his answer from another demon who was familiar with the deceased and he, in turn, passes it along to the psychic in terms of a vision or a whisper. Satan and his demons can present images [see 2 Corinthians 11:14-15]. However, the fact that demons use nonbelievers to do this does not mean that a psychic has sold her soul to the devil. In fact, the psychic probably doesn't have a clue as to how she knows these details. Many explain that their powers are a gift from God.

God's Word tells us to test the message of the prophets, whether they be preachers, priests, Bible teachers, Sunday school teachers, television evangelists, another Jim Jones or David Koresh [1 St. John 2:20-27]. To test their messages, we must be familiar with the Scriptures. In Deuteronomy Chapter 13, we learn that the LORD sometimes allows false prophets to come to us for the purpose of reminding us to test the message.

God's Word Reveals His Wonderful Promise

Have you ever heard someone say sympathetically about a friend, "I don't know what she's looking for. I just hope she will recognize it when she finds it"? Many people are searching for happiness. They change jobs, houses, cars, spouses, religions, and everything else looking for that one ever-elusive something that can satisfy them. Such a person is following the desires of his heart. Sometimes satisfaction with the new find lasts for months, sometimes years. But more is never enough and enough seems to be an unobtainable goal. God has placed a void in the human heart that only He can fill. Some will spend a lifetime looking in all the wrong places, putting their trust in all the wrong faces. On the other hand, have you ever known someone who seemed perfectly content with what he or she had? Many mistakenly assume that such a person has found the right house, spouse, or has the perfect family. We say these people are content. Their "desires" and their "haves" are synchronized. That is, they desire that which they have and they have that which they desire. God assures us that we can be in such an enviable position. The psalmist reveals:

> Take delight in the LORD, and he will grant you your heart's requests.
> —Psalms 36 (37):4

This verse is sometimes misunderstood as, "Delight in the LORD, and He will give you whatever you want." However, the idea is that He will place certain cravings into your heart. When God places desires in your heart, He only places those which He intends to equip you to achieve. Thus, your "desires" and "haves" will be in harmony.

God's Word Tells Parents How to Raise Up Godly Children

Every New Testament believer has a responsibility to teach God's precepts to his children and raise them in the discipline (*respect*) and admonition of the Lord [Ephesians 6:4]. Your child's first impression of what God is like will be based on his experiences with his earthly father: being his child; living within rules established for his protection and benefit; receiving gifts and unconditional love; and, when necessary, godly discipline. A good father never thinks: "I'll watch closely and when he messes up, then I'll jump in and criticize him." Neither does his heavenly Father think such a thing.

Atheist Friedrich Nietzsche (1844-1900) is credited with being one of the foremost thinkers of the 19th century. He was the son of a Lutheran minister. His father died when Friedrich was only five years old, leaving the boy to be raised by his mother, grandmother, two aunts, and a sister. Thus, the lad really had no exposure to a father. In time, Friedrich came to believe that his father's weaknesses had led to his death. The man who would later inspire Adolph Hitler, himself the son of an abusive father, by his concept of an "overman," which would evolve into an Aryan superman under the German dictator, concluded that God, like his earthly father, was also absent. The Prussian-born German philosopher is best remembered for his startling pronouncement: "God is dead." As far as Nietzsche was concerned, God died when his father passed away.

Jean Paul Sartre (1905-1980) is another example. This 20th century French philosopher and writer lost his father when he was only one year old. His mother remarried, but the young Jean Paul hated his stepfather. Sartre was a leading proponent of existentialism, a false alternative to worship of the true God. In his autobiography, *The Words* (1964), this modern-day atheist and cynic sadly concluded, "There is no such thing as a good father."

Dr. Benjamin Spock broke with what up to that time had been the recognized manner of child rearing since time began—literally. In his first book entitled, "Common Sense Book of Baby and Child Care," published in 1946, the pediatrician advocated a radical departure from biblical principles in raising children to one of more permissiveness. The book sold thirty million copies in the three decades following its publication. It sowed the seeds of rebellion against God's Word in the minds of millions of parents. Dr. Spock's recommended "common sense" permissiveness produced the self-indulgent flower children of the 1960s and 1970s complete with unrestrained use of drugs, sex, and rock and roll. These parents rebelled themselves against the biblical principles of child rearing.

They reaped in the following generation what they had sown. In 1972, the father of "flower power" ran for president of the United States on the left-wing People's Party ticket. After evaluating the harvest his "common sense" nostrums had produced, Dr. Spock recanted much of what he had previously advocated.

There is another book parents can get by an even more widely known Author that will give them a head start. It's the book of Proverbs. It's probably located on a bookshelf in your home between Psalms and Ecclesiastes, books by the same author. Here are some of its "not-so-common-sense" approaches to what traditionally has been called child rearing. Can you determine why the word "rearing" figures so prominently in dealing with children?

Here is a sampling of directives from God's book on child raising, the book of Proverbs.

> He who spares his rod hates his son, but he who loves him takes care to chastise him (*beginning from a young age*).
>
> —13:24

But you protest, "I would never strike my child with a rod!" Yes, and it shows! But hold on. The word rod is defined in Isaias 28:27. It means a switch. The Lord is quite specific about what He will use to rule the nations of this world when He establishes His kingdom on earth: a "rod of iron" [Apocalypse 19:15]. Thus, the Lord is not directing parents to strike their children with a rod of iron but with a switch from a tree. Satan's lie is "spare the rod and *spoil* the child." However, God's Word says if you spare the rod, you "*hate*" your child! Satan is a liar and the father of lies [see St. John 8:44].

> Folly (*foolishness*) is close to the heart of a child, but the rod of discipline will drive it far from him.
>
> —22:15

But you say you would never hit your child in anger. That's good.

> The rod of correction gives wisdom, but a boy left to his whims disgraces his mother.
>
> —29:15

Thus, one is to discipline a child—never out of anger—but to teach him, make him wise, and help him remember. In fact, the LORD warns against striking a child in anger.

> He who sows iniquity (*anger*) reaps calamity, and the rod destroys his labors.
>
> —22:8

If you strike your child in anger, you will be sowing the seeds of anger and teach him nothing. Isn't it amazing that God knew that a man who was beaten by an angry father would one day become a child beater himself. God didn't list the excuses we have today such as alcohol and drug abuse. He just warned what would happen. This intergenerational curse can only be broken by the grace of God.

We hear a lot about tough love. It's especially prominent in dealing with substance abuse among teens. Tough love is a new, enlightened approach, right? Hardly. God's message to parents is to discipline children with love, but only to the extent necessary, and never out of anger. God's measures for dispensing discipline do not include reasoning with a three-year old not to play in the street. This is one reason God made trees and placed an "herbal remedy" in your backyard.

> Withhold not chastisement from a boy; if you beat him with the rod, he will not die. Beat him with the rod, and you will save him (*his soul*) from the nether world (*hell*).
>
> —23:13-14

How far does God think parents should go to prevent their child from leading a life that eventually will lead him to hell? God says to "beat" him if that is what it takes, but points out that "he will not die" from the experiences. The word used for "beat" in these two verses connotes leaving stripes on the area beaten. A child will not die from having a switch taken to his behind. It should be noted that this is the only verse in God's Manual on Child Rearing to use the word "beat." Parents' failure to follow God's advice in this matter can be measured by the outrageous stories pertaining to our youth reported on the local and national news.

To "drill" God's law into your children, you must first know what God's Word says [Deuteronomy 6:7]. With regard to why one should train his child, God gives many reasons, including:

> Train a boy in the way he should go; even when he is old, he will not swerve from it.
>
> —22:6

The reward for the parent is reported in 23:24-25:

> The father of a just man will exult with glee; he who begets a wise son
> will have joy in him. Let your father and your mother have joy; let her
> who bore you exult.

God has some good advice for parents who resist His teaching on how
to raise children:

> The fear of the LORD is the beginning of knowledge; wisdom and
> instruction fools despise.
>
> —1:7

Hopefully you are not counted among the fools.

The underlying purpose behind raising a child to submit to parental
authority is twofold: his future in this world and the next. Each of us is under
some form of required submission: worker under boss; military man under
commanding officer; and citizen under local, state, and federal governments.
Those who are taught by parents to obey at a young age generally have less
difficulty learning to submit to other authorities later in life. Every child is
born a Nemrod, a rebel. God's Word tells us that rebellion is as of the sin of
witchcraft [see 1 Kings 15:23]. The sin of witchcraft is what cost Saul, the
first king of Israel, his crown and his life [see I Paralipomenon 10:13-14].
It is an abomination to God.

Jails, prisons, neo-Nazi organizations, halfway houses, sanitariums, and
graveyards are full of children of adult age who never learned to submit.
If God's will is that all be saved [St. John 3:16] and He has provided a way
to accomplish our salvation through the death of the Jesus of the New
Testament [St. John 14:6], but we refuse to submit to His will, then we are
rebels. Hell is filled with rebels. Heaven is populated by those who learned
to submit. If your child learns he can rebel against you in the home and get
away with it, what do you think his behavior will be like when you take
him other places? In later years with his teachers? With his boss? With the
police? With his spouse? If you do not teach your child to submit at an
early age, society will at least attempt to do so. The big difference is that you
love your child. Society does not and will use whatever means necessary to
make him submit. One who has led a rebellious life is not likely to submit
to the laws of God or recognize Jesus as his Master. One day he will stand
before God and answer for his rebellion.

Other Reasons to Know God's Word

A final reason to know the Bible may be politics. In attempting to secure
his party's nomination for office of President in the year 2000, Senator John

McCain of Arizona referred to pastors Jerry Falwell and Pat Robertson as "evil men." We must conclude from this widely reported appellation that Senator McCain was not well versed in Scripture. Isaias 5:20 warns:

Woe to you that call evil good, and good evil....

Certainly there have been some "men of the cloth" whose conduct, as reported by the national media, has been disgraceful. However, pastors Falwell and Robertson have never been identified as such until labeled so by Mr. McCain. Reporters, pundits, political analysts, and advisors all blamed McCain's Super Tuesday losses on a number of factors, none of which included God's warning to those who call good evil!

Study God's Word

In summary, we should do as the Beroeans did.

But the brethren straightway sent Paul and Silas away by night to Beroea, and on their arrival there they went into the synagogue of the Jews. Now these were of a nobler character than those of Thessalonica (*where Paul and Silas were first run out of the synagogues and later out of town*) and they received the word with great eagerness, studying the Scriptures (*the Law and the Prophets*) every day to see whether these things (*Paul's and Silas' teachings*) were so. Many of them became believers, and so did no small number of prominent Gentiles, women, and men.

—Acts 17:10-12

The author of Hebrews reveals:

For the word of God is living and efficient and keener than any two-edged sword, and extending even to the division of soul and spirit, of joints also and of marrow, and a discerner of the thoughts and intentions of the heart.

—Hebrews 4:12

The psalmist tells us how to be happy:

Happy (*is*) the man who follows not the counsel of the wicked, Nor walks in the way of sinners, nor sits in the company of the insolent, But delights in the law of the LORD and meditates (*pondering upon God's law and how it relates to one's life*) on his law day and night. Not so the wicked, not so; they are like chaff which the wind drives away.

—Psalms 1:1-4

Jesus promises believers:

> ... If you abide in my word, you shall be my disciples indeed, and you
> shall know the truth, and the truth shall make you free.
>
> —St. John 8:31-32

To *abide* in His Word, we must first *know* His Word. Finally, as
mentioned earlier, we are told:

> Take delight in the LORD, and he will grant you your heart's requests.
>
> —Psalms 36 (37):4

To delight in the LORD, we must first know Him. How do we get to
know Him? By reading and studying His Holy Word.

It is my sincerest hope that you will pick up a Bible and begin reading.
If you do, the Holy Spirit will convict your heart of sin, of righteousness,
and of judgment to turn your heart to Jesus [St. John 16:8-11]. I suggest you
start with chapter 10 of St. John's Gospel. It's subtitled *The Good Shepherd*.
You will discover in that chapter that Jesus was not murdered. Neither was
He a victim. He is not a martyr. His life was not taken from Him. He makes
it clear that He gives His sheep eternal life (salvation—see 1 St. John 5:13)
and they shall never perish (a double promise) and no one can snatch them
from His hand or the Father's hand. This is a promise of eternal security.

> Use all care to present yourself to God as a man approved, a worker that
> cannot be ashamed, rightly handling the word of truth (*the Scriptures*).
>
> —2 Timothy 2:15

Chapter 3

THE GOSPEL OF JESUS CHRIST

IN THIS CHAPTER we want to develop a clear understanding of the New Testament gospel message and determine if the Roman Catholic Bible accurately presents that message. For those who cannot stand suspense, the answer is an unqualified yes. All citations in this chapter are from the Roman Catholic Bible.

Most people in the U.S. have heard the word "gospel." However, its meaning has been co-opted by the secular world. Someone will say, "The boss fired him on the spot, and that's the gospel." Thus, even in the secular world, the word gospel is used to mean "the truth." God uses even unbelievers to support His message that the gospel is *the truth*!

All that the word "gospel" entails in Christian doctrine is generally not understood by unbelievers. First, the Greek word for gospel is translated into English as Good News. People often use an abbreviated version of the gospel, namely, that Jesus died for our sins. However, this is not the gospel. One could allege that Buddha, another religious leader, or even the robbers on the crosses next to Jesus died for our sins. The thing that makes the gospel of Jesus Christ unique is not that He died for our sins, but that He was also *buried* and subsequently *rose bodily from the dead*. No other religious leader has risen from the dead. Check their graves. Moreover, the followers of such religious leaders have not even *claimed* that any of their masters have risen. Not only did Jesus die for our sins, get buried, and rise on the third day, He did so *according to the Scriptures*, as noted by St. Paul in 1 Corinthians 15:3-4. The prophecy that Jesus would die for our sins is expressed clearly in Isaias 53. The prophecy that He would rise from the dead is expressed clearly in Psalms 15 (16):10. No one else ever came close to fulfilling these prophecies. How could they? Moreover, God's Word records that the resurrected Jesus was seen by many [see St. John 20:11-31; 21:1-14; St. Matthew 28:8-20; St. Luke 24:13-49; 24:50-52; and Acts 1:4-9].

It is necessary to specify that Jesus was buried for three days and three nights before He rose. This is an important point since certain cults, such as Christian Scientists, teach that Jesus only "swooned" on the cross. Adherents maintain that Jesus' followers removed Him from the cross and secreted Him away to recover from His wounds. Therefore, there was no burial and, hence, no resurrection. However, as St. Paul makes clear in 1 Corinthians 15:14:

> ... if Christ has not risen, vain then is our preaching, vain too is your faith.

But the complete gospel message has its impact in our lives now and for all eternity because not only did Jesus die for our sins and then rise from the grave, He tells us that He died *for all* and offers as a free gift *to all who trust in Him as Savior and Lord* an escape from the payment of their sin debt (an eternity in hell) and the promise of eternal life with Him in heaven. This is good news. St. Paul defines the gospel in 1 Corinthians 15:3-6:

> For I delivered to you first of all, what I also received, that Christ died for our sins according to the Scriptures, and that he was buried, and that he rose again the third day, according to the Scriptures, and that he appeared to Cephas, and after that to the Eleven. Then he was seen by more than five hundred brethren at one time, many of whom are with us still, but some have fallen asleep (*died*).

The salvation message, in its simplest form, consists of five things one must *believe* and one thing one must *do* to be saved.

Five Things One Must Believe to Be Saved

(1) All Scripture is inspired by God....

—2 Timothy 3:16

This is the first thing one must believe. If the Scriptures are not the inspired Word of God but are only words of men, then our faith is indeed in vain. However, St. Peter assures us that "... no prophecy of Scripture is made by private interpretation. For not by the will of man was prophecy brought at any time; but holy men of God spoke as they were moved by the Holy Spirit" [2 St. Peter 1:20-21].

(2) In the beginning was the Word, and the Word was with God; and the Word was God... And the Word was made flesh and dwelt among us...

—St. John 1:1 and 1:14

The second thing one must believe is that Jesus is God in human flesh, the Son of Man. St. John tells us, "For God so loved the world that he gave his only-begotten Son, that those who believe in him may not perish, but may have life everlasting. For God did not send his Son into the world in order to judge the world, but that the world might be saved through him" [St. John 3:16-17].

(3) ... all have sinned and have need of the glory of God (*and come short of the glory of God*).

—Romans 3:23

The third thing one must believe is that he is a sinner. The word sin means to "miss the mark." St. Paul tells us "... as it is written, 'There is not one just man; there is none who understands; there is none who seeks after God. All have gone astray together; they have become worthless. There is none who does good, no, not even one'" [Romans 3:10-12].

(4) ... the wages of sin is death....

—Romans 6:23

The fourth thing one must believe is that he is going to die and be judged for his sins. As the author of Hebrews tells us "... it is appointed unto men to die once and after this comes the judgment..." [Hebrews 9:27].

(5) For our sakes he (*God*) made him (*Jesus*) to be sin who knew nothing of sin, so that in him we might become the justice (*righteous*) of God.

—2 Corinthians 5:21

The fifth thing one must believe is that Jesus, as *his* kinsman redeemer, died for *his* sins. He who knew no sin, Jesus, was made sin for our sakes. It was *our sins* that put Jesus on the cross. This is why one hears believers speak of having a personal relationship with Jesus. Nothing could be more personal than someone substituting His own death to spare the death of His friend. Jesus said, "Greater love than this no one has, that he lay down his life for his friends. You are my friends if you do the things I command you" [St. John 15:13-14]. St. Paul tells us, "But God commends (*demonstrates*) his charity (*love*) towards us, because when as yet we were sinners, Christ died for us" [Romans 5:8-9]. Although we cannot understand how, God placed *all* our sins on Jesus and imputed Jesus' righteousness to all who accept His free gift of salvation and ask Him to be their Lord and Savior, thereby crucifying their flesh to the ways of this world [see Galatians 5:24]. This of course is not a physical crucifixion. More will be said about "crucifying the flesh" in chapters 4 and 5.

One Thing One Must Do to Be Saved

There is one thing one must *do* after accepting the five beliefs discussed above.

> (1) For whoever calls upon the name of the Lord shall be saved.
> —Romans 10:13

Calling upon the name of the Lord is the single thing one must *do*. It is an action, not a belief. But what does it mean to call upon the name of the Lord? In the Trinity there is God the Father, God the Son, and God the Holy Spirit. These are positions, not names. All members of the Trinity have multiple titles. However, only one member has a *name* and that is "the name of the Lord." We know Him as Jesus in the English language. His Hebrew name is Yeshua.

A part of our acceptance of Jesus when we call upon Him to be our Lord and Savior is to recognize that we need to repent, that is, to change our minds. Repentance is the Greek word "*metanoeo.*" "*Meta*" means "change" and "*noia*" means "mind." We must agree with God that we are sinners in need of a Savior. We no longer justify or deny our sins. "Oh, I know it was an R-rated movie, but that's not so bad. After all, parents let their *children* see these movies." Maybe some parents don't mind their children seeing such movies, but God doesn't want His children to see them.

God's Word confirms:

> For if thou confess with thy mouth that Jesus is the Lord, and believe in thy heart that God has raised him from the dead, thou shalt be saved. For with the heart a man believes unto justice, and with the mouth profession of faith is made unto salvation.
> —Romans 10:9-10

Notice where the believer is to hold the belief that God raised Jesus from the dead. In his heart. Did you ever study for a test where you stored the material learned in your heart? Of course not. You stored it in your brain.

Thus, what is meant by "believe in thy heart" is more than intellectual acceptance. Heartfelt belief moves one to action. Heartfelt belief that God raised Jesus from the dead moves the believer to whatever action God calls him to do, no matter how seemingly impossible it may appear when viewed through the eyes of flesh. It is the inward belief that God raised Jesus from the dead that expresses itself outwardly in the profession that Jesus is Lord. If one believes Jesus to be as dead as Buddha, there is no use calling upon him to be your lord. That's why one has to believe in his heart that God raised Jesus from the dead.

The above citation reiterates God's promise of salvation. Moreover, Jesus tells us "... everyone who acknowledges me before men, I also will acknowledge him before my Father in heaven" [St. Matthew 10:32]. The gospel of the Jesus of the New Testament, the Christ, certainly is "good news" for every sinner. Finally, St. Paul tells us: "... neither death, nor life, nor angels, nor principalities, nor things present, nor things to come, nor powers, nor height, nor depth, nor any other creature will be able to separate us from the love of God, which is in Christ Jesus our Lord" [Romans 8:38-39].

These are the things one must believe and do to be saved. The Roman Catholic Bible is quite clear on these matters. Moreover, the Roman Catholic Bible presents the same gospel message as the King James Version, the New King James Version, and *The Orthodox Study Bible, New Testament and Psalms*. At this time, *you* may want to say the sinner's prayer. I encourage you to do so. It is presented below. Say it out loud to the Lord.

> Jesus, I am a sinner deserving of nothing but hell. But I believe You paid my sin debt on Calvary with Your shed blood and death. I ask You to be not only my kinsman redeemer, but also the Lord of my life. As You died for me, let the old man in me die to sin. And just as You rose from the dead, raise up Your Spirit in me so that I may walk in Your ways, living for You, crucifying my flesh day by day through the indwelling power of the Holy Spirit. I gratefully accept the free gift of salvation offered by God the Father through Your atoning death on the cross. Wherever You lead, Good Shepherd, I will follow.

If you said the prayer and meant it, you are now saved. You have passed from death to life. You have been sealed by the Holy Spirit and have become a child of God, a joint heir with Christ.

What are the *implications* of being saved? Can one *lose one's salvation*? If so, what is the meaning of Jesus' *promise of eternal life*? These questions are addressed in the next chapter.

CHAPTER 4

THAT YOU MAY KNOW THAT YOU HAVE ETERNAL LIFE

THE TITLE OF this chapter is taken from 1 St. John 5:13. In chapter 5, as in many other parts of his first epistle (letter), St. John is combating certain claims made by false teachers and encouraging believers to hold to the truth so they can be true witnesses for Christ. One reason believers can share the gospel confidently with others is because of the assurances we have from Jesus regarding eternal life [Acts 19:8]. St. John writes:

> These things I am writing to you that you may *know* that you have eternal life—you who believe in the name of the Son of God.
> —1 St. John 5:13

Note carefully the words used by the apostle John. Believers are not told to *hope* for eternal life or *pray* for it or in any way be uncertain about it. St. John tells believers they are to *know* that they have eternal life. Moreover, Jesus assures us:

> Amen, amen, I say to you, he who hears my word, and believes in him (*God the Father*) who sent me, has life everlasting, and does not come to judgment, but has passed from death to life.
> —St. John 5:24

Here again is certainty. Jesus does not say he who believes is "in the process of passing from death to life," but that he who believes "*has passed*," past tense, a completed action, "from death to life."

Some Churches and churches teach that it is presumptuous to believe that one can know he or she is saved. However, as can be verified by examining the above citation, it is no more arrogant to believe one is saved than to believe that Jesus is God in human flesh, that He died, was buried, and rose from the dead. Why believe a part of His teaching and deny another?

49

The Bad News for Sinners

Prior to Eve's creation, God placed Adam in the Garden of Eden and told him not to eat of the fruit of the tree of the knowledge of good and evil. He warned Adam, "... for the day you eat of it, you must die" [Genesis 2:16-17]. However, as we know, Adam did not go into the ground on the day he ate. Therefore, we must examine the Scriptures to determine what God meant.

Man is a tripartite being consisting of body, soul, and spirit created in the image of the Triune God [see 1 Thessalonians 5:23]. The body needs no further definition. The soul is the essence of a person. A person uses his body to carry out the will and purpose of his soul and to communicate with others. In doing so, a person reveals that which is in his heart and mind [St. Mark 7:20-23].

The spirit is what the soul uses to communicate with God, who is pure Spirit [St. John 4:24]. In turn, God speaks to man through his reborn spirit. If Adam and Eve's bodies didn't go into the grave and their personalities did not cease to exist, then it must have been their spirits that died. Indeed this is confirmed in many passages of Scripture. The result was that Adam and Eve's fellowship with the Lord, with whom they had walked in the cool of the day, was broken [Genesis 3:8]. And since man reaps what he sows, we, Adam and Eve's children, are born with *dead spirits*. Just as it is the genes of his parents that determine a man's physical traits, so it is with the condition of his spirit at the time of physical birth. Therefore, what he inherits is not an "original sin" that can be washed away by water baptism. Rather, he inherits a dead spirit and, because his spirit is born dead, he also inherits a sin nature, that is, a natural bent away from God and the things of God.

Did you have to teach your baptized children to lie, steal, or rebel? Of course not. Neither did they have to learn such things from others. They, like we, were born with a sin nature and no one had to teach us how to sin. However, we cannot put the blame for our sins solely on Adam and Eve. We, too, have sinned [Psalms 14:3 and Romans 3:23]. We are told in Ezechiel 18:20, "The soul that sinneth the same shall die." Romans 6:23 reinforces the message, "For the wages of sin is death...." Ephesians 2:1 and Colossians 2:13 confirm that we die by reason of *our* sin.

It is abundantly clear from the Roman Catholic Bible that each of us, as a child of Adam, was born with a dead spirit. Each of us is a sinner. Therefore, each of us is destined to die. However, according to the Roman Catholic Bible, the definition of death—whether it is limited to only the body or also includes the soul—depends solely on one's relationship with the Jesus of the New Testament.

We know our bodies will die. This is true for the saved, as well as the unsaved. However, as revealed in Ezechiel 18:20, our "souls" are capable of dying also. Scripture refers to death of the soul as the "second death." The second death has no power over believers. The believer's soul, through the regeneration of the spirit, does not die [Apocalypse 2:11 and 20:6]. However, for the unsaved, those who do not have regenerated spirits, the second death is defined in the context of hell and the pool that burns with fire and brimstone [Apocalypse 20:14 and 21:8]. In St. Matthew 25:41, Jesus revealed that such a place was not created for man but for the devil and his angels (messengers of the devil, demons) and that the souls of the lost will be there forever (v. 46), separated from God forever, and tormented day and night forever and ever [Apocalypse 20:10]. So while a man's body is dying from ageing and he is struggling in this world with a spirit that is dead to the things of God, condemning himself through his unbelief, receiving the consequences of sin in his flesh, he is without fellowship with God. Moreover, his soul is destined to spend eternity in hell. If this sounds like bad news, it is.

Our first parents, Adam and Eve, tried to cover their sin with fig leaves. However, God did not judge the coverings the two made for themselves, *their works*, to be adequate. Therefore, the Lord made garments of skin for them. Notice the wording carefully. God did not make garments or skins for them. Rather, He made garments of skin. It is clear that the skins came from an animal slain by God. This is the first time the Scripture associates the shedding of blood with the covering of sin. God tells us in Leviticus 17:11, "... it is the blood... that makes atonement (*for sin*)." The author of Hebrews reiterates this truth in Hebrews 9:22, "... without the shedding of blood there is no forgiveness (*of sin*)."

In summary, each of us is born with a dead spirit. Each has sinned. The wages of sin, that is, what is owed to us in return for sinning, is death. This death is the second death, the death of the soul. Those whose spirits are not regenerated (brought back to life or reborn) cannot communicate with God. Therefore, when the body of such a one dies, his soul cannot remain on earth among the living because his soul can no longer communicate with those on earth. Since his spirit has not been regenerated, so that he can communicate with God, his soul and spirit cannot go to be with the Father. Therefore, his soul and spirit have only one place to go—hell. In hell he will receive a new and indestructible body which will be tormented day and night forever and ever.

The Good News of Jesus the Christ

There is good news, literally the Good News of Jesus the Christ, the promised Messiah, the Anointed One, the promised seed of the woman in Genesis 3:15. While the first part of Romans 6:23 tells us the bad news, that the wages of sin is death, the latter part gives us the good news:

... but the *gift* of God is life everlasting in Christ Jesus our Lord.

While the first part of Ephesians tells us that we are dead in offenses and sins, St. Paul gives believers the good news:

For by grace you have been saved through faith; and that not from yourselves, for it is the *gift* of God; not as the outcome of works, lest anyone may boast.

—Ephesians 2:8-9

As recorded in St. John 6:47, Jesus tells all mankind:

Amen, amen, I say to you, he who believes in me *has* life everlasting (*eternal life*).

After feeding the five thousand near Tiberias, Jesus told those following Him:

Do not labor for the food that perishes, but for that which endures unto life everlasting, which the Son of Man *will give you*.

—St. John 6:27

Eternal life, or life everlasting, is a *gift* from God. It is not something we can labor for like food which perishes. Once received, eternal life does not spoil. God *gives believers eternal life as a gift* which *was purchased at the cross*. It is *given* to those who look upon Jesus as whom He said He was and is: a *kinsman redeemer* (Christ or Messiah) *and* Lord (*Master*) of their lives [see Leviticus 25:25]. Moreover, believers are told that through their baptism they are buried with Him and raised with Him [Romans 6:4 and Colossians 2:12]. However, baptism plays no role in salvation. This will be explained in more detail later. In St. Matthew 23:10, Jesus instructed:

Neither be called masters; for one only is your Master, the Christ.

In St. John 17:1-4, Jesus prayed:

... Father, the hour has come! Glorify thy Son, that thy Son may glorify thee, even as thou (*God*) hast given him (*Jesus*) power over all flesh, in order that to all that thou (*God*) hast given him (*Jesus*) he (*Jesus*) may *give* everlasting life. Now this is everlasting life, that they may know thee (*God*), the only true God, and him whom thou hast sent, Jesus Christ. I have glorified thee on earth; I have accomplished the work that thou hast given me to do.

Much is revealed about everlasting life in these few verses. First, life everlasting is a *gift*, as stated in Romans 6:23, above. Ephesians 2:8-9 confirms that we cannot earn it because then we could rightfully boast. Second, St. John tells us that life everlasting is a *possession* of those who believe Jesus is whom He says He is. Third, it is Jesus' right to *give* God's gift of everlasting life to whomever calls upon Him to be Lord of his or her life. And finally, everlasting life is the privilege of *knowing God and Jesus Christ*. The Greek word used in this text for "know" is "*ginosko*." It goes past mere acquaintance to intimate knowledge. For example, one would know the likes and dislikes of a spouse.

What Is One's Eternal Future Apart from the Jesus of the New Testament?

There are many "Jesuses" other than the Christ of the New Testament. Moreover, Jesus warned that false christs would come [St. Matthew 24:24]. There is the Jesus of the Latter-Day Saints, a created being and half-brother of Lucifer. This Jesus cannot save you and most of those who think of themselves as Catholic, Orthodox, or Protestant understand this. There are the Jesuses of "The Churches." Neither can any of them save you. These Churches have stolen the "power" of Christ for themselves and made Him a liar. Thus, they preach a false, impotent Jesus represented either as an infant in his mother's arms or as a helpless man nailed to a cross. St. Paul warned against those who preach such a Jesus, having a form of godliness but denying His power [see 2 Timothy 3:5 KJV]. He described these as having a zeal for God but not according to knowledge [Romans 10:2]. These Churches teach His virgin birth, death, burial, and resurrection. However these same Churches strip away His power to justify, sanctify, and preserve the sinner and give him eternal life [see Romans 8:29-30]. What you may not realize is that such a Jesus is no less false than the Jesus worshiped by the cults. Neither can this Jesus save you.

Seek Mercy Rather Than What You Are Owed

Each of us *deserves* to spend eternity separated from God in hell. This is the wage our works have earned. This is what God's justice demands. However, as God's Word reveals in St. John 3:16-18:

> For God so loved the world that he gave his only-begotten Son, that those who believe in him may not perish, but may have life everlasting. For God did not send his Son into the world in order to judge the world, but that the world might be saved through him. He who believes in him is not judged; but he who does not believe is already judged, because he does not believe in the name of the only begotten Son of God (*Jesus*).
>
> —see also Jeremias 31:31

In His mercy, God provided a plan of salvation for man because He knew man could not come to salvation on his own. St. Paul explains what it means to believe in the Jesus he knew, the Jesus of the New Testament:

> But we know that man is not justified (*saved*) by works of the Law, but by the faith of (*in*) Jesus Christ. Hence we also believe in Christ Jesus, that we may be justified by the faith of (*in*) Christ, and not by the works of the Law; because by the works of the Law no man will be justified.
>
> —Galatians 2:16

While one man's disobedience to God in eating of the forbidden tree resulted in the door to the kingdom being closed, the God-man's obedience in hanging on the tree in accordance with His Father's will resulted in the door being reopened.

Man Cannot Be Saved by the Law

The pervasive view on obtaining salvation among the Jews of Jesus' day was through keeping the Law of Moses (doing works). However, the Pharisees had replaced God's Law with their manmade traditions. Jesus taught that faith in Him, not following the traditions of men, opened the door to the kingdom of God. As recorded in St. John 5:24, Jesus said:

> Amen, amen, I say to you, he who hears my word, and believes him who sent me, has life everlasting, and does not come into judgment, but has passed from death to life.

Devout Jews prided themselves on following the Law to the most minute detail. Wealth was viewed as God's assurance of accepted behavior.

The wealthier one was, the more esteemed by God was the prevalent view. When Jesus told the crowd, "It is easier for a camel to pass through the eye of a needle, than for a rich man to enter the kingdom of God," His listeners were astonished and angered [St. Mark 10:25]. The religious leaders hardened their hearts. They simply did not believe that Jesus was who He claimed to be. Moreover, most people then, as today, feel comfortable in their time-honored traditions handed down by their fathers. If one has believed for the better part of his life that the path to God is secured by biting the heads off live chickens three times a week, it will be extremely hard to keep him out of the coop! The same is true for those who put their faith in receiving certain sacraments, lighting votive candles to the Blessed Virgin, etc. It will be extremely difficult for him to accept any other view. Sadly, few question the faith they inherited from their parents. Moreover, since such a one has resisted the "Truth," God will harden his heart against the truth of the Jesus of the New Testament, against His ability to save and give eternal life to His sheep. Jehovah God hardened Pharao's heart when he refused to let the Jews go. Even worse, God's Word tells us:

> For they have not received the love of truth that they might be saved. Therefore God sends them a misleading influence that they may believe falsehood, that all may be judged who have not believed the truth, but have preferred wickedness (*not trusted in the Jesus of the New Testament*).
> —2 Thessalonians 2:10-12

Jesus referred to the hard-hearted religious leaders in their disbelief as "serpents, brood of vipers." He asked them rhetorically, "How can you escape the condemnation of hell!" [see St. Matthew 23:1-33] It is interesting to note that Jesus never referred to non-clerical Jews or the Gentiles as "serpents" or "vipers," but as "lost sheep without a shepherd." Jesus identified the disbelieving Pharisees with the very seed of the serpent [see Genesis 3:15]. He told them:

> The father from whom you are is the devil, and the desires of your father it is your will to do ... But because I speak the truth you do not believe me.
> —St. John 8:44-45

St. Paul reiterates the *impotence* of the law to save in Romans 3:20:

> For by the works of the Law no human being shall be justified (*declared not guilty*) before him (*God*), for through law comes the *recognition* of sin.

The *purpose* of the Law is to allow man to recognize by how far he misses the mark. In fact, that is the definition of sin: missing the mark. Man could not even gauge how truly reprobate his life was until God gave him Ten Commandments. Have you ever broken even one? If you have, then you have missed the mark. Therefore, you have sinned and your infraction has earned a wage: eternal death. Prior to God's giving Moses the Ten Commandments on Mount Sinai, man lived by his conscience. He had no external gauge by which to measure his depravity. His conduct grew so horrible that God mourned that He had made man:

> ... the LORD saw that the wickedness of man on the earth was great, and that man's every thought and all the inclination of his heart were only evil, he regretted that he had made man....
>
> —Genesis 6:5-6

The Ten Commandments, the Law, was never intended to save. Rather, it is intended to work like a plumb line. A plumb line can reveal that a wall is not straight. However, it cannot straighten it.

Only God's Grace Saves

Only God's grace saves. In Galatians 2:21, St. Paul concludes:

> I do not cast away the grace of God. For if justice (*justification*) is by the law, then Christ died in vain.

The word "grace" means unmerited favor, that is, we did nothing to "earn" God's favor. In the Old Testament, the supreme example of grace was the redemption of the Hebrew people from Egypt and their establishment in the Promised Land. This did not happen because of any merit on Israel's part, but in spite of their unrighteousness [Deuteronomy 9:5-6]. Although the grace of God is always free and undeserved, it must not be taken for granted. Grace is given by God and received by man through faith [Ephesians 2:8]. As St. Paul observes above, if one throws away God's grace, then Christ's death *was* in vain! Jesus died to save St. Paul. In fact, Jesus' death on the cross paid for every past, present, and future sin of *all* mankind. However, Jesus will not force a man or woman to accept God's free gift.

In St. Luke 19:10, Jesus revealed, "For the Son of Man came to seek and to save what was lost." Jesus confirms that He does the *seeking* and the *saving*. Not the law. Not The Church. Not any church. Not any other person. The title, "Son of Man," is a messianic title dating back to the time of the major prophets. Since Jesus' birth, we understand it to mean God in

human flesh (Emmanuel–see Isaias 7:14). St. Peter confirms that there is
no other name under heaven by which men can be saved [Acts 4:12].

God Has a Plan for *Your* Salvation

God's plan for man's salvation is described in the Scriptures and, because
our minds are finite and we live in a fallen state, we must accept God's
purpose and plan on faith. There is no way our minds can reason to it or
even understand it. God tells us in Isaias 53:10-11:

> And the Lord was *pleased* to bruise him (*Jesus*) in infirmity; (*for*) if he
> (*Jesus*) shall lay down his life for sin (*as an atonement for sin*), he shall see
> a long-lived seed, and the will of the Lord (*God*) shall be prosperous in
> his (*Jesus'*) hand. Because his soul hath labored, he shall see and be filled:
> by his knowledge shall this my just servant (*Jesus*) justify many, and he
> shall bear their (*sinners'*) iniquities.

Justification is a legal term that refers to God's declaration that a man
is righteous, just, or not guilty. This means he is no longer condemned
and, therefore, there is no penalty to pay. In Romans 8:1-2, St. Paul reveals
that:

> "There is therefore now no condemnation for those who are *in Christ
> Jesus* (*believers*), who do not walk according to the flesh. For the law of
> the Spirit of the life in Christ Jesus has delivered me from the law of sin
> and of death."

Why? Because, for those who have accepted Jesus as Lord and Savior,
as *evidenced* by the fact that they no longer walk according to the flesh
(more will be said on this in chapter six), God has imputed their sins to
Jesus and Jesus' righteousness to them. God reckons their sins to Jesus'
account and Jesus' righteousness to their accounts. Notice the wording
carefully. These are not "not walking according to the flesh" in order to
be in Christ. That would be works. Rather, because they are "in Christ,"
they do not walk according to the flesh. Moreover, since Jesus died on the
cross in their place, their accounts are marked "paid in full." That is why
St. Paul asks rhetorically in Romans 8:33-34:

> Who shall make accusation against the elect (*those who have accepted Jesus
> as Lord and Savior, believers*) of God? It is God who justifies! Who shall
> condemn? It is Christ Jesus who died; yes, and rose again, he who is at
> the right hand of God, who also intercedes for us.

The question St. Paul is positing here is, "After God declares a man not guilty, who can condemn him? Who will speak counter to the Word of God?" Satan, the accuser of the brethren, for one [Apocalypse 12:10]. And, as we shall see in later chapters, many Churches and denominations also do so.

Why did Jesus go to the cross?

> For our sakes he (*God*) made him (*Jesus*) to be sin who knew nothing of sin, so that in him (*Jesus*) we might become the justice (*righteous*) of God.
> —2 Corinthians 5:21

God's justice, as recorded in His Law, demands death for the sinner. Jesus, who knew no sin, was made to be sin for us. It *pleased* God to make Jesus a sin offering to redeem all who would believe on His Son. In doing so, God tells us:

> But now the justice of God has been made manifest independently of the Law, being attested by the Law and the Prophets; the justice of God through faith in Jesus Christ upon all who believe. For there is no distinction, as all have sinned and have need of the glory of God. They are justified (*declared not guilty*) freely by his grace through the redemption which is in Christ Jesus whom God has set forth as a propitiation (*a blood sacrifice to atone for sin*) by his (*Jesus'*) blood through faith, to manifest his justice, God in his patience remitting former sins; to manifest his justice at the present time, so that he himself is just, and makes just (*declares not guilty*) him who has faith in Jesus.
> —Romans 3:21-26

Why did God choose this manner of reconciliation to save all who would believe on His Son?

> That he (*God*) might show in the ages to come the overflowing riches of his (*God's*) grace in kindness towards us in Christ Jesus.
> —Ephesians 2:7

To whom will God show in the ages to come the overflowing riches of His grace in kindness towards us? It will certainly be manifested to those in heaven. This will include Old Testament saints (believers), believers from the church age, and saints from the Tribulation period, as well as the angels that remained faithful to God during the time of Lucifer's (Satan's) initial rebellion. It will also be known to nonbelievers and demons (fallen angels), including Satan. It is interesting to note that God did not create a plan of restoration for Lucifer and his fallen angels. Their hardness of heart is past repentance.

God Established His Plan of Salvation *Before* He Created Man

When did God choose this manner of reconciliation-atonement through the blood of Jesus? John the Baptist identified Jesus as the Lamb of God who takes away the sin of the world, as recorded in St. John 1:29. Apocalypse 13:8 identifies Jesus as, "... the Lamb who has been slain from the foundation of the world." Thus, God's plan for man's salvation was determined even *before* his creation. God knew that man would fall short of the mark, that is, sin. St. Paul reveals:

> But all things are from God, who has reconciled us to himself through Christ and has given to us the ministry of reconciliation. For God was truly in Christ, reconciling the world to himself by not reckoning against men their sins and by entrusting to us the message of reconciliation (*salvation*).
> —2 Corinthians 5:18-19

Reconciliation means the establishment of friendly relations between parties who were formerly at variance. In this case, reconciliation between God and sinful man. St. Paul elaborates in Romans 5:10-11:

> For if when we were enemies we were reconciled to God by the death of his Son, much more, having been reconciled shall we be saved by his (*Jesus'*) life. And not this only, but we exult (*rejoice greatly*) also in God through our Lord Jesus Christ, through whom we have now received reconciliation.

St. Paul is explaining in the two citations above that God and man are reconciled through Jesus. Moreover, St. Paul confirms that if Jesus could reconcile us to the Father, then He can also save us. In addition, God gives all who believe in the Jesus of the New Testament a ministry of reconciliation. That is, all believers are to be witnesses for Jesus [Acts 1:8]. Believers are to preach the gospel and to be ready to do so both in season and out of season—in good times and in bad [2 Timothy 4:2]. The believer is to explain to the lost that Jesus can save them.

Some Churches misinterpret what is meant by "the ministry of reconciliation." As discussed in *The Orthodox Study Bible, New Testament and Psalms*, Orthodoxy views reconciliation as taking place between the *Church* and the sinful member. Thus, as with the Catholic and many other

Churches, the ministry of reconciliation is taught to be a sacrament and a repeated ritual necessary for forgiveness of sins (absolution). However, according to the above citations, reconciliation occurs between God and a man and is affected by the Jesus of the New Testament, not an ordained priest or Church. Moreover, according to the Scripture, this reconciliation is an accomplished act ("who has reconciled us to himself"), not an ongoing process.

Believing Jews and Gentiles Are Now in One Body

St. Peter confirms that Jesus "... himself bore *our* sins in *his* body upon the tree" [1 St. Peter 2:24]. Through Jesus' atoning work on the cross, believing Jews and Gentiles are now united as brothers. St. Paul explains:

> Wherefore, bear in mind that once you, the Gentiles in flesh, who are called "uncircumcision" by the so-called "circumcision" in flesh made by human hand—bear in mind that you were at that time without Christ, excluded as aliens from the community of Israel, and strangers to the covenants of the promise, having no hope, and without God in the world. But now in Christ Jesus (*saved*) you, who were once afar off (*Gentiles*), have been brought near through the blood of Christ. For he himself is our peace, he it is who has made both one (*Jews and Gentiles*), and has broken down the intervening wall of the enclosure, the enmity, in his flesh. The Law of the Commandments expressed in decrees he has made void, that of the two he might create in himself one new man, and make peace and reconcile both in one body (*the church general*) to God by the cross, having slain the enmity in himself. And coming, he announced the good tidings of peace to you who were afar off, and of peace to those who were near (*the Jews*); because through him we both have access in one Spirit to the Father. Therefore, you are now no longer strangers and foreigners, but you are citizens with the saints (*believing Jews*) and members of God's household: you are built upon the foundation of the apostles and prophets with Christ Jesus himself as the chief corner stone.
>
> —Ephesians 2:11-20

In the mind of a devout Jew, Gentiles were unclean. Jewish tradition demanded that Jews separate themselves from Gentiles in many daily activities. For example, Gentiles were allowed into the Court of the Gentiles at the Temple, but could go no farther. Jehovah-worshiping Jews and Gentiles were separated by "an intervening wall." St. Paul reveals that, with His death on the cross, Jesus "broke down" that wall so that believing Jews and Gentiles are now in "one body," the church general (*autos*). And both believing Jews and Gentiles have direct access to the Father. Notice how similar the concept of "both in one body" is to Jesus' teaching about the Good Shepherd in chapter 10 of St. John's Gospel. In verse 16 Jesus says, "And other sheep I have (*Gentiles*) that are not of this fold (*Jews*). Them also I must bring, and they shall hear my voice, and there shall be one fold (*Jew and Gentile believers*) and one shepherd (*Jesus*)."

The word "saints" in the above citation refers to Jewish believers. Old Testament believers were saved by God's grace received through faith, as recorded in the books of the Old Testament, just as are New Testament believers today [see Genesis 15:6]. They looked forward in time to the cross, with animal sacrifices being a foreshadowing of the ultimate propitiation of the Lamb of God. New Testament believers look backward in time to the cross and thus there are no additional blood sacrifices required:

> He (*Jesus*) does not need to offer sacrifices daily, as the other priests did, first for his own sins, and then for the sins of the people; for this latter (*sins of the people*) he did once for all in offering up himself.
> —Hebrews 7:27

St. Paul expands on how Christ removed identities and barriers for His followers:

> But before the faith came we were kept imprisoned under the Law, shut up for the faith that was to be revealed. Therefore the Law has been our tutor unto Christ, that we might be justified by faith. But now that faith has come, we are no longer under a tutor. *For you are all the children of God through faith in Christ Jesus.* For all you who have been baptized into Christ, have put on Christ. There is neither Jew nor Greek (*Gentile*); there is neither slave nor freeman; there is neither male nor female. For you are all one in Christ Jesus. And if you are Christ's, then you are the offspring of Abraham, heirs according to promise.
> —Galatians 3:23-29

God promised Abram a son. Abram means "father of many." Many years passed and still Sarai, Abram's barren wife, had not conceived. Tired of waiting for the Lord to fulfill His promise, Sarai, which means contentious, took matters into her own hands. She told her husband, who had endured many years of humiliation due to his childless life, to go into her young Egyptian slave girl, Hagar, and lay with her, that she might conceive and bring forth a son. According to the law, any child born to a slave would legally be the possession of the master, Sarai and Abram.

Hagar conceived and bore a son, Ishmael, meaning "God hears," when Abram was eighty-five. Later God again promised Abram a son at the age of ninety-nine. God told Abram his son would be born to Sarai, his wife, then eighty-nine. God also changed Abram's name to Abraham, meaning "father of a multitude." Sarai's name was changed to Sarah, meaning "princess." Because Abraham laughed with joy when God reiterated His promise, God told them to name the child Isaac, meaning "laughter." God told Abraham that His covenant would be passed down through Isaac, the son of promise, rather than through Ishmael, the slave son of Law. As revealed in the above citation, *all* believers are now children of Abraham and heirs to the covenant. Since all believers make up the church general (*autos*), this means that the church general—those in the body of Christ—are now joint heirs to the blessings under the Abrahamic covenant.

As will be discussed more extensively in the Conclusion, some denominations teach that God turned His back on the nation of Israel and that The Church has taken Israel's place in God's heart and prophetic plan. This notion was used by some Churches, as well as the Nazis, as a justification for persecuting the Jews. This false teaching is called "replacement theology" and is a doctrine of demons. God promised Abraham that his descendants would be as numerous as the "stars of the heavens" and "the sands of the seashore" [Genesis 22:17]. The stars are indicative of spiritual Israel, which includes all believers, while the sands are representative of physical Israel. However, as the stars do not replace the sands, neither do believers (the church general) replace Israel. God's prophetic attention will return to the nation of Israel after the end of the church age. If your Church teaches that "The Church" took Israel's place in God's prophetic plan, get out. You are in an apostate church! Read Romans 11.

Salvation Is by Grace Received Through Faith

After explaining that one is saved by the grace of God received through faith, rather than by works, St. Paul goes on to ask rhetorically:

> Where then is thy boasting? It is excluded. By what law? Of works? No, but by the law of faith. For we reckon (*reason*) that a man is justified by faith independently of the works of the Law. Is God the God of the Jews only, and not of the Gentiles also? Indeed of the Gentiles also. For there is but one God who will justify (*declare not guilty*) the circumcised (*Jews*) by faith, and the uncircumcised (*Gentiles*) through the same faith.
> —Romans 3:27

St. Paul affirms that we are saved by faith, not by works or faith plus works. His expository reasoning is that only the Jews are under the Law, since the Law was given only to the Jews and not to the Gentiles. Therefore, only the Jews know what works to do. The Gentiles are not under the Law, do not know the Law, and therefore do not even know what works to do to satisfy the Law. However, since God also saves Gentiles who believe in Jesus' atoning work on the cross, then man is justified by faith through God's grace alone and not by the Law or any of its works. Therefore, no man can boast of the works he has done toward *earning* his salvation. Moreover, if we boast that we "earn" any part of our salvation, then we *steal from God* a part of *His* glory and *His* mercy for ourselves and we *make Him a liar* for He tells us repeatedly that salvation is His *gift* to man through the atoning work of Jesus on the cross [see Ephesians 2:7]. As summed up in Romans 4:4:

> Now to him who works, the reward is not credited as a favor (*gift*) but as something due (*a wage*). But to him who does not work, but *believes* in him (*Jesus*) who justifies the impious, his faith is credited to him as justice (*he is justified by faith*).

The Jewish legalists of Jesus' day, the Judaizers, taught that works must be performed to enter heaven. The many pagan mystery cults that flourished in the Roman Empire taught the same. In fact, *all* false religions, starting with the first—the Babylonian Mystery Cult at the Tower of Babel—have *always* taught that man must perform works to obtain the gods' favors. Works were "known" to be a powerful tool unto salvation and the religious establishments, both pagan and Jewish, took full advantage of the people's ignorance of God's Word, recorded in the Old Testament. The religious hierarchies (Jewish and pagan) used this satanic lie to generate revenues by "selling" salvation to the "faithful." There were those who brought animals to the Temple and sold them for sacrifice at inflated prices. Some coming with worldly currency had to exchange their holdings for Temple coinage. Just as at today's currency exchanges, there was a profit to be made for providing such services. However, those selling animals for sacrifice and the money changers in the Temple charged usurious rates, a practice labeled sin in God's Word and, therefore, forbidden by Law [see Leviticus 25:36].

Some confuse the fact that one is saved by grace through *faith* using:

> So there abide faith, hope, and charity (*love*), these three; but the greatest of these is charity (*love*).
> —1 Corinthians 13:13

If love is a greater virtue than faith, then how can one be saved by faith? they ask. The answer is found in the meaning of the Greek word translated "greatest." That word is "*meizon*." It means greatest in time, that is, the most long lasting, not greatest in virtue. Prior to going to be with God for eternity, the believer has faith in and hope for same. After physical death, the believer no longer needs faith or hope. However, God will continue to love His children, and they Him, throughout eternity. Thus, while faith and hope and the need for both will pass in eternity future, love will not.

Many who subscribe to the Catholic and Orthodox faiths and their Protestant derivatives have been told erroneously that Church tradition taught that one is saved by faith plus works and that Martin Luther altered the King James Version of the Bible to read that one is saved by faith *alone*. However, this supposition presents a number of problems, not the least of which is that the King James Version was not printed and distributed until 1611, more than sixty years *after* the reformer's death in 1547! Moreover, as discussed previously, the people did not request a new translation until 1603, some fifty years after Luther's death. Therefore, the charge that Luther modified the King James Version is false. Presented below are the relevant verses from the three versions of the Bible cited in this book.

> For by grace you have been saved through faith; and that not from yourselves, for it is the gift of God; not as the outcome of works, lest anyone may boast. For his workmanship we are, created in Christ Jesus in good works, which God has made ready beforehand that we may walk in them.
>
> —Ephesians 2:8-10, Roman Catholic Bible

> For by grace you have been saved through faith; and that not of yourselves, it is the gift of God; not of works, lest anyone should boast. For we are His workmanship, created in Christ Jesus for good works, which God prepared beforehand that we should walk in them.
>
> —Ephesians 2:8-10, *The Orthodox Study Bible,*
> *New Testament and Psalms*

> For by grace are ye saved through faith; and that not of yourselves: it is the gift of God: Not of works, lest any man should boast. For we are his workmanship, created in Christ Jesus unto good works, which God hath before ordained that we should walk in them.
>
> —Ephesians 2:8-10, King James Version

None reads that man is saved by "faith" or by "faith alone." Rather, all three confirm the same message from the same perspective: one is saved by God's *grace* which is received through *faith*. The gospel message presented in all three Bibles is the same. Is one saved by grace *alone*? Absolutely! That is the message throughout Scripture. Moreover, people have great faith in Buddha, icons, deceased ancestors, and themselves. However, such faith cannot save. Only God's grace can save. Differences in denominational teaching arise due to various evolved Church (Catholic, Orthodox, Anglican, Episcopal, etc.) traditions, which will be examined in chapter five.

Many Paths to God?

As already cautioned, many Churches preach a false Jesus rather than the all-powerful Christ prophesied in the Old Testament and fulfilled in the New. Following a false Jesus is a false path which leads to hell. Also, some preach a false gospel of "brotherly love." This is an alternative to the true and saving gospel of the Christ of the New Testament. While human love may conquer all in books and movies, it is not a path to God. In a September 19, 2000 interview on *60 Minutes II*, self-admitted cafeteria Catholic and pop-star-turned-mother, Madonna, revealed to her many fans that "all paths lead to God." When the interviewer asked the "Material Girl" how her opinion squared with the position of the Catholic Church, she explained that one need not agree with everything the Church teaches to be a good Catholic. According to this singer-turned-movie-star, "love" is the key. "Some believe in Jesus," she explained, "while others believe in Buddha. At the end of the day, we all end up at the same place." Sadly, many share Madonna's view. However, there is not a single verse in Scripture to support this demonic lie. In fact, God's Word contradicts this mistaken Madonna:

> And this is the testimony, that God has given us eternal life; and this life is in his Son. He who has the Son has the life. He who has not the Son has not the life.
>
> —1 St. John 5:11-12

The only "love path" that leads to God is through the One who said, "Greater love than this no one has, that one lay down his life for his friends" [St. John 15:13]. So yes, love saves, but it is God's love for us through Jesus' shed blood that opens the door to the kingdom, not our love for one another. Believers pray that God will open the minds of those following false christs and false Gospels [2 Corinthians 4:3-4].

Salvation Is Not for Sale

The notion of buying and selling salvation is what prompted Jesus to attack those in the Temple. What God had intended for good, namely, animal sacrifices, which were to be a foreshadowing of Jesus' sacrifice on the cross, man had corrupted by his "love of money" (what St. Paul termed the root of all evil in 1 Timothy 6:10). Thus, the spiritual aspects of Temple worship had been overtaken by the pecuniary interests:

> And they came to Jerusalem. And he entered the temple, and began to cast out those who were selling and buying in the temple; and he overturned the tables of the money-changers and the seats of those who sold doves. He would not allow anyone to carry a vessel through the temple. And he began to teach, saying to them, "*Is it not written*, 'My house shall be called a house of prayer for all the nations?' But you have made it a den of thieves."
>
> —St. Mark 11:15-17

Jesus again emphasizes the importance of knowing the written Word. It is written in Isaias 56:7. The perverse religious leaders had turned their backs on God's Word in favor of selling salvation. God had revealed through the prophet Osee (Hosea in the KJV) around 750 B.C.:

> ... I desire mercy and not sacrifice: and the knowledge of God more than holocausts (*animal sacrifices*).
>
> —Osee 6:6

Temple leaders could not find a way to sell mercy or enhanced knowledge of God. However, they did find a way to hawk animal sacrifices. Moreover, God revealed through the prophet that His prime desire was for people to come to a greater knowledge of Him. How had this knowledge been lost? The things taught by man in the synagogues and in the Temple—the Old Testament analogue for The Churches—had become corrupted by manmade traditions. *Only through the Scriptures* was God's Holy Word preserved uncorrupted. However, the Pharisees had hid the Word of God from the people and, out of greed and lust for power, taught them the precepts of men. Jesus lambasted the Pharisees for withholding the truth of God's Word from the people:

> Woe to you lawyers! because you have taken away the key of knowledge; you have not entered yourselves and those who were entering you have hindered.
>
> —St. Luke 11:52

Over time, people who were following the Word of God and entering the kingdom began to be hindered by the false teachings of the Pharisees. They had established a *religious* system to serve their selfish interests. The Pharisees would not go in themselves, and their false teachings did not allow their followers to enter, either. They were bad shepherds. God's Word says, "My people are destroyed for lack of knowledge" [Hosea 4:6 KJV]. It was after Jesus upset their lucrative financial dealings that Temple leaders began plotting His death.

At the same time, the Babylonian and other mystery cults sold salvation through auricular confessions to their priests. They also hawked sacred items such as carved images and various talismans and amulets to be worn around the neck to ward off evil spirits [see Acts 19:25-40]. It was because of such widespread abuses in both Judaism and paganism that the Samarian sorcerer named Simon, when he saw the miracles of Philip and the other apostles, asked them to "sell" him some of their power, so he could sell salvation to others [Acts 8:9-20]. St. Peter told him to go to destruction, along with his money, because he thought the free gift of God could be purchased [1 St. Peter 1:18-19]. Jesus condemned the practice of selling salvation with the words, "Freely you have received, freely give" [St. Matthew 10:8].

The Jews believed a man's riches were a blessing from God and that his righteousness could be measured by his material wealth. They believed in the next life the wealthy would get the best seats in heaven, because they now got the best seats in the synagogues. Moreover, the wealthier one was, the more he could put in the religious coffers. But Jesus condemned such teachings as the "traditions of men." In fact, He told the religious leaders they would receive a *heavier sentence* (*greater condemnation*) for their sin than those who were poor [see St. Luke 20:46-47]. Jesus turned the established religious organizations, Jewish and pagan, on their heretical heads by teaching salvation as a *free gift from God*, apart from works purchased and performed. Exasperated, the Temple leaders asked Him:

> ... "What are we to do that we may *perform* the works of God?" In answer Jesus said to them, "This is the work of God, that you *believe* in him (*Jesus*) whom he (*the Father*) has sent."
>
> —St. John 6:28-29

Dissatisfied with His answer, since there was no way they could sell "belief," they asked Him what sign He would give them. This was a recurring theme among nonbelievers in Jesus' day just as it is in ours. All during His ministry the religious leaders kept asking for a sign even as Jesus healed the sick, gave sight to the blind, cast out demons, and raised the dead [St. Matthew 9:26].

Some television evangelists today shamefully hawk salvation, along with prosperity theology. "God wants you to be happy, healthy, and out of debt," they claim. "The first step is for you to send me one hundred dollars. The

Lord will bless you for your faith." These are not teaching the gospel or anything else Jesus taught. They will have much to answer for when they stand before the Lord on Judgment Day.

Works Play No Role in God's Plan of Salvation

St. Paul instructs believers on their relationship to good works and how such works are related to the life of the believer:

> For by grace you have been saved through faith; and that not from yourselves, for it is the *gift* of God; not as the outcome of works, lest anyone may boast. For his (*God's*) workmanship we are, created in Christ Jesus in (*for*) good works, which God has made ready beforehand that we may walk in them.
>
> —Ephesians 2:8-10

Notice carefully what is said. Believers are *saved*. Salvation is not through ourselves, it is a *gift* from God. It is *not* a result of works. As with God's plan for man's salvation, which was determined by God before He created man and man fell, so it is with good works. The good works the believer is to do were made ready by God *beforehand*. So not only can we not save ourselves through "our" works, we cannot even *do* good works apart from the Jesus of the New Testament. Moreover, the believer cannot pat himself on the back for the good works he does since they were made ready *by God* for him to walk in even *before* he was saved! For the believer to take any credit for any good works he performs would be to steal a part of God's glory [see 1 Corinthians 15:10]. When someone compliments a pastor on his sermon, a born-again pastor is likely to respond "Praise the Lord," giving God the glory. Jesus instructed His disciples:

> ... let your light shine before men, in order that they may see your good works and give glory *to your Father* in heaven.
>
> —St. Matthew 5:16

St. Peter confirms the purpose of good works:

> For such is the will of God, that by doing good (*performing good works*) you should put to silence the ignorance of foolish men.
>
> —1 St. Peter 2:15

If a believer can perform good works apart from God's indwelling Holy Spirit, then credit for those works should go to the individual. This is what faith-plus-works Churches and churches teach. This is why some denominations claim that man has some inherent good in him. However, the above verses make it clear. The believer can take no credit for his good works. Moreover, "good" works performed by a nonbeliever, which would by necessity be performed apart from Jesus Christ, are seen by God as the equivalent of the "rag of a menstruous woman" [Isaias 64:6]. If you are in a Church or church that preaches you *deserve* anything other than hell, get out. You are in an apostate church.

The fact that works play no role in the believer's salvation can be affirmed further from Ephesians 1:4-7 wherein St. Paul reveals:

> Even as he (*God*) chose us in him (*Jesus*) before the foundation of the world, that we should be holy and without blemish in his sight in love. He (*God*) predestined us to be adopted through Jesus Christ as his (*God's*) sons, according to the purpose of his will (*to do His good pleasure*), unto the praise of the glory of his grace, with which he favored us in his beloved Son. In him we have redemption through his (*Jesus*) blood, the remission of sins, according to the riches of his (*God's*) grace.

The first thing to note in the above passage is that it is God who chose who would be holy and without blemish in His sight. How is it that God can look upon a sinful man as holy and without blemish? Only through His imputation of Jesus' righteousness to the believer, as discussed earlier. Second, note when these were chosen—before the foundation of the world. Third, why were they chosen? Because it was God's will to do His good pleasure. Moreover, the text makes clear that God favored those He chose (graced them). Thus, again we see further confirmation from the Roman Catholic Bible that a man's works play no role in his salvation. Jesus confirms that a man's works, even though viewed as "good" by the world, cannot save him:

> "Not everyone who says to me, 'Lord, Lord,' shall enter the kingdom of heaven; but he who does the will of my Father in heaven shall enter the kingdom of heaven. Many will say to me in that day, 'Lord, Lord, did we not prophesy in thy name, and cast out devils in thy name, and work many miracles in thy name?' And then I will declare to them, 'I never knew you. Depart from me, you workers of iniquity!'"
>
> —St. Matthew 7:21-23

These are among the most frightening words in the entire Scripture. False teachers lead many to believe that their works make them followers of Jesus and that their ability to perform such works validates this view. This is analogous to the Pharisees' belief that their wealth was confirmation of their good standing with God. Jesus corrected their misunderstanding. As can be seen from the above verses, He will do so again. One can say Jesus is Lord with his lips, but reject the Lord in his heart and still perform works if it suits God's purposes. God can and does use evil men to accomplish His good pleasure, as the above citation makes clear. The Old Testament records many examples of wicked rulers being used by God to accomplish His will. The New Testament reveals incidents of Jesus using demons to accomplish His purposes. Men who think they are prophesying, casting out demons, and working miracles in their own power are only fooling themselves. The feeling of power is a drug to which they become addicted. Jesus' disciples, on the other hand, walked in submission to God, humbled themselves, crucified their flesh daily, and found their strength in the might of the power of the Lord [see Ephesians 6:10]. Unless we do likewise, as prompted by the indwelling power of the Holy Spirit, then Jesus does not *know us* even though we may be great name droppers!

Whatever You Did For The Least of These, My Brethren, You Did For Me

In the latter part of chapter 25 of St. Matthew, Jesus describes the future Judgment of the Nations. In Scripture, "the nations" generally refer to the Gentile nations, as distinct from the nation of Israel. Similarly, there are only two peoples: Jews and Gentiles (sometimes called Greeks). When Jesus returns to earth to end the battle of Armageddon and establish His earthly kingdom, He will come at the most reprobate time the earth has ever experienced. During the preceding seven-year period of Tribulation, 144,000 Jews will have been sealed with the Holy Spirit (these are discussed more fully in chapter six and Appendix A). They will be witnesses for Christ among Jews and Gentiles and will convert many. However, since these will be acting in direct opposition to the world ruler, the Antichrist, they will be persecuted by his one-world government. Therefore, it will be difficult for Christ-believing Jews to obtain any of life's necessities. Some will help them to survive. Jesus refers to these as sheep. Others will shun them and report any contact to the authorities, who will then hunt them down and throw them into prisons and kill them. Jesus refers to these as goats. Thus, when Jesus returns, he must deal with living sheep and goats. He must determine who will enter into and populate His earthly millennial kingdom. The criteria He will use to make His decision are recorded in Scripture:

> "... for I was hungry and you gave me to eat; I was thirsty and you gave me to drink; I was a stranger and you took me in; naked and you covered

me; sick and you visited me; I was in prison and you came to me. Then
the just will answer him saying, 'Lord, when did we see thee hungry, and
feed thee; or thirsty, and give thee drink? And when did we see thee a
stranger, and take thee in; or naked and clothe thee? Or when did we see
thee sick or in prison, and come to thee?' And answering, the king (*Jesus*)
will say to them, 'Amen I say to you as long as you did it for one of these,
the least of my brethren, you did it for me.'"

—St. Matthew 25:35-40

The sheep, whose actions are described in the above citation, are invited
to enter into the kingdom. The goats are sent to everlasting punishment
[St. Matthew 25:46]. Some argue that, at least in this instance, eternal
destinies are based on works: feeding, clothing, and visiting, rather than
grace through faith. Viewing the above verses in isolation, it would appear
to be so. However, numerous other verses reveal that such an interpretation
is incorrect. There is only one true gospel and, thus, only one entrance to
the kingdom. We have no less authority on this matter than the Jesus of the
New Testament: "I am the way, and the truth, and the life. No one comes to
the Father but through me" [St. John 14:6]. Moreover, God's Word refers
to the one and only gospel—the "everlasting gospel"—in Apocalypse 14:6.
Further confirmation that there is only one true gospel is provided by Jesus
Himself, "And this gospel of the kingdom shall be preached in the whole
world, for a witness to all nations; and then will come the end" [St. Matthew
24:14]. It is clear. The sheep are those whose hearts were transformed by the
gospel, the good news of Jesus resurrected preached by the Jewish witnesses.
This change of heart resulted in changed lives and attitudes as it always
does and, in this instance, bold actions to help persecuted Jewish witnesses
and new believers. Confirmation that these are believers who accepted the
gospel can be seen from the way they preface their question with the title
"Lord," the same way Saul did on the road to Damascus [Acts 9:4-5]. After
seeing how the sheep address the king as "Lord," the goats do likewise. As
Satan mimics God, so the goats mimic the sheep. They ask:

"Lord when did we see thee hungry, or thirsty, or a stranger, or naked, or
sick, or in prison, and did not minister to thee?"

—St. Matthew 25:44

However, these goats never recognized Jesus as Lord. Their actions
toward the Jews of the Tribulation period *prove it*. As St. James reminds us,
"Faith without works is dead" [St. James 2:26]. The goats failed to recognize
Jesus as Lord when presented with the gospel time and time again. As we
just saw above, Jesus said: "Not everyone who says to me, 'Lord, Lord,' shall

enter the kingdom of heaven" [St. Matthew 7:21]. Only those who do the will of the Father will enter. And what is the will of the Father? That they *believe* in Him whom the Father has sent: that Jesus is Lord [St. John 6:28]. This is both the *will of the Father* and the *work of man*: to trust in Jesus. Thus, as in the church age, the sheep are saved by grace received through faith in the Jesus of the New Testament.

The Believer Is an Adopted Child of God

What is the believer's relationship to God through Jesus? Adopted sons and daughters. We are no longer enemies against God as we were when we were born with dead spirits [Romans 8:7]. What do we have as a result? Redemption through our kinsman redeemer Jesus the Christ who paid our sin debt at the cross so God could mark our accounts "paid in full." How do we become adopted children of God through Jesus? One of the Beatitudes Jesus preached to the multitudes was, "Blessed are the peacemakers, for they shall be called children of God." The biblical meaning of "peacemaker" is very much misunderstood today and the appellation often is used incorrectly. When two leaders of murderous factions who are known not to be believers in Jesus sit down at the "peace table" to negotiate an agreement, the media often quote those who make reference to Jesus' teaching. During Israeli and Palestinian peace negotiations several years ago, President William Jefferson Clinton commented on their progress and remarked before the television cameras, "Blessed are the peacemakers, for they shall inherit the earth." However, the president got the beatitudes mixed up. Jesus said it is the meek who will inherit the earth. No one came forward to correct the president. In a sense, his words may prove to be prophetic. If the Israelis accept the bad idea of trading land for peace, then indeed the Palestinian peacemakers will inherit more of the earth! However, God's Word tells us He will not let such a "deal" stand [see Isaias 28:14-15]. The true meaning of peacemaker is found in St. John 1:12-13:

> But to as many as received him (*Jesus*) he gave the power (*right*) of becoming sons (*children*) of God; to those who believe in his (*Jesus'*) name: Who were born not of blood, nor of the will of the flesh, nor of the will of man, but of God (*born from above*).

Thus, the one with whom the peacemaker has made peace, and is therefore blessed (happy), is God. How? By receiving Jesus as Lord and Savior. Thus, we become sons and daughters of God by believing in (trusting) Jesus. He tells us:

"... Amen, amen, I say to you, everyone who commits sin is a slave of sin. But the slave does not abide in the house forever; the son abides there forever. If therefore the Son makes you free, you will be free indeed."
—St. John 8:34-36

A slave might live in his master's house until the master puts him out or sells him. God told Abraham to send Hagar and Ishmael away. Both were slaves. However, the master's son lives in the house as long as he desires. Through Jesus' atoning death on the cross and our acceptance of Him as Lord and Savior, we become sons and daughters of God. There is a tremendous difference between a man and his slave as opposed to a man and his child. Jesus illustrated this beautifully in the parable of the Prodigal Son [St. Luke 15:11-32].

Jesus Reveals the Only Sin that Leads to Eternal Death

What sin can send one to hell? Murder? Adultery? Fornication? No one is in hell for these or similar sins. Moreover, many are in heaven who have committed murder, adultery, and fornication. King David is but one example. St. Paul is another [Acts 9:1-2]. All in hell will be there for the *same sin*. Jesus tells us in St. John 16:9 that the sin of the world is that it "... does not believe in me." The reason nonbelievers commit these acts is because, contrary to God's will, they do not believe in the Jesus of the Scriptures. They are rebels.

The Unpardonable Sin

As recorded in St. Matthew 12:24, the Pharisees, after seeing Jesus cast out demons from a possessed man, said He did so through the power of Beelzebub, a devil. Beelzebub means "Lord of Dung." This was a deliberate denigration of the name of the god of the hated Philistines, Baalzebub, which means "Lord of the Flies." Jesus' response is recorded in St. Mark 3:28-29:

Amen I say to you that all sins shall be forgiven to the sons of men, and the blasphemies wherewith they blaspheme; but whoever blasphemes against the Holy Spirit never has forgiveness, but will be guilty of an everlasting sin.

The Holy Spirit is in the world convicting sinners of sin, of righteousness, and of judgment [St. John 16:8]. This stiff-necked group of disbelieving Pharisees not only refused to listen to the convicting power of the Holy Spirit, they attributed to Satan the power Jesus exhibited in casting out demons. This reveals a hardness of heart and spiritual perversion accumulated over a lifetime of disbelief and disobedience that would make it virtually impossible ever to repent, to change their minds. If you are concerned that you have committed the unpardonable sin, you demonstrate by such concern that you do not have such hardness of heart. Therefore, you could not have committed the unpardonable sin.

The Roman Catholic Church uses a verse on blasphemy against the Holy Spirit to argue that certain *sins* can be forgiven in this age but others can be forgiven only in the next age. The Church uses this teaching to support its argument on purgatory (see Catechism of the Catholic Church, paragraph 1031):

> "And whoever speaks a word against the Son of Man, it shall be forgiven him; but whoever speaks against the Holy Spirit, it shall not be forgiven him, either in this world (*age*) or in the world (*age*) to come."
> —St. Matthew 12:32

Note that St. Mark 3:28-29 and St. Matthew 12:32 are in agreement. Moreover, this same truth is recorded also in St. Luke 12:10:

> And everyone who speaks a word against the Son of Man, it shall be forgiven him; but to him who blasphemes against the Holy Spirit, it will not be forgiven.

All three Gospel accounts are in accord. Notice, however, that none addresses *sins* that can be forgiven in one age versus another, as the Catholic Church posits. The subject in each citation is forgiveness of *one* sin: blasphemy against the Holy Spirit. All three accounts make clear that this sin cannot be forgiven. Why? Because blasphemy against the Father and the Son will result in the Holy Spirit convicting the blasphemer of his transgression. However, if one blasphemes against the very One who convicts of sin, then he will certainly not hear the convicting voice of that same Holy Spirit. And it is for this reason that blasphemy against the Holy spirit cannot be forgiven. The Roman Catholic Bible nowhere teaches that sins can be expiated after one's death.

Jesus Tells Us One Must Be Born Again to Enter into the Kingdom of God

In order to make peace with God and become His adopted children and joint heirs with Christ [Romans 8:17], we must first be spiritually regenerated. This is referred to as being "reborn." No less authority than

St. Peter confirms that believers "... have been reborn" and he emphasizes that their rebirth was "not from corruptible seed but from incorruptible (*seed*) through the Word of God who lives and abides forever" [1 St. Peter 1:23]. Those who do not consider the Holy Bible to be the authoritative Word of God often scoff when asked if they've been born again. However, when a Pharisee named Nicodemus, a leader of the Sanhedrin, asked Jesus what a man must do to enter into the kingdom of God, Jesus did not scoff. Rather, He responded:

> "... Amen, amen, I say to thee, unless a man be born again, he cannot see the kingdom of God."
>
> —St. John 3:3

It is interesting that Jesus answered Nicodemus this way. Jesus said that without being born again, a man cannot even *see* the kingdom of God. One cannot enter what one cannot see. This is explained by St. Paul:

> But the sensual man does not perceive the things that are of the Spirit or God, for it is foolishness to him and he cannot understand, because it is examined (*discerned*) spiritually.
>
> —1 Corinthians 2:14

Obviously, Nicodemus was not born again because he could not discern that he was standing in the very presence of the King and His kingdom. His inability to discern spiritual things is confirmed in St. John 3:9 where, after Jesus explained the things of the Spirit, Nicodemus asked further, "How can these things be?" St. Paul tells us:

> For if thou confess with thy mouth (*speak aloud*) that Jesus is the Lord, and believe in thy heart that God has raised him from the dead, thou shalt be saved. For with the heart a man believes unto justice (*righteousness*), and with the mouth profession of faith is made unto salvation.
>
> —Romans 10:9-10

Nicodemus addressed Jesus as Rabbi, teacher, and as one with whom God abides. But Jesus is much more. Jesus told them at the feast of the dedication (celebration of the rededication of the Temple—Hanukkah) in Jerusalem, as recorded in St. John 10:30, "I and the Father are one."

Jesus continued His discussion with a bewildered Nicodemus:

> "... Amen, amen, I say to thee, unless a man be born again of water and the Spirit, he cannot enter into the kingdom of God."
>
> —St. John 3:5

Here Jesus notes that a man must be born again (*anothen*) of water and the Spirit. The Greek word "*anothen*" has two meanings: "again" and "from above." In his first birth, a physical birth, man is born of water. The breaking of a woman's water is a sign that her delivery is near. At the time of Nicodemus, John the Baptist was baptizing people in the Jordan River much to the agitation of the religious establishment. It was widely understood that submergence beneath the water was a symbolic representation of an internal spiritual washing. Namely, in being baptized by John, the person was making a public statement that he was repenting, changing his mind about his own righteousness. John's baptism had nothing to do with salvation, only repentance. The purpose of John's ministry was to prepare the way of the Lord, the promised Messiah. It was to John's baptism that Jesus was referring when He said that one must be born again of water. In other words, he must repent. Admitting one's sin is a prerequisite for accepting Jesus as Lord and Savior and inviting Him into one's life. If one does not first change his mind and admit that he is a sinner in need of a Savior, he cannot legitimately ask Jesus to come into his life.

The word baptism comes from the Greek word *baptizo*, which means to immerse or submerge. This is why John was conducting his baptisms at a riverbank rather than at one of the ceremonial basins in the Temple. Further verification is gained from Acts 8:38-39 wherein St. Luke records the baptism of the eunuch by St. Philip:

> ... both Philip and the eunuch went *down into the water*, and he baptized him.... when they came *up out of the water*....

The second step Jesus referred to was being reborn of the Spirit. As discussed earlier, each of us is born with a spirit that is dead, a condition we inherit from the first Adam. Our first and physical birth included water and a dead spirit. In order to enter the kingdom of God, one's spirit must be regenerated, that is, raised from the dead. One must be born of the (second) last Adam. St. Paul elaborates:

> ... If there is a natural body, there is also a spiritual body. So also is it written, 'The first man, Adam, became a living soul'; the last Adam (*Jesus*) became a life-giving spirit. But it is not the spiritual that comes first, but the physical, and then the spiritual.
> —1 Corinthians 15:44-46

So the physical man is born first (with his dead spirit) and then the spiritual. However, both the rebirth via water (repentance) and the Spirit (spiritual regeneration) come not from ourselves or any other man but *anothen,* from above, from God.

Nicodemus appears one last time in Scripture. He was among those who came to retrieve Jesus' body from the cross [St. John 19:39]. He brought a mixture of myrrh and aloes weighing about one hundred pounds. It is unlikely that a ruling member of the Sanhedrin would have come with expensive burial elements in hand to remove from the cross the dead body of an itinerant preacher and render himself unclean for a period of days. Therefore, it is likely that Nicodemus recognized Jesus for whom He was and is: the Savior.

Jesus Is the Rock

The Feast of Tabernacles is a jubilant celebration commemorating God's preservation of the Israelites in the desert on their way from Egypt to the promised land. On the last day, Jesus provided new understanding for one of the solemn rituals. Each day the priest would fill a gold pitcher with water from the Gihon Spring and lead a large procession back to the Temple. Along the way, they would sing a hymn of praise to the Lord based on Isaias 12:3. The pouring out of the water from the golden pitcher into the basin in the Temple reminded the people of how their ancestors got water during their long trek through the desert. The story is recorded in chapter 20 of the book of Numbers. Psalms 78:15-16 also speaks of this phenomena, water flowing from the cleft in the rock. God told Moses to bring forth water from the rock by striking it. Moses did so and the water came forth [Exodus 17:6]. Later, God told Moses to only speak to the rock to bring forth water. However, in a fit of anger against the murmuring throng, Moses struck the rock. For being unfaithful in showing God's sanctity before the Israelites, God told Moses he would not accompany them into the promised land [Numbers 20:11-12]. With the Jews fully aware of this history, and with the rabbis seated in solemn fashion, Jesus stood up in their midst and announced loudly:

> "If anyone thirst, let him come to me and drink. He who believes in me, as the Scripture says, 'From within him (*out of Jesus' heart*) there shall flow rivers of living water.'"
>
> —St. John 7:37-38

Again, Jesus stressed the importance of knowing Scripture [Isaias 44:3]. The crowd understood Jesus to be equating Himself with Jehovah God who had led the Israelites through the desert by day as a cloud and by night as

a column of fire. Some said Jesus was a prophet. Others said He was the
Christ (Messiah). Some questioned whether or not the Christ could come
from Galilee, a largely Gentile area. When allegations were brought before
the Sanhedrin, the attendants were called to testify. They said, "Never has
man spoken as this man." Instead of being able to condemn Jesus, all the
Sanhedrin could do was criticize the witnesses for not knowing the Law
(Torah). Nicodemus, however, defended Jesus, saying, "Does our Law
judge a man unless it first give him a hearing, and know what he does?"
[St. John 7:37-53] In 1 Corinthians 10:4, St. Paul identifies the rock from
which his ancestors drank:

> ... they drank from the spiritual rock which followed them, and the rock
> was Christ.

Jesus was the source of their water in their desert wanderings. That is
why Jesus is identified as the "Rock of Ages, Cleft for Me." Moses' treatment
of the rock is symbolic of the shepherd being struck, the Christ dying only
once for all, and after this coming to us not again on the cross but by the
Word (speak). The centurion who came to Jesus in Capharnaum seeking
help for his sick servant told Jesus there was no need for Him to come to
the home of an unworthy man like himself (Gentiles recognized that Jews
were forbidden to enter their homes) but if He would only *speak the Word*
his servant would be healed [St. Matthew 8:5-13].

Good Works Are the *Result* of Salvation, *Not Its Cause*

God promises eternal life to His *children* because they *believe*. However,
St. Paul warns:

> Let no one lead you astray with empty words; for because of these things
> (*sin*), the wrath of God comes upon the children of disobedience.
>   —Ephesians 5:6

St. Paul tells us further in Colossians 3:6:

> ... the wrath of God comes upon the unbelievers....

We learn from these two verses something surprising: the opposite of
belief is not disbelief, unbelief, or nonbelief, but disobedience! This is not
surprising since God's *will* is for *all* to come to salvation [St. John 3:16].
Children of God are joint heirs with Christ and have an inheritance in the
kingdom. However, as explained in chapter two, believers do not have a

share in His divinity. Believers do not ascend to godhood. The children of disobedience, on the other hand, have no inheritance:

> For know this and understand, that no fornicator, or unclean person, or covetous one (for this is idolatry) has any inheritance in the kingdom of Christ and God.
> —Ephesians 5:5

Moreover, Jesus tells us in St. John 14:23:

> ... If anyone love me, he will keep my word, and my Father will love him, and we will come to him and make our abode with him.

St. John illuminates in 1 St. John 5:3-4:

> For this is the love of God, that we keep his commandments; and his commandments are not burdensome. Because all that is born of God overcomes the world; and this is the victory that overcomes the world, our faith.

Some who do not understand the teaching of Scripture mistakenly think that believers have a "license to sin." This is not true, as will be made clear later in this chapter. Certainly one who claims to be a believer but lives like the world would leave most wondering if he were truly "born again." The believer is expected to walk the Christian talk he professes. Moreover, the believer is to be a light in a world walking in darkness. Jesus commands believers to, "... let your light shine before men..." [St. Matthew 5:16]. Why? "... in order that they (*men*) may see your good works...." So that a man can receive praise? No. So that God in heaven will be glorified [see Acts 4:21 KJV].

> ... let your light shine before men, in order that they may see your good works *and give glory to your Father in heaven*.
> —St. Matthew 5:16

The only way God can receive glory from works a believer performs is if those works are the ones prepared by God beforehand for the believer to walk in [see Ephesians 2:10]. Thus, it is clear that good works are *not a prerequisite or requirement for salvation*, but *a result of salvation*. Churches that teach salvation by works or faith plus works do not understand this. It is analogous to the proverbial question: "Which came first, the chicken or the egg?" In the instant case, Which comes first, salvation or good works? Errant Churches and churches teach that good works come first. However,

God's Word reveals that salvation comes first and that apart from salvation there is no such thing as "good" works. Moreover, if a believer is not walking in the works God prepared for him, but is walking in his own, then his works cannot be called "good" [see Ephesians 2:8-10]. They are made of hay, wood, and straw and will be consumed [see 1 Corinthians 3:15].

Believers Are to Be Salt

Jesus commands believers to be the salt of the earth [St. Matthew 5:13]. Salt was so important to the ancients that it was used in making covenants [Numbers 18:19 KJV]. Every man carried a pouch of salt. When two men agreed on a matter, similar to a contract today, each would take a pinch of salt from his pouch and drop it into the other's pouch. Then they would agree that until they could identify whose salt belonged to whom and separate the grains, they would adhere to the agreement. A salt covenant was a perpetual one.

Salt was used also as a preservative. Without salt, there was no hope of preserving meat and other foods. Without salt, neither the bread nor the vegetables tasted good. Salt was used also for medicinal purposes and in Temple worship. Salt was so necessary to the preservation of life, both man and animal, that it was a medium of barter. The city of Sodom made its wealth selling salt [see Genesis 14]. Salt is still used as a preservative in areas where refrigeration is not available.

The problems the U.S. faces today have nothing to do with the way the world acts and everything to do with the way many Christians behave. Today, people who call themselves Christian do things Christians a generation ago wouldn't even talk about. The salt has lost its flavor because it has been diluted with other spices such as apathy, immorality, doctrinal error, etc. Many today are trying to reintroduce a sense of morality into society through a number of secular initiatives. Some hold hope for a return of Christian morality through the electoral process. However, this is man's way, not God's. God's Word reveals:

> "If my people, which are called by my name, shall humble themselves, and pray, and seek my face, and turn from their wicked ways; then I will hear from heaven, and will forgive their sin, and will heal their land."
>
> —2 Chronicles 7:14 KJV

Humble themselves, as used in the above citation, means to admit and confess their sins. The problem today is that too many Christians *justify* their sins. Many say, "Oh, I don't really get drunk, just a little high sometimes. Besides, it's not like getting drunk is a big sin. It's no big deal to God." However, God's Word warns:

> ... neither fornicators, nor idolaters, nor adulterers, nor the effeminate, nor sodomites (*sexual perverts*), nor thieves, nor the covetous, nor drunkards... will possess the kingdom of God.
>
> —1 Corinthians 6:9-19

Note the company God places drunkards in: idolaters and sexual perverts. To God, seeing His children get drunk and knowing the consequences that inevitably follow *is* a big deal.

Salt also creates thirst. By walking in a Christlike manner and exhibiting the fruits of the Holy Spirit—love, joy, peace, longsuffering, gentleness, goodness, faithfulness, meekness, and temperance—there is created in those around the believer a thirst for such fruits.

Believers Are to Live by Faith, Not by Sight

Believers are to stand on the promises of God for security rather than rely on ever-changing circumstances. St. Paul exhorts believers to be courageous and walk by faith rather than sight [2 Corinthians 5:6-7]. When St. Peter asked Jesus to bid him to come to Him (walk) on the water, Jesus did so, as recorded in St. Matthew 14:28-31. St. Peter walked on the water while his focus was fixed on Jesus. However, when he took his eyes off the Lord and looked at the winds and the waves, his circumstances, he began to sink. If the believer keeps his focus on Jesus, rather than circumstances, the believer will continue to walk in the right path.

Believers Are to Walk in the Spirit

St. Paul exhorts believers to:

> ... Walk in the Spirit (*Holy Spirit*), and you will not fulfill the lusts of the flesh. For the flesh lusts against the spirit, and the spirit against the flesh (*a man's flesh and spirit are in constant struggle*); for these are opposed to each other, so that you do not do what you would. But if you are led by the Spirit (*born again*), you are not under the Law.
>
> —Galatians 5:16-18

Again, St. Paul encourages believers:

And be not conformed to this world, but be transformed in the newness of your mind, that you may discern what is the good and acceptable and perfect will of God.

—Romans 12:2

The newness of mind refers to the fact that, as a believer, one sees the world differently. The believer now has eyes to see and ears to hear. His mind is renewed continuously by reading the Scriptures and, hopefully, through attending regular services at a Bible-believing, Bible-preaching church. Is the believer ever tempted to sin? Of course. St. James confirms in his epistle, "But everyone is tempted by being drawn away and enticed by his own passion (*flesh*)" [St. James 1:14]. How is the believer to prepare to recognize and respond to temptation? St. Peter answers:

Be *sober*, be *watchful*! For your adversary the devil, as a roaring lion, goes about seeking someone to devour. Resist him, steadfast in the faith....

—1 St. Peter 5:8-9

Believers Are to Confess Their Sins to God

Temptations occur within trials. Trials come along, sometimes from God, sometimes from circumstances. God doesn't tempt anyone [see St. James 1:13]. God does send trials our way, though, to strengthen believers in areas where we are weak and to more closely conform us to Jesus [see Romans 8:29]. Within the context of a trial, Satan (a general reference to his demons) will tempt the believer. How strong can the temptation be? St. Paul assures us:

... God is faithful and will not permit you to be tempted beyond your strength, but with the temptation will also give you a way out that you may be able to bear it.

—1 Corinthians 10:13

Thank God for the words "God will not permit you (*the believer*) to be tempted beyond your strength (*in Him*)." However, the believer doesn't always avail himself of the strength available to him. For example, let's say a believer runs into money problems because he has run up too much debt on his credit cards. In God's view, he has become a bad steward and is on his way to becoming a worse one. God may bring a trial his way to chasten him [see Hebrews 12:6]. God may also let Satan turn the trial into a temptation. How can the believer escape the temptation? St. James reveals:

Be subject therefore to God, but resist the devil, and he (*the devil*) will
flee from you.
                                                                —St. James 4:7

Do we always escape? No. Why? Because a man's flesh is continually
at war with the will of his spirit (the spirit is willing but the flesh is weak).
St. Paul felt so strongly about the separation between the will of a man's
flesh which dwells in his members and the will of his spirit that he taught
that the sins a believer commits are committed by the flesh apart from the
will of his spirit. St. Paul shares with us his lament for the actions of his
members (the makeup of his physical body) and his hope for release from
his earthly body which seeks only after death (sin):

> For we know that the Law is spiritual but I am carnal (*weak in the flesh*),
> sold into the power of sin. For I do not understand what I do, for it is not
> what I wish that I do, but what I hate, that I do. But if I do what I do not
> wish, I admit that the Law is good. Now therefore it is no longer I that do
> it, but the sin that dwells in me. For I know that in me, that is, in my flesh,
> no good dwells, because to wish is within my power, but I do not find the
> strength to accomplish what is good. For I do not the good that I wish, but
> the evil that I do not wish, that I perform. Now if I do what I do not wish,
> it is no longer I who do it, but the sin that dwells in me. Therefore, when
> I wish to do good I discover this law, namely, that evil is at hand for me.
> For I am delighted with the law of God according to the inner man, but I
> see another law in my members, warring against the law of my mind and
> making me prisoner to the law of sin that is in my members. Unhappy
> man that I am! Who will deliver me from the body of this death? The
> grace of God through Jesus Christ our Lord. Therefore I myself with my
> mind serve the law of God, but with my flesh the law of sin.
>   —Romans 7:14-25

St. Paul explains that while his renewed mind wants to do the right
things, his physical body wants to continue in sin. He reasons that if he
does with his body what he does not wish to do in his spirit, then it is not
he who does it—because it is not done freely—but the sin that dwells in
him. It would be analogous to someone putting a gun to your head. At
that point, you likely could be forced to do something with your body that
your mind really didn't wish to do. For example, if someone were holding
your child hostage, you might be willing to rob a bank to redeem her, even
though you had never purposed in your spirit to do such a thing.

What is the believer to do about his sin? St. John answers:

> If we acknowledge (*confess*) our sins, he (*God*) is faithful and just to forgive
> us our sins and to cleanse us from all iniquity.
>
> —1 St. John 1:9

Why would the devil flee from a believer? Because the believer is in submission to God through belief in His Son Jesus and all that such belief entails. Moreover, if the believer has no unconfessed sin in his life and is walking in the will of God (daily prayer and Scripture reading), then his fellowship with God is not broken. Therefore, Satan has no power over the believer unless the believer purposefully allows Satan to enter into his life. Why can Satan not dominate the life of the believer? St. John reveals:

> You are of God, dear children, and have overcome him (*the devil*), because
> greater is he who is in you (*the Holy Spirit*) than he who is in the world
> (*Satan*).
>
> —1 St. John 4:4

Some mistakenly believe that Jesus established auricular confession of one's sins to a priest. Certainly this was a feature of pagan religions of Jesus day and before. They recall having heard or read where Jesus told someone to go and tell it to the priest. However, Jesus never told anyone to confess his sins to a priest. Moreover, as revealed in 1 St. John 1:9 above, God not only forgives our sins when we confess to Him, but also cleanses us from all iniquity.

After curing a leper, Jesus told the man:

> "... go, show thyself to the priest, and offer the gift that Moses commanded,
> for a witness to them."
>
> —St. Matthew 8:4

The curing of leprosy was rare in ancient times and people considered it to be a miracle from God. Moses had recorded the gift a cured leper would offer in Leviticus 14:1-7. Also, Leviticus requires that the priest verify the cure. Thus, Jesus' words to the restored leper harkened back to the Law of Moses and had nothing to do with confessing sins to a priest. Moreover, now every believer is a priest [Apocalypse 1:6]. This means the believer can approach God directly. That is why we pray to God in Jesus' name and confess our sins directly to God. In Old Testament times, God was approached by a man with a blood sacrifice to have his sins forgiven. Our blood sacrifice is Jesus. This is what is meant by praying in His name.

The Believer Is a Purchased Property and Is Sealed by the Holy Spirit for the Day of His Redemption

How can it be that the devil and his demons have no power over the believer unless the believer willfully submits to the temptation? It is not through his own power but through the power of Him who lives within, the Holy Spirit of God. St. Paul tells us that in the day of our belief we were "... sealed (*by the Holy Spirit*) for the day of redemption" [Ephesians 4:30]. St. Paul explains further:

> In him, I say, in whom we also have been called by a special choice, having been predestined in the purpose of him who works all things according to the counsel of his will, to contribute to the praise of his (*God*) glory—we who before hoped in Christ. And in him you too, when you had heard the word of truth, *the good news of your salvation*, and believed in it, were sealed with the Holy Spirit of the promise, who is the pledge of our inheritance, for a redemption of possession, for the praise of his (*God's*) glory.
> —Ephesians 1:11-14

Here St. Paul reveals why some are saved: to contribute to the praise of God's glory. He also explains that the Holy Spirit's sealing of the believer is a type of pledge of his salvation which is his inheritance. When the believer accepts Jesus as Lord and Savior, his salvation is established at that moment. However, it most often is not effected at that moment, the repentant robber on the cross being a notable exception [see St. Luke 23:42]. Therefore, as a pledge of salvation and inheritance, the believer is sealed by the Holy Spirit of God. The sealing serves as a type of earnest money in the purchase of a property. This is particularly fitting since the believer is a purchased property: "You have been bought with a price..." [1 Corinthians 7:23]. And what was that price and who paid it? St. Peter reminds believers:

> You know that you were redeemed (*purchased for a price*) from the vain manner of life handed down from your fathers (*traditions*), not with perishable things, with silver or gold, but with the precious blood of Christ, as of a lamb without blemish and without spot (*Jesus was without sin*).
> —1 St. Peter 1:18-19

The author of Hebrews reminds us who the beneficiaries are in Hebrews 9:15. He explains that "... they who have been called may (*will*) receive eternal inheritance according to the promise." To whom is the author referring when he speaks of those "who have been called"? He is referring to those who have answered "Yes, Lord."

Will *You* Answer, "Yes, Lord"?

After departing from where He had raised a young girl from the dead, two blind men followed Jesus and cried out, "Have pity on us, Son of David!" When Jesus asked them if they believed He could cure their blindness, they answered, "*Yes, Lord*" [St. Matthew 9:28].

After being taunted in Galilee by Jewish leaders sent from Jerusalem, Jesus traveled to the region of Tyre, some thirty-five miles north. The area was a Gentile coastal region of Phoenicia. There, a Canaanite woman (Gentile) called to Jesus, "Have pity on me, O Lord, Son of David. My daughter is sorely beset by a devil" [see St. Matthew 15:21-28]. As a non-Jew, this distraught mother had no way of approaching God. She had no Temple, no Holy of Holies, no altar, no sacrificial offering, and no high priest to intercede with Jehovah God on her behalf. Her spiritual condition was one of utter hopelessness.

Jesus told her He was not sent except to the lost sheep of the house of Israel. But the woman fell down before Him and begged, "Lord, help me!" Jesus told her that it would not be right to take the children's bread and give it to dogs. Bread, of course, was the primary staple supporting life. She did not argue. She agreed with Him, saying, "*Yes, Lord*; for (*yet*) even the dogs eat of the crumbs that fall from their master's table." Jesus responded, "O woman, great is thy faith! Let it be done to thee as thou wilt." And her daughter was healed from that moment.

This story is all the more poignant in light of the cultural background. The Jews did not consider the Canaanites, the cursed decedents of Noe's (also spelled Noah) wicked son Ham, whom the Jews had to fight to enter the promised land, to be on their spiritual level [Genesis 9:25]. In fact, many of the Jews referred to Gentiles as "dogs." In this story, Jesus verbally paints a scene of a family gathered around the table for the meal. The dogs of course would be prancing anxiously around the table, waiting impatiently for their opportunities. In His analogy, Jesus is telling the woman that it would not be right to bring blessings upon her, a Gentile, before first bringing such blessings upon Israel. It would not be right to feed the dogs (Gentiles) with the bread (Jesus) intended for the children (Israel). The woman agreed, "Yes, Lord." However, picturing herself not as a child at the Master's (Jesus') table, for those at the table were of the house of Israel, but as the family's pet under the table, the woman responded that even as a dog she was eligible to receive the crumbs. Jesus commended her *faith*. It must have seemed all the more precious to Him in light of the fact that the religious leaders of the house of Israel were, for the most part, rejecting His claim of being the Master, the promised one—the Son of David, a messianic title [see St. Matthew 23:10]. This is one of the many places in Scripture where Jesus referred to Himself as "bread." The significance of His many references to Himself as bread will become clear in later chapters.

When Jesus arrived at the house of His friend Lazarus, He found Mary and Martha mourning the death of their dear brother. Martha told Jesus she was sure that He could have prevented Lazarus' death had He been there. Jesus assured Martha that Lazarus would rise. Martha agreed that her brother would one day in the far future take part in the resurrection. Jesus corrected her misunderstanding:

> "*I am the resurrection* and the life; he who believes in me, even if he die, shall live; and whoever lives and believes in me, shall never die. Dost thou believe this?" She said to him, "*Yes, Lord*, I believe that thou art the Christ, the Son of God, who hast come into the world."
> —St. John 11:25-27

Lazarus' coming forth from the tomb after four days was a foreshadowing of how God would work His plan of salvation during the church age, the present age of grace. First, a man is called by God while he is spiritually dead and bound in sin. Lazarus was dead and bound in burial bandages. Jesus called, "Lazarus, come forth" [St. John 11:43]. Lazarus heard the call. He responded "*Yes, Lord*," rose, and came out of the tomb. Jesus told them: "Unbind him, and let him go" [St. John 11:44]. This is what Jesus does for the sinner when he responds "Yes, Lord." He frees the sinner from death and the bondage of sin and the grave and gives him a new and *eternal* life.

Who Can Answer, "Yes, Lord"?

The blind men, the Canaanite woman, and Martha all answered, "Yes, Lord." The Holy Spirit is in the world convicting *all* of sin, of a righteous judge, and of a coming judgment [St. John 16:8]. As the Jews were encouraged by John the Baptist, so are we encouraged to agree with God that we are sinners in need of a Savior, the Christ of the New Testament. Which of us can answer, "Yes, Lord"? Jesus gives the answer in St. John 6:44-47:

> "No one can come to me (*answer Yes, Lord*) unless the Father who sent me draw him, and I will raise him up on the last day. *It is written* in the Prophets, 'And they all shall be taught of (*by*) God.' Everyone who has listened to the Father, and has learned, comes to me… (*and*) he who believes in me has life everlasting."

How are we taught by God today? As Jesus notes above, "It is written." He teaches us through our Bible study. We are also taught during services if we attend a Bible-believing, Bible-preaching church. If the preaching at your church is from some source other than Scripture or if the preaching contradicts the Scriptures, then you are not in a Bible-believing church. Many Churches and churches have moved away from teaching Scripture and are instead teaching as doctrines the traditions of men. They do not preach the Jesus of the New Testament, but an antichrist. They hide God's Word from the people. The Pharisees taught the people to love their neighbors but to hate their enemies. Jesus corrected this errant teaching as recorded in St. Matthew 5:43-45. St. Peter was so concerned that false teachers had and would in the future continue to malign the gospel that, near the time of his death, he warned of false doctrines that destroy and pointed to the inerrancy and supremacy of Scripture:

> This, then, you must understand first of all, that no prophecy of Scripture is made by private interpretation. For not by will of man was prophecy brought at any time; but holy men of God spoke as they were moved by the Holy Spirit. But there were false prophets also among the people, just as among you there will be lying teachers who will bring in destructive sects (*teachings*). They even disown the Lord who bought them, thus bringing upon themselves swift destruction. And many will follow their wanton conduct, and because of them the way of truth will be maligned.
>
> —2 St. Peter 1:20-2:2

It is important to *know* the Scripture. It is the responsibility of the believer to determine if the teaching he is hearing or reading is in accordance with God's Word. If it isn't, he needs to find a new teacher.

Some who argue that it is possible to lose one's salvation often look to 2 St. Peter 2:1 for support: "... there will be lying teachers who will bring in destructive sects (*teachings*). They even disown the Lord who bought them, thus bringing upon themselves swift destruction." Viewed in isolation, it would appear that this verse does allow for loss of salvation since they definitely were "bought." However, as 1 St. John 2:2 confirms "and he (*Jesus*) is a propitiation for our sins (*believers*), not for ours only but also for those of the whole world (*nonbelievers*)." Thus, Jesus died for *all*-believers *and* nonbelievers. *All* were bought at the cross. However, only believers accept His payment. Therefore, St. Peter is not teaching that a believer can lose his salvation, but that nonbelievers preach false gospels and bring upon themselves swift destruction.

As recorded in the New Testament, Jesus often prefaced His words with, "It is written." Some argue that Jesus was referring to the Old Testament since the writings that one day would comprise the New Testament hadn't yet been written. This is true. However, note what St. Peter says in the above citation: "... no prophecy of Scripture *is* made by private interpretation" [2 St. Peter 1:20]. While Jesus was speaking of the Old Testament, St. Peter is not. He is talking about the epistles and Gospels that he and others wrote that were in circulation among the churches. In fact, in 2 St. Peter 3:16, St. Peter referred to St. Paul's writings as *Scriptures*, as discussed in chapter one. Moreover, St. Paul told believers to stand firm on the things they learned by epistles [see 2 Thessalonians 2:15]. What St. Peter and St. Paul are teaching is that believers are to compare what is being taught with the writings in circulation among the churches. During this time, there were some preaching errors. Some doing so intentionally and other not. Apollos provides an excellent example of the latter:

> Now a certain Jew named Apollos, born at Alexandria, an eloquent man... instructed in the way of the Lord; and being fervent in spirit, he spoke and taught accurately the things of the Lord, though he knew only the baptism of John. So he began to speak boldly in the synagogue. When Aquila and Priscilla heard him, they took him aside and explained to him the way of God more accurately. And when he desired to cross to Achaia, the brethren wrote, exhorting the disciples to receive him; and when he arrived, he greatly helped those who had believed through grace; for he vigorously refuted the Jews publicly, showing from the Scriptures that Jesus is the Christ.
>
> —Acts 18:24-28 NKJV

Comparing the spoken word to the written Word is precisely what many of the Jews failed to do with regard to the Law and the Prophets that allowed their corrupted teachers to move them away from God's Word to the traditions of men which Jesus condemned [St. Matthew 15:3; St. Mark 7:7-9; and St. Mark 7:13].

A controversy in some Christian theological circles concerns election and predestination, that is, who can come to Jesus. At first glance, verse 44 of St. John, chapter 6, quoted above, appears to be a threat to the concept of free will. This idea is repeated in St. John 15:16:

> "You have not chosen me, but I have chosen you, and have appointed that you should go and bear fruit...."

St. Paul brought the Good News to the Gentiles at Antioch and:

On hearing this (*the Good News*) the Gentiles were delighted, and glorified the word of the Lord, and all who were *destined* for eternal life believed.

—Acts 13:48

St. Paul summarizes important theological insights taught in Scripture:

For those whom he has foreknown he has also predestined to become conformed to the image of his Son, that he should be the firstborn among many brethren. And those whom he has predestined, them he has also called; and those whom he has called, them he has also justified, and those whom he has justified, them he has also glorified.

—Romans 8:29-30

St. Paul explains in Ephesians 1:5-6:

He predestined us to be adopted through Jesus Christ as his sons, according to the purpose of his will (*His good pleasure*), unto the praise of the glory of his grace, with which he favored us in his beloved Son.

Finally, St. Paul reveals to believers:

For God has not destined us unto wrath, but to gain salvation through our Lord Jesus Christ who died for us....

—1 Thessalonians 5:9

Some are inclined because of these verses to conclude that man does not have a free will, that whether or not he believes is determined solely by God. Others believe in karma or destiny. However, look again at St. John 6:45:

... Everyone who has *listened to the Father*, and has *learned*, comes to me.

In verse 45, Jesus affirms that the Holy Spirit of God teaches us through conviction and that this enables people to accept the truth concerning Jesus and respond, "Yes, Lord." Moreover, it is revealed through God's Word that "faith comes by hearing, and hearing by the Word of God" [Romans 10:17]. However, only those who *listen* and *learn* will respond, "Yes, Lord." The disobedient refuse to listen. They refuse to learn. Some are so busy following a false christ, an antichrist taught by a Church, that they refuse to read the Scripture and therefore cannot "listen to the Father." And if they do not listen, they cannot learn. These do not even know the Jesus of the

New Testament. Neither do they know how far from the New Testament the impotent Jesus their Church preaches is from the all-powerful Christ of the Scriptures. Therefore, these cannot respond, "Yes, Lord."

Others are enthralled listening to the cacophony of the world. As revealed in 3 Kings 19:12, God's voice is like the "whistling of a gentle air." Others simply are too busy, too involved ministering to the flesh (doing "good" works), or too caught up with the things of this life to be concerned about where they will spend eternity. St. Paul warns in 2 Timothy 3:7, some are so busy:

> ... ever learning yet never attaining knowledge of the truth.

What is the truth? Jesus said:

> "... I am the way, and the truth, and the life...."
> —St. John 14:6

Some, ever learning the useless things of this world that will perish along with this world, never come to the knowledge of truth, namely, that the Jesus of the New Testament is the way, the truth, and the life. This Jesus is the only path. Some have hardened their hearts against the convicting power of the Holy Spirit, just like Pharao [see Exodus 8:15]. A hardened heart builds up a thick layer of scar tissue. Over time it becomes less and less likely that the good news of the gospel of Jesus Christ can penetrate. St. Paul warns believers:

> Now the Spirit expressly says that in after times (*the time after Jesus' ascension*) some will depart from the faith, giving heed to deceitful spirits and doctrines of devils, speaking lies hypocritically, and having their conscience branded (*seared with a hot iron*). They will forbid marriage, and will enjoin abstinence from foods, which God has created to be partaken of with thanksgiving by the faithful and those who know the truth.
> —1 Timothy 4:1-3

As will be seen in chapter five, it didn't take long for these demonic heresies to take root.

The Biblical Meaning of Predestination

The key to understanding the biblical meaning of predestination is understanding God's foreknowledge of each of us. In the first chapter of the book of Jeremias God declared to the prophet:

Before I formed you in the womb I knew you; before you were born I
sanctified you (*set you aside for My purposes*); I ordained you a prophet
to the nations.

—Jeremias 1:5

Since God is sovereign and all-knowing, He knew before the foundation
of the world who would say "Yes, Lord" and who would not. While a man
is in this world carrying out his free will, God *was* in heaven knowing the
man's end even *before* his creation. So from God's perspective, one's answer
to Jesus appears to be predestined [see Ephesians 1:5]. From the man's point
of view, however, it is not. It is like viewing "an instant replay." The runner
is free to run right or left before the play is videotaped. However, on the
replay, he must run the same way he did originally. Nevertheless, he had a
free will and he exercised it in executing the run. One may hear the gospel
one hundred times and reject it. However, he has the free will to accept it
at the one-hundred-and-first hearing. Our God is a God of more than just
second chances. Moreover, God's will is for *all* to come to eternal life through
Jesus and this is what has delayed Jesus' return. St. Peter explains:

The Lord does not delay in his promises (*to return*), but for your sake
is long-suffering, not wishing that any should perish but that *all* should
turn to repentance.

—2 St. Peter 3:9

Thus, no one will be in hell because God predestined him to go there.
Everyone who enters hell will do so by his own choice and *against God's will*
[St. John 3:16]. Because God foreknew who would accept His free offer of
salvation and say, "Yes, Lord," He made sure the gospel message was gotten
to him. This is the biblical meaning of predestination. Some reject God's plan
of salvation by using the excuse that it's not fair since some in backward
countries have never heard of Jesus. Again, God knows who will say, "Yes,
Lord," and He gets the gospel to them. God graciously allows believing
men and women to participate in His plan of salvation. However, no one's
eternal destiny is dependent on anyone getting the gospel to him.

Believers Exhibit Changed Lives

The Roman Catholic Bible describes what happens to the man and
woman who accept the Jesus of the New Testament as Lord and Savior. St.
Paul teaches in Galatians 5:24:

And they who belong to Christ have crucified their flesh with its passions
and desires.

St. Paul is not speaking literally, of course. Rather, he is explaining that a decision to accept Jesus is at the same time a decision to reject those desires of the flesh that God has labeled sin. Therefore, believers need not automatically respond to their sin natures when tempted, as they did when they were in bondage, before the Son "made them free" [St. John 8:36].
In chapter 4 of Ephesians, St. Paul instructs believers further, encouraging them to no longer walk as those who are unsaved, chasing the worthless pleasures of this world, giving in to lewdness, and working all manner of unclean acts. He emphasizes that such things are not learned by hearing of Christ. Rather, St. Paul exhorts:

> ... as regards your former manner of life (*walking in sin*) you are to put off the old man, which is being corrupted through its deceptive lusts. But be renewed in the spirit of your mind (*your attitude*), and put on the new man, which has been created according to God in justice and holiness of truth.
>
> —Ephesians 4:22-24

St. Paul is explaining that the believer did not come to know Jesus through his flesh, the flesh representing the old man which is being corrupted by chasing after the things of this world which appear good but which, in the end, result in death. That is why such things are deceptive. Rather, the believer came to know Jesus through a renewed mind which leads to changes in one's thinking and attitudes. The believer no longer looks at the world the same way after his spirit has been regenerated and his mind renewed. For example, most among the unsaved would agree that murder is wrong. However, many would argue where to draw the line between what is a sin and what is not. Some would draw it at adultery, fornication, legalization of prostitution (which is already legal in some counties in Nevada), abortion, parental consent for an abortion for a minor, sexual relations between adults and children, bisexuality, homosexuality, or the legalization of drugs. A person's inability to distinguish between right and wrong is a characteristic God's Word calls a reprobate mind [Romans 1:28]. Since the unsaved reject God's standards presented in the Scripture, they consider totally irrelevant factors in determining morality. Some consider things like "mutual consent" to be important while others consider answers to questions like "Whom does it hurt?" It is only with a reborn spirit that a man has eyes to see and ears to hear and a renewed mind by which he can understand that what God calls sin *is* sin regardless of mutual consent or whom it may or may not hurt. God knows sin always hurts us and often others. This is why He gives us standards to live by, for our protection and happiness, not to spoil our fun. Again, one result of a reborn spirit is a reorientation of one's thinking and attitude.

St. Paul reiterates that the believer is a new creation:

> If then any man is in Christ, he is a new creature: for the former things have passed away; behold, they are made new.
>
> —2 Corinthians 5:17

Moreover, St. Paul confirms that:

> He has rescued us from the power of darkness and translated us into the kingdom of his beloved Son.
>
> —Colossians 1:13

Thus, believers do not inhabit the same dimension as nonbelievers! As early as the second century, Christians came to be called the "third race," neither Jewish nor pagan, but a community apart.[1] Their lives and conduct were radically different from those of both pagans and Jews. These early Christians truly were "not conformed" to the world. Believers are Christ's representatives on earth. As His ambassadors, we are to live our lives in a Christlike manner [2 Corinthians 5:20].

St. Paul addresses in chapter 6 of the book of Romans an old and grave error. After preaching that where sin abounds, God's grace abounds even more, some alleged that believers were free to sin with impunity so that God's grace would flow even more abundantly. Also, some who *claimed* to be believers, but were not, spread the lie that the more they sinned, the more grace God would bestow on them. St. Paul takes up this heresy in rhetorical fashion in Romans 6:1-10:

> What then shall we say? Shall we (*believers*) continue in sin that grace may abound? By no means! For how shall we who are dead to sin still live in it? Do you not know that all we who have been baptized into Christ Jesus have been baptized into his death? For we are buried with him by means of Baptism into death, in order that, just as Christ has risen from the dead through the glory of the Father, so we may also walk in newness of life. For if we have been united with him in the likeness of his death, we shall be so in the likeness of his resurrection also. For we know that our old self has been crucified with him, in order that the body of sin may be destroyed, that we may no longer be slaves to sin; for he who is dead is acquitted of sin. But if we have died with Christ, we believe that we shall also live together with Christ; for we know that Christ, having risen from the dead, dies now no more, death shall no longer have dominion

over him. For the death that he died, he died to sin once for all, but the
life that he lives, he lives unto God.

In referring to believers being dead to sin, St. Paul is expressing the fact
that believers are no longer slaves to sin. Jesus taught that everyone who is
living in sin is a slave to sin. He went on to say, as recorded in St. John 8:36,
"If therefore the Son makes you free, you will be free indeed." Therefore,
the believer is free from the bondage of habitual sin. That is why St. Paul
asks rhetorically how one who is dead to sin can live in it? For example,
if an alcoholic repents and is treated for his addiction by Jesus, he will be
made free and will no longer want to return to a life of alcoholism. How
can the alcoholic stay away from liquor day after day? Without Jesus in
his life, it would be difficult if not impossible. Jesus says the believer is to
"... deny himself, and take up his cross daily...." The cross is a symbol of
the believer's death *but only for his flesh*. If he picks up his cross daily, then
he dies daily to the sinful desires of his flesh, as St. Paul affirms he himself
does in 1 Corinthians 15:31. Prior to the Holy Spirit coming into his life,
the alcoholic was like the proverbial dog that returned to his vomit [see 2
St. Peter 2:22].

St. Paul points out that he who is dead to sin, namely the *old* man, is
acquitted of sin. Moreover, he makes it clear in the above citation that the
believer's baptism is symbolic of Jesus' burial and resurrection. That is
why when one is baptized in a Bible-believing church, one is completely
immersed, as in being buried. Also, public baptism clearly identifies the one
being baptized as a follower of the New Testament Jesus. The one doing the
baptizing asks the one to be baptized if he or she has accepted Jesus Christ
as Lord and Savior. After receiving an affirmative answer, acknowledging
Jesus before men [St. Matthew 10:32], the baptizer says: "I baptize you, my
brother (sister) in Christ, in the name of the Father, and of the Son, and of
the Holy Spirit." As the immersion takes place, the baptizer continues: "In
the name of Jesus, buried in the likeness of His death, raised in the likeness
of His resurrection." Baptisms take place with the congregation present so
that the new believer can be welcomed into the body of Christ, the local
church. Going beneath the water symbolizes the burial of the old man, the
sinner who is now dead. Coming up out of the water represents the birth
of the new man who, like Christ, is rising to new life. Since we are united
with Christ, we know that our old man was crucified with Him and we are
dead in our flesh to sin but alive in our spirits and minds to God.

St. Paul continues his exhortation of new believers in chapter 4 of
Ephesians. He instructs them to put away lying and speak the truth; to
not let their anger get control of them and lead them to sin, thus giving

the devil a foothold in their lives; to stop stealing; to stop speaking ill of others; to remove all bitterness and wrath from their hearts:

> On the contrary, be kind to one another, and merciful, generously forgiving one another, as also God in Christ has generously forgiven you. Be you, therefore, imitators of God, as very dear children and walk in love, as Christ also loved us and delivered himself up for us an offering and a sacrifice to God to ascend in fragrant odor.
>
> —Ephesians 4:32-5:2

It should be understood that St. Paul is instructing *new converts.* These are the same ones who before their conversions unwittingly walked in the darkness of this world, fulfilling the lusts of their flesh. Thus, as new believers, they needed instruction on how to walk in the Spirit. New converts, through the power of the Holy Spirit, begin putting off the old man and putting on the new. As they learn to crucify (deny) their flesh in its desire to sin, their spirits become more attuned to the "whistling of a gentle air." The noise of the world is subdued and the Holy Spirit speaks to their reborn spirits [3 Kings 19:12]. While the acceptance of Jesus as Lord and Savior, the promise of salvation, and the sealing by the Holy Spirit are instantaneous and simultaneous, knowing how to put off the flesh and walk in the Spirit as a new creation is not [see Galatians 5:16 and 5:25]. It is interesting to notice in the citation above that Christ's sacrifice on the cross is described as ascending in a fragrant odor. This contrasts sharply with God's condemnation of the burning of incense:

> Offer sacrifice no more in vain: incense is an abomination to me.
>
> —Isaias 1:13

The Pharisees hid God's Word from the people so they could sell them incense. In Isaias 66:3, God clearly ties the burning of incense to idolatry:

> ... he that remembereth incense, as if he should bless an idol.

Some Refuse to Answer, "Yes, Lord"

Some refuse to answer, "Yes, Lord," because they mistakenly believe that they would have to "clean up their act" before coming to Jesus. This is another of Satan's lies. There is not one word of Scripture that supports this notion. In fact, there is verse after verse that invalidates it. The repentant robber on the cross didn't have time to straighten out his life before coming to Jesus. Saul was on the road to Damascus not to clean up his act, but to kill more followers of the Way. It is only *after coming to Jesus* that our lives *can be* straightened out through the indwelling power of the Holy Spirit. Jesus said, "... without me you can do nothing" [St. John 15:5].

Many refuse to answer, "Yes, Lord," because they're afraid if they do some "goody two-shoes" calling himself a Christian and wearing the Law on the tip of his unceasingly condemning and self-righteous tongue will approach with a list of 126 "really fun" things they can't do anymore. But that's not the way it works. Believers have been in their shoes. They understand that it is God who changes people—not a list of prohibitions—and He does it from the inside out. Man makes only cosmetic changes. Moreover, these internal changes which result in external manifestations come about slowly, one at a time. The Holy Spirit does not set about to correct a lifetime of sin overnight. Jesus neither condemned sinners nor did He come into the world to do so. Jesus said that he who does not believe in the Son of God is already condemned [St. John 3:18]. Therefore, no further condemnation is necessary. If you consider yourself a Christian and see someone drinking a beer and decide to witness to him, don't say, "Hey. Don't you know that drinking that beer is going to send you to hell?" That's not the gospel! As already discussed, no one is or will be in hell for drinking beer or anything else. All will be there for the same reason: disbelief in the Jesus of the New Testament [see St. John 16:9].

Some refuse to answer, "Yes, Lord," because they understand only too well that having a reborn spirit and renewed mind do not fit the lifestyle they've been leading. They've seen changes in believers' lives. They understand that the believer dies to his own desires and walks in the will of the Father, but certainly not without stumbling from time to time [see Proverbs 24:16]. They are not willing to submit. They don't want to give up their sin. Some are not willing to part with their pornography collections. "I have every issue of *Playboy* going back to the first," they explain. "Do you know what that's worth?" I don't know the dollar value. However, I believe any fair appraiser would establish a dollar value certainly no greater than the dollar value of the *whole world*. While Jesus didn't address directly the monetary value of a stack of magazines, He did ask, "For what does it profit a man, if he gain the whole world, but suffer the loss of his own soul?" [St. Mark 8:36] You believe your collection is worth your soul.

Others don't want to part with their "fast-lane" lifestyles, their promiscuous sex lives, or other things which God's Word calls sin. Some make the mistake of estimating whether *they* could give up the sin that is holding them back. Many conclude—rightly—that they could not. They

fail to account for the fact that *no believer* has ever given up these things
in *his own* power. That's why Jesus invites us to:

> "Come to me, all you who labor and are burdened, and I will give you rest.
> Take my yoke upon you, and learn from me, for I am meek and humble
> of heart; and you will find rest for your souls. For my yoke is easy, and
> my burden light."
>
> —St. Matthew 11:28-30

The believer is attacked by the world, the flesh, and the devil every
single day. His soul tires from the constant war between the desires of his
flesh that dwell in his members and his renewed mind [Romans 7:23].
Jesus characterized this fight as labor for the burdened soul. He invites us
to take up His yoke which is light. That is, rest in Him as the branches rest
in the vine [see St. John 15:5]. Let Jesus take the lead and your burden.
The yoke couples two together. Where one goes, the other follows. Learn
from Him which way to go by listening to the Holy Spirit as you study the
Bible. Jesus promises this will make your burden light.

St. Paul instructs believers:

> And do not be drunk with wine… but be filled with the Spirit….
>
> —Ephesians 5:18

In comparing wine with the Spirit, St. Paul is teaching that both have
similar control over one's life. Both lower inhibitions: submit yourself to the
Spirit, not to wine, and you will walk in the will of God. The flesh desires
wine just as a renewed mind and reborn spirit desire to be controlled by
the Holy Spirit. The effect of the wine will wear off and another drink will
be required. It is likewise with the Spirit. Each day the believer must ask
the Holy Spirit to help him walk in submission.

Some Only Pretend to Answer, "Yes, Lord"

There are those who pretend to accept Jesus but do not. St. Paul gives
those who call themselves believers a test to use to determine the veracity
of their acceptance:

> But immorality and every uncleanness or covetousness, let it not even
> be named among you, as becomes saints; or obscenity or foolish talk or
> scurrility, which are out of place; but rather (*make*) thanksgiving. For know
> this and understand, that no fornicator, or unclean person, or covetous
> one (for that is idolatry) has any inheritance in the kingdom of Christ and

God. Let no one lead you astray with empty words; for because of these
things the wrath of God comes upon the children of disobedience.
—Ephesians 5:3-6

How do we know St. Paul is not talking about a believer who has
lost his salvation? Because he calls such fornicators and unclean persons
"children of disobedience." As discussed earlier, this is a biblical term for the
unsaved. What St. Paul is teaching is that if you are living for the pleasures
of this world, in habitual sin, then you are not born again and you have no
salvation. St. Peter instructs believers to:

... love one another heartily and intensely. For you have been reborn, not
from corruptible seed but from incorruptible, through the word of God
who lives and abides forever.
—1 St. Peter 1:22-23

Another test for self-assessment is found in Hebrews 12:6-8, wherein
the author reveals:

For whom the Lord loves, he chastises; and he scourges every son whom
he receives. Continue under discipline. God deals with you as with sons;
for what son is there whom his father does not correct? But if you are
without discipline, in which *all* (*believers*) have had a share, then you are
illegitimate children and not sons.

Being born again is not a license to sin. In fact, to live in the flesh after
having been reborn is an invitation for God's chastisement. A changed life
which exhibits good works made ready by God, as promised in Ephesians
2:10, is evidence of a reborn spirit. If a believer continues to lead a life of
sin in spite of God's chastisement, the Father, in His mercy, may call His
child home. This is called "sinning unto death" [see 1 St. John 5:16-17].

Some try to fool men into believing that they are born again. Others
try to fool God. Some fool only themselves. These are addressed by Jesus,
as recorded in St. Matthew 7:21-23:

"Not everyone who says to me, 'Lord, Lord,' shall enter into the kingdom
of heaven; but he who does the will of my Father in heaven shall enter
the kingdom of heaven. Many will say to me in that day, 'Lord, Lord, did
we not prophesy in thy name, and cast out devils in thy name, and work
many miracles in thy name?' And then I will declare to them, 'I never
knew you. Depart from me, you workers of iniquity.'"

Note that Jesus does not argue with their claims. As revealed in Scripture, God can and does use evil men to accomplish His good pleasure [see Romans 8:28]. Moreover, in casting out devils (demons), it is not the power of the exorcist the demons fear but the name and power of the Jesus of the New Testament. However, as Jesus said, heaven is reserved for those who do the will of the Father. And what is the will of the Father?

> "For this is the will of my Father who sent me, that whoever beholds the Son, and believes in him, shall have everlasting life, and I will raise him up on the last day."
>
> —St. John 6:40

We only have one way to behold the Son of the Scriptures and that is by reading them.

Do You Have a Personal Relationship with the Jesus of the Scriptures?

Following one's death, the Master will say one of two things:

> "Well done, good and faithful servant,"
>
> —St. Matthew 25:21

or

> "I never knew you. Depart from me."
>
> —St. Matthew 7:23

These two statements form the basis for what believers call a personal relationship with the Jesus of the New Testament. Either you have it or you don't! There's no middle ground. You can't develop it in the next life. While you may know Him, or at least think you know Him, if you are not obeying the will of the Father, by believing in the Jesus of the Scriptures, then Jesus, by His own Word, maintains He doesn't know you. Remember, too, that we are to do the *work* of God:

> "This is the work of God, that you *believe* in him (*Jesus*) whom he (*God*) has sent."
>
> —St. John 6:29

Thus, it is both the *will* of God and the *work* of God that we believe, that is, trust in the Christ of the New Testament. Most will not. Most will look to a different Jesus, others to their Church or church for salvation. All such paths lead to hell.

God Preserves Believers

How can the believer preserve his "saved" status after he has repented of his sins and accepted Jesus as Lord and Savior? He cannot. However, God can and does. This is called preservation of the saints. Jesus promised no one could snatch His sheep from His hand [St. John 10:28]. St. Paul confirms in Philippians 1:6:

"... he (*God*) who has begun a good work in you will bring it to perfection until the day of Jesus Christ (*Christ's return*)."

Believers Are to Grow in Grace and Knowledge of the Lord

If the believer is not growing, he is backsliding. St. Peter exhorts believers to: "... grow in grace and knowledge of our Lord and Savior, Jesus Christ" [2 St. Peter 3:18]. How does the believer grow in grace? Through reading the Scriptures [see 2 Timothy 3:16-17]; hearing God's Word from pastors and teachers [see Ephesians 4:11-12]; enduring trials (suffering) through His grace [see 1 St. Peter 2:19]; and by being filled with the Holy Spirit of God. Being filled with the Spirit is not a matter of how much of the Holy Spirit the believer has. Every believer has the same amount of the Holy Spirit and this cannot change. Rather, being filled with the Spirit refers to how much of the believer the Holy Spirit has, how much control over the believer's life. The believer needs to ask the Holy Spirit to control his thoughts and actions every day. An excellent book that reveals from Scripture how to allow the Holy Spirit to work in one's life is: *How On Earth Can I Be Spiritual?* by Dr. C. Sumner Wemp, published by Thomas Nelson, Inc., Nashville, Tennessee, 1978. Copies are available from Dr. Wemp for a nominal charge of $10.00 plus $1.50 for shipping and handling. Visit his website at Sumnerwemp.com or write Dr. Wemp at 10005 Chimney Hill Lane, Dallas Texas 75243. His book is about releasing the *power* of the Holy Spirit in one's life.

Believers Are to Walk in Submission

Believers are told to be submissive to the will of God; to government authorities; to those in authority, such as bosses; wives to their husbands; children to parents; and, finally, even one to another [Ephesians 5:21].

The word submissive is sometimes misunderstood. It is often thought of as "being less or not equal." However, Jesus made it clear that He was in submission to the Father [see Philippians 2:5-9]. He had come to do the will of the Father. Now certainly God the Son is in every way no less than the Father. Jesus answered any question about this in His statement "... he who sees me sees also the Father..." [St. John 14:9]. Therefore, it can be concluded that being in submission does not imply inferiority. But how can submission be accomplished when man is a rebel by nature? St. Paul answers:

> And do not be drunk with wine, for in that is debauchery (*sins of the flesh*); but be filled with the Spirit.
>
> —Ephesians 5:18

A believer who is walking in submission to the Holy Spirit will be controlled by the Spirit and, therefore, submissive. St. Paul provides an excellent example, as recorded by St. Luke in Acts 16:1-10. St. Paul purposed to take Timothy and Silas with him to preach in the region of Galatia. However, the Holy Spirit forbad them to preach the Word in Asia at that time. St. Paul then decided they would go preach in Bithynia, a coastal province in northwestern Asia Minor. However, the Holy Spirit turned them around and sent them to Philippi in Macedonia to preach the gospel there and many were saved.

St. James argues in his epistle that while we cannot *see* a person's faith, we can *see* the results of that faith, in this instance, a submissive spirit. We are told in God's Word to follow our Master's example. Jesus was submissive to the will of the Father even unto death. He never failed to pay taxes. He never called for the abolition of taxes. He never told slaves to revolt against their masters. He never advocated the overthrow of the occupying Roman army. Therefore, when the media report that some so-called Christian fundamentalist group is responsible for blowing up a government building, do not be fooled. Contrary to what the criminals and media might claim, they are not believers in the Jesus of the New Testament. Jesus never taught rebellion against authority. One of the marks of a believer is submissiveness. While we all give in to the devil's prompting to rebel from time to time, rebellion is not a way of life for the believer.

Believers are allowed to appeal to those in authority over them. Daniel did this successfully, as recorded in Daniel 1:8-16. The king's order was that the captive Daniel eat meat from the king's table. This presented a problem since the meat had been offered to a false god. Daniel did not rebel. He did not insist on his "rights." He did not initiate a strike or sit-in. Rather, he explained to his Babylonian superior that while he was in submission to him and the king, he had to follow a higher law, the law of his God. Jesus appealed to the Father to "... let this cup pass away from me..." as recorded in St. Matthew 26:39. However, Jesus ended His prayer by asking that the will of the Father be done, rather than His own.

Believers Are to Know They Are Saved

A believer is to know that he or she has eternal life. Twenty-two of the New Testament's twenty-seven books speak of eternal life in one way or another, e.g., everlasting life, kingdom of heaven, kingdom of God, salvation, justification, etc. Jesus' promise of eternal life to believers is recorded in all four Gospels [St. Matthew 19:29; St. Mark 10:30; St. Luke 18:30; and St. John 10:28]. The Jesus of the New Testament promises everlasting life to those who follow Him:

> "My sheep hear my voice, and I know them and they follow me. And I give them everlasting life; and they shall never perish; neither shall anyone snatch them out of my hand."
>
> —St. John 10:27-28

Jesus is so adamant about His promise of eternal life that He makes a double promise: (1) And I give them everlasting life, and (2) they shall never perish. To never perish is to have everlasting life! Then, to make sure the point is understood, He adds that no one—and this includes Satan—can snatch them out of His hand. The prophet reveals God's position:

> "And from the beginning I am the same, and there is none that can deliver out of my hand: I will work, and who shall turn it away?"
>
> —Isaias 43:13

These and many other verses in the Roman Catholic Bible just do not allow for the possibility of losing eternal life. This should be viewed as another argument against the notion of anyone earning any part of his salvation. It is universal in man's experience that what *he* gains, *he* can lose. Not so with a *gift from God!*

Some at the Thessalonica church were grieved because their loved ones had died and they were afraid that these had missed Jesus' promised return and the opportunity to enter into the kingdom. St. Paul corrected their misunderstanding, as recorded in chapter 4 of 1 Thessalonians. He assured them that their departed loved ones were already with the Lord and that soon they, too, would be with the Lord. Moreover, he told them to comfort one another with this assurance [see 1 Thessalonians 4:18]. There can be no comfort in the words, "you may go to heaven when you die." Neither is there comfort in the idea of going to purgatory for some indeterminate period of time.   As St. Paul neared the end of his life, he told his young protégée, Timothy:

> ... there is laid up for me a crown of justice, which the Lord, the just Judge, will give to me in that day....
>
> —2 Timothy 4:8

St. Peter, too, was no less certain about his eternal future:

> ... I, your fellow-presbyter (*elder*) and witness (*Apostle*) of the sufferings of Christ, the partaker also of the glory that is to be revealed in time to come (*kingdom of God/heaven*)....
>
> —1 St. Peter 5:1

St. Jude spoke of his and others' "common salvation," as recorded in St. Jude 3. Thus, St. Paul, St. Peter, and St. Jude were confident of their eternal destinies. And for good reason. There is no teaching by Jesus or His disciples that states, implies, or even allows for the possibility of losing salvation. The Scriptures make clear that the reason one cannot lose it is because *he did not earn it*. It was a *gift* from God with absolutely no merit on his part. Therefore, the only way one could lose his salvation would be for God to take it back. However, the prophet reveals:

> "For I am the Lord and I change not...."
>
> —Malachias 3:6

God does not change His mind. He does not give eternal life one day and rescind it the next. Unlike us, God is not double-minded [St. James 1:8]. He does all His good pleasure. Moreover, God instituted marriage to be binding until death, not binding one day and not the next. Is it possible that the Creator of the universe intends His promise of eternal life to be less binding than the man's promise to the woman in the marriage ceremony? Hardly. Jesus reassures us in St. Luke 12:32:

> "'Do not be afraid, little flock, for it has pleased your Father to *give* you the kingdom.'"

Note the word *give* in the above citation. Thus, once God justifies the sinner, the promise of eternal life is made and the seal of the Holy Spirit is down payment of later fulfillment. Moreover, the believer is also glorified at this same time. St. Paul reminds us in Romans 8:30:

> And those whom he has predestined (*to be conformed to the image of His Son-see v. 29*), them he has also called; and those whom he has called, them he has also justified, and those whom he has justified, them he has also *glorified*.

To "glorify" means to magnify God through praising His name and honoring His commandments [Psalms 85 (86):12]. Thus, those who are saved magnify God. If one can lose one's salvation, then what is God to do with the fact that, according to His Word, He has already glorified that one, that is, magnified Himself in that believer? The question is rhetorical. Its purpose is to point out the absurdity of any teaching that one can lose his or her salvation. Finally, St. Paul assures believers:

> For the gifts and the call of God are without repentance (*irrevocable*).
> —Romans 11:29

Believers are not to doubt their eternal future. Either we believe Jesus was and is who He said, as recorded in the New Testament and not diminished by some Church's teaching based on non-scriptural revelations, or we do not. If we believe Him when He says we have all sinned; that He is God in human flesh; that He was sent by the Father to seek and to save those who are lost and give His life as a ransom for many; then we *must believe*, too, that He has the authority to grant everlasting life to His followers. There simply is no other choice. Study Philippians 4:3 and Apocalypse 20:15. If your Church or church teaches that one can lose his salvation, you are in an apostate church.

Which Jesus Will You Believe In?

God's Word assures believers:

> For as in Adam all die, so in Christ all will be made to live.
> —1 Corinthians 15:22

Notice the wording carefully. Sinners are brought back to life by Christ, not by a Church or some sacramental salvation system. The disobedient have always severed what they believe about the Christ. Some believe Jesus was a philosopher who preached love. Others believe Jesus was a created being, not the Son of God. Some believe Jesus died on the cross but did not

rise from the dead bodily, but only in spirit. Too many believe that Jesus'
death on the cross did not pay their full debt for sin and that there is an
unpaid balance. Some believe Jesus lied on the cross when He cried out
"it is consummated," *finished*, referring to His work of salvation [see St.
John 19:30]. The Greek word Jesus cried out was "*Tetelestai.*" This word
was used in economic transactions and was well known to all. It meant
"paid in full."

We use the same concept today. One may make a down payment, buy
on lay-away, installment plan, or interest payments. None of these pays
the full bill. Only when one pays the full amount owed does one get a
receipt from the merchant marked "paid" which is shorthand in today's
business lexicon for "paid in full." Jesus' death on the cross at Golgotha
was not a down payment, a lay-away payment, an installment payment, or
an interest payment. The Jesus of the New Testament, the Christ, paid it
all on that old rugged cross. "There is therefore now no condemnation for
those who are in Christ Jesus" [Romans 8:1]. There is no "balance due,"
not one penny, not one prayer, not one good work by one's family, not one
day in purgatory. This is why St. Paul and St. Peter referred to believers
as "bought," past tense, a finished transaction, rather than a purchase in
process [see 1 Corinthians 6:20 and 7:23; and 2 St. Peter 2:1], which is
what sacramental salvation systems teach.

Some acknowledge Jesus' turning water into wine, healing the lame, and
causing the blind to see. Some even believe Jesus raised the dead. However,
some who believe these miracles deny His authority to grant eternal life and
preserve the believer. Jesus assures us again in St. Matthew 19:29:

> And everyone who has left house, or brothers, or sisters, or father, or
> mother, or wife, or children, or lands for my name's sake, shall receive a
> hundredfold, and shall possess life everlasting.

What would it mean if one encountered a god whose word could not
be trusted? The obvious answer is that if we cannot believe the Jesus of
the New Testament when He promised eternal life, then there would be no
basis upon which to believe the other things He taught! If we cannot believe
the veracity of Scripture wherein Jesus promises eternal life to His sheep,
then there is no basis for believing He established a church or empowered
His followers with the "Great Commission" to make disciples of all nations
[St. Matthew 28:19].

St. Paul warned against false teachers who would preach a form of
godliness but deny its power to justify the sinner, sanctify, preserve, and

save him. He directs us: "Avoid these" [2 Timothy 3:1-5]. St. Paul expresses his attitude toward such false teachers:

> But even if we or an angel from heaven should preach a gospel to you other than that which we have preached to you, let him be anathema! As we have said before, so now I say again: If anyone preach a gospel to you other than that which you have received, let him be anathema!
>
> —Galatians 1:8-9

Based on the analysis in this chapter, it is clear that the Roman Catholic Bible faithfully presents the complete gospel message:

> ... from thy infancy thou hast known the Sacred Writings (*Scriptures*), which are able to instruct thee unto *salvation* by the *faith which is in Christ Jesus*. All Scripture is inspired by God and useful for teaching, for reproving, for correction, for instructing in justice; that the man of God may be perfect (*complete*), equipped for every good work.
>
> —2 Timothy 3:15-16

Chapter 5

TRADITION

AS SHOWN IN previous chapters, there is no difference between what the Roman Catholic, King James Version, New King James Version, and *The Orthodox Study Bible, New Testament and Psalms* teach regarding salvation. All present the same gospel. However, the Roman Catholic Church, as well as the Orthodox Churches and most Protestant Churches, teach a different soteriology (manner of salvation) than that taught by independent, Bible-believing, fundamentalist New Testament churches. Somewhat surprising, however, is the fact that these Churches teach a soteriology contrary to that taught in their respective Bibles! The reason can be summed up in one word: tradition. While *The Orthodox Study Bible, New Testament and Psalms* states that, "One cannot be an Orthodox priest… and reject the divinity of Christ, His virgin birth, Resurrection, Ascension into heaven, and Second Coming," apparently one can reject the many teachings by Jesus and His disciples on eternal security. Whereas the Good Shepherd said, "And I give them eternal life, and they shall never perish; neither shall anyone snatch them out of My hand," [St. John 10:28, Orthodox Study Bible], Orthodoxy, like Catholicism and most erring Protestant denominations, teach salvation to be a *process* accomplished through receiving sacraments rather than an accomplished act by the Jesus of the New Testament at Calvary. Protestant Churches coming out of the reformation took with them many of the false doctrines that had evolved in first the Roman and then the Roman Catholic Church. Most of these make a statement of faith during their services wherein they "confess one baptism for the forgiveness of sins."

Appendix A includes a discussion on the characteristics of independent, Bible-believing, fundamentalist New Testament churches. These characteristics are extracted from the Roman Catholic Bible and confirmed in the Orthodox Study Bible, as well as the King James and New King James versions.

Jesus Condemns the Traditions of Men

The word *tradition/traditions* is used only in the New Testament and relatively few times. Tradition/traditions is used by Jesus several times and in each instance to point out the contradiction between manmade traditions and God's Holy Word. In every case, Jesus condemns the traditions:

> "You make void the commandment of God by your tradition, which you have handed down; and many suchlike things you do."
>
> —St. Mark 7:13

Jesus tells the Scribes and Pharisees, as recorded in St. Matthew 15:6-9:

> "... So you have made void the commandment of God by your tradition. Hypocrites, well did Isaias prophesy of you, saying, 'This people honors me with their lips, but their heart is far from me; and in vain do they worship me, teaching as doctrines the precepts (*traditions*) of men.'"

St. Paul Condemns the Traditions of Men

In Galatians 1:11-14, St. Paul verbalizes his anguish over his past beliefs (as Saul) in which he advanced up through the ranks of Judaism by what he calls his zeal for the *traditions* of his fathers. Those traditions caused Saul to lead his minions from town to town to arrest and murder members of the Way until that fateful day on the road to Damascus when Saul had an epiphany: he recognized Jesus as Lord. At that point, Saul put away his traditions and heard the living Word of God for the first time. This experience transformed every aspect of his life, even his name.

St. Paul again addresses the subject of traditions in Colossians 2:8:

> See to it that no one deceives you by philosophy and vain deceit, according to human traditions, according to the elements of the world and not according to Christ.

St. Paul offers the strongest words of condemnation for the traditions of men other than those spoken by Jesus Himself. St. Paul establishes two categories of instruction: (1) the teachings of Christ, and (2) those not of Christ. Those elements not of Christ include (1) philosophy and vain deceit,

(2) traditions of men, and (3) the world. St. Paul clearly places the traditions of men in the same category as "the world, the flesh, and the devil," the three things the believer knows to be the enemies of God and man.

St. Peter Condemns the Traditions of Men

In his first epistle, St. Peter writes:

You know that you were redeemed from the vain manner of life handed down from your fathers (*traditions*)....
—1 St. Peter 1:18

Apostolic Traditions Affirmed in Scripture

The King James Version uses the word tradition(s) in two places where the Roman Catholic Bible uses "teachings." The first is 2 Thessalonians 2:15. The King James Version is quoted below followed by the same verse from the Roman Catholic Bible.

Therefore, brethren, stand fast, and hold the traditions which ye have been taught, whether by word, or our epistle.
—2 Thessalonians 2:15 KJV

So then, brethren, stand firm, and hold the teachings you have learned, whether by word or letter of ours.
—2 Thessalonians 2:15 Roman Catholic Bible

Both verses give the same instruction: hold on to what you have learned (been taught) whether by word or letters of ours (epistle). Evidence that St. Paul is talking about the things *of his day*, rather than the future, is found in the use of the word learned/taught, past tense.

St. Paul again addresses traditions in 2 Thessalonians 3:6:

Now we command you, brethren, in the name of our Lord Jesus Christ, that ye withdraw yourselves from every brother that walketh disorderly, and not after the tradition which he received of us.
—2 Thessalonians 3:6 KJV

And we charge you, brethren, in the name of our Lord Jesus Christ, to withdraw yourselves from every brother who lives irregularly, and not according to the teachings received from us.
—2 Thessalonians 3:6 Roman Catholic Bible

Again, the same thought is expressed in both versions. And again the passing on of traditions/teachings is discussed in the past tense, it has been completed. No new traditions are to be expected.

In summary, the New Testament records Jesus', St. Paul's, and St. Peter's condemnation of the traditions of men. However, St. Paul endorses the traditions/teachings received from *him* and the other disciples either through direct preaching (word) or epistles (letters). Thus, it should be clear that any tradition taught by St. Paul and the other disciples is reflected in the writings that make up the New Testament. In fact, this is the standard to use to determine the veracity of any tradition, whether it is apostolic or of men. The Catholic Church labels those traditions that teach doctrines contrary to the teaching in the Roman Catholic Bible "Sacred Traditions."

Believers Have Been in Possession of All Truth Since the End of the Apostolic Age

Latter-Day Saints (LDS) teach that the Book of Mormon is another testament of Jesus Christ, a continuing revelation given by Jehovah to prophetic descendants of Israel in America between 600 B.C. and 421 A.D. According to Joseph Smith, these revelations were recorded on golden plates. However, the plates were lost some time after 421 A.D. According to Smith, an angel calling himself Moroni appeared and led him to the plates which were buried in upstate New York. According to LDS teaching, Joseph Smith translated the messages on the plates from reformed Egyptian to English "by the gift and power of God" in a 3-month period in the late 1820s. After Smith completed his translation, Moroni took the plates and left. One of the traditions taught by some sects of Mormonism is that after He grew to manhood, Jesus took three wives: Lazarus' sisters, Mary and Martha, and Mary of Magdalene. Is this teaching true? Not according to Scriptures which contain the complete teachings of Jesus and the apostles, including all the traditions taught by them. St. Jude confirms that, as of his time, there were no new revelations to be forthcoming:

> Beloved, while I was making every endeavor to write to you about our common salvation, I found it necessary to write to you, exhorting you to contend earnestly for the faith *once for all delivered to the saints.*
>
> —St. Jude 3

According to St. Jude, the faith (teachings and apostolic traditions) had been delivered (completed) by the time he wrote his epistle, which would have been no later than 95 A.D. Thus, the Scriptures, and the traditions revealed therein, do not support the teaching that Jesus was married.

In His words of comfort to His followers, Jesus revealed that He still had many things to tell them, but that they could not bear them at that time. However, He promised to send the Spirit of truth (Holy Spirit) to teach them all truth:

> "Many things yet I have to say to *you*, but *you* cannot bear them now. But when he, the Spirit of truth, has come, he will teach *you all* the truth."
> —St. John 16:12-13

Note Jesus' words carefully. He told them He had more to say to *them*, His contemporaries. He also promised that the Spirit of truth would teach *them* all the truth. It is important to understand that Jesus' words were directed to His disciples, not to some future Church, its leaders, or councils. If the Holy Spirit was coming to lead His disciples into *all the truth*, then those in subsequent generations should not expect additional truths beyond those revealed in Scripture. This is confirmed in the last chapter of the Apocalypse [see Apocalypse 22:18-19]. Failure to appreciate this fact has led to numerous false teachings which have resulted in satanic lies called post-scriptural revelations. The Koran is another example.

The Spirit of truth, the Holy Spirit, came on the Day of Pentecost when they were gathered in the house (probably the Temple) with one accord, as recorded by St. Luke in Acts 2:4. Thus, the teaching of all truth by the Holy Spirit began soon after Jesus' ascension. Moreover, Jesus promised also that the Holy Spirit would bring to *their* minds all things that He had taught them [St. John 14:26]. St. Paul knew that the Holy Spirit was working in his and the other disciples' lives to bring about the complete revelation of truth. He knew, too, that these truths were being written down as they were revealed. St. Paul noted:

> For we know in part and we prophesy in part; but when that which is perfect (*complete*) has come, that which is imperfect (*not complete*) will be done away with.
> —1 Corinthians 13:9-10

Biblical exegetes understand this verse to refer to the completion of the books of the New Testament. In the previous verse, St. Paul tells us that prophecy and speaking in tongues will cease [1 Corinthians 13:8]. He tells us in subsequent verses that, "We see now (*prior to the completion and recording of revelation by the Holy Spirit*) through a mirror in an obscure manner, but then (*when complete*) face to face" [1 Corinthians 13:12]. All would be revealed. St. John confirms:

> This is the disciple who bears witness concerning these things (*the things
> Jesus taught and did*), and who has written these things, and we know that
> his witness is true. There are, however, many other things that Jesus did;
> but if *every one* of these should be written, not even the world itself, I
> think, could hold the *books that would have to be written.* Amen.
> —St. John 21:24-25

St. John clearly reveals that many of the things Jesus did were being
written down. Also, the disciples knew that the Holy Spirit was active
in their ministries as a consolidating and integrating Spirit, as recorded
throughout many books of the New Testament. St. Luke records one of
many such testimonies, this one concerning the things new converts must
avoid:

> For *the Holy Spirit and we* have decided to lay no further burden upon
> you but this indispensable one, that you abstain from things sacrificed to
> idols and from blood and from what is strangled and from immorality;
> keep yourselves from these things, and you will get on well.
> —Acts 15:28-29

Notice the words, "For the Holy Spirit and we have decided...." This
and many other verses express an intimate working with the Holy Spirit.
Thus, it is no wonder that St. Paul confesses in 1 Corinthians 13:9-10:

> For we know in part and we prophesy in part; but when that which is
> perfect has come, that which is imperfect will be done away with.

All truths to be revealed and all apostolic traditions to be followed
had been revealed and were being followed by the end of the apostolic age
(around 95 A.D.), as recorded in the books of the New Testament. Those
individual writings were in wide circulation among the early churches.
They were later assembled into a compendium which today we call the New
Testament. Thus, things practiced under the rubric of tradition by various
denominations today may be placed in one of two categories: apostolic
tradition or non-apostolic tradition. The non-apostolic traditions may be
further divided into traditions that are not at odds with the Scriptures and
those that are counter to things taught in Scripture. Traditions practiced
that are counter to Scripture are what Jesus condemned as the "traditions
of men." Such traditions render God's Word impotent and Jesus and His
disciples therefore condemned them.

We Can Test the Traditions

Let's examine the hypothesis suggested by several denominations that it was the tradition of the early Christians to meet for worship on the Sabbath, Saturday. St. Luke reveals the answer:

> And on the first day of the week, when we had met for the breaking of bread, Paul addressed them....
>
> —Acts 20:7

Christians met for the breaking of bread (worship) not on the Sabbath, but on the first day of the week. St. Paul confirms this:

> On the first day of the week, let each one of you put aside... whatever he has a mind to, so that the collection....
>
> —1 Corinthians 16:2

St. Paul is discussing what today we call the collection plate. That day of worship is referred to as the Lord's Day [Apocalypse 1:10]. Thus, we can conclude that early Christians did not meet to worship on Saturday. If they had, it would not be recorded otherwise in the Scriptures. The New Testament records that St. Paul and the others entered the synagogues of the Jews on Sabbaths, not to worship, but to preach Jesus resurrected to the unbelieving Jews [see Acts 13:5].

It is perhaps worth noting that the early Christians did not refer to the first day of the week as Sunday. The word Sunday comes from a combination of pagan words meaning the "Sun's day." The word was coined early in the 4th century when Roman Emperor Constantine the Great (274-337 A.D.), himself a worshiper of the Roman sun god Sol, married a large segment of "Christianity" to the pagan state of Rome.[1] More will be said later about Constantine and his influence on Christianity.

Traditions not mentioned in the New Testament are acceptable as long as they are not contradicted by the Word of God. For example, many denominations meet for worship services on various days of the week in addition to the Lord's day [see Hebrews 10:25].

Let us now examine the meaning of "saint." A typical definition found in a dictionary refers to a saint as "a person considered holy and worthy of public veneration, especially one who has been canonized." According to the Roman Catholic Church, "The saints are those in heaven who came through the difficulties of this life victoriously and are now chosen friends of God."[2] Other Churches hold similar views. According to the Roman Catholic and Orthodox Churches, canonization is the final act of a lengthy and formal process that begins with beatification. The decree of beatification is an official declaration that a person lived a holy life and therefore can be venerated. Canonization conveys the title of "saint." In the Orthodox Churches, the process of canonization is less formal and is carried out by local synods of bishops. The definition of *canonization* contained in the "Catholic Doctrinal Guide" states:

> The solemn pronouncement by which the Pope declares that worship (*different kind of worship from that given to God*) is to be given to a saint... and it must be proved that two miracles have been subsequently wrought at his intercession....[3]

This is a rather impressive view of a saint. One common aspect of all these definitions is that the "saint" is deceased, that is, no longer in the body. To determine the veracity of this supposition, let's use as our working hypothesis that one requirement for being a saint is that the person to be so pronounced must be dead and, therefore, out of the body.

The word saint or saints is used in the Bible some ninety-seven times: thirty-five times in the Old Testament and sixty-two times in the New Testament. St. Paul writes in Romans 15:25, "Now, however, I will set out for Jerusalem to minister to the *saints*." Moreover, St. Paul begins many of his epistles with the word *saints* in his salutation:

> ... to all God's beloved who are in Rome, called to be *saints*....
>
> —Romans 1:7

> ... to the church of God at Corinth, to you who have been sanctified in Christ Jesus and called to be *saints* with all who call upon the name of our Lord Jesus Christ....
>
> —1 Corinthians 1:2

> ... to the church of God that is at Corinth, with all the *saints* that are in the whole of Achaia....
>
> —2 Corinthians 1:1

Without exception, the Roman Catholic Bible refers to saints as believers who are among the living and, therefore, in the body. It is recorded in St. Matthew 27:52:

> And the tombs were opened, and many bodies of the *saints* who had fallen asleep (*died*) arose.

Even in this verse, the saints are alive *and in the body*. Thus, we must conclude that the Roman Catholic, Orthodox, and others' teaching on what constitutes a saint is among the traditions of men. The earliest instance of a solemn decree of canonization is of Ulric, Bishop of Augsburg. Pope John XV declared Ulric a saint in 993, some nine hundred years after completion of the New Testament. Prior to this, there was no ritual for the designation of saints in Constantine's universal Church, or by what had evolved into the Roman Catholic Church around 450 A.D. All martyrs were considered saints.

It is ironic that St. Ulric was one of the many bishops who argued against the Roman Catholic Church's consideration of celibacy for the clergy. History records his arguments to have been based on Scripture.[4]

> Now the Spirit expressly says that in after times (*after Jesus' ascension*) some will depart from the faith, giving heed to deceitful spirits and doctrines of devils, speaking lies hypocritically, and having their conscience branded (*cauterized, which results in thick scar tissue which cannot be penetrated*). They will forbid marriage....
> —1 Timothy 4:1-3

> Let marriage be held in honor with *all*, and let the marriage bed be undefiled....
> —Hebrews 13:4

Other saints have not had such an easy time. For example, the Roman Catholic Church no longer lists the beloved St. Christopher on its calendar of feasts. At one time, he was venerated as the patron saint of travelers. The Church designated July 25 as his feast day. Parishes and book stores sold small plastic statues which the faithful placed on dashboards and hung on rear-view mirrors. Some wore talisman with his purported likeness around their necks for protection. Millions of Catholics around the world prayed to St. Christopher to protect them, their families, and their loved ones on journeys long and short. But poor Christopher faded from dashboard icon into obscurity when the Church later discovered that he never existed. Nevertheless, many Catholics continued to pray to the bearded man who, according to Church tradition, ferried the Christ child across the river on his broad shoulders. When the faithful created an uproar, Rome again went on the hunt for the sainted one and this time indeed found him. Thus, Christopher has been restored to sainthood—sort of. While the Church has now confirmed his existence, they have not placed him back on the liturgical calendar. Therefore, this quasi-saint still has no official feast day.

However, because of tradition, he is still venerated and his feast day is still celebrated among many parishes without Rome's formal consent.

Joan of Arc was labeled a heretic by the Catholic Church in 1431. Twenty-five years later, the Church revisited her case and reversed its decision. The Church found Joan not to be a heretic after all, but, in fact, a saint. Unfortunately, by the time the Church admitted its error Joan had been dead for some twenty-five years, burned at the stake. Her feast day is May 30. St. Joan rose from executed heretic to heroine and patron saint of France.

Cardinal Humbert of Silva Candida excommunicated the Patriarch of Constantinople and the entire Orthodox Church in 1054. Patriarch Michael Cerularius reciprocated several days later and excommunicated the Cardinal and the entire Roman Catholic Church. Pope Alexander III (1159-1181), in 1171, reserved the right of canonizing exclusively for the papacy. This eliminated the possibility of anyone from the Orthodox Church being canonized. Pope Urban VIII (1623-1644), in constitutions promulgated in 1625 and 1634, created more stringent requirements for canonization more than fifteen hundred years after the New Testament had been completed.[5] These requirements, in turn, have been modified by subsequent popes.

Out of the tradition of venerating men grew the "cult of the saints." The bones of "saints" were dug up, broken, and divided among competing prelates. They were displayed in local churches for public veneration. The Church makes no apology for its behavior even today. As Father E. Hayes notes:

> Some people consider it odd to venerate the relics of saints, but there is nothing odd about a practice that goes back many thousands of years. The followers of Buddha, Confucius, and Muhammed have long venerated the relics of those ancient religious leaders....[6]

Bible-believing Christians consider it odd to *create* so-called "Christian traditions" based on pagan superstitions. The Roman Church began venerating saints around 375 A.D.

Another tradition introduced from paganism was the use of prayer beads, called rosaries today. Prayer beads have been in use for thousands of years and are still used in Buddhism, Hinduism, and Islam. They are used to count a set number of repetitious prayers in a systematic order recited by rote. The pagan religions of Jesus' day also prayed long litanies to seek favors from their gods. Jesus condemned such practices:

> "And when ye pray, use not vain *repetitions*, as the heathen do: for they think that they will be heard for their much speaking."
>
> —St. Matthew 6:7 KJV

The use of prayer beads in the U.S. is most often associated with Roman Catholicism. Traditionally, use of the rosary as a form of *Christian* worship was ascribed to the Spanish theologian St. Dominic.[7] The use of "holy water" in some denominations is another tradition based on pagan superstition adopted from Hinduism. According to legend, the gods placed three drops of holy water into the Ganges and made the river "sacred." Jesus tells us He gives us *living water* [see St. John 4:10]. Living water is a reference to the Holy Spirit [see St. John 7:38-39].

With regard to the Roman Catholic definition that saints are "chosen friends of God," every *believer or born-again Christian* is a friend of God. Jesus said:

> "Greater love than this no one has, that one lay down his life for his friends. You are my friends if you do the things I command you."
>
> —St. John 15:13-14

Jesus laid down His life for the entire world [St. John 3:16]. Those who accept Jesus' finished work on the cross as full payment for their sins (*believe in Him*) and ask Him to be Lord of their lives (*call upon the name of the Lord*) are no longer children of wrath but are adopted sons and daughters of God, as was explained in chapter four. These are the ones who "... do the things I command you."

Palestine in Jesus' Day

The Romans were an occupying army and were greatly resented by the Jews. Not so with the aristocratic Herodians. They were descended from the Idumean line, the children of Esau, also called Edomites. The decedents of Jacob, the Jews, did not consider the Idumeans to be Jews, but impostors. Esau, the firstborn of Isaac and Rebecca, and therefore the rightful heir to the birthright in the line of Abraham and Isaac, sold his birthright to his fraternal twin, Jacob, for a serving of bread and lentils (peas) [Genesis 25:27-34]. The prophet records God's *hate* for Esau [Malachias 1:3]. Among the privileges of the birthright were a favored position in the family, a double portion of the father's assets upon his death [Deuteronomy 21:17], and a special blessing from the father and the privilege of leadership of the family [Genesis 43:33]. The inheritance rights of the firstborn were protected by law, so a father could not give his firstborn's benefits to a younger son [Deuteronomy 21:15-17]. Jacob obtained the birthright legally from Esau, however, and fathered the twelve tribes after God changed his name from Jacob (which means supplanter) to Israel (which means prince with God) [see Genesis 32:29]. Thus, God's blessing on the Jews came through Abraham, Isaac, and Jacob.

First governor of Galilee and later king of Judea, Herod the Great (37–4 B.C.), the title owing mostly to the fact that he was the eldest son of Herod Antipater, along with other Jewish pawns under his tutelage, played their parts in supporting Roman authorities and suppressing Jewish uprisings. They were rewarded well by Rome. Herod was in power when Jesus was born. On the positive side, he prevented the Romans from destroying the rebuilt Jewish Temple. On the negative, he had a history of eliminating whomever he pleased. Herod suspected his wife, Mariamne, was planning to betray him. He murdered her in 14 B.C. When his two sons by Mariamne discovered their father's treachery and confronted him, he had them murdered. It was said of Herod that it was better to be one of his hogs than one of his sons—he only butchered his sons and left his hogs to their own.

A relatively short time before his death, Herod dispatched his henchmen to Bethlehem to kill all male infants under two years of age [see Jeremias 30:15-17 and St. Matthew 2:13-18]. The aging king did not tolerate any threat to his throne, not even that posed by a baby playing at the hem of his mother's robe. By the time Jesus began His public ministry, one of Herod's many sons, Herod Antipas, was on the throne. Antipas outraged many in the Jewish community when he left his wife and welcomed Herodius, the wife of his half-brother, Philip I, into his marriage bed [see Leviticus 20:21]. It was John's fierce and persistent condemnation of this unholy act that cost the Baptist, the son of a Temple priest, his head. Jesus warned His followers about the treachery of Antipas [see St. Mark 8:15 and St. Luke 13:31-33].

Fomenting just under the uneasy facade of peace was the ever-present Jewish messianic expectation. It was believed by many that arrival of the long-awaited messiah would lead to Jewish autonomy. Barabbas was the latest in a long line of hopefuls. It was known that he and his small band of rebels had shed Roman blood whenever the opportunity had presented itself. Moreover, he inspired others, particularly the young and brash, to take up the sword and drive out the "Roman dogs." But alas, Barabbas' fate landed him in and out of prison. Against this backdrop of dashed messianic expectations for a promised liberator from the royal House of David [Jeremias 30:7-9], who would not only overthrow the Romans, but rule the nations with a rod of iron [Psalms 2:7-9]—particularly those that had persecuted the Jews—came a soft-spoken itinerant preacher of thirty years age with barely the required Hebrew minion who claimed the messianic title, Son of David.

Jesus Paves the One and Only Way

Rather than take up the rod of iron, Jesus took up the olive branch of peace and preached love toward even one's enemies. With regard to interacting with those in authority, He taught "do not resist an evil person"; "turn the other cheek"; "walk an extra mile with him who compels you to walk one"; and "if he sues you for your tunic, give him your cloak also." Rather than lay the sword upon the necks of the Roman centurions, He traveled about Galilee and laid His healing hands upon all who believed in Him and cured their infirmities. Most of those looking for a messiah-king, a liberator for Palestine, realized they had to look past Barabbas and the peripatetic preacher. Few were either surprised or even aware when the Romans put another messianic disappointment on the cross [see St. Luke 23:35-39].

After His death, Jesus' followers scattered as prophesied [Zacharias 13:7 and St. Matthew 26:31]. They wept and lamented, having forgotten His promise that their sorrow would be turned to joy [St. John 16:20]. A small, heart-broken cadre of family and friends removed Jesus' body from the cross and took it to a tomb donated by a rich man, Joseph of Arimathea. He had said "... the Son of Man has nowhere to lay His head" [St. Luke 9:58]. Neither did He have a place of His own in death. Defeated in mind, body, and spirit, the small band wrapped Jesus' lifeless, scared, and bloody body in fine linens and quickly departed the tomb since the beginning of a Sabbath (a set time, not necessarily a Saturday) was nearing (6 P.M.) and the Jews were preparing to eat the Passover meal the next day [see St. John 19:31]. Jesus likely was crucified on Thursday at the same time the Passover lambs were being slain, as will be discussed in the Conclusion. His friends planned to come back after the Paschal Sabbath (Friday) and the weekly Sabbath (Saturday) to prepare His body with spices and oils (Sunday morning). They had forgotten Jesus' teaching that it was impossible to plant a grain of wheat and not have something come up in its place. They had failed to understand what He meant when He told them that He was *the bread of life* [St. John 6:48].

> "Amen, amen, I say to you, unless the grain of wheat falls into the ground and dies, it remains alone. But if it dies, it brings forth much fruit."
> —St. John 12:24-25

He Is Risen—Hallelujah

Following His resurrection and appearing, Jesus followers' sorrow turned to unbounded joy. They put away their fear of men and of death and came out of hiding. They received the Holy Spirit and, because of their verve in spreading the gospel, became the men and women to whom the world referred as those "... setting the world in an uproar..." [Acts 17:6]. This is good news for sinners.

Satan Has a Plan for Your Personal Destruction

Satan viewed Jesus' death on the cross and His followers scattering as a victory and the end of God's plan for saving man. The first coming of messiah as the suffering servant, along with His death, burial, and resurrection, were both prophesied and veiled in the Old Testament. Even most of the orthodox Jews did not realize the time of their visitation [Daniel 9:25-26 and St. Luke 19:44]. Satan had tried to negate God's promise of a redeemer in Genesis 3:15 by eliminating the people of God, the Jews, through wars, idolatry, and intermarriage. He planted the seeds of jealousy in Herod's heart which led to the destruction of all newborn males in Bethlehem, the prophesied place of the redeemer's birth [Micheas 5:2]. Satan again failed in his effort.

Satan has a plan to keep man and God out of fellowship. A part of that plan has been to destroy God's chosen people, the Jews, because they play necessary roles regarding salvation during all ages [see St. John 4:22]. It was only the Jews that God trusted to write and preserve His words in both the Old and New Testaments [Romans 3:1-2]. The Jews also figure prominently in spreading the salvation message during the seven years known as the Tribulation Period which takes place some time after the end of the church age, after the Rapture. More will be said later about these things.

Satan hates man because he is jealous. Lucifer, the highest of all God's creations, was created to be a servant of the LORD. He was *created perfect* in his ways [Ezechiel 28:13-15]. However, Lucifer wanted to be "like" God. But God made *man* in His image, not Lucifer. We have what Lucifer always wanted. In his jealous hatred for mankind and God, Satan continually tries to isolate man from God's love, blessings, and salvation. Never mistake the real person of Satan for "an evil force" in the universe. You make that mistake to the detriment of your eternal soul. Realize also that God brings good from what Satan intends for evil. In other words, God uses even Satan to bring about His will.

Satan never really knew who Jesus was. It must be remembered that Jesus was not in an earthly body when Satan rebelled. In fact, Satan may not have even known about the Trinity prior to Jesus' incarnation. Also, since His body was prepared by the Father [Hebrews 10:5], Satan was not sure who Jesus was at their first encounter in the desert. God must have revealed to Satan that Jesus was His Son because Satan prefaced his first two tests of Jesus with, "If thou are the Son of God" [St. Matthew 4:3 and 6]. Remember, too, that Jesus was led into the desert by the Holy Spirit to be tested by Satan. Satan did not find Jesus. Since he did not know who Jesus was, *the Son of God*, or understand what His mission was, *to die for the sins of the world*, Satan stirred up the angry mob to call out to Pilate, "Crucify him! Crucify him!" Satan mistakenly thought that with Jesus' death would come the destruction of God's plan for reconciliation with mankind. When Satan saw Jesus die on the cross, he thought he had been successful in obviating God's plan to restore fellowship between Himself and sinful mankind. He had no way of knowing that his call for Jesus' crucifixion was actually moving God's plan for restoration forward. Satan was astonished when he learned that Jesus had *risen from the grave* and that by His death many would be saved. Satan had to devise yet another plan to keep mankind alienated from God.

Often the world and even some believers have a hard time understanding that God and Satan are not opposite sides of the same coin. There is no cosmic struggle of good against evil. God and Satan are not on the same level. The only thing they have in common is that they are both working their respective plans. God is still working His original plan to bring about the salvation of all who will accept His free gift. He has never had to change a single aspect of His plan which was drawn up in eternity past. Satan is working his plan and modifying it as necessary to destroy man's opportunity to recognize and accept that free gift.

Numerous novels, movies, and cult religions also have suggested duality between God and Satan. One so-called "Christian" ministry teaches that after Jesus died on the cross, He descended into hell where He was tortured by Satan for three days to pay man's sin debt! It should be understood, however, that the debt for sin is owed to God, not Satan. Moreover, Satan has not yet spent so much as one day in hell [Job 1:6-7 and 2:1-2]. Satan is the *god of this world* [2 Corinthians 4:4] and, during the present age, he continues to have access to earth and heaven [Job 1:6-7; 2:1-2; and St. Luke 4:1-13]. However, he is subject to the providential will of God and is therefore limited in the evil he can do. He is restrained by the power of the Holy Spirit who came at Pentecost to indwell believers. When all believers are taken off this earth at the Rapture [1 Thessalonians 4:13-18], which will be discussed more fully in the Conclusion, lawlessness will greatly increase [2 Thessalonians 2:6-10]. However, the day is coming when Satan will no longer have access to heaven [see Apocalypse 12:7-8].

Satan is a subtle seducer of souls. He wants people to believe that those under his influence are demonically possessed and that they run around foaming at the mouth, turning their heads through three-hundred-and-sixty degrees, and using telekinesis to move objects on the other side of a room. He also likes to be caricatured as the cute, comedic-looking little red fellow with a tail, horns, and pitchfork. Such portrayals lead many to dismiss his existence—a fatal error. However, Satan is referred to by name more than fifty times in the Scriptures, eighteen in the Old Testament and thirty-six in the New Testament. He is referred to as either "the devil" (there are many *devils* or demons) or as "the evil one" around forty times in the New Testament. Some believe in evil, but not in a literal Satan and his demons. Jesus believes he is a personality. In fact, Jesus referred to him by name, as recorded in all four Gospels [St. Matthew 4:10, St. Mark 3:23, St. Luke 4:8, and St. John 13:27].

No concept of duality is suggested in Scripture. Satan is not omniscient (all knowing), omnipotent (all powerful), or omnipresent (present everywhere at the same time). Neither does he know the future nor can he read your mind. What he does have is a vast army of demons to help him carry out his damnable plans. When one of Satan's cabal whispers a non-audible suggestion in your ear, it's not because he can discern what you are thinking. It is because he sees where your eyes are focused—maybe on an attractive woman, or something you want but can't afford that is within your physical grasp. "Take it," he suggests. "No one will ever know." If one is not on guard, he will soon be in the demon's snare and, without the freeing power of Jesus in one's life, the only path is down and down and down.

Neither Satan nor the demons have spirits attuned to the things of God. Their spirits were cut off at the time of their rebellion in heaven [Isaias 14:12-15]. When Satan reads the Scriptures, and he is versed in them [see St. Matthew 4:6], he gets no more understanding of the spiritual message contained within [see St. Matthew 4:7] than the man or woman who reads the Scriptures with an unregenerated spirit [see chapter four]. The promise of a new covenant in Jeremias 31:31-34 meant nothing to him. Satan has neither ears to hear nor eyes to see [Ezechiel 12:2]. Like those with unregenerated spirits, Satan believes that the Scriptures are just so much collected distillations of the minds of men. In his blinding pride, Satan believes he can defeat God. However, his final fate is clear [see Isaias 46:10]. Satan will battle God and man until finally he is cast into "... the pool of fire and brimstone..." wherein he will be "... tormented day and night forever and ever" [Apocalypse 20:9-10]. Many years ago, a popular rock group sang a song titled "Sympathy for the Devil." If these singers follow Satan to hell, they'll change their tune. One can have no sympathy for the devil.

Satan's first attempt to kill off the small community of believers known as the Way was through the efforts of some of the unbelieving, zealous Jews. One particular Jew described himself as having been:

> ... circumcised on the eighth day (*the day appointed by God for circumci-sion*), of the race of Israel, of the tribe of Benjamin, a Hebrew of Hebrews; as regards the Law, a Pharisee; as regards zeal, a persecutor of the Church of God (the *Way*); as regards the justice of the Law, leading a *blameless* life.
>
> —Philippians 3:5-6

He was the Jewish ideal. Moreover, this particular Pharisee presided over the murder of St. Stephen, the first Christian martyr [Acts 7:58-60]. Still breathing threats of slaughter against the disciples of the Lord, this Pharisee asked the high priest in Jerusalem for letters to the synagogues in Damascus such that if he found any men or women belonging to "this Way," he might bring them back to Jerusalem bound (with chains) for trial and execution [Acts 9:1-2]. This Pharisee's name was Saul. He and his compatriots were used by Satan in an attempt to kill Christianity. However, Jesus reoriented Saul's thinking one day and Saul changed his attitude. Saul thought of himself as *blameless*, that is, sinless, because the lawyers had perverted the Word of God. Whereas God's Word clearly taught that sin begins in the heart as a thought and that that thought itself is a sin, the Pharisees taught that one must actually *act* upon the thought for it to be sin. After having met the living Christ and coming to understand that even the thought of breaking God's Law is sin, St. Paul was horrified [see St. Matthew 5:28]. He repented. He realized that he was a sinner after all. Moreover, in I Timothy 1:15, St. Paul refers to himself as *chief* of all sinners.

Whereas Satan manipulated Saul to get him to kill a relatively small number of early Christians, God used St. Paul mightily to convert multitudes of Greeks and other Gentiles to grow His church. Defeated once again, Satan expanded his persecution strategy.

Judaism at the Time of Jesus' Ministry

The Roman emperor paid little attention to the goings-on among what were considered to be feuding sects of continuously feuding Jews: the Sadducees against the Pharisees, and the Scribes at times opposing both.

Among the feuding factions there was much disputation. The Sadducees came to Jesus and described a woman who had been married to seven men. They asked whose wife she would be in the next life. Jesus unloaded on these duplicitous Sadducees:

> "'... Is not this why you err—*because you know neither the Scriptures* nor the power of God? For *when they rise from the dead*, they will neither marry nor be given in marriage, but are *as the angels* in heaven. But as to the dead rising, have you not read the book of Moses about the bush, how God spoke to him saying, "I am the God of Abraham, and the God of Isaac, and the God of Jacob"? He is not the God of the dead, but of the living. You are therefore entirely wrong.'"
>
> —St. Mark 12:24-27

Jesus addressed three major errors in the Sadducees' doctrine: the importance and relevance of Scriptures, the resurrection of the body, and the existence of angels. At other times, Jesus addressed the errors of the Pharisees. By the time of Jesus' birth, centuries of internecine fighting among the various sects had led to a practiced Judaism wholly corrupted by the traditions of men [see St. Matthew 23:13-39].

After Jesus' ascension, St. Peter and the rest of the disciples, along with the newly converted St. Paul, preached the gospel to all who would listen. As long as the Pax Romana was maintained, the emperor and Judean governor were content to let the many religious factions worship in whatever manner they chose so long as it was not contrary to the interests of Rome.

Rome Begins Persecutions

This short-lived *laissez faire* policy changed when Nero became emperor (60-68 A.D.). He murdered both his wife and mother. He torched two-thirds of the city to make way for his rebuilt Rome and blamed the Christians for the conflagration. Nero began the first of ten waves of persecution by Roman emperors. Among his contrived tortures was tethering Christians to poles, covering them with pitch, and igniting their flesh to provide light in the evenings along the footpaths meandering through his gardens. Nero made Christianity an outlaw religion. It was during this time that St. Paul was beheaded and St. Peter crucified. Nero had the spirit of antichrist.

Subsequent emperors increased the types and levels of persecution for those who refused to make the required worship offerings of incense to their emperor. The Christians were not persecuted because they worshiped Jesus, but because they worshiped no other gods in addition to Him. The emperor knew he was no less a god than the crucified rabbi the stubborn Christians refused to deny. Emperors Domitian (81-96 A.D.), Trajan (98-117 A.D.), Marcus Aurelius (161-180 A.D.), Severus (193-211 A.D.), Maximinus (235-238 A.D.), Decius (249-251 A.D.), Valerian (253-260 A.D.), Aurelian (270-275 A.D.), and, finally, Diocletian (284-305 A.D.), all tried to end Christianity and its spread by maintaining its outlaw status and killing Christians. It was a simple and straightforward, satanically inspired approach.

The emperors also used Christians for sport in the arena to entertain the pagan masses. Believers were torn to pieces and eaten by wild beasts; boiled in oil in large vats over open flames; slowly roasted alive over red-hot coals; and subjected to other tortures that the most depraved minds could conjure. Persecution reached its zenith under Emperor Diocletian. He had so many tens of thousands of Christians killed that in 303 A.D. he had a state coin struck bearing the words: "Diocletian, the emperor who destroyed the Christian name."[8] Still, the faith spread and spirit-filled Christians refused to deny their Lord. This infuriated some of their tormentors but caused many to repent and accept Jesus as Lord and Savior. Believers met their fate in the arena amidst the singing of hymns and psalms. It is estimated that during the ten waves of persecution some five million Christians were martyred for their testimony of Jesus.[9]

Those Christians who escaped the persecutions fellowshipped in secret, meeting in small groups in each others' homes. They carried out the Lord's command to be witnesses and faced the possibility of death with each testimony [Acts 1:8]. Families didn't have the opportunity to bury loved ones killed in the persecutions. Their ashes and what was left of their broken bodies were disposed of by the state in the burning trash heaps outside the cities. The Christians had no certainty in this life. Their only certainty was in the life of the world to come. They could sing hymns and recite psalms as they were torn apart in the arena because, like St. Paul, St. Peter, and St. Jude, they were certain of their eternal destinies. They believed as they looked into the faces of the ravenous lions in one moment that in the next they would be looking into the face of their loving Lord and Savior. They longed to hear His promised words: "well done, good and faithful servant" [St. Matthew 25:21]. The blood of the martyrs served only to strengthen the resolve of the faithful and expand the gospel throughout the Empire. Satan realized that his plan to kill Christianity through expanded persecution was failing.

Some argue that it is presumptuous of the believer to think he knows his eternal destiny. Moreover, in Canon 30 the Council of Trent decreed:

> If anyone says that after the reception of the grace of justification the guilt
> is so remitted and the debt of eternal punishment so blotted out to every
> repentant sinner, that no debt of temporal punishment remains to be
> discharged either in this world or in purgatory before the gates of heaven
> can be opened, let him be anathema.

However, this decree is in direct opposition to the teachings contained in the Roman Catholic Bible, as evidenced by St. Paul's, St. Peter's, and St. Jude's words prior to dying, as was discussed in chapter four. Moreover, the Roman Catholic Bible assures believers that they abide in God and He in them and that love is perfected among us, one for another, through this abiding love. Therefore, God's Word assures us that "... we may have confidence in the day of judgment..." [1 St. John 4:17]. If one cannot know he is saved, then how can one have confidence in his judgment, his eternal destiny? The question is rhetorical. Its purpose is to point out how ridiculous is the notion that one cannot know of his salvation. Moreover, the Roman Catholic Bible assures believers, "exiled from the body, at home with the Lord" [2 Corinthians 5:8].

Believing God's Word is not presumptuous. Rather, it is living faith. To not believe Jesus' words on eternal life is not to be humble. It is to be disobedient! Belief is standing on the promises of God given in His Holy Word. The reason Jesus came to earth was to seek and to save that which was lost [St. Luke 19:10]. He left no room for ambiguities except for those created by the minds of those whose spirits have not been regenerated and the double-minded [St. James 1:7-8]. Jesus never once told anyone to be uncertain about his eternal destiny. He made clear to the Scribes and Pharisees their eternal destinies. He told the people "... unless your righteousness exceeds that of the Scribes and Pharisees, you shall not enter the kingdom of heaven" [St. Matthew 5:20]. On the other hand, Jesus told His followers, His sheep, "And I give them everlasting life; and they shall never perish..." [St. John 10:28]. This is a double promise-everlasting life and never perishing.

Satan Uses Constantine

Many had fallen in martyrdom to both the Jews and the Romans. St. Stephen was stoned to death. St. Mark was dragged through the streets until dead. St. Luke was hanged. Saints Peter, Simeon, and Philip were crucified. St. James was beheaded and St. Bartholomew skinned alive. St. Thomas was killed by lances and St. Jude shot to death with arrows. St. Matthias was stoned to death and St. Paul beheaded. In 313 A.D., the new western emperor,

Constantine (306-337), later known to the *world* as Constantine the Great and erroneously to many Churches as the first Christian emperor, issued a joint Edict of Toleration with his co-Emperor in the east, Licinius. The edict allowed freedom of worship for all religions in the Roman Empire. For the first time in more than two hundred years, Christianity was not an outlaw religion. Being a Christian was no longer a crime punishable by death. Prior to issuance of the Edict, the world noticed differences in conduct between Christians and nonbelievers. After, many claiming to be Christian continued to act the same way they had prior to their supposed conversions. Thus, in prompting Constantine to issue his Edict of Toleration, Satan created a *false Christianity* which has and still leads many to perdition. If there is no changed life, then there is no spiritual regeneration and, hence, no Holy Spirit working within the person to empower him to crucify his flesh [see Galatians 5:24 and 1 St. John 4:4]. Such a one is lost.

What is known about Constantine is that his mother, Helena, was a supposed Christian convert who claimed to have found the cross upon which Jesus was crucified. It is not surprising that the same cross upon which an itinerant preacher of no worldly importance was crucified, and which was subsequently lost to history for nearly three hundred years, was miraculously found by the emperor's soldiers when told by the emperor's mother to do so. Failure would have resulted in their executions.

The unbeliever will find himself standing before the Great White Throne in the presence of *His* cross and *His* shed blood [Apocalypse 20:11]. At this point, the prophecy will be fulfilled which says "every knee shall bend and every mouth confess that Jesus Christ is Lord, to the glory of God the Father" [Philippians 2:10-11]. Believers will have already confessed that Jesus is Lord while on earth [Romans 10:9]. Thus, believers do not come into judgment but have passed from death to life [St. John 5:24].

The Power Behind the Power

Constantine is renowned for being the first "Christian" emperor. History records that in the year 312 A.D., one year prior to his issuance of the Edict of Toleration, Constantine claimed that no less than Jesus appeared to him in a dream and told him to inscribe the first two letters of His name, *Chi-Rho* (XP in Greek), on the shields of his armies. Constantine claimed to have seen a heavenly vision the next day: a cross superimposed on the sun and the words "*in hoc signo vinces*"-"in this sign you will be victorious." Constantine did indeed defeat his rival, Maxentius, at the Battle of the Milvian Bridge and, as history records, became a "Christian" in that same year. Constantine generally is credited by secular historians with expanding Christianity throughout the Roman Empire. However, the sign Constantine saw had meaning not just for Christians, but also for pagans because it looked like the Egyptian "ankh." Realize, too, that Jesus' name is not Christ. Thus, Constantine's dream was phony on its face. The "Jesus" of his dream was not the Jesus of the New Testament. More is said later about the source of this and other visions. The Greek word Christ and Hebrew word Messiah are both titles. They both mean the "anointed one."

What generally is not known about Constantine among those who consider him to have been Christian is that after his supposed conversion, he continued to worship pagan gods in *their* temples along with his new-found Christian god. Constantine was the first "Christian" ecumenist and the one who introduced the heresy of ecumenism into Christianity. Moreover, his widely known vision of a cross superimposed on the sun was not his first. Two years before, in 310 A.D., Constantine had a vision of the Sun god, Sol, while worshiping in the grove (a place of pagan worship) of Apollo in Gaul. This may explain why in his second vision the cross was not alone, as it certainly would have been if the vision were from God, but superimposed *on the sun*, not replacing it. This, of course, would violate God's own commandment to have no other gods "beside" Me [Exodus 20:3]. However, it explains why Constantine went on worshiping Sol *and* his new Christian god who, in Constantine's mind, had brought him his latest victory, just as Sol had brought him earlier ones. This symbol, which honors both Jesus and Sol, is still used today by many Catholic and Orthodox churches.

Muhammad had similar visions some three hundred years later and, as a result, wrote the Koran, the holy book of Islam. A young Joseph Smith, junior, had visions in the early 1800s. As a result, he penned the Book of Mormon. Many Marian (Virgin Mary) visions have been reported since the 12th century with increasing frequency, including the Fatima appearance in Portugal. St. Dominic introduced the rosary into "Christian" worship following an apparition of the Virgin Mary in the company of demons. According to St. Dominic, Mary forced the demons to reveal to him the efficacy of prayers to her. [10] With regard to any vision, it is important to understand that there is more than one source. The veracity and message of all visions should be checked against Scripture.

Satanic Visions

We know from 2 Corinthians 11:14 that "Satan disguises himself as an angel of light." Moreover, we know that Satan is a liar and the father of lies [St. John 8:44]. These two verses tell us that Satan can present false visions to people. All visions are either from God or from Satan (his demons). In

Constantine's first vision, that of Sol, the Sun god, the source must have been Satan, for God does not present visions of false gods. His second vision, the one that showed the a cross superimposed on the sun, indicating that the Sun god and Jesus were equal, was also from Satan [see Exodus 20:5].

In Muhammad's vision, he alleged that the angel Gabriel appeared to him and dictated the Koran. This, of course, is the same Koran that contradicts the concept of the Trinity, denies the deity of Jesus, and paints a portrait of a concupiscent afterlife.

Joseph Smith's visions began when he was fourteen years old and continued until just before his martyrdom in 1844. According to Smith, Moroni, a former human and son of the LDS prophet Mormon (400 A.D.) turned angel, appeared and led him to where the "golden plates" were buried. The plates contained an encrypted message in a language Smith didn't understand. However, "by the gift and power of God," he translated the message into English and produced the Book of Mormon. Among other things, the plates revealed that both Jesus and God the Father are created beings.

The Virgin Mary appeared to three young girls several times at Fatima in Portugal in 1917. During one of her apparitions, the Virgin asked them, "Would you be willing to die for the sins of the world?" This is a strange question for a believer in Christ and His supposed mother to ask. First, the believer understands that the sacrifice for sin must be unblemished, that is, without sin [see Exodus 12:5 and 1 St. Peter 1:19]. Even though these were children, could they have been without sin? The Scriptures are clear on this. None is without sin [see Romans 3:10-12]. If we say we have no sin, then the truth is not in us and we make Him a liar [see 1 St. John 1:8 and 1:10]. There is also the matter that Jesus had already gone to the cross and *paid for the sins of the whole world* [see 1 St. John 2:2]. Given these facts, it must be concluded that the source of the Fatima visions was the same source as the visions experienced by Joseph Smith, St. Dominic, Muhammad, and Constantine. One can also determine that this vision was not from God by applying the test given us by St. John:

> Beloved, do not believe every spirit, but test the spirits to see whether they are of God; because many false prophets have gone forth into the world. By this (*test*) is the spirit of God known: every spirit that confesses that Jesus Christ has come in the flesh, is of God. And every spirit that severs Jesus (*segments the Jesus of the New Testament*), is not of God, but is of Antichrist, of whom you have heard that he is coming, and now is already in the world.
>
> —1 St. John 4:1-3

The Scriptures tell us that the Jesus of the New Testament came to save us by paying our sin debt and that He was crucified. Thus, He came in the body, for only the body can be crucified. Only the body can shed blood, which is necessary for the remission of sins. When the apparition asked the children if they would be willing to pay the sin debt of the world, it was denying that Jesus had come in the flesh and already paid that debt. Therefore, the apparition was not from God, but from Satan! As already mentioned, many Churches, too, sever Jesus. They strip away His power as the lawgiver and usurp His authority for themselves.

Many are treated to visions in this age. Several years ago a popular television series on a major network featured angels at a time when angel worship was at an all-time high. It would be difficult to deny that the show was uplifting *in the flesh*. The beginning and ending focused on a white dove. The program used many Christian words like the Father, truth, love, and good news. One of the female stars who played an angel was an ordained minister. The angels told those to whom they appeared that they had been sent by God. They were careful not to indicate which god—Allah, Buddha, Apollo, Zeus, you name it. After this revelation, a golden aura manifested around their heads and shoulders. The angels explained, "We are all his children."

The creator of this program was interviewed by Pat Robertson on his CBN telecast. She professed to be a Christian and said there was no subject the show was afraid to take on. The series dealt with many social issues. However, there were some subjects the show stayed away from: Jesus, the Son of God, His shed blood, and Him being the *only way* to the Father. At the end of each episode, when the angels revealed the truth, that they were messengers from God, they never mentioned that Jesus is the Truth. Neither did they mention that God loved the people in this corrupt world so much that He gave His only begotten Son to pay their sin debt on the cross so that any who believe in Him should not perish but have eternal life. When the angels said that there was good news, they never mentioned the Good News that God has a free gift of salvation for all through the atoning work of His Son on the cross. In fact, the "cross" was not a part of this so-called Christian series. Neither was there mention of Calvary or the shedding of blood for the remission of sin. By *erroneously* claiming that we are *all* God's children, the program misled many into believing that there are indeed many paths to heaven. Believers in Islam who worship Allah and deny the deity of Jesus naturally believed that the angels were sent from Allah. Jehovah's Witnesses who worship Jehovah and deny the deity of Jesus believed that the angels were from Jehovah. Practicing Jews who worship Jehovah and deny the deity of Jesus believed that the angels were from Jehovah God. As recorded in St. Mark 16:15, Jesus told His apostles to: "Go into the whole world and preach the gospel to every *creature*." An unbeliever is not a child of God but a creature, that is, something created by God. Because he has a dead spirit, he is considered a child of disobedience. Only by accepting the Jesus of the New Testament as Lord and Savior does the creature become an adopted child of God [see Romans 8:16]. Don't think you couldn't be deceived by a false vision. Millions were taken in every week. Most who consider themselves Christian, when asked, replied that the series is Christian. They are deceived. Satan is the prince of the power of the air, as revealed in Ephesians 2:2.

Today, television programming includes series on demons, vampires, ghosts, mediums, witches, ghost hunters, and a plethora of other paranormal phenomena. A popular children's cartoon features gargoyles and other demonic representations. A new series features a man who can raise the dead.

Constantine a Believer?

Another thing that generally is not known about Constantine is that he, a supposed "disciple of Christ," had his son, Crispus, put to death in 326 A.D., some fourteen years after his assumed conversion. Following more in the footsteps of Herod the Great and Emperor Nero than Christ, Constantine shortly thereafter had his wife, Fausta, suffocated in her bath after she was accused by Constantine's mother Helena, later designated St. Helena, of having committed adultery with a household slave.[11] Constantine also had an eleven-year-old nephew and an uncle murdered. This sounds more like palace intrigue among heathens than Christian family values. There is no evidence of a "changed life" in Constantine's history, no crucifixion of the flesh, no walking in submission, and no putting on of the new man, as would be expected if his conversion were real [see Colossians 3:5-10]. Jesus taught that one could know the tree by its fruit and multiple murders without any indication of repentance are a pretty rotten fruit by just about anyone's standard [see St. Matthew 7:17-20]. As recorded in St. John 13:35, Jesus said, "By this will all men know that you are my disciples, if you have love for one another." He further said, "If you love me, keep my commandments" [St. John 14:15]. One of Jesus' commandments was to be baptized. Baptism symbolizes the believer's faith in Jesus' death, burial, and bodily resurrection:

"He who believes and is baptized shall be saved, but he who does not
believe shall be condemned."

—St. Mark 16:16

Contrary to Jesus' command, Constantine did not follow the Lord
in believer's baptism after his supposed conversion. Rather, he waited
twenty-five years until he was on his death bed.[12]

Constantine Establishes His Universal Church

Constantine was not a follower of Jesus. He was a pagan opportunist
who saw a way of uniting a disparate and far-flung Empire through the
enthusiasm of a most resilient and coherent new force called Christianity.
Constantine viewed the Christian god as a god who could help him win
battles and wars. He invited the many disparate churches to join him and
his empire in building a unified infrastructure that would combine the
temporal power of the empire with the spiritual power of the churches.
This would make him and his empire invincible. In 313 A.D., pagan Rome
was married to those many churches that accepted Constantine's proposal.
However, as history reveals, not all churches accepted.

Constantine had the daunting challenge of combining pagan prelates,
religions, and traditions with those of the new state-sponsored religion.
Pagan traditions and rituals already had slipped into some of the churches,
but not all. This can be verified from the letters to the seven churches
addressed in chapters 2 and 3 of the book of Apocalypse. This final book
of the New Testament, which contains a warning against adding to or
subtracting from the things in the book, is generally interpreted to be a
prohibition against doing same for all of Scripture. The Apocalypse was
written by St. John while he was exiled on the Island of Patmos by Emperor
Domitian around the year 95 A.D.

Contrary to early church tradition, which is documented in the book
of Acts and elsewhere in the New Testament, some churches were not
following the simple structure of a church authorized in Scripture. Rather
than having a bishop (pastor) and several deacons (elders) to administrate
the functions of a single, autonomous church, as authorized in 1 Timothy
chapter 3 and Ephesians 4:11, these churches were constructing hierarchal
positions similar to those found today in the Roman Catholic, Orthodox,
and most Protestant Churches. Such structures and those who belonged
to them were termed Nicolaites. It is a combination of two Greek words
that translate "victory over the laity." In Apocalypse 2:6, Jesus commends
the church at Ephesus:

But this thou hast (*commendation*): thou hatest the works of the Nicolaites, *which I also hate.*

Again in Apocalypse 2:15-16, Jesus condemns the teaching of the Nicolaites in His letter to the church at Pergamum:

So thou hast also some who hold the teaching of Nicolaites. In like manner repent, or else I will come to thee quickly, and will fight against them with the sword of my mouth.

Damnable Heresies Take Root in Some of the Early Churches

Even before the time of Constantine, several heresies broke out among some of the many independent churches. Satan did his best to destroy God's plan for mankind's restoration with the Almighty by polluting the gospel with false teaching. Prior to Constantine, Satan was carrying out a dual strategy to kill Christianity. He was using the emperors to persecute Christians from without and raising up false teachers within the churches, just as St. Peter and St. Paul had warned against [see 1 Corinthians 15:12 and 2 St. Peter 2:1]. Both were aware that Satan had used the evil prophet Balaam to put into the Moabite king's head that the solution is dilution of the Jewish race [see Numbers 22-25]. St. Peter and St. Paul feared that Satan would use false ministers *within the church* to dilute the gospel message. Satan had been unable to kill the Israelites and Balaam's efforts to curse them resulted in blessings. Finally, Balaam advised king Balac to have the women seduce the Israelite men and marry them (this is addressed more fully in Appendix A). St. Peter and St. Paul feared that Satan would attack the church in a similar way and dilute the true gospel message.

Damnable heresies are teachings outside the veracity of Scripture that, if followed, lead to the second death, literal damnation. Obviously, not all heresies are damnable. Prior to unification of a large number of churches early in the 4th century by Constantine, later known as the universal Church, most of the churches were independent, fundamentalist, Bible-believing churches. In some churches, however, the heresy of "baptismal regeneration" began to take hold. Whereas Scripture teaches that the spirit is reborn by saying "yes" to Jesus, the heresy of baptismal regeneration held that the spirit was reborn by receiving water baptism. Some mystical significance was attached to water as not only a physical cleansing agent but also a spiritual cleansing agent. However, there is no scriptural support for such a view.

Integral to this heresy was another, namely, that of original sin. This damnable heresy taught that man is born with an original sin on his soul, which can be washed away by baptism. However, the Catholic and all other Bibles teach that man is born with a sin problem caused by being born with a spirit that is dead to the things of God. This misunderstanding may have been a throwback to some pagan rituals. Both the Jews and pagans relied heavily on ceremonials and rituals. However, John the Baptist never preached that his baptism brought salvation. Moreover, Jesus never taught or even suggested that baptism would allow one to enter into the kingdom of heaven. If baptism is the key to the kingdom, it is indeed strange that when asked what one must do to be saved, Jesus never once told anyone to be baptized! Many denominations erroneously teach that the spirit is reborn by water baptism. Moreover, many teach that without baptism one cannot be saved. However, the Scriptures never record Jesus or any of His disciples telling anyone he had to be baptized to enter the kingdom. Jesus promised the believing robber on the cross that they would be together in paradise that day. Moreover, as recorded in St. Mark 16:15-16, when Jesus commissioned His apostles He told them:

"... Go into the whole world and preach the gospel to every creature. He who *believes* and is baptized shall be saved, but he who *does not believe* shall be condemned."

Jesus is setting a binary condition for salvation with His words "believes" and "does not believe." The believer is saved. The nonbeliever is lost. Baptism is not the subject of these two verses. Belief in Jesus is. And the result is that those who believe in Him are saved. Jesus tied the words "believes" and "baptized" together because we are to follow His example in believer's baptism. The servant follows the lead of the master [see St. Matthew 3:13-17]. Moreover, baptism is an act of obedience, commitment, and proclamation—not salvation. Baptism is to take place as a result of salvation, not a cause of it. As recorded by St. Paul in Colossians 2:12:

For you were buried together with him in Baptism, and in him also rose again through faith in the working of God who raised him from the dead.

Thus, baptism has everything to do with obedience and proclaiming Jesus as Master and nothing to do with salvation. Baptism is symbolic of our burial with Him and our resurrection in Him.

A natural outgrowth to the heresy of baptismal regeneration was infant baptism. Since baptism had been declared to be the vehicle of salvation, it was obvious to adherents that infants should be baptized. Moreover, since immersion could be dangerous to infants, sprinkling with water replaced immersion. Independent churches, however, continued to follow the practice established in the early churches that only believers who confessed Jesus with their mouths (to the congregation) were to be baptized and then only by immersion. Infant baptism was not an option in New Testament churches. Orthodox Churches to this day baptize infants by immersion rather than sprinkling.

Another outgrowth of these damnable heresies was the logical extrapolation that if baptism could wash away original sin, then baptism could wash away other sins accumulated prior to baptism. Such a belief is ritualistic and pagan. History tells us this is why Constantine did not get baptized until he was at death's door. He believed he could sin all he wanted, order the deaths of his son, wife, nephew, uncle, co-emperor, and other "enemies" and then have the water of baptism "wash away" all those sins from his "blackened soul." It cannot and does not [see Apocalypse 1:5]. Jesus taught His followers to *love* their enemies, not dispose of them [St. Matthew 5:44].

The heresies of original sin, spiritual regeneration through baptism, infant baptism, sprinkling with water, and the soul-washing power of baptism to remove all accumulated sins prior to baptism, resulted in the first schism among the disparate, autonomous churches. The year was 251 A.D., some sixty years before Constantine entered onto the world stage.[13] The New Testament churches followed the Scriptures with regard to all aspects of baptism:

> On hearing this they were baptized in the name of the Lord Jesus; and when Paul laid his hands on them, the Holy Spirit came upon them....
> —Acts 19:5-6

Here the Scripture makes clear that baptism is not the agency by which spiritual rebirth is accomplished. Certainly St. Paul was used greatly by Jesus to bring salvation to Jews and Gentiles alike. In addressing certain heresies concerning baptism that had broken out in Corinth, St. Paul reaffirms the non-necessity of baptism for salvation:

> For Christ did not send me to baptize, but to preach the gospel....
> —1 Corinthians 1:17

Thus, St. Paul, who was instrumental in bringing new members into the kingdom, reflects the truth of Scripture, namely, that entrance is through the preaching and acceptance of the gospel, not baptism. St. Paul taught the Ephesians, "For by grace you have been saved through faith" [Ephesians 2:8]. He also preached that, "Faith then depends on hearing, and hearing on the Word of Christ" [Romans 10:17]. Thus, St. Paul gloried in the fact that he was an instrument of God by which the Good News of salvation was being heard and accepted throughout the known world.

Baptism in Early New Testament Churches

The book of Acts describes a time of growth and transition for the early churches. Many instances of baptism are recorded. In all cases, expressed belief in Jesus precedes baptism. St. Paul's rebirth experience is typical. On his journey to Damascus, Saul was knocked to the ground. Trembling and amazed, he asked, "*Lord*, what wilt thou have me do?" Thus, he confessed Jesus as Lord with his mouth [Acts 9:6]. After first believing and confessing Jesus as Lord, the Holy Spirit entered St. Paul and he was subsequently baptized:

> And so Ananias departed (*from his own house at the direction of the Lord*) and entered the house (*of Judas of Damascus where Saul was staying*), and said, "Brother Saul, the Lord has sent me—Jesus, who appeared to thee on thy journey—that thou mayest recover thy sight and be filled with the Holy Spirit." And straightway there fell from his eyes something like scales, and he recovered his sight, and arose, and was baptized.
>
> —Acts 9:17-18

Crispus' and his family's experience was similar:

> But Crispus, the president of the synagogue, believed in the Lord and so did all his household, and many of the Corinthians heard Paul, *and believed*, and were baptized.
>
> —Acts 18:8

Another clear example of the Holy Spirit being poured out prior to baptism is found in Acts 10:44-48:

> While Peter was still speaking these words, the Holy Spirit came upon all who were listening to his message. And the faithful of the circumcision (*believing Jews*), who had come with Peter, were amazed, because on the Gentiles also the grace of the Holy Spirit had been poured forth; for they (*the believing Jews*) heard them (*the Gentiles*) speaking in tongues and magnifying God. Then Peter answered, "Can anyone refuse the water to

baptize these, seeing that they have received the Holy Spirit just as we did?" And he ordered them to be baptized in the name of Jesus Christ.

Again, the order was belief, sealing by the Holy Spirit, and then baptism.

In one instance, baptism preceded the falling of the Holy Spirit. This instance is recorded earlier in Acts 8:14-17:

> Now when the apostles in Jerusalem heard that Samaria (*region in northern Israel whose inhabitants were hated by Jews, thus, the story of the Good Samaritan*) had received the word of God (*believed*), they sent to them Peter and John. On their arrival they prayed for them, that they might receive the Holy Spirit; for as yet he (*Holy Spirit*) had not come upon any of them, but they *had only been baptized* in the name of the Lord Jesus. Then they (*Peter and John*) laid their hands on them and they received the Holy Spirit.

In Samaria, belief (*had received the Word of God*), as always, came first; followed by baptism in the name of the Lord Jesus; and, lastly, the falling of the Holy Spirit upon the believers. This recorded instance makes it clear that water baptism does not bring about spiritual rebirth. Those in Samaria had believed and been baptized, but had not yet received the Holy Spirit. St. Luke records for us that the Holy Spirit was poured out only after St. Peter and St. John arrived. However, the laying on of hands should not be interpreted as a ritual, because in other verses there was no laying on of hands when the Holy Spirit fell on believers [Acts 9:17-18; Acts 18:8; and Acts 10:44-48]. Why did God wait before sending the Holy Sprit upon the believing Samaritans in this unique instance? God knew that St. Peter would resist taking the gospel to the Gentiles. To prepare him for the task, God first let him *see* the Holy Spirit falling on the hated Samaritans.

The Roman Catholic Church uses 1 St. Peter 3:21 to support its position that baptism is necessary for salvation [see *Pillar of Fire, Pillar of Truth* , Catholic Answers, page 15]. However, as already cautioned against, biblical exegesis should never be based (1) on only one verse or (2) taken out of context with surrounding verses. Ecclesiastes 8:15 provides a good example why:

> ... there is nothing good for man under the sun except eating and drinking and mirth (*merriment*): for this is the accompaniment (*his all*) of his toil during the limited days of his life which God gives him under the sun.

Even those with little Scriptural familiarity understand that this verse is not consistent with the message of the Scriptures and must therefore be understood within the context of the surrounding verses or, possibly, even within the context of the book in which it appears, or possibly within the context of all Scripture. The same is true for St. Peter's words in 3:21 which state: "Its counterpart, baptism, now saves you...." Even here the Catholic Church twists the meaning since Catholicism does not teach that baptism saves an individual. Nevertheless, either this verse contradicts all other verses on the teaching of salvation or else St. Peter is saying something else entirely. When one examines the verse in context, it becomes clear that St. Peter is using a water analogy to explain salvation. He is also affirming that it is Jesus the Christ who saves through baptism in His shed blood. Jesus mentioned this to Salome, the mother of James and John. She asked the Master if her sons could sit one on His right hand and the other on His left in the kingdom:

> But Jesus answered and said, "Ye know not what ye ask. Are ye able to drink of the cup that I shall drink of, *and to be baptized with the baptism that I am baptized with?*" They say unto him, "We are able." And he saith unto them, "Ye shall drink indeed of my cup, *and be baptized with the baptism that I am baptized with*: but to sit on my right hand, and on my left, is not mine to give, but it shall be given to them for whom it is prepared of my Father."
>
> —St. Matthew 20:22-23 KJV

The only baptism that saves a sinner is Jesus' baptism in His own blood. It is interesting to note that most versions of the Bible have identical content in the same two verses presented above, including the King James Version, New King James Version, *The Orthodox Study Bible, New Testament and Psalms*, and many of the versions not recommended for study in chapter 1. However, the Roman Catholic Bible, both the Douay-Challoner and Douay-Rheims translations, deletes Jesus' words about His baptism:

> But Jesus answered and said, "You do not know what you are asking. Can you drink the cup of which I am about to drink?" They said to him, "We can." He said to them, "Of my cup you shall indeed drink; but as for sitting at my right hand and at my left, that is not mine to give you, but it belongs to those for whom it has been prepared by my Father."
>
> —St. Matthew 20:22-23,
> Douay-Challoner version

This is the baptism that saves to which St. Peter refers in 1 St. Peter 3:21:

Its counterpart, baptism, now saves you also (not the putting off of the filth of the flesh, but the inquiry of a good conscience after God), through the resurrection of Jesus Christ.

The key to interpreting this verse correctly is understanding what is meant by "the filth of the flesh." The Catholic and many other Churches misinterpret this verse to mean dirt on the body. However, it is a reference to *sins of the flesh*. The Greek word used for filth here is *rhupos*. It means moral depravity. St. Peter clearly states in this verse that baptism does not remove the sins of the flesh. In the previous verses St. Peter is talking about how the physical lives of Noe and his family were "saved through water." How did the water save them? The water lifted those "in the ark" above the flooded world. The water condemned those not "in the ark." In verse 21 St. Peter turns his attention from the physical realm to the spiritual. He notes that baptism is the counterpart to water in the above verse. Jesus' blood (a type of water) lifts those who are "in Christ" (a type of ark) above spiritual death (a type of physical death). Those not "in Christ" are condemned by His blood. Apocalypse 1:5 confirms that Jesus "washed us from our sins in his own blood." Baptism in New Testament churches today is the same as it was in these early churches.

What Is Baptism?

The concept of "*baptizo*," a Greek word meaning "submerge," "dip," or "immerse," was not invented by either John the Baptist or Jesus. A person wishing to abandon idol worship and convert to Judaism had to get circumcised and perform a number of Jewish ceremonies, including a covenant meal and a ritual bath. The bath was an outward sign that the convert was washing away things associated with the old life of idol worship and being transformed into a child of the covenant. Both John and Jesus incorporated this ceremonial *baptizo* in their teachings. In John's teaching, baptism was symbolic of changing one's mind about his self-righteousness and need for a Savior. In Jesus' teaching, baptism was public affirmation that one was His follower. Neither John the Baptist, Jesus, nor His apostles ever taught that baptism played any role in gaining entrance into the kingdom. New Testament churches understood that baptism by immersion symbolized Jesus' death, burial, and bodily resurrection. Following Jesus in believer's baptism affirmed, in a symbolic way, their identification with Jesus' burial (of the old man) and resurrection (of the new man in Christ) [Romans 6:4-7 and 2 Corinthians 5:17].

With these heresies concerning baptism, Satan had sown the first bad seeds which over time would grow into bad trees and produce the rotten fruit of a sacramental salvation system. Baptism was only the first of several sacraments to come. Contrary to God's plan of salvation taught by Jesus and His disciples, the erring Churches evolved to teach that salvation is a "process" toward which one progresses by participating in the sacraments. Different denominations created different sacraments that are themselves divided into several categories which allegedly transmit *grace* (a different concept of grace than taught in Scriptures) to participants through ordinary elements such as water, wine, bread, and oil. Thus, God's free offer of salvation through Jesus' atoning death on the cross was set aside and religious establishments—each calling itself "The Church" and run by sinful men—became the dispensers of salvation. This concept resulted in a false soteriology where one could be saved one day, lost the next, and saved again the following day and so on.

The Persecuted Churches Become the Persecuting Church

Only a few decades after the *worldly* power of the Roman Empire was married to the spiritual power of the universal "Christian" Church created by Constantine, New Testament churches that continued to resist false teachings on original sin, baptismal regeneration, and infant baptism, were labeled heretical and persecuted for not *conforming* their beliefs to the *new world* religion headed by the emperor. In 416 A.D., the Roman Church, whose roots were established only one hundred years earlier by the pagan Constantine, made infant baptism compulsory.[14] Soon after, the formerly autonomous persecuted churches that now made up the universal persecuting Church evolved by 450 A.D. into the Roman Catholic Church. Whereas Jesus said:

> "If the *world* hates you, know that it has hated me before you. If you were *of the world*, the *world* would love what is its own. But because *you are not of the world but I have chosen you out of the world, therefore, the world hates you*. Remember the word that I have spoken to you: No servant is greater than his master. If they have persecuted me, they will persecute you also... But all these things they will do to you for my name's sake, because *they do not know him who sent me (God the Father)*."
> —St. John 15:18-21

Those who would not follow the Roman world's dictum in the matter of infant baptism were put to the "Christian" sword. During the persecution of believers and The Inquisition that began shortly thereafter, and lasted more than twelve hundred years, the Roman Catholic Church *legislated* additional required beliefs contrary to the doctrines in the Catholic Bible. In the process, it created more martyrs for the testimony of Jesus than all the pagan Roman emperors combined![15] The Roman Catholic Church had accepted many of Constantine's ideas, but not freedom of religion as expressed in his 313 A.D. Edict of Toleration. Despite fierce persecution, God saved a remnant for His own, as He always does [see 4 Kings 19:31; Isaias 10:20-22; Jeremias 6:9; Joel 2:32; Romans 9:27 and 11:5; and Apocalypse 7:2-8]. Today's New Testament churches are direct descendants of these persecuted churches. Each reproduces after its own kind [Genesis 1:21].

The Confused Church

Pope Innocent I (401-417) pronounced that babies were obliged to receive communion in addition to being baptized. The Pope warned that if they died baptized but "uncommunioned," they would go to hell. With this new pronouncement, the Church changed from its previous position that baptized babies who die go to heaven. Pope Gelasius I (492-496) announced his agreement with Innocent's position. However, both popes' positions on the matter were condemned at the Council of Trent (1545-1563). Prior to Trent, Pope Gregory I, also know as Gregory the Great (590-604), modified Innocent's and Gelasius' position. He decreed that unbaptized babies who die go to hell and suffer there for all eternity. He rescinded the requirement to receive communion to avoid damnation.[16] Some two hundred years after Trent, the Church changed its teaching yet again. Pope Pius VI (1775-1799) decreed that those who die unbaptized go to Limbo where they suffer the pain of loss (of the Beatific Vision, that is, they do not see God), but not the pain of fire.

Limbo is mentioned briefly in the *Catechism* of the Catholic Church under baptism. It is not listed in the subject index. However, the Church's position on Limbo appears also to have been replaced. According to paragraph 1261 of the *Catechism* of the Roman Catholic Church:

> As regards children who have died without Baptism, the Church can only entrust them to the mercy of God, as she does in her funeral rites for them. Indeed, the great mercy of God who desires that all men should be saved, and Jesus' tenderness toward children which caused him to say: "Let the children come to me, and do not hinder them," allow us to hope that there is a way of *salvation* for children who have died without Baptism. All the more urgent is the Church's call not to prevent little children coming to Christ through the gift of holy Baptism.

God's Word tells us that babies who die go to be with God. You may recall the story of king David and Bethsabee (also spelled Bathsheba). The king routinely accompanied his army into battle. On this particular occasion, however, he remained behind in Jerusalem. One evening David was walking along his lofty palace veranda. He looked down and noticed a beautiful woman taking a bath on the roof of her house. That was the custom on warm evenings. David summoned her. Her name was Bethsabee, the wife of Urias, one of his field generals. The two entered into a clandestine relationship which was hidden from men's eyes until Bethsabee became pregnant. Upon discovering her condition, David immediately recalled Urias and his troops from battle. He ordered Urias to go home to the comfort of his bed and wife, hoping the general would think in coming months that he was the father. However, Urias did not go home. David asked him to explain his disobedience. Urias replied that he felt if his men were denied the comfort of their beds and wives that he should deny himself those same pleasures. David sent Urias back to the battle with a sealed letter to his commanding officer. It directed that Urias be placed on the front line. Urias was slain by the enemy and David took Bethsabee into his palace as one of his wives. Bethsabee gave birth to their son. However, the child soon became ill. David fasted and prostrated himself before the Lord. However, God took the child as a chastisement. Upon hearing of his son's death, David ceased his grief, rose up, and ate. When questioned about his conduct, David replied calmly:

> ... now that he is dead, why should I fast? Shall I be able to bring him back any more? *I shall go to him* rather: but he shall not return to me.
> —2 Kings 12:23

David could have recorded this in Scripture *only* if God revealed it to him. Thus, David had every reason to be certain of his and his dead child's eternal destinies. David's lamentation for his sin of adultery is recorded in Psalm 50 (51). In verse 14 he states:

> Give me back the *joy* of your salvation....

Notice that David does not ask God to restore his *salvation*. David, despite his wicked sins of lust, adultery, and murder knew he had not lost his salvation. Rather, he asked God to cleanse his heart and restore to him his *joy* that came from knowing his eternal destiny. David paid dearly for his sins during his lifetime. His children's conduct made his one of the most "dysfunctional families" in history.

Anabaptists—God's Preserved Remnant

Anabaptist churches insisted that converts make a public profession of faith and be scripturally baptized. Apostate Churches referred to such churches as re-baptizers since most of these converts had been baptized as infants. The Roman Catholic Church simply labeled them heretics. They referred to themselves as New Testament churches and held their testimony for Jesus more sacred than their own lives, as evidenced by their martyrdom.

It should be understood that Anabaptists did not come about as a result of the 16th century Protestant Reformation. Unlike Catholic and most Protestant Churches, Baptists do not "confess one baptism for the forgiveness of sins." Anabaptists were there from the beginning, before the notion of a universal, Roman, or Roman Catholic Church. They were found in independent, fundamentalist, Bible-believing New Testament churches. Often the "ana" was dropped and they were referred to simply as Baptists. Cardinal Hosius, who became the president of the Council of Trent said in 1524:

> Were it not that the baptists have been grievously tormented and cut off with the knife during the *past twelve hundred years*, they would swarm in greater number than all the Reformers.
> —Hosius, Letters, Apud Opera, pages 112, 113[17]

The cardinal confirms that Baptists date back to the time of Constantine's unification of many of the formerly independent churches into a universal Church. Independent, fundamentalist, Bible-believing Baptist churches are the only ones never to have created a denominational organization (hierarchy) or symbolized with Rome.

An Emperor Calls the First of Many Councils

Constantine's plans to consolidate his power were moving forward. He finally was successful in uniting the eastern and western halves of the Empire in 324 when he had his eastern co-emperor, Licinius, killed. Shortly after, Constantine invited representatives of all the autonomous churches to convene at a council in Nicea in 325. Many responded in the affirmative. However, a good number did not. Many followed Jesus' teaching that church leadership and state leadership should not be combined [St. Mark 12:17]. Moreover, with the issuance of the Edict, many in the pagan world saw the writing on the wall and jumped to the new, state-sponsored religion headed by Constantine, the Pontifex Maximus. These included not only ordinary practitioners but also priests and hierarchal leaders in the many pagan mystery religions (mystery refers to secret rights and rituals) that prospered in Rome during the Christian persecution and before. To accelerate such "conversions," Constantine ordered tax breaks given to "Christian" prelates.

A hierarchy was formed among those who attended Constantine's first ecumenical council. This led to a Church structure that included real but erring Christians in positions of authority along with unconverted pagan religious leaders in others. Christ was dethroned as head of the formerly autonomous churches and the emperor installed as its new head. Under the headship of the emperor, the universal Church soon began to act not only in an executive manner, but also in a legislative one, setting aside the teaching and laws of God and substituting in their place manmade traditions such as infant baptism. After assuming headship of the universal Church, Constantine accepted the pagan title of his predecessors, Julius Caesar and Augustus, Pontifex Maximus, the head of all state religions. Under this title he selected young girls for service as Vestal Virgins who served at the public shrine to Vesta, the goddess of the hearth. Moreover, Constantine continued in pagan worship and practiced pagan rituals used to bless crops, animals, homes, and other things.[18] Additional elements of pagan ceremonies, rituals, and articles of worship began to be brought into the universal Church by "converting" pagans.

The Emperor Becomes "The Vicar of Christ"

Constantine, like all Roman emperors before him, was infallible. The universal Church recognized that Constantine needed a Christian title as head of the "Christian" Church to go with his pagan title of Pontifex Maximus. Church hierarchy honored him with the title "Bishop of bishops." Constantine, however, claimed an even higher title: *Vicarius Christi*, "Vicar of Christ." It means "in the place of Christ."[19] Since the Greek word for Vicar is Anti, the Emperor and anyone else who claims the title Vicar of Christ is, by simple translation, an antichrist. It means "in the place of Christ." It is not necessarily a pejorative term meaning "against Christ," but such is the context within which it is generally used. Thus, for the first time in history, the world had an unrepentant, multiple-murderer claiming to stand in the place of Christ! There have been many homicidal maniacs since who have claimed to be the Christ, or vicars of Christ, as was discussed in chapter two. Prior to his death, Constantine also usurped St. Paul's title by referring to himself as "the 13th apostle."

The Emperors Successors

Successors to Constantine to this very day carry *his* claim of infallibility and *his* titles of Pontifex Maximus and Vicar of Christ, along with many of the ceremonials such as having their rings kissed. The reigning emperors continued to exercise the office of Pontifex Maximus until 376 A.D. when Emperor Gratian, for Christian reasons, refused it. Gratian did much to remove paganism from its new home in Constantine's universal Church. However, by this time and with much of the universal Church hierarchy consisting not of real Christians, but opportunists from the pagan mystery cults, his accomplishments were limited. He ended state-provided financial support for the pagan cults. This action resulted in the unintended consequence of driving prelates from cash-starved cults into the cash-rich universal Church. Gratian tried unsuccessfully to disassociate the Roman state from pagan religions.[20] When he refused the title of Pontifex Maximus, Damasus, the Bishop of Rome, graciously accepted it, along with the emperor's other titles of Bishop of bishops and Vicar of Christ, along with his cloak of infallibility. St. Peter never held such titles. Neither did he claim to be infallible. This degree of hubris was reserved largely for the leaders of the secular world, the Roman emperors and the pharao's before them, along with the Moslem Abbasid Caliphs after.

The First Small Compromise

Constantine's "conversion" and subsequent elevation of Christianity to the preferred state religion aggravated many of the pagan prelates. As a matter of tradition, these priests, magicians, soothsayers, and astrologers had been valued advisors to the emperors. On the other hand, these same "lowly" Christians had been used for sport in the arena. In order to placate that portion of the pagan upper crust who did not "flee" to Christianity, Constantine created a placebo, a new name for the day on which the sun god was worshiped—Sunday. By no coincidence, this was the same day on which the Christians worshiped. Not long after this accommodation by the Pontifex Maximus, Bishop of bishops, and Vicar of Christ, those churches who had joined Constantine in uniting Church and pagan state began to refer to the first day of the week as Sunday. True Christians in the universal Church felt it was a small compromise. But it was a large step toward ecumenism, a danger which they did not recognize. Whereas Jesus, the servant with no place to lay His head, had said "Render, therefore, to Caesar the things that are Caesar's, and to God the things that are God's," and St. Paul had taught, "And be not conformed to this world," and St. John had warned, "Go out from her (*the world*)," [21] all indicating a clear separation of Church and state, Constantine combined the two and, over time, many so-called Christians began to be conformed not to Christ but to the pagan world. It started with a small compromise here and then a compromise there and so on. Within a relatively short time, the leaders of the universal Church would become the rulers not only of the Catholic Church, but also of the entire world. Kings and princes would bow before them literally and figuratively. Charlemagne was crowned emperor by Pope Leo III on Christmas Day in the year 800. To this day, all Christian denominations, even those who broke away from Rome after the Reformation, indirectly and unknowingly pay homage to a false sun god by referring to their day of worship as *Sunday*. Constantine had put the god Mars on Empire coins in his pre-Christian years. In later years, the "Christian" Constantine chose not to honor Jesus on state coins, but instead honored his greatest god, the alpha and omega of his true faith, Sol. [22] Constantine's baptism on his death bed was no act of following Jesus. Rather, it appears that Constantine, to use the parlance of our day, wanted to cover his bets, just in case this Jesus was the god those who had gone gladly to their martyred deaths thought him to be. Constantine believed that if the Christian god accepted the riffraff of Jewish and Roman society into his kingdom, he would be more than exuberant to welcome an exalted Emperor.

The Babylonian Mystery Cult

One of several prominent pagan mystery religions over which the Pontifex Maximus ruled was the Babylonian Mystery Cult. This cult was the first apostasy recorded in the Old Testament. It is discussed in chapters 10 and 11 of Genesis. It was the first postdiluvial world empire consisting of combined religion and state. Its founder was Nemrod (also spelled Nimrod).

King Nemrod (Nemrod means rebel), Noe's great grandson (Noe, Ham, Cush, Nemrod), was a mighty hunter before the LORD. This usually is interpreted to mean a "hunter of men," a tyrant and a murderer. The first potentate recorded in history built many cities, as well as the tower of Babel. The tower was a foreshadowing of man's rejection of God's free gift of salvation and a prideful attempt to work his way to heaven, at least symbolically, and to "make a name" for *himself* [see Genesis 11:4] rather than glorify God [see Ephesians 2:4-7].

Nemrod married Semiramis. Shortly after his death, Semiramis found herself pregnant. The queen explained that Nemrod had ascended into the heavens to become the sun god and that he had impregnated her with a sunbeam. She claimed the child, whom she named Tammuz, was conceived miraculously. She revealed that Tammuz (referred to in the Greek as Adonis [23]) was, in fact, the promised seed of the woman who would redeem all mankind [see Genesis 3:15]. Sometimes Satan's imitations come frightfully close to the real thing [see Apocalypse 6:2 and 19:11]. However, God promises to protect His elect (believers) from such deceptions [St. Matthew 24:24]. Centuries later the prophet Ezechiel lamented when he saw the women of Jerusalem weeping in Solomon's Temple for the god Tammuz [Ezechiel 8:14]. Tradition taught that Tammuz was betrayed by his lover, Ishtar, and, as a result, died each year only to be resurrected in the spring. His set days of mourning are forty, a period of time and season that coincide with Lent.

Some thirty years earlier, the prophet Jeremias had lamented when he saw the people worshiping and making little wafer cake offerings to Semiramis who was referred to as the "queen of heaven" [24] [Jeremias 7:18 and 44:17-19, 25]. Our word Easter comes not from anything having to do with Jesus' resurrection, but from Ishtar, the goddess of love and fertility. This is why eggs and rabbits are associated with Easter. They are ancient symbols of fertility. Thus, another small compromise with pagan religion was introduced into the universal Church which made Resurrection Sunday coincide with Ishtar's feast day. Ishtar is the Assyrian name for the Babylonian goddess Semiramis, also known as the Egyptian goddess Isis. [25] All held the title "Queen of Heaven."

The Babylonian gods Semiramis and Tammuz were also worshiped as Isis and Osiris by the Egyptians, as Ishtar and Bacchus by the Assyrians, as Isi and Iswara by practitioners in India, as Cybele and Deoius by Asians, as Aphrodite and Eros (or Adonis) by the Greeks, and as Venus and Cupid by the Romans. At no time in history have Semiramis and Tammuz, even though worshiped under other names, been without worshipers. And today is no exception.

Jehovah God condemned these acts of idolatry through the Old Testament prophets. Nevertheless, this mother-son religion, the Babylonian Mystery Cult, was the first alternative to the worship of Jehovah God recorded in Scripture. Apocalypse chapter 17 describes the false, one world religion (called the harlot) of the Tribulation period (end times), a period of time yet future. Verse 5 reveals the name written upon her forehead: "... Babylon the great, the mother of harlotries and of the abominations of the earth." It was this first apostate religion that gave birth to all others.

The Babylonian Mystery Cult, started more than four thousand years before the birth of Jesus, employed many practices that are used in various denominations to this day. There was a priestly hierarchy that ruled over

the laity, a precursor to the Nicolaites discussed earlier. The priests had the
power to hear and forgive (or not forgive) sins and dictate fines (penance).
Worship services were ritualistic and included elaborate processions in
which wooden and stone images were elevated and venerated. Incense was
burned before the altar [see Isaias 1:13] over which hung the Chaldean tau,
"T," which stood for the god Tammuz! Cultists crossed themselves with
the "T" when they felt in danger and wished the "spirit of Tammuz" to
protect them. By the time Jesus started His ministry, the Babylonian Cult
had introduced prayer beads [see St. Matthew 6:7], prayers for the dead
[see Isaias 8:19], and forced celibacy for certain levels of the priesthood
as with the Vestal Virgins [see 1 Timothy 4:1-3]. [26] The Cult continued to
teach salvation by works just as it had during the building of the tower.

Cyrus the Great, King of Persia, overtook the Babylonians in 539 B.C.
He drove out the cultists and their high priests and destroyed their graven
images. Cyrus recognized Jehovah as God and was also used by Him to
carry out His good pleasure toward His chosen people, the Jews. He let
the Jewish captives from the southern kingdom of Judah taken away by
Nabuchodonosor (also spelled Nebuchadnezzar) to Babylon, the capital
of the Babylonian Empire, return to Jerusalem to rebuild the city and the
Temple. Cyrus provided the building materials and technical assistance
needed for the restoration. He also had the returning captives take back
the sacred articles of gold and silver removed from the Temple by the
Babylonians in 587 B.C. [Esdras (Ezra) 1-6]. God refers to Cyrus as His
"shepherd" and His "anointed," as recorded in Isaias 44:28 and 45:1,
respectively.

Paganism Flourishes in the Universal Church

With the rout of the Babylonian Cultists by Cyrus, Satan moved his seat
of power from Babylon to Pergamum (also spelled Pergamos). The Roman
Catholic Bible confirms this in Apocalypse 2:12-13:

> And to the angel (*messenger*) of the church at Pergamum write... I
> know where thou dwellest, where the throne of Satan is... where Satan
> dwells.

The cultists also moved the seat of their heathen practices to Pergamum
in Asia Minor, about fifteen miles from coast of the Aegean Sea. The
Babylonians worshiped a number of gods, including the "fish god" Marduk.
The same god had been worshiped as Dagon by the Philistines hundreds of
years earlier [Judges 16:23]. The chief priests who officiated at the various

ceremonies were identified by their peculiar headdress which bore the title "Keeper of the Bridge." To the uninitiated, the Bridge was thought to be between Marduk and man. However, to those initiated in the mystery rituals, the Bridge was known to be between Satan, the real founder of the cult and all other false religions, and man. Some five hundred years later, the Roman emperors unwittingly would accept this title with a slight modification. They referred to themselves as the "Major Keeper of the Bridge." In Latin, *Pontifex Maximus*. Thus, the emperors acted as heads of *all* pagan religions. It is no small coincidence that we see the Nicolaites, a hierarchal religious organization ruling over the laity, mentioned in the letter to the church at Pergamum. God's Word condemns this practice [see Apocalypse 2:15-16]. Moreover, Jesus taught His disciples that they were not to rule over one another like the Gentile powers. He told them that the greatest was the one who was the servant of all [see St. Matthew 20:25-28]. Only a little more than three hundred years later, the popes would ignore God's condemnation, set up an even more elaborate hierarchal system to rule over the laity, and take the pagan title of Pontifex Maximus.

The headdress of the chief priests of Marduk resembled a fish. Have you seen such a headdress? Consider a bishop's miter. Picture it rotated about the head by ninety degrees so that it is now horizontal rather than vertical. Now rotate it ninety degrees about its longest axis. You now are looking at a headdress that resembles a fish complete with a pink mouth! When the Bishop of Rome, Damasus, accepted the title of Pontifex Maximus and Head of the Babylonian Order in 376 A.D., Satan combined apostate Christianity with the Babylonian Mystery Cult, both under the direction of Bishop Damasus. Thus, Satan again moved his seat of power, this time from Pergamum to Rome.

A relatively few years later, it was "Pope" Damasus I (366-384) that suggested an inherited spiritual authority for the Bishop of Rome as successor to St. Peter. It was at that time that the Petrine text, "Thou art Peter," began to be used as a foundation for claims of primacy. [27] He dared not base his claim on its true, historical source, the Roman emperors, all of whom were infallible. However, it didn't really matter. Damasus was unsuccessful in that Church councils continued to hold sway over the popes, thus limiting their power and wealth for many more years. Romanism was still evolving toward Catholicism.

Constantine's Universal Church Evolves into the Roman Church (Romanism) and Then the Roman Catholic Church

Damasus I was later canonized. During his pontificate, he promoted the *worship* of saints, angels, and martyrs (more will be said on this later).

Also at this time, stone carvings of the goddess Semiramis and her godly son Tammuz, in what formerly had been pagan temples, were brought into the Roman Church for "Christian" worship. The statues were simply renamed Mary and Jesus. Many of the carved images portrayed Semiramis holding a baby in her arms. Some of the former members of the Babylonian Cult easily transferred their adoration from Tammuz and Semiramis to Jesus *and Mary*. [28] The pagan Greeks thought of Mary and Jesus as Aphrodite and Eros. The Romans thought of them as Venus and Cupid. By 428 A.D., the Roman Church, just a few short years away from its metamorphosis into the Roman Catholic Church, had decreed Mary to be not only the mother of Jesus, which she certainly was, but also the *Mother of God* and "honored" her further with the title *Queen of Heaven*. [29] True Christians venerated the Virgin Mary, the woman chosen by God above all others to be the mother of His only-begotten Son. However, pagans transformed her into a false deity who, like Semiramis and all the other names by which she had been worshiped, was now called the Mother of God and Queen of Heaven. She was worshiped as such by the pagan "faithful" within the Roman Church.

The date of Jesus' birth had been changed earlier by Constantine, probably from the Feast of Tabernacles [see Leviticus 23:39-43] in the seventh month of the Hebrew calendar. This feast was also referred to as Sukkot and, unlike other major Jewish feasts, this Feast of Lights, as it was also called, included the Gentiles. St. John records in the gospel that bears his name: "And the Word was made flesh, and dwelt among us..." [St. John 1:14]. The Greek word translated "dwelt" is *skenoo* which means "tabernacled." Moreover, God's Word tells us that Jesus is the Light of the world [St. John 9:5]. How fitting that the Light of the world would be born on the Feast of Lights. However, Jesus' birthday was changed from September to December 25th which is the date of Tammuz's birthday (also known as Dumuzi and by some cults as the Sun god), another small compromise.

As has been shown, many of the dates and celebrations in various sects of so-called "Christianity" happen to coincide with the dates and celebrations of pagan gods. Such include Easter (Ishtar) and Christmas (Tammuz's birthday). For years, the Catholic Church defended this practice by stating that Christians chose them during times of persecution to coincide with pagan days of celebration so as not to be noticed. Christians could celebrate Jesus' birthday at the same time pagans celebrated Tammuz's birthday, and not be persecuted. This sounds logical. However, it is not true. These practices and dates were developed not during times of persecution, but during Emperor Constantine's rule and later. All Saints Day, modeled after the Romans' celebration of the pagan god Saturn, was incorporated into Catholicism by Pope Gregory IV in 835. In order to avoid further persecution by the universal Church, New Testament churches accepted the changed dates for Easter and Christmas. However, they refused to celebrate the eve of All Saints Day, originally celebrated as the Roman Harvest Festival on November 1. This day is now celebrated the evening before as Halloween. The roots of Halloween date back to the 2nd century practice of Druidism in Rome. Today, Wiccans (witches), Satanists, Druids, and many Churches celebrate this day. New Testament churches do not.

Just a few hundred years after Christ's ascension, the Roman Church, whose roots had been established by Emperor Constantine in a pagan universal Church, was becoming more paganized than the pagans were becoming Christianized. By the middle of the fifth century, the Roman Church had more pagan members than Christian. As more and more pagan titles, ideas, ceremonials, and rituals—including purifications, sacrificial offerings, and other "sacraments"—were adopted by Church leaders, the theology and soteriology became more and more corrupted. Practitioners of paganism looked at their friends in the state-favored Roman Church, whom they had known as fellow worshipers and leaders of the mystery cults, and saw that their lives were unchanged. These "Christians" were no longer referred to as the "third race" or "the Way." Rather, they "were the world." St. Paul had directed the churches to expel those who lived like the world.

St. Paul established a flourishing church at Corinth around 51 A.D. The church was made up of those who formerly had been blinded to the truth of God by the attractions of the world. Many were trying to walk in the spirit, having put off the old man and put on the new in Christ [Ephesians 4:22-24]. However, it was difficult for new believers and many were being lulled back into their heathen ways. People from all over the known world flocked to Corinth to participate in its allures, which included temple prostitution, organized gambling, and other worldly amusements, much like today's Las Vegas. After he left Corinth, St. Paul heard that some converts were still behaving as heathens. The story is recorded in chapter 5 of First Corinthians. While it appears textually as a single letter, it is actually a series of letters, as can be concluded from the text:

> It is actually reported that there is immorality among you, and such
> immorality as is not found even among the Gentiles, that a man should

have his father's wife. And you are puffed up, and have not rather mourned so that he who has done this deed (*taking his father's wife*) might be put away from your midst (*expelled from the congregation*). I indeed, absent in body but present in spirit, have already, as though present, passed judgment in the name of our Lord Jesus Christ on the one who has so acted—you and my spirit gathered together with the power of our Lord Jesus—to deliver such a one over to Satan for the destruction of the flesh (*not destruction of the soul in hell*) that his spirit may be saved in the day of our Lord Jesus Christ. Your boasting is unseemly. Do you not know that a little leaven (*sin*) ferments the whole lump (*the entire congregation*)? Purge out the old leaven, that you may be a new dough, as you really are without leaven. For Christ, our Passover, has been sacrificed. Therefore let us keep festival, not with the old leaven, nor with the leaven of malice and wickedness, but with the unleavened bread of sincerity and truth. I wrote to you in the letter (*the first letter, he is now beginning the second*) not to associate with the immoral—not meaning, of course, the immoral of this world, or the covetous, or the greedy, or idolaters; otherwise you would have to leave the world. But now I write to you not to associate with one who is called brother (*believer*), if he is immoral, or covetous, or an idolater, or evil-tongued, or a drunkard, or greedy; with such a one not even to take food. For what have I to do with judging those outside (*nonbelievers*)? Is it not those inside (*your church*) whom you judge? For those outside God will judge. "Expel the wicked man from your midst."

—1 Corinthians 5:1-13

St. Paul's direction is clear. Those who behave wickedly should be expelled from the church else the whole congregation might become corrupted in their flesh. Those committing incest, those who commit other forms of sexual immorality, those who are greedy, those who are drunkards and otherwise walking in the flesh, are to be expelled and not take the Lord's Supper with believers who are walking in the spirit. Failure to expel such a one could ruin the whole lump, the entire congregation. If he refuses to reform, such that he can come back into the church, he is to be turned over to Satan for the destruction of his flesh. This means expelled from the congregation. This in no way implies that he has lost his salvation. St. Paul is clear about this. St. Paul says to turn him over to Satan for the destruction of his flesh *that his spirit may be saved*.

The Lord Protects His Obedient Children

As long as the believer walks in submission to God's will, he is protected by the providential arm of God. The Old Testament contains many stories where the LORD extended His protective arm to His children who were walking in obedience. Young David fighting Goliath [1 Kings 17:37], Daniel in the lions den [Daniel 6:22], the three Hebrew children in the fiery furnace [Daniel 3:25 NKJV], and Job [Job 1:12] are but a few of the better known examples. Because of the LORD'S protection, neither the Philistine giant, the kings of Babylon, nor Satan could inflict death on God's children. In telling the church to expel the man from the fellowship of the congregation (physical realm), St. Paul is trying to present to the man living in sin a foreshadowing of what will happen to him in the spiritual realm if he does not turn from his sin. If the man walks in the world without the protection of God, his flesh will come to its end, though his soul will be saved. This is a concept not different from that of sinning unto death, discussed later in this chapter.

In his second letter, St. Paul clarifies his earlier message. Believers cannot separate themselves from the heathens of the world. However, they are to separate themselves from fellow believers who are living like the world [1 Corinthians 5:9-11].

The Qualities of a Good Shepherd

With regard to the conduct of the "Christian" Roman clergy, former Catholic priest and author Peter De Rosa notes:

> Things became still worse by the end of the fourth century. The Church was then respectable, with rich endowments and plenty of real estate. She did not want a married priest bequeathing it to his wife and children. Further, the ascetic ideal became more demanding at the very moment when the wrong kind of candidates, greedy and ambitious, were taking up the ministry as a career. Celibacy without chastity became the norm.[30]

By contrast, the Catholic Bible says a pastor (bishop or presbyter, all were used interchangeably in the Scripture and mean overseer in the sense of a shepherd):

> ... must be blameless, married but once (*not divorced*), having believing children who are not accused of impurity or disobedience. For a bishop must be blameless as being the steward of God, not proud, or ill-tempered, or a drinker, or a brawler, or greedy for base gain; but hospitable, gentle, reserved, just, holy, continent; holding fast the faithful word which is in accordance with the teaching (*Christ's teaching*), that he may be able both to exhort (*persuade*) in sound doctrine and to confute (*rebuke*) opponents.
>
> —Titus 1:6-9

A pastor should be a man who could be held up as an example to his flock, walking apart from the world. Moreover, St. Paul points out that the pastor must hold fast to the faithful Word of God so that he can preach, lead by example and, if necessary, rebuke members of the flock to bring them back to the walk God has prepared for them. St. Paul writes to a young pastor Timothy and warns against placing new converts in positions of authority. Specifically, St. Paul says to be considered for the position of pastor, the candidate:

> ... must have a good reputation with those who are outside (*non-Christians*), that he may not fall into disgrace and into a snare of the devil.
>
> —1 Timothy 3:7

Further Paganization of the Evolving Church

Contrary to Scripture, the Roman Church was filling religious offices with new converts who were greedy and ambitious. Many pagans fled to the empire-favored Church. The more doctrinal errors it embraced, the more pagan it became. Today we view gods such as Hercules, Mars, Jupiter, Apollo, Diana, Artemis, Pluto, Bacchus, and others as only harmless mythology. However, the worship of dozens of false gods *was the theology* of the Roman Empire before, during, and after the time of Jesus. Worship of these gods was thought to provide paths to the hereafter. Great pagan temples no less in grandeur than those built later by "Christians" existed in every city of the Empire. St. Paul refers to such a temple in Corinth [see 1 Corinthians 8:10-13]. Upon observing the beautiful temples in Athens and the many altars and icons within, St. Paul compliments those assembled at Mars Hill, the center for debate of emerging ideas, for having an altar to the "unknown god." St. Paul then proceeds to explain to them that the unknown god is Jesus resurrected. Some sneered, but others believed [Acts 17:34].

Some of those pagan temples are still standing, at least in part. Many were converted to "Christian" cathedrals beginning as early as the 4th century. The statues inside were simply renamed with "Christian" names such as St. Peter, St. Paul, St. Joseph, etc. At that time, there was no formal Church ritual for bestowing sainthood. The people simply esteemed such Christians without any sense of ritual. The formal process of canonization was not established until 993. The highly decorative, elevated altars and censers used to worship false gods were incorporated into the rituals of the Roman Church.

Another important component in many pagan religions was temple prostitution. The rulers of the temples used prostitution to make money for the temples and themselves. It is no wonder that many of the Jews considered the Gentiles to be little more than "dogs." In contrast to the temples to false gods, St. Paul taught that each Christian was a temple and that it was important to carefully control what was brought into the temple and how the temple was used. In this way, St. Paul taught that there were more Christian than heathen temples and that Christian temples must be kept clean [1 Corinthians 6:19]. Jesus said to His disciples:

> "You are the salt of the earth; but if the salt loses its flavor, how shall it be seasoned? It is then good for nothing but to be thrown out and trampled underfoot by men"
>
> —St. Matthew 5:13 NKJV

Salt is a preservative. It does not lose its flavor. In fact, it is very old when it is mined. The only way salt can lose its distinctiveness is if it is corrupted by other seasonings. The only way the believer can lose his effect on the world is by mixing with the world.

Worship of Mary began in 431 A.D. after the Council of Ephesus deposed the Nestorians. Nestorius, Bishop of Constantinople, and others took exception to their Church's according Mary, the Mother of Jesus, the pagan title "Mother of God." Under the leadership of an opposing bishop, Cyril of Alexandria, the Nestorian "heresy" was taken up at the Council of Ephesus (431), called by Theodosius II, Emperor of the East, and his counterpart, Valentian III, Emperor of the West. The Bishop of Alexandria prevailed and the Nestorians were labeled heretics. Many were cut down with the sword. Those who survived were driven from the Empire. By the time the Roman Church evolved into the Roman Catholic Church, around 450 A.D., members of the clergy and laity paid special homage to the *Mother of God*. They knelt to pray in front of the idols previously known as Semiramis. God's command, "... you shall not carve idols for yourselves... you shall not bow down before them..." [Exodus 20:4-5] was ignored. Emperor Leo III (680-741) tried to redress the wrong in 726. He demanded that all icons be removed from the churches and broken, thus the origin of the word iconoclast. However, the paganized "faithful" sent up a hue and cry. Many of these "converts" viewed the icons of Mary and Jesus as Semiramis and Tammuz, Aphrodite and Eros, Venus and Cupid, etc., the same gods they had worshiped in their pagan temples. Pope Gregory II (715-731) weighed in on the issue. He told the emperor that the icons were only reverenced, not worshiped. However, the truth escaped not from his lips, but from his pen. He wrote to Leo and explained that "... the statue of St. Peter is esteemed... as a god on earth" and warned of the terrible consequences the Church would pay if St. Peter's and the other icons were removed. [31]

Leo disagreed. Gregory excommunicated Leo in 731. Today, the Church calls these images "Sacred Images." The Catholic, Orthodox, and all other Bibles still call them idols and warn Christians to flee from them! [See 1 St. John 5:21; 1 Corinthians 10:14; and 1 Thessalonians 1:9.]

When one thinks of the cultures that have produced the world's great art, one nation is conspicuously absent. That nation is Israel. The subjects for art, sculpture, and paintings, from the time of the ancients to the Romans, were their gods. However, Jehovah God warned the Israelites not to make images or bow down before those produced by others [Deuteronomy 5:8-9]. Some argue that they are not bowing down to a statue, but to whom the statue represents. This is the same thing the pagans did with their gods. The pagans created the statues with their hands. The images were only visual representations of their gods. But should one bow down even to the one the statue represents? It is revealing to note that when St. Peter entered the home of Cornelius, the Gentile dropped to St. Peter's feet. St. Peter quickly pulled him up and explained that he, too, was just a man, not one to be worshiped [Acts 10:25-26].

New Age Paganism and the Catholic Church Today

When a practitioner of voodoo in one of the Caribbean islands converts to Catholicism, he adds icons of Mary and Jesus to his collection of other loa. The loa represent the spirits of deceased African tribal gods. This form of Catholicism is called eclectic Catholicism. Eclectic, of course, means the opposite of catholic, that is, there are many elements from varying sources, rather than a universal element. Eclectic Catholicism refers to the absorption of Catholic practices and rituals into existing pagan religions of indigenous cultures.

These territories were conquered by the Spanish conquistadors in the 16th century. Catholic missionaries accompanying the invaders force-converted surviving denizens under threat of death. Soon after, slaves were brought in from various African countries to work the plantation fields and mines. These captives brought their voodoo religion with them. The Catholic missionaries tried to convert the Africans. However, they refused. The missionaries were not allowed to kill the slaves for economic reasons. To get them into the Catholic Church, the missionaries agreed to certain compromises whereby elements of Catholicism were incorporated into the practice of their voodoo rituals. These included the use of "Christian" icons, candles, bells, crucifixes, prayers for the dead, and making the sign of the cross.

Santeria, an African-based religion similar to voodoo, is a rapidly-growing influence in predominantly Latin American countries. It is a combination of theologies represented by the Spanish word *Santos*, meaning saints, and an African word, *orishas*, meaning spirits. Santeria means "Way of the Saints." Icons are used to represent the saints or spirits. In practice, an adherent develops a special relationship with a particular orisha. During the ritual, the orisha enters and takes control of the practitioner's body. Of course, the force that takes possession is not that of any saint, but that of a demon!

Salvation Through the Sacraments—A Process

In the 6th century, the clergy began dressing differently from the laity. Convents were established for women, and the female monastic movement adopted certain ideals from Hindu and Buddhists' convents established long before the birth of Jesus. A new sacrament, Extreme Unction, was created. It is now referred to as Anointing of the Sick. It is categorized as a Sacrament of the Living because, according to the Church, one must be "spiritually alive," already in the state of grace and free from "mortal sin," to receive it. Of course, this presents a significant soterilogical problem. Neither Jesus' preaching nor the Scriptures allow for the "death" of a reborn spirit. Jesus did not say that to enter the kingdom of heaven one must be in a state of grace. Moreover, the Scriptures do not categorize sins into varying levels of offenses such as "mortal" and "venial" [see 1 St. John 1:9]. When Ananias and Sapphira lied to St. Peter and, as St. Peter pointed out, to the Holy Spirit about the amount of money they received from the sale of their land, the result was not that they were convicted of a mortal sin. They were struck dead [see Acts 5:1-11]. This is a scriptural concept referred to as "sinning unto death." There is no indication in the Scriptures that they lost their salvation, and neither is there the expectation of the same based on Jesus' many words regarding eternal security. However, God will only allow His unrepentant child to continue in sin without chastisement for so long [see Hebrews 12:6]. If the chastening fails to correct his behavior, God, in His mercy, will take His child from this earth to be with Him. Thus, it is difficult to understand how one can at one moment be a child of God and at the next be a lost sinner again, which is what death of a reborn spirit would result in [see St. John 1:12].

Salvation for Sale

Toward the end of the 6th century, the concept of purgatory was introduced by Pope Gregory I, the Great (590-604). It is based on a departure from Scripture that suggests Christ's atoning death on the cross did not pay the *full* debt for sin. The concept is without apostolic support [see St. John 19:30]. St. John assures believers that the blood of Jesus "cleanses us from *all* sin" [1 St. John 1:7]. The economic utility of purgatory was not fully realized until the reign of Pope Sixtus IV (1471-1484). After purgatory was incorporated as a doctrinal tenant at the Council of Florence (1438-1443), its true efficacy became apparent to Sixtus. With the sale of indulgences having been established some time earlier, around 1190, Sixtus reckoned that such indulgences could be applied not only to the living, but also to the dead, to release them from purgatory. And what good son and loving family member would not be willing to spend a sizeable portion of his or her income to get a dearly departed mother and father, sister and brother, or spouse out of such a horrid place? Moreover, the teaching was and still is that while souls in purgatory cannot pray for themselves, they can pray for those yet living. Furthermore, what soul *prayed out of his suffering in purgatory* into heaven would dare forget to pray daily for the one or ones who affected his escape from that dreadful place?

One troubling aspect of this doctrine was that while the priests could tell the bereaved how much an indulgence or Mass cost and by how many days their loved one's suffering would be reduced, they could not say how long a sentence in purgatory lasted. Therefore, the faithful never knew when a loved one was released or, fortuitously for Church coffers, when to stop purchasing indulgences. Another aspect was that there were different levels of suffering in purgatory. One started at the bottom where suffering was least. To get out, one had to move up through successive levels, but the suffering intensified with each increasing level. [32] This ensured that those who initiated efforts to get their loved ones out could hardly stop after some period of time, because that would leave their loved ones suffering more than before. Moreover, the lower levels were populated largely by those from the lower socioeconomic classes. It was only logical that it would take longer for poor families with relatively limited resources to buy their deceased relatives out of the lower levels. Thus, more aristocratic families were inclined to pay more money more quickly, so that their more affluent departed family members would not have to spend any more time than necessary with the riffraff. The proverbial well-off were thought to move up the purgatorial ladder more rapidly than the poor. But still, neither the priests nor the Church could say who would be released sooner, the rich or the poor, since purgatorial sentences were assumed to vary among individuals. The Orthodox and Protestant Churches do not subscribe to either the doctrine of purgatory or the sale of indulgences.

In addition to using purgatory as a revenue generator, Sixtus also licensed the brothels of Rome. The most infamous of all Roman emperors, and one of Sixtus' predecessors, Caligula (37-41 A.D.), best remembered for his acts of extreme debauchery, had taxed Rome's temples of prostitution fourteen hundred years earlier to raise revenues for the state. The fact that the First Lateran Council (1123 A.D.) had adopted doctrines forbidding marriage of the clergy, but not requiring chastity, allowed Sixtus to also impose steep taxes on priests who kept mistresses. Another source of his income was arranging visits "... for rich men to enable them to solace certain matrons in the absence of their husbands." [33]

The Church placed the Roman Catholic Bible on its *Index Librorum Prohibitorum* or Index of Forbidden Books in 1229. Already the seeds of discontent were growing within. While few literates had Bibles or access to them, those who did noticed differences between what was taught from the pulpit and what was taught in Scripture. Many Catholics were calling for reform. As long as the faithful didn't have access to a Bible, the Church could teach anything that was to its benefit, even if contradicted by Scripture. Many things being taught by the 13th century were contrary to Scripture. These included prayers to and for the dead, a place of temporary suffering for the saved prior to entering heaven, and the sale of indulgences and Masses. The faithful were kneeling in front of graven images taken from pagan temples and relocated in Catholic churches or, in some instances, simply left in pagan temples that were converted to cathedrals. Salvation had been declared to be a life-long "process" that could be accomplished only through a sacramental salvation system administered by the Church. But if salvation is a process, what are we to do with:

... Behold... now is the *day* of (*your*) salvation!

—2 Corinthians 6:2

This and many other verses make clear that salvation is instantaneous. It is not a process.

Prayer beads, holy water, and incense were sold and used in worship services. Indulgences were purchased by the faithful in advance so that planned sins could be committed without guilt or spiritual consequence. If one intended to commit adultery with a neighbor, he could simply dispatch the associated guilt with as little effort as might be expended in purchasing a chicken in the marketplace. Each church published a list of sins, along with the costs of their associated indulgences. Absolution and, therefore, salvation came with a price. The more the faithful sinned, the wealthier the Church became. Even Church offices were for sale to the highest bidder, with the popes getting most or all of the proceeds.

More Changes—More Confusion

While the Mass had been instituted by the Roman Church around 394, and attendees participated in fellowship and in the breaking of bread, just as had early church members at Jerusalem [see Acts 2:42], the doctrine of transubstantiation was formulated some eight hundred years later and incorporated as doctrine at the Fourth Lateran Council (1215).[34] Thus, from its establishment in 450 A.D. till 1215, the Church did not require the faithful to believe that the bread and wine were transformed into Jesus' body and blood. In response to the reformers' position against transubstantiation two hundred years later, the doctrine was reconfirmed in 1551 at the Council of Trent.

The "Great Schism" was the split in the Catholic Church when it broke into the Western Roman Church and the Eastern Orthodox Church in 1054 A.D. Each excommunicated the other. Catholic apologists argue that the schism was over papal infallibility. However, this is not true. The doctrine of papal infallibility was not adopted by the Church until 1870 at the First Vatican Council, more than 800 years *after* the schism. Moreover, as already discussed, the Old Catholics broke from Rome shortly thereafter in 1871. The schism was initiated by a difference in the One from whom the Holy Spirit proceeds. This was the battle over the Latin word *Filioque* which means "and the Son." The Westerners held that the Holy Spirit proceeded from both the Father and the Son. This is repeated at Sunday worship services in Catholic and most Protestant Churches. The Easterners held that the Holy Spirit proceeded only from the Father. This argument, along with Constantinople's belief that Rome was cheating them out of their rightful share of the Church's wealth, led to the Great Schism. These mutual anathemas were rescinded some nine hundred years later in 1965.

The second part of the Great Schism occurred several centuries following the mutual excommunications and lasted more than thirty years. Urban VI was elected pope in 1378. The peasants had rioted in the streets to get a Roman or at least an Italian pope. Urban disliked the pretentious French cardinals and lectured the prelates on the virtues of poverty in his lavishly appointed Vatican quarters. He excommunicated former friends and foes alike. His behavior became so erratic that many thought him to have gone mad. The cardinals withdrew their support and selected a new pope, Clement VII. In retaliation, Urban formed his own college of cardinals and promptly excommunicated Clement and his followers. Clement moved to Avignon where he won support from the French king who was immediately excommunicated by Urban. Representatives from both sides met in Pisa in 1409. Their efforts resulted not in reconciliation but in the naming of a third contemporaneous pope. The Council of Constance (1414-1480) deposed both Urban and Clement and installed Pope Martin V (1417-1431). The chaos surrounding the schism intensified calls for reform. [35, 36] While a number of reforms were proposed at the council, there was not enough agreement on any to arrive at a consensus. God's Word assures us that, "... God is not the author of confusion but of peace..." [1 Corinthians 14:33 NKJV].

Calls for Reform Intensify

As early as the middle of the 14th century, an Englishman, John Wycliffe (1330-1384), an Oxford professor and priest, criticized *his* Church for its abuses in the selling indulgences; excessive veneration of the saints; and the moral corruption of Church prelates, many of whom carried on open relationships with consorts and frequently took prostitutes to their celibate but certainly not chaste beds. He also denied the authority of the religious hierarchy. Wycliffe translated the Bible from Latin into English and, much to the delight of his parishioners, preached sermons in English. Another early reformer, Jan Hus (1372-1415), maintained ideas similar to those of Wycliffe. Hus, a Bohemian, was executed by the Church as a heretic in 1415. This led directly to the Hussite Wars which were eventually suppressed by a joint effort between the Holy Roman Empire and the pope. The Dutch scholar, Desiderius Erasmus (1466-1536), reasoned that dogma must be understandable to ordinary people because God certainly would not hold someone responsible for not believing what he could not understand. He argued, too, against the doctrine of transubstantiation, calling it sophistry, and maintained that Christ is present in the Eucharist only in a spiritual rather than substantial sense. [37] These are only a few of the very many early reformers. It should be noted that they all came from within the Roman Catholic Church, not from New Testament churches. Not only did the Church hierarchy fail to listen, they escalated the abuses.

Church Abuses Multiply

One of the most egregious examples of abuse came during the term of Pope Leo X (1513-1521), one of the infamous de' Medici popes. Albert of the House of Hohenzollern, although not yet of age to be a bishop, was bishop of Magdeburg and Haloberstadt. He aspired to be made archbishop of Mainz and primate of Germany. With these two titles, the House of Hohenzollern would have power over its political rival, the House of Hapsburg. The normal fee to a pope for installation to the see of Mainz was enormous.

Albert borrowed the required sum from the banking house of Fugger in Augsburg and paid Leo in full. To enable Albert to repay the loan, Leo permitted a special indulgence to be purchased throughout Albert's territories for eight years, with half the proceeds going to the Fuggers and the other half to himself for his building projects. To create the flow of revenues necessary to repay the Fuggers, Albert, with the blessing of Leo, exaggerated the efficacy of the new indulgence. Albert pitched to eager listeners that his indulgence would remit not only the penalties for sins but also the sins themselves and would give preferential treatment to one who sinned in the future. To help hawk his *spiritual wares*, Albert enlisted the help of Dominican Father Johann Tetzel. Tetzel added that this costly but special indulgence had the unique power to ensure immediate release from purgatory. He promoted this "new and improved" indulgence with the charming jingle:

> *As soon as the coin in the coffer rings,*
> *The soul from purgatory springs.*[38]

Gutenberg Prints the Bible

A confounding problem for the Catholic Church was the increase in the number of Bibles available due to the invention of Gutenberg's printing press. A significant number of Bibles had been printed and distributed among the literate between 1450 and 1456. It was now obvious to more than the educated reformers, most of whom were also priests and teachers, that the Church had drifted far away in its teachings, traditions, practices, and ceremonies from the teachings and traditions documented in the Scriptures. This is why each reformer who left the Roman Catholic Church took with him an already large following, so large in fact, that the Church could no longer kill all the "heretics."

The Reformation

On the eve of All Saints Day, October 31, 1517, former monk and Friar, Martin Luther, nailed his ninety-five theses against the sale of indulgences to the door of the church in Wittenberg, a city in east central Germany on the Elbe River. Among other things, Luther claimed that the pope had no power over an imaginary purgatory and, if he did, he should certainly open the doors for free and release all held within. Finally, he stressed that the real treasure of the Church, which the popes overlooked, was the gospel, not the enormous content of their growing treasuries. Over time, Luther went on to preach what he had been reading in the Bible all those years when he served as head of the theology department at the University of Wittenberg. Whereas the Roman Catholic Church was selling salvation, Luther began to comprehend his Lord's command:

> "And when you go, preach the message, 'The kingdom of heaven is at hand!' Cure the sick, raise the dead, cleanse the lepers, cast out devils. **Freely you have received, freely give."**
>
> —St. Matthew 10:7-8

Luther also came to understand that man cannot merit salvation through his own efforts; and, finally, that all authority rests in Scripture, not the hands of men or any Church. This principle is called *Sola Scriptura*, "by Scripture alone." This theological principle eliminates looking outside the Scripture to the Koran, the Book of Mormon, or any post-scriptural traditions:

> Jesus therefore said to the Jews who had come to believe in him, "If you abide in my *word*, you shall be my disciples indeed, and you shall *know the truth*, and the truth shall make you free."
>
> —St. John 8:31-32

It should be noted that Luther's protests addressed only a relatively few of what he and many other reformers considered to be Rome's many significant errors leading to the second death, namely, the scandalous sale of salvation. Somewhere along life's journey, Luther's spirit had been reborn from above. As a gift from the Holy Spirit of God, Luther finally had eyes to see as he read the Scriptures. The blinders had been removed from his mind [see 2 Corinthians 4:3-4]:

> Now a man named Simon had previously been practicing sorcery in that city (in *Samaria*) and astounding the people... claiming to be someone great... and had bewitched them with his sorceries... but (*Simon*) believed Philip as he preached the kingdom of God... and after his (*Simon's*) baptism... saw that the Holy Spirit was given through the laying on of the apostles' hands, he offered them money, saying, "Give me also this power, so that anyone on whom I lay my hands may receive the Holy Spirit." But Peter said to him, "Thy money go to destruction (*hell*) with thee, because thou hast thought that the *gift* of God (*salvation*) could be *purchased* with money. Thou hast no part or lot in this matter (*salvation*); for thy heart is not right before God."
>
> —Acts 8:9-21

Salvation is not for sale by anyone or to anyone. Another lesson from these verses is that baptism does not regenerate the spirit because, according to the Scripture cited above, Simon clearly was baptized. However, St. Peter tells us that Simon's heart was not right with God and that he was on his way to destruction (hell). St. Peter also reminds us:

> You know that you were redeemed from the vain manner of life handed down from your fathers *traditions*), not with perishable things, with silver or gold, but with the precious blood of Christ....
>
> —1 St. Peter 1:18-19

Fierce Wolves Come in Among the Flock

St. Paul warned his friends from Ephesus when he called them to meet with him in Miletus:

> I know that after my departure fierce wolves will get in among you, and will not spare the flock. And from *among your own selves* men will rise speaking perverse things, to draw away the disciples (*followers of Jesus, believers*) after them.
>
> —Acts 20:29-30

Note where these fierce wolves come from—from a community that calls itself Christian! These are not believers, but men who walk among believers claiming to be believers. St. Peter gives us the reason:

> ... there will be lying teachers who will bring in destructive sects (*future tense*). They even disown the Lord who bought them... And many (*of the flock*) will follow their wanton conduct (*promiscuous lifestyles*), and because of them (*lying teachers*) the way of truth (*the gospel*) will be maligned (*Christianity will be viewed with contempt*). **And out of greed they will with deceitful words use you for gain.** Their condemnation, passed of old (*their condemnation, like others' salvation, was determined before the foundation of the world*), is not made void (*their condemnation cannot be reversed*), and their destruction does not slumber.
>
> —2 St. Peter 2:1-3

This is an accurate description of the universal Church initiated by Constantine in the early 4th century and, later, the Roman Catholic Church. Martin Luther was horrified when his eyes were opened and he saw what he, as a former monk and priest, had been a part of. Luther did not address the licentiousness of the clergy. Neither did he address the sale of Church offices to undeserving and profligate members of wealthy families. There were numerous examples. Giovanni de' Medici was made abbot at age 7; cannon of every cathedral in Tuscany at age 8; head of the Monte Cassino

Abbey at age 11; Cardinal at age 13; and, finally, Pope Leo X at age 38. He is said to have lamented that he was beaten to the title of youngest pope. Pope Benedict IX (1032-1044) held that title. He became pope at age 11, thus beating out Pope John XII (955-963) who ascended to the office at age 16. History records John's papacy as one filled with debauchery, including sleeping with his mother, two of his sisters, and a niece. John's end came at age 24 when a jealous husband returned home one night to find his "Holiness" in bed with his wife.[39]

Luther had no intention of leaving the Roman Catholic Church. He only wanted *his* Church fixed. Like other reformers, he wanted reforms made for those doctrines that were so blatantly counter to Scripture. However, Pope Leo X branded Luther a heretic and excommunicated him in 1521, thus creating the schism for which Luther is blamed by the Catholic Church.[40] Unlike most "heretics," Luther died a natural death. The decrease in revenues forced the Church at last to address the spreading reformation in an attempt to replenish retreating coffers. Prior to becoming Pope Paul III (1534-1549), Cardinal Alessandro Farnese had been a vocal supporter of reform. However, *Pope* Paul was no reformer. He called the Council of Trent (1545-1563) to deal with the hemorrhaging. He directed council members to hold the line. Numerous prelates came forth from within holy mother Church and pleaded their cases. They quoted the Scriptures to support their positions. The bishops listened attentively. What was made clear by the petitioners was that the Roman Catholic Church in its teachings, practices, ceremonies, and rituals, had moved far from the teachings and traditions contained in the Roman Catholic Bible. Many advocated a return to Scripture alone, just as had Luther and earlier reformers.

The choice to Council members was clear: (1) admit that the Roman Catholic Church had added to Constantine's errors and make the necessary reforms to move it back to God's Word and admit that its false doctrines had sent millions upon millions to hell, or (2) reject the reformers' petitions. With the first choice would come an end to the prelates' regal positions, accumulated riches, and, possibly, their lives. The bishops voted to "place tradition on the same level of authority as Scripture," at least more or less. This is the way it is recorded in most history books. In actuality, greater significance was placed on tradition and less on Scripture. In practice, the Scriptures were made subordinate to Catholic tradition in that the council stated that the Scriptures could be understood only within the context of the traditions of the Roman Catholic Church. [41] There is no scriptural support for such a position. The psalmist speaks to the contrary:

A lamp to my feet is *your word*, a light to my path.

—Psalms 118 (119):105

The Council's ruling meant that Scriptures had no meaning for New Testament churches or for the Orthodox, Anglican, or Protestant Churches! It also meant that the Old Testament had no meaning to the Jews except as understood within the context of Roman Catholic tradition, which had persecuted them nearly to extinction during the Inquisitions in many parts of Europe. According to the pronouncement of the council, when Jesus said of His sheep, "And I give them everlasting life; and they shall never perish, neither shall anyone snatch them out of my hand" [St. John 10:28], it meant nothing outside the "tradition" of the Roman Catholic Church that taught that, not only did they not have everlasting life, they could be snatched facilely as well as frequently! This is difficult to understand, particularly since Jesus spoke these words long before the establishment of the Roman Catholic Church and the *creation of "Catholic tradition."* It is also hard to understand how traditions could be used to interpret other Scriptures that were written and widely distributed hundreds of years or more before the manmade traditions were created! Moreover, as discussed earlier in this chapter, all teachings and traditions to be followed were identified in the books of the New Testament. Not only did the Church not reform, it continued down the legislative path that had taken God's Word out of its teachings and practices and substituted the traditions of men, thus usurping the power and authority of the Christ of the New Testament and making Him a liar!

The Evolving Traditions of the Roman Catholic Church

The Catholic Church claims that it is the same today as it was yesterday and will be the same tomorrow. The veracity of this claim can be evaluated by noting the evolving traditions listed below. Many of these already have been discussed.

- Baptism of infants (220)
- Spiritual regeneration by baptism (220)
- Prayers for the dead (300)
- Making the sign of the cross (300)
- Worship of saints and angels (375)
- Mass as daily ritual (394)
- Infant baptism made compulsory (416)
- Worship of Mary (431)

- Introduction of purgatory (593)
- Prayers directed to Mary (600)
- Worship of images and relics (786)
- Use of holy water (850)
- Canonization of dead saints (993)
- Fasting during the season of Lent (998)
- Celibacy for the priesthood (1079)
- Use of prayer beads (1090)
- Seven sacraments suggested by Peter Lombard, Bishop of Paris (circa 1150)
- Sale of indulgences (1190)
- Transubstantiation defined by Pope Innocent III (1215)
- Confession of sins to a priest instituted by Pope Innocent III (1215)
- Bible added to Index of Forbidden Books (1229)
- Cup forbidden to laity at communion by Council of Constance (1414)
- Doctrine of seven sacraments affirmed (1439)
- Doctrine of purgatory (1439)

The traditions listed above were started by errant pastors or by Constantine's universal Church. They were later inculcated into their offspring, the Roman Church and, later, the Roman Catholic Church, and expanded. Traditions *created* during and after Trent include:[42]

- Scripture to be interpreted only within context of Catholic tradition (1545)
- Apocryphal books declared to be inspired (1545)
- Immaculate conception of Mary revealed by Pope Pius IX (1854)
- Doctrine of infallibility of Pope by Vatican Council (1870)
- Bodily assumption of Mary into heaven revealed by Pope Pius XII (1950)
- Mary proclaimed the Mother of the Church by Pope Paul VI (1965)

With every new "tradition" created, another group wishing to be true to the teachings of Christ left the Roman Catholic Church. While most did not have access to a Bible and many could not read anyway, the gospel was continuing to be preached by those in New Testament churches. These were their friends and relatives, the re-baptizers, labeled heretics first by the universal Church and then by the Roman Catholic Church, and, at every opportunity, burned at the stake. These were the ones who took Jesus' command seriously "... and you shall be witnesses for me in Jerusalem and in all Judea and Samaria and even to the very ends of the earth" [Acts 1:8].

The Catholic Church and Abortion

As can be understood from the above discussion, the Roman Catholic Church has undergone many changes since its inception in the middle of the 5th century. One of particular interest is its position on abortion. Paragraph 2271 of the Catechism of the Catholic Church states:

> Since the first century the Church has affirmed the moral evil of every procured abortion. This teaching has not changed and remains unchangeable....

However, this is not true. St. Thomas Aquinas (1225-1274) subscribed to an earlier teaching of Aristotle (384-322 B.C.) on human embryonic recapitulation. This theory taught that a fetus did not become human (infusion of a soul) until it had completed several evolutionary stages. How could this have happened? you may ask. Both Church leadership and membership were saturated with pagans and their heathen influence, such as that from Aristotle. According to these early evolutionists, the embryo *evolves* through successive stages—gills, creeping thing, vertebrate, etc.—until it finally becomes human. St. Aquinas added that the male embryo becomes human at forty days, the female at eighty. Even Emperor Gratian, who history leads us to believe may have been a true Christian, said, "He is not a murderer who brings about abortion before the soul is in the body." Pope Gregory XIII (1572-1585) affirmed that it was not murder to kill an embryo less than forty days old. Gregory's successor, Pope Sixtus V (1585-1590), who inserted many errors into his re-translation of the Vulgate, disagreed and in 1588 decreed that all abortions were murder and those participating in same were worthy of excommunication. His successor, Gregory XIV (1590-1591), disagreed and, once again, there was a shift in Church position in favor of abortion. Finally, in 1869, after the civil war in the U.S., Pope Pius IX (1846-1878) decreed that any abortion for any reason was murder and its participants were worthy of excommunication.[43] His pronouncement remains the official position of the Roman Catholic Church to this day, except for excommunication. Had the earlier popes and St. Aquinas been as familiar with Scripture as they were with Aristotle's teaching, they might have recalled several pertinent verses that make the matter of abortion crystal clear.

> And God created great whales, and every living creature that moveth, which the waters brought forth abundantly, *after their kind*, and every winged fowl *after his kind*... Let the earth bring forth the living creature *after his kind*; cattle and creeping thing, and beast of the earth *after his kind*... And God made the beast of the earth *after his kind*, and cattle *after their kind*, and everything that creepeth upon the earth *after his kind*... And God said 'Let Us make man in our image, *after our likeness*....
> —Genesis 1:21-26 KJV

Do you see the pattern? Each animal was formed *after its kind*. One animal did not evolve or devolve into another. Each is according to its *own* kind. There is no evolution from gills to lungs. Man, however, was formed not in the image of any animal, but in the image of *God, in His likeness*. Failure to understand and believe this leads not only to an ungodly position on abortion, but also to acceptance of cults and New Age religions that teach that man can, through his aspirations, *evolve* into a god.

> Before I formed thee in the bowels of thy mother, I knew thee....
> —Jeremias 1:5

God knew each of us even before He formed us.

> If men fight and hurt a woman with child, so that she gives birth prematurely, yet no harm follows (*the infant survives*), he shall surely be punished accordingly as the woman's husband imposes on him; and he shall pay as the judges determine. But if any harm follows (*the baby she is carrying dies*), then you shall give *life for life*....
> —Exodus 21:22-23 NKJV

The penalty is based on the damage. If a death occurs to the baby in her womb, the loss shall be paid for with the life of the one who caused her to lose her baby. Note there is no stipulation that the baby in her womb must be must be forty or more days old:

> All flesh is not the same flesh, but there is one flesh of men, another of beasts, another of birds, another of fishes.
> —1 Corinthians 15:39

This verse speaks directly to Aristotle's theory of embryonic recapitulation and contradicts it for those who perhaps missed the point in Genesis 1:21-26.

Some ask if evolution and creation can coexist, if maybe God didn't use evolution to develop man. This is referred to as theistic evolution. The answer is a clear "no" as seen from Scripture. Also, Jesus said we would know the tree by its fruit. The fruits of the tree of evolution are atheism, secular humanism, abortion, and, soon, broad acceptance and practice of euthanasia. These, in turn, produce even more rotten fruit after their kind. Do you think God would plant a tree that would yield bad fruit? By the *wisdom* of this tree, children today are taught that they are nothing more than animals, the current chapter in the book of evolution. They are not taught that evolution is just a *theory* and a poor one at that. In fact, there is far more evidence to support creation than evolution, and the theory behind evolution itself is the only thing that is evolving! First it was argued by evolutionists that the reason one cannot find the missing links in the fossil record is because the evolutionary process proceeds too slowly. However, according to the most recently evolved theory, the "new and improved" reason is that the evolutionary process proceeds too quickly to leave any evidence in its wake.

The secondary fruits of this tree include drug abuse, rape, incest, sexual promiscuity, sexually transmitted diseases, suicide, drive-by shootings, and a host of other modern-day maladies and perversions featured on afternoon talk shows. Teens take guns to school and "blow away" teachers, students, and others who have hurt them, thus, destroying lives, futures, and families. But the worst fruit of all is the eradication of the understanding that man is a being created in God's image, living in a fallen state as a sinner, that there is a wage for sin, that each sinner will one day stand before a righteous God to receive his due for works committed in the flesh (either at the Bema or Great White Throne), and that, through the Christ of the New Testament, he can be saved. Thus, the rotten fruit of evolution can even steal a man's eternity. God did not plant the rotten tree of evolution. Satan did. Isn't it wonderful that God knew at the time He was inspiring His prophets to write down His Holy Words that men would create all manner of deviant behavior and ungodly theories, and He spoke to us about them through the Scriptures *even before* they were thought of by men.

The Roman Catholic Church—A Legislating Church

Many born into the Roman Catholic faith look to the Church for salvation and believe her to be the "one, true, unchanging Church" despite her well-documented past. Why? Because they have been taught incorrectly, as was I, that Jesus established the Roman Catholic Church and that He promised never to leave her. However, this teaching is as incorrect and misleading as the Church's teaching that Catholics wrote the Bible. Despite Jesus' prophecy that not one jot or one tittle of the law would pass away before all be fulfilled [St. Matthew 5:18], which would include His Second Coming as King of kings and Lord of lords [Apocalypse 19:16], the Catholic Church teaches that Jesus gave her the right to change God's Laws as she pleases. Father E. Hayes confirms:

> The Church is not only the guardian and teacher of the ten Commandments, but she also carries on the work of Christ by making additional rules and precepts to help her members live this present life in a way that will best prepare them for the life to come. Where does the Church get the authority to do such a thing? From Christ, of course.[44]

This claim reveals the Church's lack of trust in Jesus. The Scriptures confirm that Jesus and His apostles thought the Scriptures and revelations contained within were sufficient to teach His followers how to live in the present life and to prepare them for the next. Moreover, St. John reveals that those who have the anointing of the Holy Spirit dwelling inside have no need of anyone to teach them apart from God's Word, and that if anyone attempts to do so, they are commanded to compare his teaching with that found in Scripture:

> Dear children, it is the last hour; and as you have heard that Antichrist is coming, so now many antichrists have arisen... They have gone forth... But you have an anointing from the Holy One and you know all things (*nothing has been held back*)... let that which you have heard from the beginning abide in you... let the anointing which you have received from him, dwell in you, *and you have no need that anyone teach you....*
> —1 St. John 2:18-27

However, according to Father P. Stravinskas, "... Catholics do not view the Scriptures as self-explanatory but as requiring the community that formed the Bible to interpret it." [45] In his book, Father Stravinskas uses the meeting between Philip and the Ethiopian eunuch as an example:

> This problem is faced squarely in the Acts of the Apostles when Philip asks the Ethiopian eunuch if he understands the *Scriptures* he is reading. Unashamed, the man says, "How can I, unless someone instructs me?"[46]
> —Acts 8:27-39

The actual text from the Roman Catholic Bible presents a somewhat different story than that described by Father Stravinskas:

> And the Spirit said to Philip, "Go near and keep close to this carriage." And Philip, running up, heard him reading the prophet Isaias, and he said, "Dost thou then understand what thou art reading?" But he said, "Why, how can I unless someone shows me?" And he asked Philip to get up and sit with him. Now the passage of Scripture which he was reading was this: "He was led like a sheep to the slaughter; and just as a lamb dumb before its shearer, so did he not open his mouth. In humiliation his judgment was denied him; who shall declare his generation? for his life is taken from the earth." And the eunuch answered Philip and said, "I pray thee, of whom is the prophet saying this? Of himself or of someone else?" Then Philip opened his mouth and, beginning from *this Scripture*, preached Jesus to him.
>
> —Acts 8:29-35

The text makes clear that the eunuch was an educated man entrusted with his mistress' wealth. In that day it was customary for those who could to read out loud. As they rode along, Philip told the eunuch how Jesus fulfilled this and other prophecies. Philip also taught the eunuch of Jesus' mission from the Father and of His death, burial, resurrection, and ascension. When they reached water, the eunuch asked Philip to baptize him. After the eunuch *believed* and *confessed Jesus with his mouth*, Philip baptized him [Acts 8:36-39].

These verses make several things clear. First, it was not that the eunuch did not understand the entire body of *Scriptures*. In fact, what is made clear is that the eunuch worshiped at the Temple in Jerusalem (v. 27). Therefore, he had heard the words of the prophets read many times. There were only two verses of Scripture in this instance that had him perplexed and they both dealt with Old Testament prophecy concerning the Messiah. The vast majority of the Jews, too, failed to comprehend the significance of these same verses that baffled this Jehovah-worshiping Gentile. In fact, most of the Jews who witnessed Jesus' literal fulfillment of this prophecy could not identify Jesus as the Christ. In this case, having the community that wrote this Old Testament prophecy interpret it would have been antithetical to understanding its meaning! Why? Because they, like the eunuch, did not have eyes to see or ears to hear. They did not recognize the time of their visitation [St. Luke 19:44]. Finally, in the parable of the vine and the branches, Jesus told His disciples, "If you abide in me, and if *my words* abide in you..." [St. John 15:7]. If we cannot interpret His words, then how can His words abide in us? So much for Father Stravinskas' thesis that the community that "formed" the Scriptures is necessary for its interpretation. Moreover, as already noted, neither the Catholic Church nor any of its members wrote the books of the New Testament. After the eunuch *believed*, he, like all believers, received the anointing of the Holy Spirit spoken of by St. John and quoted above. It is after such anointing that the believer has no need of anyone to teach him.

It was the Holy Spirit of God that called the eunuch to salvation, not Philip, and not the eunuch himself [Acts 8:26-29]. Philip was simply God's facilitator, just as believers are used by God today to bring the gospel to those who will accept it. These verses clearly demonstrate that one does not need to understand the entire body of Scriptures or belong to a particular denomination to be saved. The text makes it clear that Philip started teaching the eunuch from these two prophetic Old Testament verses, and he must have preached Jesus up to the significance of believer's baptism since the eunuch asked to be baptized. It is true that if one wants to grow in his spiritual walk, he needs to be fed. However, one with a reborn spirit cannot be taught, and thereby grow spiritually, by one with an unregenerated spirit. Thus, if after becoming a believer one stays in a Church or church that preaches a false gospel, such as salvation by faith plus works—or possible loss of salvation—he will be frustrated in his spiritual growth. That's why it is important for a believer to get into a Bible-believing, Bible-preaching New Testament church where he can be fed the bread of life, not the feel-good-for-the-moment fodder of this world.

Father Stravinskas' position is that the community that formed the Bible is needed to interpret it. If the Catholic Church followed this advice, it would not bring graven images into its churches, since the community that wrote the Old Testament has no images in their synagogues even to this day:

> You shall not carve idols for yourselves in the shape of anything in the sky above or on the earth below or in the waters beneath the earth; you shall not bow down before them or worship them. For I, the LORD, your God, am a jealous God....
>
> —Exodus 20:4-5

Galileo and the Catholic Church

The Catholic Church insists that only Church hierarchy are led by the Holy Spirit in interpreting Scripture. The story of Galileo Galilei (1564-1642) makes an interesting case for evaluation. In 1632, Galileo concluded that the earth revolved around the sun. Such a theory was *not* contradictory to

Scripture, but was contradictory to Catholic tradition which held that the planets revolved around the earth. This fit nicely with the Church's errant teaching that man has some inherent good in him and, therefore, must be the center of God's physical universe.

Pope Urban VIII (1623-1644), one of the infamous de Medici popes, called the ailing 68-year-old astronomer to stand before the Holy Office of the Inquisition. He was charged with "grave suspicion of heresy." Rather than live out his few remaining years in prison, the frightened old man recanted. He died ten years later. The Church's investigation of Galileo was reopened by the Vatican in 1979. In 1992, following years of discussion and more investigations, the famed scientist and inventor, like earlier heretic-turned-saint, Joan of Arc, was pronounced innocent of the charge by a papal commission. Following the Church's mishandling of the Galileo "heresy," the Second Vatican Council clarified that scriptural inerrancy is limited to matters pertaining to faith and morals. Thus, rather than take responsibility for its 17th century error, the Church pointed its finger deceitfully at the Scriptures as though they were *in error*.

Men's Traditions Make God's Word Void

St. Jude tells us in verses 3-4 (the book of St. Jude contains only one chapter):

> Beloved, while I was making every endeavor to write to you about our common salvation, I found it necessary to write to you, exhorting you to contend earnestly for the faith once for all delivered to the saints. For certain men have stealthily entered in, who long ago were marked out for this condemnation, ungodly men who turn the grace of God into wantonness (*greed*)....

Once again, just as Jesus warned in His day, the traditions of men make God's Word void [see St. Mark 7:13]. As noted earlier by Father Hayes, the Catholic Church believes she has the authority from Christ to obviate old laws and make new ones. The Church bases her position on St. Matthew 16:13-19. Verses 13-18 deal with St. Peter and the rock. The authorizing verse for the claimed authority is derived from verse 19, wherein Jesus told St. Peter:

> "And I will give thee the keys of the kingdom of heaven; and whatever thou shalt bind on earth shall be bound in heaven, and whatever thou shalt loose on earth shall be loosed in heaven."

It would not be unreasonable to conclude *from this single verse* that Jesus is indeed turning *everything* over to St. Peter. Jesus seems to be saying to St. Peter, "You are in charge. The door to the kingdom is locked and here are the keys. However, if you decide that you do not like these particular keys, you have authority from Me to change the lock and make new keys."

The dangers of interpreting a few verses of Scripture in isolation was discussed earlier. There are many other verses that invalidate such an interpretation. Before examining that question, however, it is worth noting that even the most liberal interpretation of the above verse does not support the Church's claim incorporated as doctrine at the First Vatican Council in 1870 that St. Peter's authority was passed on to his successors. Moreover, no verse in the New Testament gives St. Peter the title of pope, first among equals, Bishop of Bishops, *Pontifex Maximus*, Vicar of Christ, or any other such title. The only title for St. Peter appears in I St. Peter 5:1 wherein St. Peter refers to himself as a "fellow-presbyter," an elder. Therefore, the claim of papal succession comes not from Scripture but from post-biblical traditions, what Jesus condemned as the traditions of men.

The Keys to the Kingdom

In justifying its authority to eradicate old laws and make new ones, the expositors have tied two unrelated things together, namely, (1) the keys to the kingdom, and (2) the power of binding and loosing. To determine the meaning of Jesus' words, we must search the Scriptures objectively. The first thing one notices in the subject verse [St. Matthew 16:19] is the use of the word "keys." Why not simply "the key" to the kingdom of heaven? One hears of a mayor giving someone the "key" to the city. And the use of the singular "key" would do no damage to the subject verse if the Catholic Church's interpretation is correct. In fact, it would be even more appropriate: one Church, one key. Bible students are taught to use the literal meaning first to interpret Scripture and check to see if that interpretation can be confirmed by other verses in Scripture.

The word key or keys is used eight times both in the Catholic and the King James Version of the Bible. The word "key" appears two times in the Old Testament: (1) "And I will lay the *key* of the house of David upon his shoulder..." [Isaias 22:22], and (2) "Since he did not open the doors of the upper room, they took the *key* and opened them..." [Judges 3:25]. In the first instance, the word key is used as a figure of privilege, as can be determined by the context in which it is used. God says He will call His servant Eliacim, clothe him, strengthen him, give him power, and give him the key to the house of David (the southern kingdom of Judah). In other words, He will use him to bring about Judah's destiny (privilege). In the second instance, key is used in a literal sense by concerned servants to open doors behind which they find the dead body of their master.

The word "key" appears four times in the New Testament: (1) Jesus says, "Woe to you lawyers! Because you have taken away the key of knowledge…" [St. Luke 11:52]; (2) Jesus says, "Thus says the holy one, the true one, he who has the key of David, he who opens and no one shuts, and who shuts and no one opens…" [Apocalypse 3:7]; (3) St. John says, "And the fifth angel sounded the trumpet, and I saw that a star had fallen from heaven upon the earth, and there was given to him the key of the bottomless pit" [Apocalypse 9:1]; and (4) St. John says, "And I saw an angel coming down from heaven, having the key to the abyss and a great chain in his hand" [Apocalypse 20:1]. In the first instance, Jesus uses "key" as we might today in saying that a good education is the key to a good job. Jesus accused the religious leaders of taking away the key of knowledge from the people, thus keeping them in the dark about God's will rather than teaching them, as they should have. God's Word tells us, "My people are destroyed for lack of knowledge" [Hosea 4:6 KJV]. In the second instance, the word key is used as a symbol of authority rather than privilege. In this verse can be seen the fulfillment of Isaias 22:22. Moreover, verses 20-23 make it clear that only Jesus opens and shuts, not St. Peter, his successors, or any Church.

In the third and fourth instances, the word key is used in a literal sense to open the pit or abyss. Concerning the above, the construction is one key to knowledge, one key to the house of David, one key to the bottomless pit, and one key to the abyss.

The word "keys" appears only twice in the New Testament. In Apocalypse 1:18, Jesus says "… I am living forevermore; and I have the *keys* of death and of hell." One key is of death, the other of hell. The pattern with the use of the word *key* for one item and *keys* for two is consistent. Thus, in seven of eight instances examined, there is a consistency in the use of the words key and keys.

In the eighth instance, Jesus tells St. Peter, "And I will give thee the keys of the kingdom of heaven…" [St. Matthew 16:19]. Based on the pattern seen above, we might expect that such a pattern would continue. The task at hand now is to identify two things associated with St. Peter and the plural *keys*.

Binding and Loosing

A possible starting point is "binding and loosing." These are *two* things mentioned in the same verse. Let's see if we can find the words binding and loosing used again in the Scriptures and whether or not they are associated with "keys." Jesus says to His *disciples*:

> "Amen I say to you, whatever you bind on earth shall be bound also in heaven; and whatever you loose on earth shall be loosed in heaven."
> —St. Matthew 18:18

The first thing to be noted is that the power to bind and loose was given to *all* Jesus' disciples. The promise to St. Peter was twofold, namely, that (1) he would have the keys to the kingdom, and (2) the power to bind and loose. Considering St. Matthew 16:19 and 18:18 together, one has to conclude that the two items, keys and the power to bind and loose, are not related since only the second part of the promise to St. Peter is made also to Jesus' disciples. In other words, if keys were associated with binding and loosing, then Jesus would have promised both keys and the power to bind and loose to all His disciples in St. Matthew 18:18, rather than just binding and loosing.

Binding and loosing are discussed by Jesus in the above citation within the context of forgiving sin. This can be confirmed by examining St. John 20:22-23. Jesus is again speaking to His disciples shortly after His resurrection. Prior to His ascension:

> ... He breathed upon them, and said to them, "Receive the Holy Spirit; whose sins *you* shall forgive (*loose on earth*), they are forgiven them (*loosed in heaven*); and whose sins *you* shall retain (*bind on earth*), they are retained (*bound in heaven*)"

This view is supported in St. Matthew 10:14-15, wherein Jesus tells His apostles:

> "And whoever does not receive you, or listen to your words—go forth outside that house or town, and shake off the dust from your feet. Amen, I say to you, it will be more tolerable for the land of Sodom and Gomorrah in the day of judgment than for that town."

What has been demonstrated thus far is that St. Peter's keys and his power to bind and loose are not related. Moreover, Jesus' disciples were all given the same power to bind and loose. Thus, we must examine the Scriptures further to discover the meaning of the "keys to the kingdom."

The Meaning of the Keys Revealed

When one thinks about who will inherit the kingdom, it is obvious that there will be only two classes of persons: believing Jews and believing Gentiles [see Colossians 1:26-27]. It was in just such a binary way that the Jews viewed the world. The Jews would be saved and the Gentiles lost! In St. John 10:16, Jesus revealed a startling mystery:

> "And other sheep I have that are not of this fold (*believing Jews*). Them (*believing Gentiles*) also I must bring, and they (*Gentiles*) shall hear my voice, and there shall be one fold (*believing Jews and believing Gentiles*) and one shepherd (*Jesus*)."

Jesus is saying that He has two sheepfolds, believing Jews and believing Gentiles, and that He must combine them into one sheepfold. He will be the one shepherd. Since this is the story of the Good Shepherd, it is obvious that *Jesus is that Good Shepherd.* He is the only One who could be the Good Shepherd since God tells us that there is none among men who is *good*, no not one [see Psalms 13 (14):3; Psalms 52 (53):2; and Romans 3:10-12].

Let's see if there are any two outstanding things in St. Peter's life to which the keys could relate. And, of course, the answer is "yes." St. Peter was the first to preach Jesus resurrected to the Jews, as recorded in the book of Acts [Acts 2:14-41], and the Lord added (to His church) that day about three thousand souls. The number of souls saved on this first Christian Pentecost contrasts with the three thousand souls slain by the Levites at Moses' command, when Moses came down from Mt. Sinai and found the people worshiping a golden calf. They had crafted it *not to represent a false Egyptian god, but rather the God that had brought them out of the land of Egypt*—Jehovah God. They had built an altar before it. Aaron had proclaimed, "Tomorrow is a great feast of the LORD." The next day the people offered gifts to the image, ate, and then worshiped it. Upon seeing this, God's anger blazed up and He sent Moses back down to the "stiff-necked" people [Exodus 32:1-28]. St. Peter used the first key to unlock the door to the kingdom of heaven to these stiff-necked people [see Jeremias 17:23].

Since people were saved in Old Testament times, as confirmed in the Old and New Testaments, why was it necessary for St. Peter to open a door that previously had been open? Jesus explains:

> "Woe to you lawyers! Because you have taken away *the key of knowledge*; you have not entered (*into the kingdom*) yourselves and those who were entering you have hindered."
>
> —St. Luke 11:52

The Pharisees had not been teaching the Jews from God's Word how to enter the kingdom. Rather, as Jesus noted, they had been teaching the traditions of men and making God's Word of no effect [St. Mark 7:13]. Thus, these erring Pharisees had shut the door to the kingdom. St. Peter used the first key to open it again to believing Jews.

Despite having seen the Holy Spirit come upon the Samaritans, as recorded in Acts 8:14-17, St. Peter resisted taking the gospel to the Gentile "dogs" [Acts 10:9-16]. However, his reluctance was overcome by God in the form of a thrice-repeated vision. St. Peter then obeyed and went to the house of the centurion, Cornelius, who had prayed to the Jews' God just several days before. Upon entering his home, St. Peter preached Jesus resurrected to Cornelius and his family and friends. While he was still speaking, the Holy Spirit came upon all who were listening to (believing in) his message. The Jews accompanying St. Peter were amazed to see that salvation had come to the Gentiles [Acts 10:21-48]. St. Peter used the second key to unlock the door to believing Gentiles. St. Peter's use of the keys to open the doors to the kingdom for *all* by preaching Jesus is referred to among Bible-believing Christians as the Petrine privilege. It is the duty of every believer to share the gospel with nonbelievers:

> ... but you shall receive power when the Holy Spirit comes upon you, and you shall be witnesses for me in Jerusalem and in all Judea and Samaria and even to the very ends of the earth.
>
> —Acts 1:8

The keys were used by St. Peter. They fulfilled their function and are not mentioned again in the Scripture.

All Believers Are St. Peter's Successors

Believers today receive power when they accept the Jesus of the New Testament as Lord and Savior. It should be noted that the above verse is not prophecy, but a command from the Master. Witnessing is the obligation of every believer. The fact that the message is to be taken to the ends of the earth demonstrates the veracity of such an interpretation. In Jesus' time, it was not possible to take the message to the ends of the earth. Moreover, we know that the gospel has not been preached throughout the whole world because the end has not yet come:

> "And this gospel of the kingdom shall be preached in the whole world, for a witness to all nations (*Jews and Gentiles*); and then will come the end."
>
> —St. Matthew 24:14

St. Paul reminds the leaders of the church at Ephesus prior to his last departure:

> ... I am innocent of the blood of all (*men*); for I have not shrunk from declaring to you the whole counsel of God... that for three years night and day I did not cease with tears to admonish (*warn*) every one of you (*to accept Jesus as Lord and Savior or else face the fires of hell*).
>
> —Acts 20:31

St. Paul's claim that he is innocent of the blood of all men is based on Ezechiel 33:7-9. Ezechiel was a prophet taken from the southern kingdom (Judah) to Tel Abib near the Chebar river during the Babylonian captivity (597 B.C.):

> "Son of man (*Ezechiel*), I (*God*) have made thee a watchman to the house of Israel: and thou shalt hear the word out of my mouth and shalt tell it (*to*) them (*the Israelites*) for me. If, when I say to the wicked, Thou shalt surely die: thou declare it not to him, nor speak to him, that he may be converted from his wicked way, and live: the same wicked man shall die in his iniquity, but I will require his blood at thy hand. But if thou give warning to the wicked, and he be not converted from his wickedness and from his evil way: he shall indeed die in his iniquity, but thou hast delivered thy soul."

The above verses present two possible scenarios. In the first, the sinner is not warned by the watchman that his ways are evil and that if he does not change, he will die in his sins. While the wicked man shall die in his sin, the watchman shall give an accounting also. In the second, the watchman warns the wicked man but he continues his evil ways and dies in his sins. In this case, the watchman did his duty and is innocent of the blood of this man. Ezechiel, as the watchman, is accountable for the faithful *deliverance* of God's message. Thus, St. Paul could say that through his persistent delivery of the complete gospel (the whole counsel of God) to all men with whom he came in contact during his three year mission in Ephesus, sometimes to the point of tears, that he was innocent of the blood of any who perished [Acts 20:27]. Would that all who call themselves Christian could say as much. Unfortunately, most of us cannot.

Jesus Is the Way—the Only Way

ABC aired a segment on its *20/20* news show in May of 2000. The story revolved around the conversion of a thirteen-year old boy by the youth group of a Baptist church in Dallas, Texas. The boy was invited to a teen gathering by his Baptist friends. A gospel call was given and the boy came forward and answered, "Yes, Lord." The boy's divorced mother and father made an issue out of the matter. They appeared on *20/20* to criticize the church's practice of proselytization. The pastor of the church readily admitted that their intent is *always to make converts for Jesus*, that this is their charge from the Lord. When the ABC correspondent asked the pastor why he wasn't content to let others take their own paths to heaven, the pastor answered that there is only one path and that Jesus is that one path. Then the pastor quoted Jesus: "I am the way, and the truth, and the life. No one comes to the Father but through me" [St. John 14:6]. This brave pastor was following the Master's command with regard to binding and loosing, with regard to whose sins are forgiven and whose are retained. Moreover, when Jesus' disciples tried to stop the children from approaching the Lord, Jesus said to them:

> "... Let the little children be, and do not hinder them from coming to me, for of such is the kingdom of heaven."
>
> —St. Matthew 19:14

At the end of the segment, the correspondent appeared back in the studio with Ms. Barbara Walters. The correspondent told Ms. Walters, with some degree of surprise, that the pastor took Jesus' statement that *He was the only way* literally. Ms. Walters looked shocked. She inquired if all Christian churches took Jesus' words so literally. The correspondent smiled, shook her head, and answered, "No."

Christians are often surprised when those with dead spirits cannot understand the spiritual significance of things. However, we should not be surprised that some media persons "just don't get it" when it comes to spiritual matters. Candidate George Bush was asked during a televised debate during his first campaign for president to explain the meaning of his being born again. "If I have to explain it," the Governor answered, "you won't get it." Mr. Bush wasn't being evasive. He was simply giving a modern translation of Jesus' words: "That which is born of the flesh is flesh; and that which is born of the Spirit is spirit" [St. John 3:6]. Those who were reborn or "born from above" would understand and those who were not could not no matter how many follow-up questions they might ask [see 2 Corinthians 4:3-4].

God says to the overseers in charge of His flock:

> Cry, cease not, lift up thy voice like a trumpet, and show my people their wicked doings and the house of Jacob their sins.
>
> —Isaias 58:1

Many pastors and denominations that call themselves Christian do not take Jesus' words literally, as the ABC correspondent confirmed to Ms. Walters. Many, unlike St. Paul, have blood on their hands. And, as the Scriptures testify, they will answer for it.

There Are Many Paths to Perdition

Today, the world celebrates diversity. This activist agenda is being pushed hardest by those who are spiritually dead. In November 1993, the World Council of Churches (WCC) sponsored a women's conference in Minneapolis. The theme of the gathering, which was attended by more than two thousand women, was "re-imaging." The objects to be "re-imaged" were no less than *Christ and Christianity*. The dais was filled with activists and noted feminist writers from what many consider to be mainstream denominations, including United Methodist, Lutheran, United Presbyterian, Church of Christ, and Roman Catholic. These women represented "diverse views" with regard to spiritual matters, but all approved of pantheism, existentialism, abortion, lesbianism, homosexuality, and bisexuality, just to name a few. Various speakers took turns emasculating God and Jesus and religious organizations run largely by what they termed "patriarchal males." The activists honed their words carefully so as to solicit approval from their "sisters." One of the women took the podium and informed her listeners that: "I don't think we need a theory of atonement at all… I don't think we need folks hanging on crosses and blood dripping and weird stuff… we just need to listen to the God within." Another speaker clarified for her listeners that Lazarus' sisters, Martha and Mary, were actually lesbian lovers, not familial sisters. A group of approximately one hundred "lesbian, bi-sexual, and transsexual" women were called to the stage for special recognition. They were celebrating the "miracle" of being *lesbian, out, and Christian*. The conferees applauded them for being *lesbian, out, and Christian*.

Some of the most vociferous and impassioned speakers were Catholic nuns who railed against old fuddy-duddy popes for keeping them out of the Church hierarchy. Quiet submission to authority was not one of the marks of faith for these conferees. Proverbs 31:30 tells us: "… the woman who fears (*respects*) the LORD is to be praised." Why? Because if she respects the LORD, she will respect also His authority over her, she will obey Him and respect other authorities God has placed over her. But just as nuns are throwbacks to the atavistic Vestal Virgins, so the words spoken at the conference hearken back to the themes and times of the first apostate religion, the Babylonian Cult. This was mostly a "women's following," with the mother-goddess Semiramis being in charge of the her god-son Tammuz.

Attendees in Minneapolis put forth an old goddess for worship under a new name: Sophia (Greek, means *wisdom*). One of the speakers explained that Sophia was the suppressed part of the "biblical tradition" and the female face of the human psyche. On Sunday morning, the "faithful" met to pray:

> "Our maker Sophia, we are women in your image... Sophia, creator God.... shower us with your love... we invite a lover, we birth a child; with our warm body fluids we remind the world of its pleasures and sensations... Our guide, Sophia, we are women in your image... With the honey of wisdom in our mouths, we prophesy a full humanity to all the peoples."[47]

It is likely that none of the speakers remembered Romans 1:22-32:

> For while professing to be wise, they have become fools, and they have changed the glory of the incorruptible God for an image made like to corruptible man and to birds and to four-footed beasts and creeping things. Therefore God has given them up in the lustful desires of their heart to uncleanness, so that they dishonor their own bodies among themselves, they who exchanged the truth of God for a lie, and worshiped and served the creature rather than the Creator who is blessed forever, amen. For this cause, God has given them up to shameful lusts... for their women have exchanged the natural use of that which is against nature... Although they have known the ordinance (*laws*) of God, they have not understood that those who practice such things are deserving of death. And not only do they *do* these things (*themselves*), but they *applaud* others doing them.

How's that for an *old-imaged* God? He addressed the lies of the New Age feminists nearly two thousand years before their conference to celebrate and *applaud* lesbianism. With regard to their mouths being filled with the *honey of wisdom*, God's Word warns:

> The lips of an adulteress drip with honey, and her mouth is smoother than oil; But in the end she is as bitter as wormwood (*hemlock*), as sharp as a two-edged sword. Her feet go down to death, to the nether world her steps attain.
>
> —Proverbs 5:3-5

The old name for the "new goddess" Sophia is none other than Semiramis, the goddess of the oldest apostate religious system, Babylon. It is interesting that these women should choose to call upon the goddess Sophia. According to Greek mythology, Sophia was the one who created the evil, materialistic world in which human souls are trapped. Emperor

Justinian (483-565) injected Sophia into Catholicism when he constructed a great edifice at Constantinople called Hagia Sophia, the Church of the Holy Wisdom in 538. It is now a Mosque.

This is where the false teaching of Mary as *Mother of God* and *Queen of Heaven* has taken many unsuspecting women. But how did this false teaching, once confined to the Roman Catholic Church, penetrate other denominations to the extent that women from Lutheran, Presbyterian, Methodist, and other Protestant organizations would embrace a goddess? The long answer involves a falling away from fundamentalism by some Protestant churches; inculcation of the false doctrines of Darwinism, evolution, and humanism; and the injection of liberalism and modernism, under the banner of Textual Criticism, into mainstream Churches. This has created a false religion of neo-fundamentalism that is more concerned with social issues than soteriology. The short answer is ecumenism, a damnable heresy that says, "there are many paths, each can take his own way, let's not argue over irrelevant doctrinal points. Rather, let's put aside trivial differences and concentrate on common social goals." However, St. Jude exhorts us to "... contend earnestly for the faith once for all delivered to the saints" [St. Jude 3]. Jesus said those who were not with Him were against Him and that those who did not help Him gather were scatterers of the flock [see St. Luke 11:23]. Thus, ecumenism is a doctrine of devils [see 1 Timothy 4:1].

The United Nations, an organization condemned to failure from its inception by its compromise with communist countries not to put the word "God" in its charter or on its building, declared 1986 to be the International Year of Peace. Pope John Paul II set aside December 24, 1986 as a Day of Prayer for World Peace. On February 10, 1986 the Pope invited leaders from "Christian" denominations and other religions to participate in that Day of Prayer. Some 160 participants representing virtually all "Christian" organizations, including the Roman Catholic Church; the World Council of Churches; the National Council of Churches; the YMCA and YWCA; Quaker; Mennonite World Conference; Reformed Ecumenical Synod; Baptist World Alliance; Disciples of Christ; Lutheran World Federation; Anglican Communion; Old Catholic Union of Utrecht (a sect of Old Catholics); and the Greek, Russian, and Eastern Orthodox Churches to meet in Assisi, Italy on December 24th. Also participating were about forty leaders from eleven non-Christian religions, including Hindus; Sikhs; Buddhists; Judaism; Islam; African and North American animists who worship spirits and nature; ancestor-worshiping Japanese Shintoists; fire-worshiping Zoroastrians; Baha'i; and the Dalai Lama.

According to an Associated Press report:

"ASSISI, Italy-Chants, temple bells and pagan spells echoed around the Roman Catholic shrines of Assisi yesterday as Pope John Paul II and his 200 guests from the world's 12 main religions prayed for world peace...

The medicine man of the Crow Indians [spirit worshipers], Chief John Pretty-on-Top, offered to cast out evil spirits. Many came forward, among them a young Franciscan monk.

In a chapel down the road, the head of the Zoroastrian church in Bombay prayed before a fire that symbolized his God.

Next door, six turbaned Sikhs—all Italian converts—sat chanting their prayers in the lotus position to gramophone music.

At an old Roman temple, shoeless Moslems sat on prayer mats.

The 14th Dalai Lama, exiled god-king of Tibet, headed the strong Buddhist contingent, mumbling sutras amid tinkling bells at the Basilica of St. Peter.

In the gardens outside, a Shinto sect called Tenrikyo, in black kimonos, swayed to temple music.

African animists, their togas the envy of any designer, invoked the spirits of trees and plants to come to the aid of peace...
                                —Christian Beacon (Dec. 25, 1986, p. 7)

God warns in Proverbs 14:12:

Sometimes a way seems right to a man, but the end of it leads to death.

Ecumenism is a satanic philosophy put into the hearts of men who mistakenly believe there is some inherent good in all men and that such men are capable of performing good works apart from the Jesus of the New Testament [see Colossians 2:8]. However, we know that apart from Jesus, no work is really good. It is painful for any believer to tell someone he or she loves or even a stranger that he is on the path to hell and that only Jesus is the Way, the Truth, and the Life [see St. John 14:6]. Yet this is exactly what our Lord commands of *every* believer. Jesus prophesied:

"Do not think that I have come to send peace upon the earth; I have come
to bring a sword, not peace. For I have come to set a man at variance with
his father, and a daughter with her mother, and a daughter-in-law with her
mother-in-law; and a man's enemies will be those of his own household.
He who loves father or mother more than me is not worthy of me; and
he who loves son or daughter more than me is not worthy of me. And he
who does not take up his cross and follow me, is not worthy of me."

—St. Matthew 10:34-38

Ecumenism is a satanic alternative to being His witness. In taking up
our crosses, we must not shrink from the fear and pain associated with
being witnesses for Him. Moreover, we owe it to all to tell them about
Jesus. Jesus told a story—not a parable—about a rich man tormented in
hell. The rich man had concern for his nonbelieving brothers who were
still alive. He asked Abraham to send someone to tell them so they could
avoid his fate. The story is recorded in St. Luke 16:19-31. One can almost
hear the cries of those in hell asking of us still alive, "Why didn't you tell
me? I was your friend." Share Jesus' saving power with your friends and
others. If some deride you and label you a proselytizer, wear the moniker
with pride realizing that with their mouths they confess that you are doing
the Lord's work [see St. Matthew 10:32]. Never give them reason to call
out, "Why didn't you tell me?" St. Paul told those at Miletus:

... I am innocent of the blood of all (men); for I have not shrunk from
declaring to you the whole counsel of God.

—Acts 20:26-27

St. Paul tells believers that if those to whom they witness reject the
message, then:

Do not bear the yoke with unbelievers. For what has justice in common
with iniquity? Or what fellowship has light with darkness? What harmony
is there between Christ and Belial (Satan)? Or what part has the believer
with the unbeliever? And what agreement has the temple of God with
idols? For you are the temple of the living God, as God says, "I will dwell
and move among them, I will be their God and they shall be my people."
Wherefore, "Come out from among them (unbelievers), be separated says
the LORD, and touch not an unclean thing; and I will welcome you in,
and will be a Father to you, and you shall be my sons and daughters, says
the LORD almighty."

—2 Corinthians 6:14-18

Could it be any clearer? Believers are not to participate with pagans in worship. While many may feel that it is acceptable to agree with nonbelievers on some common ground in order to accomplish some "good," look again at what God says through St. Paul: "What agreement has the temple of God with idols?"

Concerning ecumenism and coming together to pray, God says:

> "If My people who are called by My name will humble themselves, and pray and seek My face, and turn from their wicked ways, then I will hear from heaven, and will forgive their sin and heal their land."
> —2 Chronicles 7:14 NKJV

This is an invitation from God to *His people* and His people only. Worshipers of Isis and Horus and other false gods are not invited. Can you imagine the prophet Elias (also spelled Elijah) calling for joint prayer with the high priests of Baal? Hardly. Instead, Elias made fun of their god, suggesting that they call louder to him, that perhaps Baal was sleeping [see 3 Kings 18:27]. Elias did not demonstrate an ecumenical spirit. Neither did he celebrate the diversity of paths. It is indeed difficult to imagine that there was not a single believer at that 1986 Prayer Day gathering willing to stand up and say, "Friends, I see that you are in every respect extremely religious. Let me tell you about Jesus and the wonderful things He did for me and you...." Does such an idea sound foreign to you? Or even crazy? I hope not, because that is exactly what St. Paul said to the men of Athens on Mars Hill:

> "... Men of Athens, I see that in every respect you are extremely religious."
> —Acts 17:22

Then St. Paul preached Jesus resurrected and the Good News of the gospel. It is hard to believe that the *one* who claims to stand in the shoes of St. Peter, the *one* who claims to be the Vicar of Christ on earth, infallible, and led by the Holy Spirit, failed to stand up and preach Christ crucified, buried, and raised from the dead bodily! Instead, Pope John Paul II acted like his predecessor, the Pontifex Maximus, the head of all pagan religions. Not a single bishop of the Protestant faith stood up to preach Jesus. No Patriarch of the Orthodox faith came forward. In an age when many of these denominations have taken a stand supporting premarital sex, homosexuality, abortion, bisexuality, divorce, and the ordination of women, homosexuals, and lesbians to the pulpit, no one stood up for Jesus [see Philippians 2:14-16]. Not the Reverend Robert Runcie, Archbishop of

Canterbury. Not Gunnar Stalsett, head of the Lutheran World Foundation. Not Bernice Schrotenboer, leader of the Reformed Evangelical Synod. Not Allan Boesak, head of the World Alliance of Reformed Churches. And not the late Mother Teresa, a renowned Catholic nun who in numerous interviews with the world spectrum of publishers *boasted* that she had never even once tried to proselytize anyone! She proudly informed her interviewers that she simply tried to make the Hindu a better Hindu and the Buddhist a better Buddhist. Compare this soon-to-be saint's attitude with that of another saint, St. Paul:

> ... I have kept back nothing that was for your good, but have declared it to you and taught you in public and from house to house.
> —Acts 20:20

Jesus did not go to the cross to make a Hindu a better Hindu. He went to the cross to give a spiritually dead Hindu new and everlasting life! St. Paul preached Jesus to anyone who would listen. At the end of his life he found himself "innocent of the blood of all men" because he had revealed the whole counsel of God [Acts 20:26-27]. While Mother Teresa's failure to follow the Lord's command to be a witness for Him [Acts 1:8] is shocking to any believer, it is not surprising. As foretold by St. Paul in 2 Thessalonians 2:3:

> Let no one deceive you in any way, for the day of the Lord (*His second coming*) will not come unless the apostasy comes first....

In 1997, Mother Teresa traveled to Washington, D.C. to receive the Congressional Gold Medal for her humanitarian works. She explained to the Congressmen her motto: "all for Jesus." No one can question that Mother Teresa did a lot for humanity and no doubt, from her perspective, she did it all for Jesus. However, while Mother Teresa understood the words "all for Jesus," she apparently didn't understand the eternal significance of turning those words around: "Jesus for all." Those sick and dying Hindus, Buddhists, and others were not only sick in body but also dead in spirit, according to the Catholic Bible. While Mother Teresa's works are laudable in the flesh, Jesus' words speak to her failure to follow His command to be a witness: "These things you ought to have done (*tending to the sick*), while not leaving the others (*being His witness*) undone" [St. Matthew 23:23].

Be not deceived, the prophesied apostasy has arrived. And it will only grow stronger in the fertile soils of ecumenism and diversity. The ecumenical movement will turn into an ecumenical, universal Church which will become the One World Religion, the woman who rides the beast in chapter

17 of the book of Apocalypse. This apostate religious system will exercise control over the beast (world leader and his One World Government) during the first half of Daniel's 70th week of years [Daniel 9:24-27], a three-and-a-half-year period of time known as the Tribulation. During the second half of the 70th week, that is, the last three-and-a-half years, known as the *Great Tribulation* and the time of Jacob's Trouble [Jeremias 30:7], the world leader will be killed but then miraculously resurrected and literally possessed by Satan. He will then throw off the shackles of the apostate, universal Church and destroy it [Apocalypse 17:16].

Jesus Came to Seek and to Save That Which Was Lost

Catholic and many other Churches erroneously teach that Christ came into this world to "establish The Church." However, there is not one word of Scripture to support this thesis. Moreover, given the important roles each of these "Churches" has usurped with regard to salvation, it is little wonder they teach this and other errors. God's Word tells us why the Jesus of the New Testament entered the world:

... the Son of Man came to seek and to save what was lost.
—St. Luke 19:10

... I... have come to save the world.
—St. John 12:47

For God did not send his Son into the world in order to judge the world, but that the world might be saved through him.
—St. John 3:17

This saying is true and worthy of entire acceptance, that Jesus Christ came into the world to save sinners....
—1 Timothy 1:15

Jesus sent His disciples into the world to preach the gospel [St. Mark 16:15]. He did not tell them to promote the concept of a universal Church with a hierarchy that would include priests, bishops (pastors over other pastors), archbishops, cardinals, curia, and a pope. He did not tell them to establish a sacramental salvation system. If salvation is an accomplished fact for each believer through Jesus' atoning death on the cross, as the Catholic, Orthodox, and all other Bibles clearly teach, then certainly such a complex organization and soterilogical scheme are unnecessary. On the other hand, if salvation was not accomplished by Jesus on that cross but is, as the Churches teach, a life-long process for the individual, then such a complex institutional organization and soterilogical scheme would be necessary.

Finally, when the local church—in Greek, the *ekklesia*—is referred to as Jesus' body, it is not a reference to some universal mystical collection of people, some on earth and others in heaven or elsewhere. Rather, it means a body of people on earth called out for a special purpose. Jehovah God called out the Jews in the Old Testament. The *ekklesia* is the body of Christ on earth. Jesus' body left this earth. However, before leaving, He promised to establish His church [see St. Matthew 16:18]. And it was established at Jerusalem on Pentecost. What did the body of Christ do when He walked this earth? He sought to save that which was lost. He preached sin, repentance, and eternal life. What are the members of His *ekklesia*, believers, to do? The same thing. Take His message of salvation to a lost world.

Jesus *Is* the Rock

Another source of controversy is the traditional claim by some Churches that Jesus built His church upon St. Peter. These Churches base their teaching on several verses of Scripture, including:

> Now Jesus, having come into the district of Caesarea Philippi, began to ask his disciples, saying, "Who do men say the Son of Man is?" But they said, "Some say, John the Baptist: and others, Elias; and others, Jeremias, or one of the prophets." He said to them, "But who do you say that I am?" Simon Peter answered and said, "Thou art the Christ (*Messiah*), the Son of the living God." Then Jesus answered and said, "Blessed art thou, Simon Bar-Jona, for flesh and blood has not revealed it to thee, but my Father who is in heaven. And I say also to thee, thou art Peter, and upon this rock I will build my Church, and the gates of hell shall not prevail against it."
>
> —St. Matthew 16:13-18

Prior to arriving at Caesarea Philippi, Jesus had spent the previous three days healing the lame, blind, dumb, maimed, and others brought to Him by the throngs of people who followed after Him hoping for a miracle. Prior to dismissing the large gathering, Jesus, for the second time in His public ministry, multiplied the loaves and fishes and fed the crowd of more than four thousand (not including women and children) so they might be sustained during their journeys home [St. Matthew 15:38]. When Jesus and His disciples arrived at Caesarea Philippi, they were met by a group of Pharisees and Sadducees. The Pharisees were no doubt more than a little agitated. Just days earlier they had accused Jesus of casting out devils by the power of Beelzebub, the prince of devils [St. Matthew 12:24]. In response to the hardness of their hearts, Jesus had referred to them as a "generation of vipers" and children of the devil [St. Matthew 12:34 and 23:33 and St. John 8:44]. This must have cut the Torah-schooled Pharisees to the quick and brought their anger to a quick boil. Jesus labeled them—the holy ones of Israel—the spawn of Satan, the seed of the serpent referred to in Genesis 3:15. It is interesting to note that Jesus never referred to Gentiles or non-clerical Jews as the seed of Satan. Rather, He referred to the Gentiles (who practiced paganism) and to the non-clerical Jews as lost sheep without a shepherd. Jesus' harshest words were reserved for the religious leaders of His day who openly exhibited a hardness of heart and made the Word of God void by their manmade traditions.

The Pharisees and Sadducees again confronted Jesus with their request for a "sign." In light of the many miracles Jesus had performed, their demand was nothing less than an insult to Jesus and His ministry. Jesus knew that if He produced a sign, there would be no end. The next group of nonbelievers would demand an even more convincing sign and so on, and His ministry would be turned from preaching the kingdom into a sideshow. Jesus chided the Pharisees and Sadducees by affirming that they could discern the weather by the face of the sky. He asked them how it was that they did not recognize the time of their visitation (by the Messiah) [see Daniel 9:24-26]. Because of their unbelief, Jesus referred to them as a wicked and adulterous generation and promised there would be no sign except the sign of the prophet Jonas. By this, Jesus meant that just as Jonas had spent three days and nights in the belly of the great fish prepared by God [Jonas 2:1], so He would spend three days and nights in the heart of the earth.

Jesus warned His disciples to beware of the leaven of the Pharisees and Sadducees, that is, beware of the Pharisees' unbelief and the Sadducees' false teachings. Then Jesus asked His disciples who people thought Him to be. They replied John the Baptist, or Elias, or Jeremias, or one of the other prophets. Jesus queried them further, asking who *they* thought Him to be. It was in response to this question that St. Peter replied, "Thou art the Christ, the Son of the living God" [St. Matthew 16:16]. Jesus' response to St. Peter's confession of faith acknowledged that St. Peter was blessed with the answer and that he had not arrived at it through his own abilities [St. Matthew 16:17]. In addressing St. Peter as Simon Bar-Jona, Jesus may have been using a double reference. Bar means "son of." Peter's father's name was Jona. However, just as the prophet Jonas disobeyed God's command to take a message of repentance to the people of Nineveh, the capital of the much-feared Assyrians, until God prepared a great fish to assist in carrying out His will [Jonas 1:2-3], so Jesus knew, too, that St. Peter would resist God's will that he take the gospel message to the Gentiles, as discussed earlier [see Acts 10:9-16, and 28]. It is at this point that Jesus said, "And I say to thee, thou art Peter, and upon this rock I will build my church (*ekklesia*), and the gates of hell (*hades*) shall not prevail against it" [St. Matthew 16:18].

There has been much debate as to the meaning of Jesus' words. Some interpret this verse as, "Peter, I will build my church (*ekklesia*) upon you." If this is the message Jesus intended His followers to understand, however, He probably would have said so simply and clearly. Some argue that Jesus would not have chosen to build His church on St. Peter because he can be seen from Scripture often to have been rash, ill-tempered, and headstrong not only prior to Jesus' resurrection but also after [Acts 10; Galatians 2:11; and St. John 21:20-22]. Some Catholics have been taught that the "fact" that Jesus appeared to St. Peter first following His resurrection is proof that Jesus had designated St. Peter to be the rock upon which He would build His church. This teaching, however, is based on false tradition. As recorded in St. Matthew, "... Mary Magdalene..." was the first to see the resurrected Jesus [St. Matthew 28:1-10]. St. Mark's Gospel confirms this [St. Mark 16:1-9]. St. Luke records in his Gospel account that the resurrected Jesus appeared first to Mary Magdalene [St. Luke 24:1-10]. And finally, St. John, the "beloved apostle," confirms that it was first to Mary Magdalene that Jesus appeared [St. John 20:1-17]. Thus, all four Gospels in the Roman Catholic Bible confirm that following His resurrection, Jesus appeared first to Mary Magdalene.

The Catholic Church also uses St. John 21:15-17 to argue that Jesus placed St. Peter as head of The Church. According to Rome's interpretation, Jesus confirmed to St. Peter three times that he was to be head of The Church. Presented below are the relevant verses from the Roman Catholic Bible:

> When, therefore, they had breakfasted, Jesus said to Simon Peter, "Simon, son of John, dost thou love me more than these do?" He said to him, "Yes, Lord, thou knowest that I love thee." He said to him, "Feed my lambs." He said to him a second time, "Simon, son of John, dost thou love me?" He said to him, "Yes, Lord, thou knowest that I love thee." He said to him, "Feed my lambs (*Tend my sheep*)." A third time he said to him, "Simon, son of John, dost thou love me?" Peter was grieved because he said to him for the third time, "Dost thou love me?" And he said to him, "Lord, thou knowest all things, thou knowest that I love thee." He said to him, "Feed my sheep."
>
> —St. John 21:15-17

First, note that nowhere in this passage does Jesus indicate that He is placing St. Peter in charge of The Church. In fact, the word "Church" is not even mentioned. Rather, this passage is known to biblical scholars as "the restoration of Peter." The second thing to note is that Jesus refers to Simon as the *son of John*. Jesus knew Jona was Simon's father and always referred to him as the "son of Jona." However, in the above citation, as well as in St. John 1:42, the Vulgate incorrectly refers to Simon as the son of John. This is one of the errors in the revised Vulgate inserted by Pope Sixtus V which was not caught during its hurried correction by Gregory XIV. However, the St. Matthew 16:17 text correctly identifies Simon as the son of Jona.

St. Peter had denied Jesus as Lord three times. Moreover, St. Peter boldly told Jesus that even if the others denied Him, he would not. He would be willing to die for Him! In the above citation, Jesus asks "Simon" three times if he loves Him. Jesus had called him Peter or Cephas, meaning stone, prior to the night He was betrayed. In this instance, however, Jesus calls Peter by his formal name, Simon, rather than by his nickname. Also, it is important to understand that in Greek there are three words translated "love." First, there is *agapao*, which means unconditional love in a moral sense. This is the word used in St. John 3:16, "For God so loved the world ...." The second is *eros*, which means physical love, as between a married man and woman. The third word translated as "love" is *phileo*, which means a fondness or liking, more akin to brotherly love. Some men feel uncomfortable using the word love, *agapao*. St. Peter was no exception. If the Greek is substituted back into the above verses, here is how the conversation sounded:

> When, therefore, they had breakfasted, Jesus said to Simon Peter, "Simon, son of John, dost thou love me more than these do?" He said to him, "Yes, Lord, thou knowest that I *like* thee." He said to him, "Feed my lambs." He said to him a second time, "Simon, son of John, dost thou love me?" He said to him, "Yes, Lord, thou knowest that I *like* thee." He said to him, "Feed my lambs (*Tend my sheep*)." A third time he said to him, "Simon, son of John, dost thou *like* me?" Peter was grieved because he said to him for the third time, "Dost thou like me?" And he said to him, "Lord, thou knowest all things, thou knowest that I *like* thee." He said to him, "Feed my sheep."
>
> —St. John 21:15-17

The fact that Jesus asked him three times was not lost upon Simon. He knew Jesus was reminding him that he had denied him three times. This is why the text records that "Peter was grieved ...." If these verses reveal Jesus giving The Church to St. Peter, as the Catholic and some other Churches argue, then why would this "grieve" him? The question is rhetorical.

There is no plausible answer. But if the church is built on someone, which candidates should be considered?

It is revealed in the original Greek that Jesus used a play on words, using the word *petros*, which means a small stone, to refer to Peter, and *petra*, which means a large stone or bolder, to refer to that, whatever *that* was, upon which He would build His church. Some argue that the foundation upon which Jesus would build His church was St. Peter's confession of faith. Others believe that Jesus was referring to building the church upon Himself. St. Peter himself gives some insight into this matter:

> Lay aside therefore all malice, and all deceit, and pretense, and envy, and all slander. Crave, as newborn babes, pure spiritual milk, that by it you may grow to salvation (*thereby grow*); if, indeed, you have tasted that the Lord is sweet [*see Psalm 33(34):9*]. Draw near to him (*Jesus*), a living stone, rejected indeed by men but chosen and honored by God. Be you yourselves as living stones, built thereon into a spiritual house, a holy priesthood, to offer spiritual sacrifices acceptable to God through Jesus Christ. Hence Scripture says, "Behold I lay in Sion (*Mount Zion*) a chief corner stone, chosen, precious; and he who believes in it shall not be put to shame." For you, therefore, who believe in this honor; but to those who do not believe, "A stone which the builders rejected, the same has become the head of the corner," and, "A stumbling-stone, and a rock of scandal (*offense*)," to those who stumble at the word, and who do not believe. For this also they are destined.
>
> —1 St. Peter 2:1-8

It should be noted that, "Draw near to him (*Jesus*), a living stone" does not refer to the initial response of a repentant sinner coming to Christ for salvation. These instructions are for believers and address growth in holiness. As can be discerned from the context, this "draw" refers to intimate and continuing fellowship with the Lord. Earlier, in 1 St. Peter 1:3, St. Peter referred to Jesus as the living hope. In 2:4-5, St. Peter refers to coming to Jesus as coming to a living stone. He calls Jesus' followers, who are conforming their walks to His will, lively stones. In other words, there is no spiritual stagnation in their lives. They are allowing the Holy Spirit to work every day to more greatly conform their lives to Jesus' will [see Romans 8:29].

In the cited text, St. Peter makes known his view of what Christ's church is built upon. Of course, as a student of the Torah, St. Peter knew the answer long before Jesus' words to him. The answer is found in Psalm 117(118):21-23, "I will give thanks to you, for you have answered me and been my savior. The stone which the builders rejected has become the cornerstone. By the LORD has this been done; it is wonderful in our eyes." These verses make clear that salvation has come through a marvelous doing by the LORD (sending His son, Jesus, to pay the sin debt of the world) and the stone which the builders (Pharisees and Sadducees) considered worthless (that same Jesus) has become the chief cornerstone (upon which salvation is anchored). In Jesus' time, builders knew that if they set the chief cornerstone properly, the adjoining walls would line up correctly.

Many other places in Scripture affirm that the church (both *ekklesia* and *autos*) is built upon none other than Jesus. One clear example is the judgment of a believer's works, also known as the Bema judgment, discussed by St. Paul:

> According to the grace of God which has been given to me, as a wise builder, I laid the foundation, and another buildeth thereon. But let everyone take care how he builds thereon. For other foundation no one can lay, but that which has been laid, which is Christ Jesus. But if anyone builds upon this foundation, (*with*) gold, silver, precious stones, wood, hay, straw-the work of each will be made manifest, for the day of the Lord will declare it, since the day is to be revealed in fire. The fire will assay the quality of everyone's work: if his work abides (*survives*) which he has built thereon, he will receive reward; if his work burns he will loose his reward, but himself *will be saved*, yet so as through fire.
>
> —1 Corinthians 3:10-15

In addition to showing clearly that Jesus is the one and only foundation upon which the believer is to build, not St. Peter, not any Church or church, these verses also confirm that we are His workmanship created in Christ Jesus unto good works [Ephesians 2:10]. Ephesians 2:20 confirms that the church is built upon the foundation of the apostles and the prophets with Christ Jesus Himself as the "chief corner stone." Until we become followers of Jesus, and build on that foundation the good works prepared by Him beforehand that we may walk in them as He foreordained, God considers each of us to be an unclean thing and our acts of righteousness (good works) of equal value with the "... rag of a menstruous woman..." [Isaias 64:6]. Thus, apart from that foundation which is Jesus, we are unclean and can perform no good works. Therefore, those who are looking for salvation based not on the grace of God [see Ephesians 2:8 and 1 St. Peter 1:9], but on their own good works are deceiving themselves [see Ephesians 2:9]. The phrase "yet so as through fire," may be a reference to what we see in the Judge's eyes at the Bema. Jesus' eyes are described as "a flame of fire" in Apocalypse 1:14.

St. James was the leader of the church at Jerusalem. This statement is disputed by the Roman Catholic Church. She claims that St. Peter was the infallible leader of the universal Church. However, as already shown, there was no universal Church for St. Peter or anyone else to head. Further proof that St. Peter was not the infallible leader of even the apostles is recorded in Galatians 2:11-21. When St. Paul returned from Jerusalem where he had heard of St. Peter's association with the Judaizers, and the false gospel they had been spreading, St. Paul confronted St. Peter:

> But when Cephas (*Peter, see St. John 1:42*) came to Antioch, I withstood him to his face, because he was deserving of blame. For before certain persons came from James, he used to eat with the Gentiles; but when they came, he began to withdraw and to separate himself, fearing the circumcised. And the rest of the Jews (*Jewish converts*) dissembled (played the part of the hypocrite) along with him, so that Barnabas also was led away by them into that dissimulation (*hypocrisy*). But when I saw that they were not walking uprightly according to the truth of the gospel, I said to Cephas before them all: If thou, though a Jew, livest like the Gentiles, and not like the Jews, how is it that thou dost compel the Gentiles to live like the Jews (*under the Mosaic Law*)?
>
> —Galatians 2:11-14

Apparently St. Peter mistakenly believed, or was led to believe by the Judaizers *claiming* to speak for St. James, that St. James did not think believing Jews should eat with even believing Gentiles. Thus, through fear, St. Peter began to separate himself from the Gentiles. Barnabas and other of St. Peter's associates followed suit. However, St. Paul rebuked St. Peter and the others for having abandoned the truth of the gospel [see St. John 10:16 and Romans 10:12]. Thus, again, we see that St. Peter was neither infallible nor the leader of any Church or church. Moreover, the veracity of the claim that St. James was the leader of the Jerusalem church can be evaluated by simply reading the relevant text in chapter 15 of the book of Acts. As recorded therein, the question being debated at the Jerusalem church was, "What must Gentile converts do with regard to circumcision and following the Law of Moses." Certain converts from among the Pharisees insisted that Gentile converts be circumcised and follow the Law. Various disciples put forth their positions in an open forum. Then, St. Peter stood to speak. He recounted his experience converting Gentiles. Then St. Paul and Barnabas stood and told how God had performed great signs and wonders in their witnessing to the Gentiles. After all had put forth their testimonies:

... James made this answer, saying, "Brethren, listen to me. Simon (*Peter*) has told how God first visited the Gentiles to take away from among them a people to bear his name. And with this the words of the prophets agree, as it is written, 'After these things I will return and will rebuild the tabernacle of David which has fallen down, and the ruins thereof I will rebuild, and I will set it up; that the rest of mankind may seek after the Lord, and all the nations upon whom my name is invoked, says the Lord, who does these things.' "To the Lord was his own work known from the beginning of the world." Therefore, *my judgment* is not to disquiet those who from among the Gentiles are turning to the Lord; but to send them written instructions to abstain from anything that has been contaminated by idols and from immorality and from anything strangled and from (*the drinking of*) blood.

—Acts 15:13-20

St. James is the only one who dealt with the question in a doctrinal manner, citing the relevant portion of the Old Testament being fulfilled [see Amos 9:11-12]. Also, it was *his judgment* on the matter that prevailed. And, per *his judgment and direction*, a letter explaining the conclusions reached at the meeting was prepared and delivered to those at Antioch. It is interesting to note that the Jerusalem church mentioned no requirement for baptism or communion with regard to salvation which is consistent with the Scriptures but contrary to what many Churches teach.

"The Gates of Hell Shall Not Prevail"

After affirming that He would build His church upon Himself, Jesus stated that the "gates of hell" would not prevail against it. The translation of the original Greek word "*Hades*" into English as "hell" is misleading. The Greek word Hades is the equivalent of the Hebrew word Sheol. They both refer to the abode of the dead, not a place of eternal punishment. They both differ from the word Gehenna.

In biblical times, the Valley of Gehenna (Greek, Hinnom in Hebrew) was the place where garbage and refuse from the city of Jerusalem were burned. The fires raged and smoke rose day and night. Jesus often discussed hell in terms of Gehenna [see St. Matthew 5:22]. Therefore, a better translation would be that "the gates of Hades" shall not prevail against it. To the Jew of Jesus' day, the gates of Hades would have been understood to mean death, the grave. Jesus was saying was that He would establish His church and that they should not fear that His death would negate His will.

"Thou Art Peter"

With regard to the Roman Catholic tradition of papal succession, there simply is no support for such a claim in the Roman Catholic Bible. Moreover, it is worthy of note that none of the early Christian leaders including Origen (185-254), Cyprian (200-258), Hilary (315-367), Cyril (315-387), Ambrose (340-397), Jerome (347-420), and Augustine (354-430) applied, "Thou art Peter" to anyone but St. Peter. Thus, there is no support outside that *fabricated* by later popes (false decretals) for the claim of papal succession.[48] As noted earlier, the title, "pope," which means "father" or "papa," was used during the 3rd and 4th centuries to refer to numerous bishops (pastors). The first bishop of Rome to claim the title exclusively for himself was Pope Leo I (440-461). Forty-five previous bishops of Rome had not claimed papal succession or infallibility. Leo proclaimed himself "Lord of the whole Church" and announced that resistance to his decree was a sure path to hell.[49] While Leo claimed to be the first infallible head of the Roman Church and others followed in his footsteps, the claim of infallibility did not become Church doctrine until more than 200 popes later in 1870, some five years after the conclusion of the civil war in the U.S. Moreover, contentions within the Church regarding the claim resulted in a schism in 1871 when "Old Catholics" broke away. While the Catholic Church claims the Scripture is the source of papal infallibility, history records otherwise. Of the 1050 eligible bishops, only around 800 attended the First Vatican Council. There was much disagreement among participants over the justification for infallibility. When the issue came to a vote on July 18, 1870 nearly half of the 800 bishops were absent. The vote was 433-2 in favor of *Pastor Aeternus*. Thus, support for papal infallibility came not from Scripture or the divine inspiration of the Holy Spirit, but from a minority of bishops![50]

The Acorn Doesn't Fall Far from the Tree

When the reformers broke away from the Roman Catholic Church, they took with them many of the errors that had crept into the early universal Church established by Constantine and flourished under Romanism. These doctrinal errors blossomed within the Roman Catholic Church. When the Orthodox Church split in 1054, it took with it many of the erroneous teachings of Catholicism. Examples include bowing down before icons; a sacramental salvation system, and a non-belief in the Jesus of the New Testament; inheritance of original sin, including spiritual regeneration by baptism; continuation of divine revelation to Church leaders; and acceptance of the traditions of men. On the other hand, the Orthodox

Churches rejected the concepts of purgatory and indulgences. However, Orthodoxy endorses prayers for the dead:

> But the soul of the deceased is aided by the prayers of the Church, of all those who knew and loved him, and also by acts of charity carried out for his sake. By doing good works for the sake of those who are dead, we are, as it were, completing what they left undone, paying their debts and offering our own sacrifices to the Merciful Lord on their behalf.
> —The Journal of Moscow Patriarchate, No. 10, 1976

The Roman Catholic Church teaches that the faithful must make up by good works and suffering in purgatory where Jesus' sacrifice on the cross was deficient. Orthodoxy teaches that the Lord does permit those with balances owed into the kingdom based on the idea that their loved ones remaining on earth, in concert with the Church, will "complete what they, the deceased, left undone" by "good works." However, as has been made clear from God's Word, one cannot save himself through "good works." Therefore, it is not scripturally plausible that one's "good works" could contribute to someone else's salvation! While the section titled, "Introducing the Orthodox Church," in *The Orthodox Study Bible, New Testament and Psalms* maintains that the Orthodox Church is the only true Church, true to the teachings of Jesus and the apostles, this anti-scriptural teaching alone belies such a claim. Contrary to the teachings of both Catholicism and Orthodoxy, nowhere is it recorded in Scripture that Jesus or the apostles preached that there is a balance due, purgatory, prayers for the dead, or that anyone enters into the kingdom by anything other than the grace of God received personally through faith in Jesus' atoning death [see Acts 4:12].

The Catholic Church's Justification for Prayers to the Dead

Praying to the dead is based on the idea that Scriptures support intercessory prayer. The Church's position is articulated by Father Stravinskas:

> 18. *Why do Catholics pray to the saints, when the Bible tells us Jesus is the sole mediator between God and man?*
>
> Catholics agree that Jesus is the sole mediator... but that belief in no way makes prayer to the saints useless or wrong.
>
> Many times one finds the New Testament recommending intercessory prayer [see Colossians 1:9; 2 Thessalonians 1:11; 3:1; James 5:16], and very few Christians seem to have a problem with seeking the prayers of

a fellow believer. A difficulty appears to emerge only when that believer
has left the earth....[51]

Not a single scriptural reference cited by Father Stravinskas involves the
dead. Moreover, none involves the prayers of those in purgatory for those
still in the body (on this earth). The Father is correct in that the Scriptures
do teach the value of intercessory prayer. Galatians 6:2 exhorts believers to,
"Bear one another's burdens...." Therefore, most churches pray together
congregationally. In many churches, each member has a prayer partner.
There are also prayer "warriors." All are among the living, however. Father
Stravinskas is correct when he states that a difficulty emerges when the
recipient of that prayer has left the earth. In other words, the one whose help
is being sought is dead. The reason Father Stravinskas does not cite a single
verse of Scripture supporting intercessory prayer to or for the deceased is
because there is none. Moreover, the Old Testament condemns any attempt
to communicate with the dead for any reason, as was explained in chapter
two [see Isaias 8:19]. Further, since the Catholic Church teaches that no
one can know if *he* is saved, then how can one know that *someone else* is
in purgatory, which would mean, according to Catholic teaching, that he
is *saved* but not yet with Christ in heaven? According to the Church, the
answer is that he cannot! And Father Stravinskas confirms in his book that
Church teaching is that no one can know whether or not he is saved. So is
it possible that one praying to the dead is actually praying to someone in
hell? The answer has to be yes!

There is a very practical problem with prayers to the dead. Can God hear
and answer the prayers of three people at the same time from three different
continents? Yes. Why? Because He is omnipresent and omnipotent, that
is, He is everywhere at the same time and all powerful. If three people are
praying to the Virgin Mary at the same time on three different continents,
what attributes would she need to hear and answer them? She would need
to be omnipresent and omnipotent. But these are the attributes of God.
Therefore, for Mary or any dead saint to hear and answer the prayers of
the living, he or she would have to be a god. St. Aquinas taught that, "The
only-begotten Son of God, wanting to make us sharers in his divinity,
assumed our nature, so that he, made man, might make men gods." Also, St.
Athanasius taught that, "For the Son of God became man so that we might
become God." As mentioned earlier, both of these teachings are endorsed in
paragraph 460 of the Catechism of the Catholic Church. Thus, the reason
Mary can hear such prayers is because she has been made a goddess! And
"The Litany of Our Lady" is proof that the Church has raised Mary to the
level of God and Christ. She is referred to among other things as: the Ark

of the Covenant [see Numbers 10:33]; Gate of Heaven [see Genesis 28:17]; Morning star [Jesus claimed this title, see Apocalypse 22:16]; Refuge of sinners [see Jeremias 16:19]; and Comforter [the Holy Spirit claims this title, see St. John 14:26 KJV, Catholic Bible refers to the Comforter as the Advocate]. For Mary to be the ark of the covenant, the gate of heaven, or the refuge of sinners, she would have had to have preexisted prior to her physical birth! The "Hail, Holy Queen" refers to Mary as our "hope." Yet, this is the way St. Paul refers to Jesus [see 1 Timothy 1:1]. The Church also refers to her as our "Advocate." St. John identifies Jesus as our Advocate [see 1 St. John 2:1]. A deceased saint can hear and answer prayers only if he or she has been made a god!

As St. Paul was facing death, he said:

> "... I am innocent of the blood of all (*men*); for I have not shrunk from declaring to you the whole counsel of God... that for three years night and day I did not cease with tears to admonish (*warn*) every one of you (*to accept Jesus as Lord and Savior or else face the fires of hell*)."
> —Acts 20:31

St. Paul declared that he held nothing back but declared "the whole counsel of God." If believers at the time of St. Paul subscribed to prayers to the dead, as the Roman Catholic Church insists, one has to wonder why St. Paul, who said he pleaded with even "tears," didn't instruct believers on the utility of praying to him and the other apostles after their deaths. Not a single verse in the New Testament directs believers to pray to the dead—not a single one! St. Peter did not suggest that anyone pray to the dead. Neither did St. John, St. James, or St. Jude seek prayers from the living after their deaths. In fact, no New Testament saint suggested that anyone pray to anyone other than the living God. As pointed out in chapter two, God condemns such abominations. Believers share in Jesus' inheritance, not His divinity, as the Catholic Church and the Latter-Day Saints teach. Thus, the dead cannot even hear the prayers of the living, let alone answer them. An often overlooked aspect of this pagan practice is that there are those *who can answer* the living on behalf of the dead. Demons. While a demon cannot read your mind, he can see in front of whose icon you kneel to pray. And if permitted by the providential will of God, the demon may be allowed to answer your prayer. This will reinforce your belief that the one whom the icon represents has heard and answered your prayer. It also glorifies one of God's creatures rather than God. This is why prayers to the dead, rather than to the living God, are an abomination to Him:

For they have not received the love of truth that they might be saved.
Therefore God sends them a misleading influence (*strong delusion*) that
they may believe falsehood, that all may be judged who have not believed
the truth, but have preferred wickedness.

—2 Thessalonians 2:9-12

The Catholic Church would have one believe that the authors of the
New Testament who warned believers to stay away from idols in their
writings went home at night and knelt before them to pray [see Acts 15:20,
15:29; 1 Corinthians 10:14, 10:28, 12:2; 2 Corinthians 2:16; Galatians 5:20;
1 Thessalonians 1:9; 1 St. John 5:21; and Apocalypse 9:20]. If you pray to
the dead, expect an answer. But it won't be from God!

The Catholic Church's Justification for Purgatory

The Catholic Church claims that its teaching on purgatory is based
on Scripture, specifically, the apocryphal book of 2 Machabees. A story is
recorded in 12:39-46. After fighting against an enemy, Judas Machabees
returns later with his army to:

> ... take away the bodies of them that were slain... And they (*Judas and
> his men*) found under the coats of the slain some of the donaries of the
> idols of Jamnia (*scapulas or talismans to the god Jamnia*), which the law
> (*Jewish law*) forbiddeth to the Jews (*idolatry*): so that *all* plainly saw, that
> for this cause (*for wearing medallions to a false god*) they were slain (*it
> was God's will that they be slain*)... And making a gathering (*taking up a
> collection*), he sent twelve thousand drachmas of silver to Jerusalem for
> (*animal*) sacrifice to be offered for the sins of the dead... It is therefore
> a holy and wholesome thought to pray for the dead, that they may be
> loosed from sins.

After Judas' friends were slain in battle according to the providential will
of God because they were wearing medallions to a false god (for this cause
they were slain), a sin which Judas knew to be an abomination before the
Lord, Judas took up a collection and sent it back to Jerusalem for animal
sacrifices in the Temple, so that the souls of his friends might be saved after
all. Then he concludes that it is a good thing to pray for the dead.

As discussed in chapter one, neither the Hebrew Bible nor the writings
of the Jews considered the apocryphal books to be inspired. They considered
them to be heretical. In fact, it is stated in 1 Machabees 9:27 that there
was not a prophet in Israel at that time. Who wrote the Old Testament?
Only the prophets! Thus, without a prophet, the book could not possibly

be the inspired Word of God. The author of Macabees doesn't claim that his writing is inspired. Moreover, he asks the reader's forgiveness for any included errors:

> So these things being done with relation to Nicanor, and from that time the city being possessed by the Hebrews, I also will here make an end of my narration. Which if I have done well, and as it becometh the history, it is what I desired: but if not so perfectly , it must be pardoned me. For as it is hurtful to drink always wine, or always water, but pleasant to use sometimes the one, and sometimes the other: so if the speech be always nicely framed, it will not be grateful to the readers. But here it shall be ended.
>
> —2 Macabees 15:38-40

There is no provision in the Mosaic law to atone for the sins of the deceased. Thus, Judas' writings do not represent the mind of God and are, in fact, contradictory to His Law contained in His Word. Moreover, the Catholic Church would be hard pressed to make a case for purgatory consistent with its teaching based on these verses. The Church teaches that worshiping a false god—breaking the first commandment—is a mortal sin. According to Catholic teaching, these men died with mortal sins on their souls. This puts them in hell according to Church doctrine, not purgatory. Thus, there is no support for purgatory found in 2 Machabees unless one perverts both God's truth and Roman Catholic teaching. Another verse used by the Church to support its doctrine on purgatory is 1 Corinthians 3:13:

> the work of each will be made manifest, for the day of the Lord will declare it, since the day is to be revealed in fire. The fire will assay the quality of everyone's work.

Since the Catholic Church teaches a faith-plus-works-based, process-oriented doctrine of salvation, it is not surprising that she ties "work" and "fire" together in the above verse. But is this a good way to interpret Scripture? As stressed throughout this book, the correct meaning of God's Word can be derived only by examining the verse in its context and in the overall context with the remainder of Scriptures. Let's look at this verse in context:

> According to the grace of God which has been given to me, as a wise builder, I laid the foundation, and another builds thereon. But let everyone take care how he builds thereon. For other foundation no one can lay, but that which has been laid, which is Christ Jesus. But if anyone builds upon this foundation, (*with*) gold, silver, precious stones, wood, hay straw–the

work of each will be made manifest, for the day of the Lord will declare
it, since the day is to be revealed in fire. The fire will assay the quality of
everyone's work; if his work abides (*survives*) which he has built thereon,
he will receive reward; if his work burns he will lose his reward, but
himself will be saved, yet so as through fire.

—1 Corinthians 3:10-15

The above verses refer to the Bema judgment. It is clear that St. Paul
is speaking figuratively in this passage. No one can build upon Jesus with
gold, silver, precious stones, or anything else. The foundation laid in the
believer's life is Jesus Christ and His teachings. Every believer will build
upon that foundation. If he builds with his own works, God considers his
works to be of wood, hay, and straw, and they will burn up. He will not
receive rewards. However, if the believer builds with the works prepared by
God [Ephesians 2:10]—gold, silver, and precious stones—his works will
survive and he will receive rewards. Thus, this passage does not support a
doctrine of purgatory.

Some try to argue that St. Paul's discussion of his suffering in Colossians
is, as with suffering in purgatory, making up for where Jesus' suffering on
the cross was insufficient to pay the sin debt in full:

I rejoice now in the suffering I bear for your sake; and what is lacking
in the suffering of Christ I fill up in my flesh for his body, which is the
Church.

—Colossians 1:24

Such an argument is false for a number of reasons. First, note the tense
used: "is lacking." Since Jesus had been not only off the cross but also
risen and ascended by the time St. Paul wrote this, his suffering cannot
be referring to Christ's suffering on the cross. Second, if St. Paul had been
intending to say that Jesus' suffering on the cross was in some way lacking,
he would have said "was" lacking. Thus, St. Paul is talking about something
else. The Greek *thlipsis*, meaning suffering or affliction used here, is not
the word Scripture uses to describe Jesus' suffering on the cross. Rather,
St. Paul is rejoicing that he is fulfilling his mission, namely, bringing the
Good News of Christ resurrected to others, and he views his suffering in a
Roman prison as confirmation of his success. Is St. Paul a masochist? No.
He is glad because he knows, as recorded in 2 Timothy 3:13, "And all who
want to live piously in Christ Jesus will suffer persecution." Therefore, his
circumstances confirm that he is living piously in Christ. Moreover, he
knows he is blessed (happy) for his suffering in spreading the gospel, as
recorded in 1 St. Peter 3:14, "But even if you suffer anything for justice's

sake, blessed are you. So have no fear of their fear and do not be troubled." Many more verses could be cited but these suffice to demonstrate that St. Paul is not speaking of suffering for sin where Christ's atonement was not sufficient. If Jesus' atonement for sin had been anything other than fully sufficient, He could not have called out from the cross, "It is finished." He could not have risen from the dead. He could not have taken His seat at the right hand of the Father. St. Paul is suffering for the spreading of the gospel, not for the sins of the world.

Bad Fruit From the Reformation

Unbiblical teachings rooted in Catholicism carried off by various denominations in the Reformation include the following. Some became state Churches. For example, the Lutherans became The Church of Germany; the Presbyterians became The Church of Scotland; and the Anglicans became The Church of England, although not officially as a result of the Reformation, since their split from Rome had more to do with Henry VIII's marriage plans. This establishment of state Churches was not in accordance with the separation between state and church taught by Jesus [St. Matthew 22:21].

In 1560, the Scottish Parliament abolished the Roman Catholic form of worship. The first general assembly of the Church of Scotland met that December in Edinburgh and established Presbyterian Calvinism as the official religion of Scotland. The Church of Scotland was quick to mimic some of the negative characteristics of its mother. After establishing a Church hierarchy based on an Episcopal system, it published a list of prescribed and proscribed activities. Among those things required was regular church attendance. Failure to tithe was an offense punishable by imprisonment. Church offices were bought through a patronage system that had drifted far from scriptural teaching. The state Church then set about the task of routing the Catholics. The Church intimidated state officials in order to accomplish Church objectives. Before many years, the fear associated with Catholic oppression was replaced by Church of Scotland oppression. As the tasks placed on the faithful grew more and more onerous and the worldliness of Church officials became more and more egregious, the spirit of rebellion came to a boil. A series of reformations took place in the 17th and 18th centuries resulting in the creation of the Reformed Presbyterian Church of Scotland and the Associate Presbytery. As noted British historian Lord Acton (1834-1902) would later warn, "Power tends to corrupt; absolute power corrupts absolutely." Acton's warning was directed at the idea of papal infallibility.

Whereas St. Peter tells believers to walk in Jesus' footsteps [see 1 St. Peter 2:21], the Church of Scotland followed in her mother's footsteps. Whereas the mother had persecuted believers after labeling them heretics, the daughter labeled the former persecutors heretics and persecuted them [see Galatians 6:8]. The Church of Scotland, like her mother, labeled herself the only true Church and claimed only she had authority to interpret Scripture. As with her mother's abuses, she allowed them to get so out of hand that reformation was only a matter of time.

Today, there is little interest among most Scotsmen in the hereafter. They've had a warring history of too much of the here-and-now. Most people are familiar with the fact that Christian churches send missionaries to exotic parts of the world where the gospel has seldom, if ever, been heard. However, most probably are not aware that such missionaries are also sent to Scotland because large segments of the population have never heard the true gospel. They have never heard of the Jesus of the New Testament, the Christ.

Other churches coming out of the Reformation established hierarchical church governments where the head of one local church ruled over the heads of other local churches, much like the condemned Nicolaites [see Apocalypse 2:6 and 2:15-16]. Others carried over aspects of a sacramental, grace-bestowing system of salvation that relied, at least to some degree, on works. Thus, the errors inculcated into the Roman Catholic Church from the pagan universal Church established by Emperor Constantine spread like leaven among the Orthodox Churches, the Anglican Church, and most Protestant denominations. Perhaps one of the more surprising characteristics to be carried away from Catholicism was the tendency to persecute those who were not adherents to *their* beliefs, as seen in the case of the Church of Scotland. Thus, these state Churches are found persecuting independent, fundamentalist, Bible-believing New Testament churches, including the Anabaptists, just as, first, the universal Church, and later, the Roman Church, and, finally, the Roman Catholic Church, had taught them. Each reproduces after its own kind [see Genesis 1:24-25].

The Pure and Spotless Bride of Christ

The universal Church had evolved into the Roman Catholic Church by the middle of the 5th century. It was created by the fusion of pagan religions with apostate and true churches following the first schism in 251 A.D. Rather than confining its activities to the execution of God's law, the Catholic Church turned legislative, disposing of certain of God's laws for convenience and creating new ones to satisfy her pecuniary needs. This is what Jesus condemned the Pharisees for having done. Through their false teachings, they had made void the Word of God. Whereas Jesus had said that He chose His followers *out of* the world and that the world would *hate* them, just as the world *hated* Him [see St. John 15:18-21], only several hundred years later the Catholic Church was exerting control *over* the world and its rulers. Rather than being a persecuted Church, the Roman Catholic Church was the persecutor of true Christians. Jesus taught that those who lived by the sword would die by the sword [St. Matthew 26:52]. He preached that those who *were persecuted* for righteousness sake were blessed [St. Matthew 5:10]. The Roman Catholic Church passed out indulgences to bless those *who persecuted* Christians and Jews during the Inquisition. God's Word tells us that friendship with the world is enmity with God and that whoever wants to be a friend to the world becomes an enemy of God [see St. James 4:4]. The Catholic Church brokered power to the world's leaders. St. Peter warns us of corruption in the world [2 St. Peter 1:4]. History records that many of the popes descended to new levels of corruption and depravity. St. John warns us not to love the world or the things of the world and tells us if we do, the love of the Father is not in us [1 St. John 2:15-16]. The popes and the Vatican collected more worldly treasures than the combined riches of all the world's moguls at any time. St. John also tells us that whoever is born of God overcomes the world [1 St. John 5:5]. The popes ruled the world through their accumulated wealth and power and manipulated those who believed the pope could determine their eternal destinies by excommunication. This is witchcraft! With its bloody history, the Roman Catholic Church can hardly be identified as the pure and spotless bride of Christ [see Ephesians 5:27].

Who Can Be Saved?

With this background, one might ask, "Is it possible for a Catholic to be saved?" To put this question in context, one should ask, "Is it possible for a Catholic, or a Baptist, or a Presbyterian, or a Lutheran, or a Methodist, or an Orthodox, or a Hindu to be saved?" Happily, the answer is "yes." How for each? Same for all—by the grace of God, not one thing less, not one thing more [Ephesians 2:8].

Chapter three discussed what one must believe and do to be saved. The five things to be believed and the one thing to do to obtain eternal life are the same for all. While some denominations teach a soteriology different from that taught by Jesus and His disciples and recorded in Scripture, many sitting in the pews on the Lord's day do not know what their church teaches. But by some means the Holy Spirit has gotten the gospel to them and opened their eyes and ears. They believe in the Jesus of the Scriptures; that Jesus paid their sin debt in full at Calvary; and they have asked Him to come into their lives and be their Lord and Savior. God reaches even into false religions to save those who are willing to say, "Yes, Lord." To deny this would be to deny God's providential sovereignty. It should be understood that false religions are dead and a dead faith cannot regenerate a dead spirit. Only the power of the Holy Spirit can do so. However, one cannot accept God's free offer of salvation through faith and at the same time hold to a false soteriology taught by a false Church. A believer who stays in a church that preaches a false gospel cannot grow spiritually, for he is not being fed the true bread of life. If he picks up a Bible and starts reading, God will use his new-found spiritual discernment to open his eyes. God communicates with His children through His Word.

Dissension Within the Roman Catholic Church Today

While the Roman Catholic Church may consider its teachings and beliefs to be universal or catholic, they are not universally accepted by Catholic prelates or the faithful. Most are familiar with priests who condone artificial birth control. There are a few priests also, particularly in the West, who teach justification by faith alone, *Solo Fide* [see Ephesians 2:8-10] and the assurance of salvation. These can generally be classified into one of two teachings: liberal Catholicism or evangelical Catholicism.[52]

Liberal Catholicism is a post-Vatican II, progressive Roman Catholicism that to varying degrees rejects the traditional doctrines of the Church. Evangelical Catholicism consists of those who reject the unbiblical teachings of Rome, but remain in their local church to evangelize others to help bring about reform from within.

The official teaching of Rome is that salvation is a process requiring sacraments administered by the Church. Many denominations teach the same heresy. Again, no church or Church ever saved anyone, nor could it. With regard to eternal security, the Church's position, as reiterated at the Council of Trent, is that anyone who says he or she has eternal security is anathematized, condemned to hell, since such a declaration excludes one from the Church and her sacraments. Thus, in today's Catholicism, St. Peter, St. Paul, and St. Jude would be condemned to hell by Rome! These were certain of their salvation as revealed in 1 St. Peter 5:1, 2 Timothy 4:6-9, and St. Jude 3 and discussed in chapter four. Moreover, Rome teaches that if one has ever heard of the Roman Catholic Church, one must be a member and *stay a member* to have any possibility of being saved. [53] Contrary to this official teaching, however, the Catholic Church decided to end its efforts to convert Jews several years ago, as reported in the *Las Vegas Review Journal*, August 18, 2002. The Church has reversed its earlier position, held for some fifteen hundred years, and now concluded that the Jews are saved under the old covenant and therefore there is no need for them to accept Jesus Christ as their Messiah. This is yet another manmade teaching contrary to the teaching found in the Roman Catholic Bible. Jesus' teaching on salvation is clear: "I am the way, and the truth, and the life. *No one* comes to the Father but through me" [St. John 14:6]. This would include the Jews. Jesus said: "... I was not sent except to *the lost sheep of the house of Israel*" [St. Matthew 15:24]. In His final commission to His disciples, Jesus said: "... and you shall be witnesses for me in Jerusalem and in all Judea (*the southern kingdom of Israel*) and Samaria (*the northern kingdom of Israel*) and even to the very ends of the earth" [Acts 1:8]. Jesus clearly taught that the Jews needed to come into the new covenant *in His blood* to be saved.

While the Catholic Church insists that it opposes abortion, many Catholics disagree with their Church's position. Moreover, many Catholics in the U.S. House and Senate also disagree. On March 1, 2006 a group of Catholic Democrats in Congress released a "Statement of Principles" defending their pro-abortion voting records. These Catholic senators and representatives claim that they personally oppose abortion, but that they must lay aside their personal convictions when they vote. The margin on abortion votes is slim. Without the Catholic vote, pro-abortion bills would not pass. The Catholic Church could end abortion in the U.S. by telling Catholic congressmen that they will be excommunicated if they continue to vote in favor of abortion. As mentioned earlier in this chapter, Pope Pius IX (1846-1878) decreed that those involved in abortion were worthy of excommunication.

Faith and Works

The Roman Catholic Church is not the only Church to teach that salvation comes through a sacramental system beginning with baptism and that eternal life is gained and lost over and over again because of one's works, or failure to perform them. Thus, there is no assurance of salvation. Many of these errant churches adopt this position because they misinterpret Philippians 2:12:

> ... work *out* your salvation with fear and trembling.

The meaning of this isolated verse has been perverted by some to justify a works-based theology foreign to the doctrine of salvation taught by Jesus and His disciples and documented in the New Testament. Some misquote it as "work *for* your salvation with fear and trembling." Father Stravinskas uses this verse to argue that one cannot be certain of his salvation. He suggests that St. Paul believed that one could not know of his salvation and cites 1 Corinthians 10:12 as proof.[54]

> Therefore let him who thinks he stands take heed lest he fall.

However, the contexts from which the two cited verses are taken make it clear that the subject is the Christian walk, not salvation. We know the individuals to whom St. Paul is speaking are saved in both instances by the context:

> Wherefore, my beloved, *obedient* as you have always been,… work out your salvation with fear and trembling For it is God who of his good pleasure works in you both the will and the performance.
> —Philippians 2:12-13

Only believers are called "obedient." Moreover, God does not work His will and His performance in the unsaved. Ephesians 2:8-10 reinforces the message that only the saved can walk in His will and perform His works. St. Paul explains the reason why one should work out his or her salvation in fear and trembling:

> For it is God who of his good pleasure *works in you* both the will (*faith*) and the performance (*good works*). Do all things without murmuring and without questioning (*as directed by the Holy Spirit*), so as to be blameless and guileless, children of God without blemish in the midst of a depraved and perverse generation. For among these you shine like stars….
> —Philippians 2:13-15

St. Paul identifies the ones who are to "work out their salvation in fear and trembling" as those who are saved and already in possession of eternal life, those who have "*passed from death to life*" [see St. John 5:24]. St. Paul again refers to those who are working out their salvation as "children of God" [verse 15]. Thus, it is clear that achieving salvation is not the subject of Philippians 2:12.

In order to hear God's message, we must turn off the things of this world, crucify our flesh [Galatians 5:24-26] to those things which call to it at the expense of the spirit, which drown out God's voice which is like the "whistling of a gentle air," [3 Kings 19:12], and be ever-concerned (fear and trembling) that we are walking in the works *He prepared for us* rather than *in our own works*. St. Paul tells us that when we walk in His works, we shine like stars [see Daniel 12:3]. What do stars do when they shine? They reflect the glory of God [1 Corinthians 15:41]. St. Paul also tells us that if we listen for God's direction in our Christian walk and are obedient to His will, at the end of life we will not feel as though our lives and labors have been in vain. St. Paul is revealing a deeply personal experience in this teaching. God told him to preach to the Gentiles. However, St. Paul wanted to walk in his own works. He wanted to preach to his fellow Jews. He boldly opposed God's will and preached in Jerusalem. Prior to this, St. Paul had made many Gentile converts. However, in Jerusalem he made none. God had to rescue him before the Jews could kill him. St. Paul is simply warning believers to walk not in their own but in God's will.

With regard to the context of 1 Corinthians 10:12, "Therefore let him who thinks he stands take heed lest he fall," again, the subject is not salvation. The next verse goes on to comfort believers:

> May no temptation take hold of you but such as man is equal to. God is faithful and will not permit you to be tempted beyond your strength, but with the temptation will also give you a way out that you may be able to bear it.
>
> —1 Corinthians 10:13

The unsaved not only have no assurance from God that they will not be overtaken by temptation but, in fact, are told that they will be. The promise of escape is only for believers, and then only if the believer is walking in God's will (confessing his sins, praying, and reading the Bible daily). The sentiment expressed in the above verse is the same expressed by St. Paul in Romans 12:3:

> By the grace that has been given to me, I say to each one among you: let no one rate himself more (*highly in his ability to defeat temptation*) than he ought, but let him rate himself according to moderation, and according as God has apportioned to each one the measure of faith.

Those who have no assurance of salvation typically do not follow the Lord's command to be witnesses for Him. If one believes what the Catholic Church teaches, then there is no good news. The best one could do is tell someone that if he places his faith in the Catholic Church, attends Mass regularly, performs enough good works, receives the sacraments, confesses his sins to a priest and performs the required penance, and dies in a state of grace, he will suffer in Purgatory for an indeterminate period and eventually get to heaven. However, if he dies with a mortal sin on his soul, he will go to hell despite all his good works. This is not the good news of the gospel! The good news is:

> ... *Christ died for our sins* according to the Scriptures, and that he was buried, and that he rose again the third day, according to the Scriptures.
>   —1 Corinthians 15:3-4

Put On the Whole Armor of God

Both citations in the previous section encourage the believer to be strong in resisting temptation. But they caution that no one should get a "big head" concerning *his own strength*. St. Jude gives a powerful example in St. Jude 9:

> Yet when Michael the archangel was fiercely disputing with the devil about the body of Moses (*the two were struggling for possession of Moses' body after his death*), he did not venture to bring against him an accusation of blasphemy, but said, "May the Lord rebuke thee."

If Michael, an archangel and one who is much more powerful than we, did not resist Satan in his own strength, then we should understand that we cannot resist Satan in our fleshly strength. As the well-known and oft-sung standard, *Stand Up, Stand Up for Jesus*, written by George Duffield and Adam Geibel, tells us, "The arm of flesh will fail you, Ye dare not trust your own." How can *we* be strong in *our* resistance? *We can't.* However, God's Word tells us:

> ... be strong *in the Lord* and in the *power of his might.* Put on the whole armor of God, that you may be able to stand against the wiles of the devil. For we do not wrestle against flesh and blood, but against principalities, against powers, against the rulers of the darkness of this age, against spiritual hosts of wickedness in the heavenly places.
>   —Ephesians 6:10-12 NKJV

How strong is the "power of His might"?

> ... and what is the exceeding greatness of His power toward us who believe, according to the working of His mighty power which He worked in Christ when He raised Him from the dead and seated Him at His right hand in the heavenly places, far above all principality (*principality is the highest tier of spiritual power*) and power and might and dominion, and every name that is named, not only in this age but also in that which is to come. And He put all things under His feet, and gave Him to be head

over all things to the church, which is His body, the fullness of Him who
fills all in all.

—Ephesians 1:19-23 NKJV

In the power of His might, God the Father raised Jesus from the dead;
seated Jesus at His right hand; placed all things in the spiritual realm under
Jesus, including the kingdom of God; and made Jesus all in all! In that
same power He also:

"... made us worthy to share (*partake in the inheritance of*) the lot of
the saints in light. He has rescued us from the power of darkness and
transferred us into the kingdom of his beloved Son, in whom we have
our redemption, the remission of our sins."

—Colossians 1:12-14

St. Paul reveals in Ephesians 6:12 that our fight is not with flesh and
blood. The devil only makes it *appear* that way. We are to walk by faith, *not
by sight* [2 Corinthians 5:7]. St. Paul tells us why many are in darkness:

... our gospel is veiled only to those who are perishing. In their case, the
god of this world (*Satan*) has blinded their unbelieving minds, that they
should not see the light of the gospel of the glory of Christ, who is the
image of God.

—2 Corinthians 4:3-4

If one understands these verses, it is clear who the enemy is. Believers
have been rescued from the power of darkness. It is even clearer that
threatening the unbeliever with the sword to force his conversion, as was
done during the Inquisition and Crusades, is futile. One can scream at a
blind man in an attempt to force him to describe the scene which surrounds
him. One can even threaten his family and their lives. However, even with
the knife to his throat, a blind man cannot tell you what color your coat
is.

In our flesh we cannot stand against the attacks of the devil. We stand
only in His strength. Therefore, we should not get a "big head" as St.
Paul warns in Romans 12:3 and 1 Corinthians 10:12. St. Peter gives us an
excellent example of what can happen when, with all good intentions, we
try to be strong in our own strength:

And he began to teach them that the Son of Man must suffer many things,
and be rejected by the elders and the chief priests and Scribes, and be put
to death, and after three days rise again. And what he said he spoke openly.
And Peter taking him aside, began to chide (*rebuke*) him. But he, turning

and seeing his disciples, rebuked Peter, saying, "Get behind me, Satan, for thou dost not mind the things of God, but those of men."

—St. Mark 8:31-33

St. Peter, with only the best of intentions, stood in *his own* strength. This allowed Satan to whisper in his ear. Jesus knew the source. That is why He directed His rebuke to Satan, rather than St. Peter.

We must put on spiritual armor to withstand spiritual attacks, as described in Ephesians 6:14-18: the girdle of truth; the breastplate of righteousness; the shoes of the gospel of peace; the shield of faith to quench all the fiery darts of the wicked one (Satan and his demons); the helmet of salvation; and the sword of the Spirit, which is the Word of God. The battlefield is prayer. Our single offensive weapon is the sword. Not the sword of the Inquisition and Crusades, which ended men's lives, but the sword of Lord, that is, the Word of God, which gives eternal life!

For the word of God is living and efficient and keener (*sharper*) than any two-edged sword, and extending even to the division of soul and spirit, of joints also and of marrow, and a discerner of the thoughts and intentions of the heart.

—Hebrews 4:12

In chapter two we saw how Jesus answered all three of Satan's temptations with the sword of God, citing the Word of God, the Scriptures. This is how we are to be strong, in *His* strength using *His* armor for our defense and *His* sword (the Scriptures) to convert an unbelieving world.

Beginning in Ephesians 4:17 and ending in Ephesians 6:9, St. Paul tells us to change ourselves, to be renewed in the spirit of our minds and to put on the new man and avoid vices. He tells us to walk in love. He advises wives and husbands to be subject to one another. He tells parents how to raise children and children to obey parents. He tells slaves to obey masters as they would obey Christ, with a good heart, not a treacherous tongue. He tells masters to treat slaves kindly and to remember that the slave and the master are the same before the Lord, for God is no respecter of privilege. And how can people achieve such lofty behavior with Satan there to influence their flesh? St. Paul explains how beginning in verse 10, through the power of the Lord and the power of His might, for we cannot behave in such a manner in our own strength. We can apply the same principles today. For example, when the boss gets in your face because a demon is using him, realize that your desire to punch him is normal. In your own strength, that is exactly what you would do. However, a child of God is not to react in the normal way. The believer is to understand that it is the power (Satan) behind the power (boss) that is tempting him. And it doesn't matter whether or not your boss is a Christian. When we fail to humble ourselves before the Lord and instead use our own armor to resist Satan, we fall into Satan's trap and he can use us to hector fellow believers, including spouses.

There Is Laid Up for the Believer a Crown of Justice

As mentioned before, Father Stravinskas' attempt to use St. Paul's words from 1 Corinthians 10:12 to convince us that St. Paul taught that one could not know the certainty of one's salvation is misleading. St. Paul's teaching on the certainty of the believer's salvation was discussed in chapter two. As he was in prison waiting to die, St. Paul, like St. Peter and St. Jude, expressed his belief in the certainty of his salvation:

> As for me, I am already being poured out in sacrifice, and the time of my deliverance is at hand. I have fought the good fight, I have finished the course, I have kept the faith. For the rest (*his eternal destiny*), there is laid up for me a crown of justice (*at the Bema*), which the Lord, the just Judge, will give to me in that day; yet not to me only, but also to those who love his coming.
>
> —2 Timothy 4:6-9

Had St. Paul not believed in the certainty of his eternal destiny, he could not have said:

> For me to live is Christ and to die is gain.
>
> —Philippians 1:21

Even the unsaved understand that it would be better to live than to die and go to hell. The book of James also contains verses whose meanings sometimes are perverted by the legalists of our day (Judaizers of Jesus' day) to justify a works-based or faith-works-based *religion*. First, it should be reiterated that no religion, no religious system, and no Church or church ever saved anyone. All manmade religions represent men's futile attempts to "build up" to God with their works, just as the Babylonians tried and failed [Genesis 11:1-9]. Moreover, God's Word tells us that there is nothing "good" in man whereby he can do good works apart from Christ.

Salvation Is a Gift

Biblical Christianity is the only portrait among a diverse plethora of "religions" that portrays a loving God reaching down in *His* mercy to wicked sinners through *His* grace afforded by the blood atoning death of *His* Son. We were still sinners when we were saved [see Romans 5:8-9]. As St. Paul asked rhetorically: Where is *your* boasting of *your* works by which *you* have obtained *your* salvation? Then he answered simply and without equivocation: **It is excluded** [see Romans 3:27]. These three words are hardly subject to misinterpretation. The portrait of a loving God reaching down to lost mankind is a *gift* of living faith to the believer but *foolishness* to the world [see I Corinthians 1:18-25 and 2:14].

Salvation *Results* in the Performance of Good Works

St. James tells us:

> You see that by works a man is justified, and not by faith only.
> —St. James 2:24

This verse is misinterpreted by the Roman Catholic Church [see *Pillar of Fire, Pillar of Truth* , Catholic Answers, page 22] to read as indicated by the italics used below:

> You *understand* that *by works* a man is justified, *and not by faith* only.

The Catholic Church and its errant offspring place the emphasis on doing *works* to obtain salvation in their interpretation since these Churches look for some scriptural support for their non-scriptural teachings. However, if a man is justified by *works*, what are we to do with St. Paul's teachings?

> For by grace you have been saved through *faith*; and that not from yourselves, for it is the gift of God; *not as the outcome of works*, lest anyone may boast.
> —Ephesians 2:8-9

Also:

> For we reckon that a man is *justified by faith independently of the works of the Law*.
> —Romans 3:28

Are St. James' and St. Paul's teachings on justification and salvation contradictory? No. As discussed earlier, verses should be interpreted within the context in which they appear and examined for consistency with other messages on the same subject discussed throughout the entire Scripture. When this is done, it becomes clear that St. James' message is consistent with that of St. Paul's. St. James is not talking about performing works in the context of being justified (declared not guilty) and obtaining salvation as a result of having been so declared. St. Paul *is!* St. Paul is saying expressly that *salvation does not come from works, but from faith.*

Some teach that salvation is the result of good works. However, the converse is true: good works result from salvation. The Greek word for "see" is *horao.* It means to "stare at." Look at the same citation again, but with an understanding of what he means by "see."

> You *see with your eyes* that by works a man is justified, and not by faith only.
>
> —St. James 2:24

St. James is discussing a "living faith." A living faith produces good works. Without such good works, St. James says, "faith" is dead. Therefore, he concludes, while he cannot *see with his eyes* someone's faith, he can *see with his eyes* someone's good works. And since the good works the believer does were prepared by God beforehand, then seeing someone's good works visually confirms his verbal confession of Jesus as Lord [see Ephesians 2:8-10]. Jesus said we will know the tree by the fruit it produces, not by what kind of tree it professes to be [see St. Matthew 7:17].

Consider Constantine's works versus the secular world's claim that he was the first Christian emperor. St. James certainly would not have concluded that Constantine was a Christian by *seeing* his works, which included multiple murders. There was no "crucifixion of the flesh," no death of the "old man," the sinner. Neither was there a rebirth of a "new man" in Christ demonstrated through the indwelling power of the Holy Spirit. Nevertheless, some argue that while Constantine might not have been a Christian himself, despite his deathbed baptism many years after his alleged conversion, he did stop the persecution of believers, and spread the Christian faith to other parts of the world. However, an examination of history reveals that Constantine temporarily ended persecution of believers by the state, only to restart it after he had created his pagan-filled universal Church. Moreover, the persecutions were expanded under the Roman and, later, the Roman Catholic Church. Those Bible-believing Christians who refused to accept the anti-scriptural teachings of Constantine's universal

Church, then the Roman, and finally the Roman Catholic Church, were labeled heretics and put to the flames, along with their Bibles. The vast majority of those murdered by the universal State-Church were Bible-believing, Bible-preaching Christians who refused to deny their witness for the Christ of the New Testament. What spread from Constantine's "works" and universal Church was not the saving gospel of Jesus the Christ, but a false, legalistic religion similar to that of the Pharisees, which Jesus condemned [see St. Luke 11:52].

St. James asks in 2:14 what profit will it be to a man who "... *says* he has faith but does not have works?" St. James notes that *saying* one has faith does not clothe the naked or feed the hungry [see St. James 2:15-16]. One who professes to have faith but shows no fruit is a liar. Just as the body is dead without a reborn spirit, so faith is dead without accompanying good works [see St. James 2:26]. His epistle addresses the implementation of a living faith which *produces* good works. It must be remembered, however, that the believer must be walking in fellowship with the Lord in order to produce the good works prepared beforehand by the Lord. Things that take us out of fellowship with the Lord, such as living carnal lives [see 1 Corinthians 3:1-4] or carrying unconfessed sin [see 1 St. John 1:9], rob us of His intended works and we are left only with our own pitiful works to perform. Any works other than those *God* wants us to perform are pitiful, no matter how grand they may be in our own eyes or the eyes of the world. King David, a man whom God said was "a man after His own heart" [1 Kings 13:14 and Acts 13:22], wanted to build a mighty temple to the Lord. However, God told David that he was not to, but that his son would build a house to the Lord [1 Paralipomenon 22:6-19]. Certainly king David thought God would be pleased if he built Him a glorious temple. Nevertheless, David followed God's will.

The Jesus of the New Testament

The Roman Catholic Church has insisted that Mary be ever virginal, despite clear contradictions to this teaching provided in the Roman Catholic and all other Bibles [see St. Matthew 13:55; St. Mark 3:31; St. Luke 8:19-21; St. John 2:12; and 7:3-10]. The Church posits that it was the custom of Jews to call cousins and other relatives "brothers or sisters." The veracity of such a statement can be evaluated by simply reading St. Luke 1:36, "And behold, Elizabeth thy kinswoman also has conceived." If the Church's posit were correct, then St. Luke would have referred to Elizabeth as Mary's sister!

One of the barriers to acceptance of Jesus' teaching that all men are "brothers" was Jewish tradition. Tradition taught tribal pride. Family birth records and ancestral trees were meticulously recorded, kept, and guarded in the Temple. While Jesus tried to get men to understand that in God's eyes all were brothers, most resisted this teaching and, in fact, such resistance was what caused St. Peter to remove himself from associating with the Gentiles until St. Paul rebuked him, as discussed earlier. St. Paul exhorts believers to "... avoid foolish controversies and genealogies (*familial identification*)... for they are useless and futile" [Titus 3:9]. Moreover, while some of Jesus' followers sometimes referred to one another as brother, those who referred to Jesus' brothers generally were not believers [see St. Matthew 13:57]. Moreover, if one accepts the thesis that biblical references to Jesus' brothers were actually His disciples, then what are we to do with St. John 2:12?

> After this he went down to Capharnaum, he and his mother, and his brethren, and his disciples....

Before His resurrection, Jesus' brothers rejected His claim to be the Christ, the prophesied Messiah and king of the Jews who would restore Israel to greatness. There likely was more than a little jealousy among brothers, just as there was between Joseph and his brothers who hated him so much that they sold him into slavery [see Genesis 37:5-8]. The "good" advice of Jesus' brothers is recorded in Scripture:

> Now the Jewish feast of the Tabernacles was at hand. His brethren therefore said to him, "Leave here and go into Judea that thy disciples also may see the works that thou dost; for no one does a thing in secret if he wants to be publicly known. If thou dost these things (*miracles*), manifest thyself to the world." For not even his brethren believed in him.
> —St. John 7:2-5

After performing many miracles in Judea and curing a cripple on the Sabbath [St. John 5:8-16], Jesus retreated to Galilee, the area where He had been raised and where His brothers and sisters still lived. The purpose of His retreat was not fear, though the Jews sought to kill Him. Rather, His time had not yet come to manifest Himself to the world. However, His brothers advised Him to go and "show off His powers" in Judea under the guise that the world cannot accept what it does not see. It was only after His resurrection that Jesus' brothers recognized Him as Lord. In the salutation of St. Jude's epistle (Judas in English), he refers to himself as "the servant of Jesus Christ and the brother of James." St. Jude, like St. James, was another of Jesus' brothers.

Finally, if Jesus had no brothers and sisters, how are we to interpret His words in St. Matthew 13:57? "… But Jesus said to them, 'A prophet is not without honor except in his own country, and in his own house." If Jesus had no siblings, then who in His house held Him without honor, Joseph or Mary?

More Changes Ahead for the Roman Catholic Church?

There are those within the Roman Catholic Church still calling for reform. Many of the reforms being sought, however, go not only against Roman Catholic traditions but, unfortunately, against the Scriptures as well. It is not likely that Pope Benedict XVI will admit women to the priesthood. The Church now admits men independent of sexual orientation, since both heterosexuals and homosexuals are supposed to lead chaste lives. The notion of a universal or Catholic Church under centralized Vatican control is losing ground each day. Priests in some parishes throughout the Western Rite are returning to Scripture for their sermons. Prelates are deserting the Church in record numbers. Moreover, fewer and fewer young men are entering the vocation. More and more of the "faithful" are leaving the Church with each new sexual abuse scandal revealed.

I escorted my father to Mass during one of his visits to my home in Las Vegas several years ago [see Deuteronomy 5:16]. The priest preached on St. John 10, the Good Shepherd. To my surprise, he seemed to be giving an exegesis, although a little garbled, I would expect to hear only from a fundamentalist, Bible-believing Christian. He talked about Jesus *not being a martyr* [see St. John 10:17-18]. The traditional Catholic teaching is that Jesus' life *was taken from Him*, that He was a *martyr and a victim*.[55] As recently as fifty years ago, Catholic hierarchy still referred to the "perfidious Jews" who murdered Jesus. They called them "Christ killers."

The priest also talked about Jesus *giving His sheep eternal life* and how Jesus said *no one could snatch them out of His hand or the Father's hand* [see St. John 10:28-29]. As we exited the church, I mentioned to the priest that he sounded more like a Christian than a Catholic. He looked at me warmly and said, "Jesus was a Christian, not a Catholic." Following up with the priest, however, my hopes were dashed. "Jesus' death on the cross was necessary," he explained. "Jesus did His part. Now it's up to each of us to do ours."

I asked a practicing Catholic friend, one of the old-fashioned kind
who still believes in a sacramental salvation system, the infallibility of
popes, praying the rosary for those in purgatory, and asking the dead for
help in this life, to explain the contradiction between some popes putting
the "perfidious Jews" to the sword during the infamous auto-da-fé (acts of
faith) of the Spanish Inquisition and Pope John Paul II referring to them
in an avuncular manner as "older brothers" and apologizing for past "sins
of the Catholic Church."

"What contradiction?" he asked wearing a puzzled look. "The Holy
Spirit led past popes to convert the Jews under pain of torture and Pope
John Paul to apologize for those actions," he replied without a hint of
discomfort. "Where's the contradiction?" he asked. "They all followed the
leading of the Holy Spirit."

The late Pope John Paul II surprised many in December of 2000 when
he joined pop-singer Madonna and others in proclaiming that belief in Jesus
Christ is not necessary for salvation. According to a December 9, 2000 LA
Times story, the pontiff explained that "all who live a just life will be saved,
even if they do not believe in Jesus Christ and the Catholic Church." The
pope made this startling pronouncement before 30,000 pilgrims gathered
in St. Peter's Square. This position stands in opposition to current Church
teaching (see paragraph 846 in the Catechism of the Catholic Church).
Moreover, John Paul's statement contradicts a previous September 5, 2000
declaration, Dominus Iesus, issued by the Vatican's Congregation for the
Doctrine of the Faith, previously known as The Inquisition. That declaration
addressed many of the "errors" resulting from the Second Vatican Council
(1962-1965) that modernized the Church. The declaration affirmed that the
Roman Catholic Church is the only true Church, apart from the Catholic
Church there is no salvation, and that other denominations are illegitimate.
The 2000 declaration, ignored by John Paul, was written by Cardinal Joseph
Ratzinger. The declaration was re-released on July 10, 2007 by Pope Benedict
XVI, the former Cardinal Ratzinger. Among other changes, Pope Benedict
intends to bring back the Latin Mass.

Chapter 6

FOR OUR SAKES HE MADE HIM TO BE SIN WHO KNEW NOTHING OF SIN

THE TITLE OF this chapter is taken from 2 Corinthians 5:21:

For our sakes he (*God the Father*) made him (*Jesus*) to be sin who knew nothing of sin, so that in him we might become the justice (*declared righteous*) of God.

The concept of justification used in Scripture is a legal declaration by God that a man is not guilty. It is not a pardon. A pardon admits guilt but remits the associated punishment. Most know of criminal trials where the accused was guilty. However, due to any number of extenuating circumstances, the court declared the defendant "not guilty." This legal declaration is analogous to God's declaration that the believer is not only not guilty, but that he is "righteous." The believer's extenuating circumstance is that he has admitted his guilt and accepted another's payment for his sins. When God looks at the believer, He sees not a creature clothed in sin, but His child arrayed in the imputed righteousness of the Jesus of the New Testament. One can be declared righteous by God only by the shed blood of Jesus at Calvary—the most unique and singularly unselfish act of love man has ever known. There is no other way.

Satan Mocks God

Satan is jealous of God. He mimics God. Just as God spoke to Adam and Eve in the Garden, Satan deceived Eve in the Garden. Jesus said, "... I am the light of the world" [St. John 9:5]. Satan disguises himself as an angel of light [2 Corinthians 11:14]. God sent His anointed One to earth [St. John 3:16-17]. Satan will send his son, the Antichrist [Apocalypse 6:2]. The Antichrist will come on a white horse and offer a false peace

[Apocalypse 6:2]. Jesus will come on a white horse with a peace the world has never known [Apocalypse 19:11]. Jesus is the lion of the tribe of Judah [Apocalypse 5:5]. Satan goes about as a roaring lion, seeking whom he can devour [1 St. Peter 5:8].

Satan Uses Men to Mock The Christ

Some deny they are sinners. Others believe they can atone for their sins in their own way. They refuse to accept the righteousness offered by God as a free gift through faith in Jesus' atoning death on the cross. Every year around the time the world calls Easter, the media carry stories of Roman Catholic men in predominantly Catholic countries who have themselves affixed to crosses for several hours on what the Church calls Good Friday. They tell the media they want to "imitate" Christ's suffering. Most are secured with tape or rope. However, a few use nails. San Fernando, in the Philippines, is renowned for such crucifixions. Volunteers are nailed to crosses for several hours to "reenact" the crucifixion.[1] One man has been quoted as saying he doesn't want Jesus to pay his debt. He wants to pay his own.

Many believe incorrectly that the stigmata, the marks and bleeding on a person's body resembling the wounds of Jesus in the crucifixion, date back to the time of the early Christians. However, this is not true. St. Francis of Assisi (1182-1226) displayed the first known case.[2] St. Francis wanted to go farther than those in San Fernando, however. His heart's desire was to be martyred, "like Jesus," and, in fact, he rejoiced upon hearing that five Franciscan friars had been murdered in Morocco.[3] However, martyrdom was not his future. Instead, he became the first stigmatic in 1224 just shortly before his death. Since St. Francis there have been another 400 or so stigmatics, over 100 in the last century, and the number is increasing. All claimed they "shared" Jesus' suffering. Most have been Catholic, with a few Pentecostals in the latter part of the 20th century. All have displayed marks and bleeding from the palms of their hands. This is curious since the Roman practice of crucifixion involved driving spikes through the wrists, not the more fragile palms which would have torn away. This common feature is probably best explained by examining the crucifix which shows nails driven through the palms. Given this discrepancy, one must question the source of this sanguine phenomenon. Is it from the One who cried out from the cross "It is finished"? Or is perhaps this imitation of Jesus' suffering a part of St. Paul's warning concerning the approach of end times?

> And his (the antichrist's) coming is according to the working of Satan with
> all power and signs and lying wonders, and with all wicked deception to

those who are perishing. For they have not received the love of truth that
they might be saved. Therefore God sends them a misleading influence that
they may believe falsehood, that all may be judged who have not believed
the truth, but have preferred wickedness (*unrighteousness*).

—2 Thessalonians 2:9-12

Can Satan cause a stigmata? Yes, in those who have rejected the Jesus
of the New Testament. Neither Catholics nor Pentecostals teach that Jesus
has the authority to do for them what He clearly did for the robber on
the cross: *give eternal life*. If one continues to reject the gospel, the truth,
preferring unrighteousness instead, that is, relying on one's own righteousness rather than the imputed righteousness of the Christ, then God will
send false signs to bolster his false faith in his false works which will lead
to judgment. Notice how God refers to these in the above citation: "those
who are perishing." The judgment referred to is the Great White Throne,
the judgment of the damned. God's children will not be judged. Only
the children of disobedience will stand before the Great White Throne.
By encouraging some to have themselves affixed to crosses and others to
"share" in Jesus' suffering through the stigmata, Satan attempts to show
the world that Jesus' suffering was common, rather than the unique act of
ultimate love for mankind. Moreover, many flock to see these "curiosities"
which edify men, rather than glorify God. Walking submissively in His will
glorifies God [see St. Matthew 5:16].

God tells us in the Old Testament that the sacrifice for sin must be a
lamb without blemish. Jesus was that Lamb. Thus, the Scriptures make
clear that only the blood of Jesus washes away our sins [see Apocalypse 5:6,
and 12]. Therefore, no one can pay his own sin debt since none is without
blemish. All have sinned and are therefore blemished [Romans 3:23]. In
his greetings to the seven churches in the book of Apocalypse, St. John the
revelator includes the following:

... and from Jesus Christ, who is the faithful witness, the firstborn of the
dead, and the ruler of the kings of the earth. To him who has loved us
(*Jesus*), and *washed us from our sins in his own blood*....

—Apocalypse 1:5

It was learned in chapter four that "... without the shedding of blood
there is no forgiveness (*of sins*)" [Hebrews 9:22]. So if one turns away
from the atoning blood of Jesus, where can he turn to obtain forgiveness?
Nowhere.

The King Hosts a Marriage Feast for His Son

Chapter 22 of St. Matthew records the beautiful parable of the marriage feast, as told by Jesus:

> "... The kingdom of heaven is like a king who made a marriage feast for his son. And he sent his servants to call in those invited to the marriage feast, but they would not come. Again he sent out other servants, saying, 'Tell those who are invited, Behold, I have prepared my dinner; my oxen and fatlings are killed, and everything is ready; come to the marriage feast.' But they made light of it, and went off, one to his farm, and another to his business; and the rest laid hold of his servants, treated them shamefully, and killed them. But when the king heard of it, he was angry; and he sent his armies, destroyed those murderers, and burnt their city. Then he said to his servants, 'The marriage feast indeed is ready, but those who were invited were not worthy; go therefore to the crossroads, and invite to the marriage feast whomever you shall find.' And his servants went out into the roads, and gathered all whom they found, both good and bad; and the marriage feast was filled with guests. Now the king went in to see the guests, and he saw there a man who had not on a wedding garment. And he said to him, 'Friend, how (why) didst thou come in here without a wedding garment?' But he was speechless. Then the king said to the attendants, 'Bind his hands and feet and cast him forth into the darkness outside, where there will be the weeping, and the gnashing of teeth.'"
>
> —St. Matthew 22:2-13

The king in this parable is God the Father. The king's son is God's Son, Jesus. The first two invitations were to the nation of Israel. The first invitation was given by John the Baptist. Herod had him killed. The second was extended by Jesus and His disciples. Those who refused the second invitation were too busy tending their farms, businesses, and going about happily in their usual ways. Jesus and His disciples were murdered [see St. Matthew 23:37]. This angered the king so he burned their city and destroyed those who had murdered his servants. The Romans sacked and burned Jerusalem, along with the Temple, in 70 A.D. The king sent his servants a third time but this time into the crossroads to invite whomever they could find. This invitation is made to individual Jews (as opposed to the nation of Israel) and Gentiles and represents the church (*autos*) age. Both the good and the bad were brought in to the feast. The view of those who were good and bad was from the perspective of the servants, not the king.

It was the custom of Eastern kings to provide proper attire for guests at festive occasions. When the king greeted the guests, he noticed one who was not wearing the garment provided by his graciousness. Instead, the man was wearing his own. The man's failure to wear the garment provided was an act of pride [see Sophonias 1:8 (Zephaniah in the KJV)]. When the king questioned the man about this breach of sartorial protocol, the man stood speechless. At that moment, he knew there was no justification for his having turned down the king's free offer. The king's sole criterion for guests attending the feast was not whether the guests were well dressed (good or sinners). The king knew none had such finery as he provided (the righteousness of Jesus). One guest thought *his own* garment (works) was good enough. He mistakenly believed he had no need of the king's free gift. This man was following his own path. However, he paid the price for his willful conduct. This man's philosophy was "my will be done," rather than "the king's will be done." Since this man chose to reject the king's free offer, the king granted the man's wish, but this resulted in his being removed from the marriage feast (the kingdom) and thrown into the darkness outside (hell).

God stopped dealing with Israel as a nation when Messiah was cut off, when Jesus was crucified [see Daniel 9:26]. God's prophetic clock for dealing with the nation of Israel is still stopped. God will again address Israel as a nation after the Rapture, at the end of the church age, during the Tribulation period. The nation of Israel will receive a third invitation to enter into the kingdom. The book of Apocalypse reveals that there will be 144,000 Jews sealed with the Holy Spirit during the Tribulation period, twelve thousand from each of the twelve tribes [see Apocalypse 7:4]. The Tribulation period is the last seven years before Jesus returns to earth to establish His 1,000-year rule on earth. Like all who accept the Jesus of the New Testament as Lord and Savior, these will be witnesses for Him, as will the two Jewish witnesses spoken of in Apocalypse 11:3. Many prophecy scholars believe these two witnesses will be Moses and Elias (spelled Elijah in the KJV). The 144,000 witnesses produce so many converts from every nation, tribe, people, and tongue that no man can number them [see Apocalypse 7:9]. These Tribulation saints are the ones who respond to the third invitation. These are not part of the church general, the bride. They, along with the Old Testament saints, are the invited guests to the marriage feast. Today, God deals with individual Jews in the same way He deals with individual Gentiles: all are called to repentance and acceptance of Jesus as Savior. The Jews returning to Israel today are doing so in unbelief. However, the day is coming when God will breathe His Spirit into them and they shall believe [see Ezechiel 37:14]. The church age will end with the Rapture, prior to the initiation of the seven-year Tribulation period and the sealing of the 144,000.

God Freely Offers Us His Son's Robe of Righteousness

Satan puts into the minds of men that they have no need of God's robe of righteousness provided through the atoning death of His Son on Calvary. Apocalypse 6:11 reveals:

> And there was *given* to each of them a *white* robe.

Note the words carefully. These robes were *given*, not earned. They were *gifts*, not wages. Eternal life is a *gift* from God received through faith, but sin brings a wage—death. Death is something we *earn*! How were these robes made *white*? They were washed white in the red blood of the Lamb [see Apocalypse 7:14]. It is heartbreaking that so many are so easily fooled by Satan. It was Satan's pride that caused his fall and sealed his eternity. It was Adam and Eve's pride that caused them to eat of the forbidden fruit. As a result, their spirits died and they could no longer communicate with their Creator. Another consequence is that their children and all subsequent generations are born dead spiritually. And Satan is still deceiving many today, causing them to rely on their own goodness, their own garments to *earn* eternal life [see Proverbs 16:25].

In his book, cited earlier, Father Stravinskas provides some insights he believes Catholics need to be aware of when talking with fundamentalists, what Father Stravinskas believes to be errors in fundamentalist thinking:

> *Regarding the nature of man: Man is totally corrupt.* Hence there arises the tendency to limit religion to matters of sin and justification: repentance, conversion, making a decision for Christ, bewailing one's sins, condemning as evil what common experience and Catholic doctrine teach to be good.
>
> If this tenet is correct, then what is one to make of such lines in the Scriptures as Psalm 8:5-6? "What is man that you should be mindful of him, or the son of man that you should care for him? You have made him a little less than the angels, and crowned him with glory and honor." The inspired Psalmist clearly held this to be true—even after the Fall.[4]

Several of Father Stravinskas' observations are correct. Although we don't spend time talking about religion, something that has never saved anyone (if it could, Jesus would not have had to go to the cross), we are guilty, by the grace of God, of following our Lord's command to preach His gospel to every creature [see St. Mark 15:16]. In accordance with Scriptures, we also confess our sins directly to God [see 1 St. John 1:9]. Father Stravinskas refers to this as bewailing, which means "expressing sorrow for." To this charge, too, we plead guilty. As believers, we understand that it was *our sins* that nailed Jesus to that cruel cross. With regard to his allegation that we condemn as evil what common experience… teaches to be good, the Father does not provide examples. Certainly if New Testament Christians are doing this, we are guilty of sin, for to call what is good evil is condemned in God's Word, as was discussed in chapter two:

> Woe to you that call evil good, and good evil….
>
> —Isaias 5:20

While Father Stravinskas tells us that common experience and Catholic doctrine teach what is "good," God's Word reveals:

> … *all* that is not from faith is sin.
>
> —Romans 14:23

Thus, fundamentalists use *faith*, that is, the Scripture, rather than common experience and traditions contained in Catholic or other Church doctrine, to determine what is good and what is evil. Our faith tells us that if God's Word calls something evil, then *it is evil*. No experience, Catholic or other Church doctrine, reasoning, reassessment, or rationalization can change that [Malachias 3:6]. With regard to the Father's interpretation of Psalm 8:5-6, that man is not inherently evil, he chose a verse that, if viewed out of context, might impart the notion that man has some inherent good in him. However, as already cautioned against, one must be careful when using a single verse to prove a point. The Father has done exactly this. Moreover, there are a plethora of other verses that contradict Father Stravinskas' thesis. Psalm 52 (53):4 states, "*All* have gone astray; they have become *perverse*; there is *not one who does good, not even one.*" Others include: "as it is written, '*There is not one just man*; there is *none* who understands; *there is none who seeks after God*" [Romans 3:10-11]. Again: "*All* have gone astray together; they have become *worthless*. There is *none* who does good, *not even one*" [Romans 3:12]. The heading over Romans 3:9-18 in the Roman Catholic Bible is: "*The Scriptures Attest Universal Sin.*" And so they do. As a final note on this subject, God's Word reveals:

> How much less man, who is but a maggot, the son of man (*Jesus*), who is only a worm.
>
> —Job 25:6

In the above verse, God's Word refers to man as a "maggot." Maggots are the first-stage offspring of flies. And who is the Lord (Master) of the flies? Baalzebub! [4 Kings 1:2; St. Matthew 10:25; St. Mark 3:22; and St. Luke 11:15] What is being revealed here is that all men are born of their father: Satan. Thus, how could there be any inherent good in a man? The "son of man," in the above verse, refers to Jesus as a worm. Thus, in this single verse, God has described the nature and future of all flesh without the soul-saving power of the Jesus of the New Testament in their lives.

Red dye was made from blood obtained by mashing a certain kind of worm in Old Testament times. It is in this sense that the flesh of the "son of man" is a worm. Jesus shed His blood for all sinners. In Psalm 21 (22), the great revelation that prefigures Jesus' crucifixion, verse 6 confirms: "But I am a worm, not a man; the scorn of men, despised by the people."

Contrary to Father Stravinskas' hypothesis, what David is saying in Psalm 8 is not that man is in any way deserving of God's care, but that God is so majestic in His love and mercy that He is even mindful of undeserving man! David, as one of God's creations, is praising his Creator, not justifying or edifying himself. In fact, Psalm 8 is considered by Bible scholars to be one of the greatest recorded expressions of man's praise for his Creator.

God's truth reveals that men's garments are "filthy rags." You may be the most sartorially resplendent one in your church, but God sees that you are either wearing the imputed righteousness of Jesus and the whiteness of His robes or your own filthy rags, stylish though they may appear to the world. Wearing your own garment is folly [see Proverbs 15:21]. If you are not clothed in His righteousness, then you stand naked indeed and you will be thrown into the darkness of hell.

"They Crucified Him There"

Most people do not begin to understand what Jesus bore for sinners. When one looks at a crucifix, it is no wonder God's Word forbids graven images. Jesus never has been portrayed accurately on the crucifix, nor can the *price* He paid for all mankind, saved and unsaved, ever be comprehended by the limited mind of man. While the crucifix presents a man with a strong jaw and facial features, Isaias 52:14 (NKJV) reveals: "... His visage (*face*) was marred *more than any man*." Moreover, David declared in a future-truth prophecy recorded in Psalms 22:14 (NKJV): "And all My bones are out of joint." Neither of these features is revealed in the crucifix. Moreover, while the Scriptures do not address this point, most students of that period of Roman history believe that those crucified were naked on the cross as a final humiliation. The image on the crucifix is modestly clothed.

After Jesus was delivered into Pilate's hands, the soldiers scourged Him. The Scriptures do not tell us how many stripes Jesus received at the hands of sinners [Isaias 53:5]. Under Jewish law, no more than forty stripes could be given [Deuteronomy 25:2-3]. That's why St. Paul tells us in 2 Corinthians 11:24, "From the Jews five times I received forty lashes less one." It is reasonable to assume that Roman law carried out by battle-hardened Roman soldiers had no such concern. Moreover, the scourge used by the soldiers was a cat-o-nine-tails. Nine leather thongs, each about eighteen inches long, were attached to a wooden handle. At the end of each thong was attached a piece of metal or bone designed to tear away flesh. Thus, the scourging turned Jesus' back into something resembling bloody, raw meat.

The soldiers made a "crown" for Him following the scourging. However, Jesus' crown was made of thorns, possibly from the sharp prongs of the date palm, the same plant that produced the palm branches the people waved upon His triumphal entry into Jerusalem. The soldiers used rods to position it upon His head. The length of the rods provided a safe distance from which the two-inch thorns could be beaten down into His scalp until stopped by the bones of His skull. As the blood from His scalp clotted around the piercing thorns, it anchored the crown in place. They put a cloak of royal color on Him and placed a reed in His hand for a scepter [see Genesis 49:8-10]. The soldiers blindfolded Him and took turns slapping His face and spitting on Him and asking Him to prophesy whom it was that struck the "King of the Jews." While the soldiers were engaged in this torment, the blood and raw flesh on Jesus' back were beginning to clot and stick to the cloak.

The soldiers also pulled out Jesus' beard [Isaias 50:6]. Most adult male Jews had long beards. A beard was a mark of pride in one's heritage. To pull out any part would bring disgrace. His face was now raw, swollen, and bleeding. Prior to leading Him away to Golgotha, they removed the cloak and dressed Jesus in His own clothes. Removing the cloak tore additional flesh from His back and restarted the bleeding. Dressing Him in His own clothes reinitiated clotting. When He was stripped again to be nailed to the cross, more raw flesh was ripped from His back and bleeding was reinitiated [see St. John 19; St. Matthew 27:31; and St. Luke 22:64].

> And when they came to the place called the Skull, they crucified him there,
> and the robbers, one on his right hand and the other on his left.
> —St. Luke 23:33

The words, "they crucified him there," do not begin to tell of the excruciating agony associated with being crucified. Dr. C. Truman Davis, an M.D., provides the following description of a crucifixion from a physiological perspective:

The cross is placed on the ground and the exhausted man is quickly thrown backwards with his shoulders against the wood. The legionnaire feels for the depression at the front of the wrist. He drives a heavy, square, wrought-iron nail through the wrist and deep into the wood. Quickly he moves to the other side and repeats the action, being careful not to pull the arms too tightly, but to allow some flex and movement. The cross is then lifted into place.

The left foot is pushed backward against the right foot, and with both feet extended, toes down, a nail is driven through the arch of each, leaving the knees flexed. The victim is now crucified. As he slowly sags down with more weight on the nails in the wrists, excruciating, fiery pain shoots along the fingers and up the arms to explode in the brain—the nails in the wrists are putting pressure on the median nerves. As he pushes himself upward to avoid his stretching torment, he places the full weight on the nail through his feet. Again he feels the searing agony of the nail tearing through the nerves between the bones of the feet.

As the arms fatigue, cramps sweep through the muscles, knotting them in deep, relentless, throbbing pain. With these cramps comes the inability to push himself upward to breathe. Air can be drawn into the lungs but not exhaled. He fights to raise in order to get even one small breath. Finally carbon dioxide builds up in the lungs and in the blood stream, and the cramps partially subside. Spasmodically he is able to push himself upward to exhale and bring in life-giving oxygen.

Hours of this limitless pain, cycles of twisting, joint-rending cramps, intermittent partial asphyxiation, searing pain as tissue is torn from his lacerated back as he moves up and down against the rough timber. Then another agony begins: a deep, crushing pain deep in the chest as the pericardium slowly fills with serum and begins to compress the heart.

It is now almost over—the loss of tissue fluids has reached a critical level—the compressed heart is struggling to pump heavy, thick, sluggish blood into the tissues—the tortured lungs are making a frantic effort to gasp in small gulps of air. He can feel the chill of death creeping through his tissues.... Finally, he can allow his body to die. [We know that the Lord Jesus Christ dismissed His spirit from His body; He was in complete control even of the time of His death.

—St. John 19:30[5]

It was standard practice to give those nailed to the cross a drug to dull their senses and speed up death. Jesus was offered "wine mixed with gall" but refused it [see St. Matthew 27:34]. He, rather than a drug, would choose the exact moment His Spirit would be dismissed. Surrounding the foot of the cross were Roman soldiers. They continued to mock Him and cast lots for His garments even after they had nailed His limp and bloody body to a rugged, splintered cross that cut into His already raw back with every strained, agonizing breath. Stretched out naked on the cross, Jesus could barely identify the local citizens and their rulers sneering and wagging their tongues at Him as He made out their blurred forms from behind rivulets of blood meandering down His eyes.

From below His nail-pierced feet they looked up at His bleeding body hanging helplessly on the cross. "He saved others; let him save himself, if he is the Christ, the chosen one of God," they called with disdain. Yet others remarked, "If thou art the King of the Jews, save thyself" [St. Luke 23:35-37]. The two robbers also began to revile Him [St. Matthew 27:44]. The zealots were watching, too, from a distance. Barabbas was in their company, keeping the caldron of Jewish discontent boiling. They likely remarked among themselves, "If this man *is* the Messiah, the *Christ,* surely he will call upon the God of Israel to send legions of angels to smite these Roman dogs and free himself and us."

Amid the hatred, the horror, the pain, and the dashed messianic expectations, Jesus finally responded. He did not hurl obscenities or rain down curses on His tormentors. Neither did He call upon legions of angels. Rather, He took compassion on them all. Jesus lifted His disfigured, bloody face toward heaven and asked:

... Father, forgive them, for they do not know what they are doing.
—St. Luke 23:34

Not all had ears to hear:

Now one of those robbers who were hanged was abusing him, saying, "If thou art the Christ, save thyself and us!"
—St. Luke 23:39

A Sinner Was Reborn at Calvary

Among many within earshot, one heard Jesus' prayer:

But the other (*robber*) in answer rebuked him (*the abusing robber*) and said, "Dost not even thou fear God, seeing that thou art under the same sentence? And we indeed justly, for we are receiving what our deeds deserved; but this man has done nothing wrong." And he said to Jesus, "Lord remember me when thou comest into thy kingdom."
—St. Luke 23:40-42

The second robber gives us a perfect example of how a trusting belief in the true Christ results in a changed life. The robber had little life left. However, after *hearing* Jesus' words, "he made a decision for Christ," to use Father Stravinskas' words. That decision changed not only the few remaining moments of his life, but also his eternal destiny. The robber was a fundamentalist. He changed his mind about Jesus being a condemned criminal and recognized Him as Lord and Savior. At that moment, the Holy Spirit entered into the robber and sealed him for the moment of his redemption. Jesus' words confirm:

"... Amen I say to thee, this day thou shalt be with me in paradise."
—St. Luke 23:43

The words this repentant robber spoke magnify the Lord even to this day. Note that Jesus did not place any conditions on his salvation. He did not tell him, "if only you could be baptized, or join a certain Church, or receive certain sacraments, then you could be with Me this day in paradise." Neither was Jesus expecting the robber to do good works to *earn* any part of his way into Paradise. Neither did Jesus reveal that the robber would be allowed into Paradise based on the notion that the robber's family would complete those good works the robber left undone in this life, as Orthodoxy teaches, or spend so much as an hour in purgatory. We know the robber only did one "good" thing in his life: he recognized Jesus as Lord. One day, all believers will have the privilege of meeting this sinner turned saint who still speaks to us today through the recorded Word of God! The gospel was presented in its simplest form at Golgotha. A child of disobedience heard the Word of God, changed his attitude toward the person of Jesus, confessed Him with his mouth ("Lord remember me..."), and received the promise of salvation ("... this day thou shalt be with me in paradise"). Although the robber didn't have much time to allow the Holy Spirit to work in his life, many of us do. Does your church allow Jesus to exercise His power to save and preserve or has it, like many Churches, robbed Him of the power He exercised on the cross to save a sinner?

The Hosts in Heaven Rejoiced When Jesus Cried Out, "It Is Finished"

Jesus' bodily suffering on the cross (six hours) was excruciating. However, it was not His physical suffering alone that paid the sin debt of the world. The wages of sin is death, that is, eternal separation from God. This death, of course, includes death of the body. Moreover, the death of the body must be experienced by blood loss, for without the shedding of blood there is no atonement for sin [see Hebrews 9:22]. In some manner which the human mind in its fallen state cannot fathom, Jesus was, for the first time in eternity, separated from God the Father as He was dying on that old rugged cross. Jesus cried out: "My God, my God, why hast thou forsaken (*left*) me?" It was at that wonderful moment that the sin debt of all the world, for all people, for all sins, for all time was paid in full. His words were prophesied in the 22nd Psalm:

> "My God, my God, why have you forsaken me, far from my prayer, from the words of my cry?"
>
> —Psalms 21 (22):1-2

While we cannot fully comprehend or appreciate what wondrous thing happened at the cross, we can fully *believe*. When Jesus cried out, "It is finished," Satan thought he had won the battle. However, angels in heaven were singing and the hosts were celebrating in the presence of God the Father. The Father's will had been carried out by the Son even to delivering His soul unto death [see Isaias 53:10-12]. Romans 8:28 teaches:

> And we know that *all things* work together for good to those who love God, to those who are called according to His purpose.

There are many who doubt the literal interpretation of this verse. While Satan thought he had won the victory, God was working even Jesus' death for good for those who love God and would accept His plan for their salvation. Jesus' death on the cross is the greatest fulfillment and proof of the veracity of Romans 8:28.

The Curtain Is Torn—Barriers Between God and Man Are Removed

At the moment of Jesus' death, the curtain (also called the veil) separating the Holy Place in the Temple from the Holy of Holies within, was torn top to bottom [see St. Matthew 27:51]. The Holy of Holies was the innermost sanctuary where only once a year, on the Day of Atonement, only the high priest could enter to make an offering for the sins of the nation of Israel [see Leviticus 16:2-3]. The high priest would slay the designated animals in the designated manner, enter the Holy of Holies with the blood, and sprinkle it on the Mercy Seat, which was the covering on the Ark of the Covenant [see Leviticus 16]. It was precisely because God dwelled above the Ark on the Mercy Seat that only the high priest could approach and then only once a year. Before the high priest went in, a golden rope was tied around his waist because if God found him to be unworthy, He struck him dead and no man could enter to remove the body—wherefore, the golden rope.

With Jesus' death on the cross, the curtain, that barrier that had existed between sinful man and a Holy God from the time of the Tabernacle (Dwelling–see Exodus 25:9), was torn. The significance of its being torn top to bottom is that no man could have torn it top to bottom because of the height. Man could only have torn it bottom to top. Thus, we are to see God's hand at work in this tearing of the veil. Prior to Jesus' atonement, the only way to approach God was through blood sacrifice, the high priest, and the veil. Now, however, our only way to God is through Jesus: "... I am the way, the truth, and the life. No one comes to the Father but through me" [see St. John 14:6]. Jesus has become our sacrificial Lamb and High Priest forever, "reaching even behind the veil" [see Hebrews 6:19-20]. Every believer can approach the Father based on Jesus' atoning death. However, if one rejects His finished work on the cross as paying his sin debt in full, then he rejects the Jesus of the New Testament. Many cults and Churches do exactly this. When a believer prays (asks for something), he prays to the Father and ends his prayer "in Jesus' name." If one does not accept the Jesus of the New Testament, then one cannot pray in His name and if one does not pray in His name, then the Father does not hear [see St. John 15:16]. The veil separating the people from God was not torn by God just to be replaced by a sacramental salvation system, the Mass, a new order of high priests, or a new holy of holies known as some particular denomination or Church!

And You Shall Be Witnesses for Me

Believers are often labeled intolerant, narrow-minded, divisive, and even hateful because of their insistence that Jesus is the only way—no other god, no Church, or church, no denomination. In fact, the early Christians were not persecuted for worshiping Jesus. They were thrown into the arena because they worshiped *only* Jesus. They refused to offer incense once a year to the god Caesar, as required by Roman Law. What is not understood by the world, what cannot be understood by the world is that no believer ever approaches a nonbeliever out of hate to share with him or her the Good News of Jesus Christ—that he or she can have eternal life through Jesus. Anyone who hates another is probably not a believer in the first place and certainly would not be witnessing to others [see St. Luke 11:4]. Only those in submission to the Lord's command bear Him witness. Jesus said:

"If the world hates you, know that it has hated me before you. If you were
of the world, the world would love what is its own. But because you are
not of the world, but I have chosen you out of the world, therefore the
world hates you."

—St. John 15:18

Know this. The world loves *icons* of a dependent baby confined to its
mother's arms, an infant laying in a manger, and a helpless man hanging
on a cross. Most even celebrate to some extent the time of year mistakenly thought to be His birthday. They greet one another not with "Merry
Christmas," but with "Happy Holidays." Many do not realize He's the reason
for the season. Others mistakenly associate the word Mass with Christmas
and erroneously explain that that's what Christmas means—"Christ's
Mass." However, this term did not come into existence until the Middle
Ages. Christmas simply means Christ's coming. However, the world *hates*
the Jesus of the New Testament. They reject the *Son of God* who said, "I am
the way, the truth, and the life. No one comes to the Father but through
me." We hear His name profaned and blasphemed everywhere. It is nearly
impossible to watch television without hearing blasphemy, in addition
to profanity, and the ever-increasing vulgarity. One of the many aspects
believers enjoy about church services is hearing the name of Jesus lifted
up, praised, and glorified in hymns and sermons.

When You Think of Jesus, What Image Comes to Mind?

I recently heard of a lady who entered a jewelry store. She told the
salesman she wanted to buy a cross like all the rock and roll and movie
stars wear. He asked, "Do you want a plain one or one with the little man
on it?" Perhaps this is why God tells us over and over again in His Word
not to make images. This is what image making and image worship has
led to—the Creator of the universe; the Second Person of the Trinity and
only-begotten Son of God; the One who left His glory in heaven for our
sakes; the One who formed us with His hands in our mothers' wombs; the
author and finisher of our faith; our sacrificial Lamb without blemish; our
Lord and kinsman redeemer; the One who defeated hell, Satan, and all his
demonic forces at Calvary; the One who won victory over death and the
grave; the One who refers to Himself no less than four times in the book
of the Apocalypse as the Alpha and the Omega; and the King of kings and
Lord of lords succinctly summed up as the "little man" on the cross.

Some say they like the crucifix because it reminds them of what Jesus
did for them. However, the same people who make this claim often believe

that Jesus did not do all that was required. They deny Jesus' words, "It is consummated (*finished*)," and make Him a liar [St. John 19:30]. They do not believe their debt has been "paid in full." Some believe where Jesus' suffering was lacking, they can make up for His shortfall through their good works, suffering in purgatory, and the treasury of grace of the saints in heaven. Others believe the "good" works of their families, when added to Jesus' death, will allow them entrance into the kingdom.

One day each of us will be judged not by the Jesus taught by his Church, but by the Jesus of the New Testament. Jesus will judge the *works* of believers. He will determine whether the believer walked in the good works prepared for him by God before the time of his salvation [Ephesians 2:10] or in his own works which, by definition, cannot be good [Isaias 64:6]. Crowns will be awarded to lay at the feet of Jesus for those who walked in the good works He prepared [1 Corinthians 3:10-14]. These good works are referred to as "gold, silver, and precious stones." A man's works, on the other hand, are referred to as "wood, hay, and straw." The believer will not receive a reward (crown) for walking in his own works. However, he will be saved [1 Corinthians 3:15]. Moreover, a believer can lose his reward, his crown, if he quits the Christian walk. However, he cannot lose his salvation. That's why Jesus tells believers to "... Hold fast what you have, that no one may take your crown" [Apocalypse 3:11].

Nonbelievers will be judged at the Great White Throne. This is the judgment of the damned [Apocalypse 20:11-15]. It occurs at the end of the millennial kingdom, just prior to the beginning of eternity. Are you prepared to say to Jesus, "Thank you for what you did. But where your sacrifice fell short, I made up the deficit with *my* 'good works.'" Like the guest wearing his own garment at the marriage feast, such an individual will stand speechless before the Judge-King [see St. John 5:22]. He will immediately realize that he has transgressed *God's plan* for his salvation. God help those who place their trust in anything other than, or in addition to, or less than the grace of God provided through Jesus' atoning death at Calvary. Whose garment will you wear on Judgment Day? The one provided by the King of kings? Or your own?

CONCLUSION:
BUT WHO DO
YOU SAY THAT I AM?

THE ABOVE QUOTE is from the Gospel of St. Matthew. When they had come into the district of Caesarea Philippi, Jesus asked His disciples who others thought Him to be. They replied that some thought Him to be John the Baptist returned, while others thought Him to be one of the prophets, Elias, or Jeremias. Then Jesus asked, "But who do you say that I am?"

The answer to that question changed not only the lives and eternal destinies of the disciples, but also the world. This is a very personal question each of us must answer. It is no less personal than asking, "Will you marry me?"

Eat My Flesh, Drink My Blood

Jesus told His followers not to labor for food which perishes, but to seek that which endures forever which He would *give* to them. Jesus then talked about how their ancestors were fed manna that fell from heaven in the desert. He revealed that *He* was the true bread of life "come down from heaven" and that anyone who comes to Him will not hunger, and that he who believes in Him will never thirst [St. John 6:27-35]. The crowd began to murmur. Jesus knew there were doubters. And where there are doubters, Satan moves in [St. Luke 8:5]. To separate those who had ears to hear from those who did not:

> Jesus therefore said to them, "Amen, amen, I say to you, unless you eat the flesh of the Son of Man, and drink his blood, you shall not have life in you. He who eats my flesh and drinks my blood has life everlasting and I will raise him up on the last day. For my flesh is food indeed, and my blood is drink indeed."
>
> —St. John 6:53-56

Was Jesus lying about eating His flesh and drinking His blood? No. But as recorded in St. Mark 4:10-12, the message of the kingdom could not be understood by all. Those at Capharnaum without discerning spirits could only understand His words literally. They found them offensive. They muttered among themselves as they left the synagogue, "This is a hard saying; who can hear (*understand*) it?" This fulfilled the prophecy of Isaias, "And he shall be a sanctification to you (*to believers*), but for a stone of stumbling, and for a rock of offence to the two houses of Israel, for a snare (*trap*) and a ruin to the inhabitants of Jerusalem" [Isaias 8:14]. Moreover, His audience understood that eating human flesh was a curse from God [see Leviticus 26:29 and 4 Kings 6:26-30]. Jesus turned to those who remained. "Does this scandalize (*offend*) you?" He asked [v. 62].

The Law and the prophets (the Scripture) condemned the eating and/ or drinking of blood. Toasting the gods with blood was a pagan ritual. The first proscription is found in Genesis 9:4. Prior to the flood, the people were vegetarians [Genesis 1:29]. After the flood, God told Noe they could eat meat [Genesis 9:3]. However, Jehovah put a limitation on the meat: "But flesh with the life—that is, its blood—you shall not eat" [Genesis 9:4]. In Leviticus 17:11-12 God's Word says, "Since the life of a living body is in its blood, I have made you put it on the altar, so that atonement may thereby be made for your own lives, because it is the blood, as the seat of life, that makes atonement. That is why I have told the Israelites: No one among you, not even a resident alien, may partake of blood." This prohibition was so strong that, under the leadership of the Holy Spirit, St. James included it as a prohibition for Gentile converts, some of whom thought it acceptable to toast their new god, Jesus, with blood just as they had their former gods [see Acts 15:20].

Jesus' followers were familiar, too, with His affirmation that He had come to fulfill the Law and the prophets and that "… not one jot or one tittle…" would pass from the law until all things be fulfilled [see St. Matthew 5:18]. They had heard Jesus refer to Himself as the bread of life [St. John 6:35]; the light of the world [St. John 8:12]; the door to the sheep gate [St. John 10:7]; and the vine [St. John 15:5]. But His disciples realized that if Jesus were speaking of eating His flesh and drinking His blood in a literal sense, then He had just done away with much more than a jot and a tittle. After those without ears to hear departed, Jesus explained to His disciples, "It is the spirit that gives life; the flesh profits nothing. The words that I have spoken to you are *spirit* and life" [St. John 6:63-64]. His beleaguered followers must have breathed a sigh of relief. Jesus' words prepared them for what they would later hear at their last supper with Him.

Few verses have been so misconstrued as Jesus' command to eat His flesh and drink His blood. Even today, some still ignore that He said in verse 63 that His words were *spiritual*. Those who interpreted His words literally walked away. Those who interpret His words literally today have also walked away from the Jesus of the New Testament. Jesus spoke of Himself as bread again at the Last Supper:

> And while they were at supper, Jesus took bread, and blessed and broke, and gave it to his disciples, and said, "Take and eat; this is my body." And taking a cup, he gave thanks and gave it to them, saying, "All of you drink of this; for this is *my blood* of the new covenant, which is being shed for many unto the forgiveness of sins. But I say to you, I will not drink henceforth of this fruit of the vine, until that day when I shall drink it new with you in the kingdom of my Father."
>
> —St. Matthew 26:26-29

Various world religions have treated Jesus' spiritual words within the context of magical incantations which turn the bread and wine into His flesh and blood. Some teach that a priest or minister can say certain words over the bread and wine today and perform some mystical metamorphosis. This generally is referred to as transubstantiation by some and as consubstantiation by those who have less confidence in transubstantiation. However, there was no metamorphosis. The answer to whether Jesus thought He and His disciples had drunk blood is answered in verse 29, "But I say to you, I will not drink henceforth of this *fruit of the vine*, until that day when I drink it new with you in the kingdom of my Father." Thus, Jesus made it clear that His disciples had just drunk the fruit of the vine—not blood! Moreover, in none of the gospel accounts did Jesus even suggest He was giving those present, much less some priests or ministers in the future, the power to change bread and wine into His body and blood. Neither is this suggested by any writers of the epistles. Moreover, Jesus' death on the cross brought about the end of the priestly system with its blood sacrifices where the high priest stood between God and man. Furthermore, Scripture describes the early churches as continuing steadfastly in the apostles' doctrine and fellowship, and in breaking of bread (communion), and in prayers. None refers to anything approaching transubstantiation or consubstantiation [see Acts 2:42 and 46]. Why would they? Jesus clarified:

> "It is the spirit (*Holy Spirit*) that gives life; the flesh profits nothing. The words that I have spoken to you are *spirit* and life."
>
> —St. John 6:64

The Old Covenant required the priest who offered the sacrifice for sin to eat it:

> And the LORD spake unto Moses, saying, "Speak unto Aaron and to his sons, saying, 'This is the law of the sin offering: In the place where the burnt offering is killed shall the sin offering be killed before the LORD: it is most holy. *The priest that offereth it for sin shall eat it:* in the holy place shall it be eaten, in the court of the tabernacle of the congregation.'"
> —Leviticus 6:24-26 KJV

Who are the priests in the New Covenant? All believers [see 1 Peter 2:5 and Apocalypse 1:6]. Under the Old Covenant, the priest offered a lamb as a sin offering. Under the New Covenant, believers bring the true Lamb as a sin offering. And since the priest must eat the sin offering, we must eat Jesus' body. When Jesus said we must eat His flesh, He was saying that we must recognize Him as the sin offering, the true Lamb who takes away sin. All the animal sacrifices were merely types and shadows. Their blood only *covered sin*. He was the true sacrifice. Jesus' blood didn't just cover our sins, His blood *took them away* [see Colossians 2:13-14]. The bread and wine are spiritual representations of His body and blood, not substantial ones. Jesus and His disciples likely celebrated Passover with grape juice since leaven was prohibited during Passover. It is the leaven (yeast) that turns the grape juice into wine. That's why Jesus referred to it as the "fruit of the vine" rather than wine, which was what they normally drank [St. Matthew 26:29].

No Scriptural Support for Transubstantiation or Consubstantiation

Some have attempted to support the notion of transubstantiation with a verse from 1 Corinthians 11:29:

> For he who eats and drinks unworthily, without distinguishing the body, eats and drinks judgment to himself.

They argue that the word "body" in the above verse supports the doctrine of transubstantiation. However, this is not the case. It is a danger to one's eternal destiny to use verses out of context to support non-scriptural positions.

The keys to interpretation of verse 29 are found in verses 33 and 34:

> Wherefore, my brethren, when you come together to eat, wait for one
> another. If anyone is hungry let him eat at home (*before coming to the
> service*), lest you come together unto judgment (*chastisement*)....
> —1 Corinthians 11:33-34

St. Paul is addressing a problem in the Corinthian church. Some
were forgetting the serious nature of partaking in communion, which is
representative of the Lord's body and blood. Some were coming together
more in the fashion of eating a meal rather than as a single body (church) to
partake of the Lord's Supper. They were coming through the church doors
hungry. Bread and wine were basic staples. Some were eating and drinking
to satisfy their flesh, rather than for spiritual edification. They were not
waiting for their brothers and sisters *in Christ* before starting [v. 33]. What
they were eating and drinking was not a small piece of bread, matzo, or
wafer and a small sip of wine or grape juice, as we do today. Rather, they
were coming to the table ravenous, not discerning that they were supposed
to be coming together as *one body, the body of Christ*, to partake in spiritual
edification. This is the body referred to in 1 Corinthians 11:29. St. Paul
warns errant Corinthians to realize that participation in the Lord's Supper
requires preparation and confession of any unconfessed sin. He tells them
not to come to the Lord's Table unworthily. He warns further that failure
to distinguish between supper (food for the body) and the Lord's Supper
(food for the spirit) has already led some to the grave [v. 30].

The Celebration of Passover

Contrary to traditional teaching, Jesus did not celebrate the Passover
with His apostles on the traditional Jewish Passover. Jesus was crucified the
same day the Passover lambs were being slaughtered throughout Jerusalem,
on Thursday. Jesus said He would be three days and three nights in the heart
of the earth [see St. Matthew 12:40]. Jesus was in the tomb Thursday, Friday,
and Saturday nights. Jesus celebrated the Passover as the Last Supper with
His apostles on Wednesday evening. This is why they were able to rent a
room on such short notice [St. Matthew 26:18].

As recorded in St. Luke's Gospel, Jesus said, "... do this in remembrance
of me" [St. Luke 22:19]. The Jews were commanded by God to celebrate
annually their exodus from Egypt with the Passover meal [Exodus 12:42].
Jesus told those present to remember Him and what He did for them at
future Passover celebrations. 1 Corinthians 11:26 teaches that every time
we celebrate the Lord's Supper we are affirming His death, a death He freely
died for us, until He returns. As we saw in chapters four and five, we affirm
Jesus' burial and resurrection through baptism.

The Christian experience of salvation finds a great many parallels with the Israelites' release from bondage by Pharao. God told the Israelites that each family should slay a lamb without blemish and place its blood upon the doorposts and lintel of every house [Exodus 1:7]. This, of course, was a foreshadowing of our Paschal Lamb, Jesus [St. John 1:29]. God told them further that death would stop at each house but for those marked with the blood, death would pass over. This, too, is a foreshadowing. Death, eternal death, an eternity in hell separated from God forever is the wage each of us has earned because of our sin [Romans 6:23]. However, God's Word tells us that for those under the blood of the Lamb, eternal death will pass over. Like the Israelites passing into and out of the Red Sea, we go into and come out of the water at baptism. Also, as the Israelites journeyed to the Promised Land, believers journey to the promised heaven.

But if Jesus' words about eating His flesh and drinking His blood were not literal, then what did He mean? To answer this question, we need to examine Jesus' words within the context of the customs of the Jewish people. The meaning of "eat My flesh" is revealed through the Passover celebration. The meaning of "drink My blood" is seen through the marriage customs.

Jesus Is the Bread of Life

St. Matthew 26:26 begins with a peculiar wording, "And while they were at supper, Jesus took bread...." It is clear from preceding verse 23 that they had already begun eating bread. However, the bread that Jesus broke and gave to His disciples was distinguished from other bread in the Passover celebration. Moreover, it was over this particular piece of bread that Jesus recited the traditional Jewish thanksgiving for food.

At Passover, the father of the house takes three pieces of unleavened bread (matzo) and places them, one each, into three compartments of a single linen satchel. Prior to the beginning of the meal, he retrieves the second piece, referred to as the Afikomen, from the middle compartment and wraps it in a special piece of linen and "hides" it. The two remaining pieces of matzo are retrieved from the first and third compartments and eaten along with the other prepared foods. Prior to the end of the meal, the father "finds" the Afikomen, which means *he who comes*, still wrapped in linen, and there is much rejoicing.

It is not difficult to see the three pieces of matzo in one satchel as representative of the Triune God: Father, Son, and Holy Spirit, particularly in light of the fact that it is the second piece of matzo (the Son) that is separated from the other two and then wrapped in linen, hidden away, then later found among great rejoicing. On the cross, Jesus was separated from the

Father and the Holy Spirit. He cried out "My God, my God, why hast thou forsaken me?" Shortly thereafter, Jesus dismissed His Spirit and died.

If you have seen matzo and can discern the symbolism in the Passover meal, then you can see great similarities between Jesus' body and the matzo He called His body. Jesus tells us in St. John 6:48 that He is the bread of life. Moreover, He was born in Bethlehem, which translates into "house of Bread." Matzo is an unleavened bread. In His teaching, Jesus equated leaven with sin [see St. Matthew 16:6]. Like the matzo, Jesus' body was without leaven. Because matzo is cooked on a grill, it bears stripes, just as would the body of Jesus [see Isaias 53:5 and 1 St. Peter 2:24]. To aid in cooking, the matzo is pierced throughout, just as Jesus' body would be pierced by nails, the lance, and the crown of thorns [see Zacharias 12:10].

The father breaks the Afikomen and gives a piece to each participant at the Passover meal, just as Jesus' body would be broken for us [see Isaias 53:10]. The Afikomen is wrapped in linen and hidden away, just as Jesus' body would be wrapped in burial linen and placed in a tomb. As with the joy of "finding" the Afikomen, there would be much rejoicing by Jesus' disciples after they found the tomb empty and saw the risen Christ [see St. Matthew 28:8].

We know from Scripture that Jesus took the Afikomen and blessed it. But what was that blessing? What words did He say? The answer to this question again confirms how much Jesus' body was like bread. The blessing Jesus said was the standard blessing all Jews said: "Blessed are You, O LORD our God, King of the universe, Who brings forth bread from the earth." Jesus was telling His friends that just as bread is brought forth from the earth by His Father, so would His dead body be brought forth. Moreover, Jesus had told His followers, "Verily, verily, I say unto you, Except a corn (*grain*) of wheat fall into the ground *and die*, it abideth alone; but if it die, it bringeth forth much fruit" [see St. John 12:24]. Jesus' followers did not fully understand His words until they stood face to face with the risen Christ [see St. Matthew 28:9 and St. John 20:28].

Jesus Is Our Bridegroom

The analogy between our Lord's blood and the wine can be understood in a similar context. The Abrahamic covenant and the Jewish marriage proposal figure prominently in understanding this symbolism. As described in chapter 15 of Genesis, God made a blood covenant with Abram to seal His promise of an heir to come from Abram's own body. Blood from a heifer, goat, ram, turtledove, and pigeon was shed to seal the covenant. God made other covenants with Abram's descendants and all were sealed by the blood of animals. Centuries later, Jeremias prophesied a "new covenant" would come to the Northern kingdom of Israel and the Southern kingdom of Judah [see Jeremias 31:31].

When Jesus said, "For this is my blood of the new covenant," it is likely He placed the emphasis on the words "my blood," to distinguish the basis for this new covenant (His blood) from the old covenant (animal blood).

Jesus gave thanks over the cup as He did over the bread: "Blessed are You, O LORD our God, King of the universe, Who brings forth the fruit of the vine." Eleven apostles drank from the cup. Judas had already departed. In order to understand the importance of drinking from the cup, or declining, we must understand the traditional Jewish marriage proposal.

When a boy wanted to marry a girl, he approached the girl's father. He discussed his intentions, as well as the price he would pay. Then the girl was summoned. The father explained the circumstances to his daughter and the three sat down at the table. The boy poured a cup of wine and sat it before his intended. The girl would indicate her acceptance by picking up the cup and drinking from it.

The analogy to God's offer of salvation to each of us is clear. Who is the intended bridegroom? The King's Son, Jesus [see St. Matthew 22]. Each of us is analogous to the girl. Like the girl, we were purchased with a price: Jesus' death on the cross. As with the pouring of the cup of wine, Jesus poured out His life's blood and died in our place. Symbolically speaking, He fills the cup with His blood and places it in front of us. He invites each to accept His proposal: full payment of one's sin debt and His free gift of eternal life [see Romans 6:23]. He gives each the choice whether or not to pick up the cup and drink or, like Judas, walk away. If we accept, then we become a part of His bride, the church, and He becomes our Bridegroom. We forsake all others for our bridegroom and He becomes our Lord, our Master.

John the Baptist refers to Jesus as the Bridegroom and to himself as the Bridegroom's friend in St. John 3:29, "He who has the bride is the bridegroom; but the friend of the bridegroom, who stands and hears him, rejoices exceedingly at the voice of the bridegroom. This my joy, therefore, is made full." Moreover, Isaias says, "I will greatly rejoice in the Lord, and my soul shall be joyful in my God; for he hath clothed me with the garments of salvation and with the robe of justice he hath covered me: as a bridegroom decked with a crown, and as a bride adorned with her jewels" [see Isaias 61:10]. Who other than believers are described in the Scriptures as being clothed in the garments of salvation and covered with the robe of righteousness? No one! Thus, it is clear that Jesus is the Bridegroom and the church general (*autos*) is His bride. Jesus did not pour out wine in

His proposal. He poured out His life's blood. When we eat this bread and drink this cup, we affirm Jesus' death until He comes again [1 Corinthians 11: 26].

If the girl accepted the boy's proposal, the boy would depart to his father's house to prepare the bridal chamber where the couple would spend their honeymoon. That bridal chamber was called a mansion [see St. John 14:1-3]. The boy would collect the materials necessary to construct the small, one-room addition to his parents' house. The boy's father would carefully check the progress. If a friend asked when the wedding would be, the boy would answer that only his father knew since it was the responsibility of the father, and the father alone, to determine when construction of the mansion was complete [see St. Matthew 24:36 and Acts 1:6-7].

When the moment came and the father gave the nod, the boy would round up his friends. With lighted torches they would proceed with much noise and gaiety through the streets toward the girl's house. When they were a short distance away, they would begin calling out her name to let her know her bridegroom was near. The blowing of the shofar, made from a ram's horn, left no room for doubt. And if she was prepared, the lamp in her room was burning throughout the night each night so that there would be no stumbling in the dark. Her clothes were packed, for she did not know the hour of his coming [see St. Matthew 25:1-13]. After collecting his bride, the entire party went back to the boy's parents' house where a *seven-day* celebration began. After the father of the boy placed the hand of the girl into his son's hand, the two were married and they entered into the mansion to consummate the marriage. It is at this door which his friends stood and rejoiced at hearing the voice of the bridegroom [St. John 3:29].

In our culture, we honor and celebrate the bride. In Jewish culture, it is the bridegroom. Therefore, these customs may seem strange to us. But to the people of Jesus' time, the customs and ceremonies were well known. When Jesus told his parable, relating Himself to the bridegroom and His followers to the bride, His listeners understood the analogy. They also understood the significance of drinking from the proffered cup. Before He went to the cross, Jesus told His worried disciples:

> "Let not your heart be troubled. You believe in God, believe also in me. In my Father's house are many mansions. Were it not so, I should (*would*) have told you, because I go to prepare a place for you. And if I go and prepare a place for you, I am coming again, and I will take you to myself; that where I am, there you also may be.
>
> —St. John 14:1-3

Jesus made a number of "hard sayings" in addition to stating that believers must eat His flesh and drink His blood. He told people that if their eye sinned, pluck it out [St. Matthew 18:9]; and if their hand sinned, cut it off [St. Matthew 5:30]. The same people who interpret Jesus' words about eating His flesh and drinking His blood literally understand His words to be symbolic in these instances.

The Pre-Tribulation Rapture of the Church

In His Olivet discourse, Jesus discussed the prophetic signs that will signal His return [St. Matthew 24]. While the context of the discussion revolves around His return to earth to establish His earthly kingdom, referred to as His "glorious appearing" [see Titus 2:13] and distinct from His coming "in the clouds" [see 1 Thessalonians 4:17] to rapture His church, His words have relevance to both prophetic events since He said, "But of that day and hour no one knows, not even the angels of heaven, but the Father only" [St. Matthew 24:36]. Clearly, Jesus' language here in referring to "only the Father knowing" parallels the role of the bridegroom's father in determining when the bridegroom could go to retrieve his bride.

The Rapture is a reference to all believers who are in the body (alive) from all denominations, not an organizational or institutional Church. Only those who have picked up the cup and said, "Yes, Lord," will be raptured. Those who believe that their belonging to a certain denomination, or church, or Church, or having been baptized and received certain sacraments, or singing in the choir, or tithing saves them will be left behind. Bridegrooms are particular about whom they take as brides and Jesus is no exception.

The coming of the Bridegroom is explained by St. Paul:

> But we would not, brethren, have you ignorant concerning those who are asleep, lest you should grieve, even as others who have no hope (non-believers). For if we believe that Jesus died and rose again, so with him God will bring those also who have fallen sleep through Jesus (*Christians whose souls and spirits are with Jesus but whose bodies are in the ground*). For this we say to you in the word of the Lord, that we who live, who survive until the coming of the Lord, shall not precede those who have fallen asleep. For the Lord himself with cry of command, with voice of archangel, and with the trumpet of God will descend from heaven; and the dead in Christ will rise up first. Then we who live, who survive (*those who are living at the time of the Rapture*), shall be caught up together with them in clouds to meet the Lord in the air and so we shall ever be with the Lord. Wherefore, comfort one another with these words.
> —1 Thessalonians 4:13-18

The above citation is what the Catholic Bible teaches and what believers call the "Rapture." That is, Christ will "snatch" His followers off the face of the earth prior to the beginning of the seven-year Tribulation period prophesied in both the Old and New Testaments, especially the book of the Apocalypse. This will mark the end of the church age. The Lord will appear in the clouds (only to those who have eyes to see) and the graves of the dead in Christ (deceased believers) will be opened and their bodies will go up with the bodies of those in Christ who are still alive to be united for all time with the Lord. At this same time, the quick and the dead will receive their new and eternal bodies.

After baptizing the eunuch, the Spirit of the Lord took (caught) Philip away and the eunuch saw him no more, as recorded in Acts 8:39. In other words, Philip was raptured. The same Greek word," *harpazo*," is used to describe Philip's being caught away, as well as "caught up together" in the above citation. St. Paul revealed additional aspects of the Rapture:

> Behold, I tell you a mystery: We shall not all sleep (die), but we shall all be changed, in a moment, in the twinkling of an eye, at the last trumpet. For the trumpet will sound, and the dead shall rise incorruptible, and we shall be changed.
>
> —1 Corinthians 15:51-52

Some followers will be alive at the time of Jesus' return in the air to rapture His church. Therefore, each believer has a "blessed hope" that he or she will not die but be alive in the body on the day of Rapture.

Note the parallels with the coming of the Bridegroom for his bride. The Bridegroom departs to fetch His bride only at the day and hour designated by the Father. The Bridegroom comes Himself. He brings His friends with Him. The Lord alerts His bride that He is coming with a shout. The bride is ready and has oil (the Holy Spirit) in her lamp. The shofar is blown when the Bridegroom is only a short distance away (in the clouds). We go to the mansions prepared for us by the Lord Himself, to the seven-year marriage feast of the Lamb [see St. John 1:29 and Apocalypse 19:7].

The words of thanks Jesus said over the bread and wine at the Last Supper, combined with His other teachings discussed above and in previous chapters, reveal a beautiful portrait of salvation: how it is offered and how it is accepted. There are no magical words, no mystical metamorphic murmurings, and no rituals or ceremonials. Salvation is a free gift offered by God to each of us, received through faith, based on the finished work of His Son, the Jesus of the New Testament, at Calvary [see St. John 19:30]. Will you accept His proposal? Will you pick up the cup and drink?

Errant Teachings on End Time Events

While the Bema judgment of the believer's works and the receiving of crowns and the subsequent marriage feast of the Lamb are occurring in heaven, those not raptured from the earth will experience the most awful and terrifying period of history. Not all Churches or denominations believe in the Rapture and end times prophecy. As many depart from biblical truth in other areas, many depart from the truth of the Rapture and end times prophecy. The Catholic, Orthodox, and many Protestant Churches are examples.

The Orthodox Churches teach that there will be no Rapture preceding the end times and that the faithful will go through the Tribulation, along with nonbelievers. The Churches justify their teaching based on the Greek word for Tribulation used in Scripture. As recorded by St. Matthew 13:21 in *The Orthodox Study Bible, New Testament and Psalms*, Jesus said, "... For when tribulation... arises... he stumbles." The Greek word for tribulation is "*thlipsis*" which is translated as "pressure, persecution, affliction." However, the Orthodox Churches fail to distinguish between tribulation, which the Scripture teaches *all* will go through, such as that cited above, and the Great Tribulation. The Orthodox Study Bible reveals in Revelation 7:14, "... These are the ones who come out of the *Great Tribulation*...." The Greek for Great Tribulation is "*megas thlipsis*." This is the root word from which we get the English prefix "mega." It means "large, one million." Thus, the Scripture reveals that all believers will go through tribulation but that the tribulation experienced during the Great Tribulation will be a million times worse! Also, Orthodoxy mistakenly interprets 1 Thessalonians 4:15-17 (see above) as the Second Coming of Jesus to establish His earthly kingdom.

The Orthodox Churches' teaching is based on non-scriptural traditions, what Jesus called the traditions of men. The Scripture is clear. God has already rained down His wrath on Jesus, our substitute, at Golgotha. Believers have repented of their sins and accepted Jesus payment at the cross for their debt. God has accepted that payment. Just as Moses was to strike the rock for water the first time and to speak to it in future times, so it is with the Shepherd. The body of the Shepherd has been smitten once for our sakes. Our kinsman-redeemer bore our sins and our punishment. There is no balance owed. The purpose of God's pouring out His wrath during the Tribulation is to get sinners' attention and turn them toward Himself. Believers will have already done this. Therefore, why would God leave believers, the body of Christ on the earth, to experience the end-time destruction described in the book of the Apocalypse? He wouldn't. It would be analogous to striking the Rock a second time.

Churches that teach "replacement theology," that is, that the Church has replaced the nation of Israel in the New Testament, lose perspective on end times prophecy because end times prophecies deal with the *end of the church age* and *God's returning His focus to the nation of Israel*. That God will deal with Israel in the end times is prophesied by major and minor prophets in the Old Testament, as well as the authors of the New. If one does away with Israel in interpreting end times prophecy and substitutes the Church, as does Orthodoxy, which mistakenly calls the Church the "New Israel," there is no interpretation consistent with the teaching in the Orthodox Bible. The prophet Zacharias recorded God's Word in the end times prophecy:

> And I will pour out upon the house of David, and upon the inhabitants of Jerusalem the spirit of grace... and they (*Jews*) shall look upon me, whom they have pierced....
> —Zacharias 12:10

The house of David cannot be interpreted as anything other than Israel. It cannot reasonably be interpreted as the Church. Moreover, it certainly was not the Church that "pierced" Him. Again, this prophecy points to the Jews, not the Church. No Church was established prior to Jesus' crucifixion. Moreover, God's dealing with the Jews in the end times is confirmed by St. Paul in Romans 11:26, "And so all Israel will be saved." This verse pertains to Jews who come to believe in Jesus during the seven-year Tribulation. Failure to understand that the Church did not supplant Israel as God's chosen people leads to false interpretations of end times prophecy.

The Roman Catholic and many Protestant Churches, too, subscribe to the ungodly theory of replacement theology. Before proceeding to examine the Church's teaching on end times, it should be mentioned that the Catholic Church refers to the same thing, but with the words "end of the world." However, the Catholic Church does not teach that the world will end. What actually ends is the age, and this initiates eternity.

An article titled, "What Catholics Believe About Prophecy, the Second Coming of Jesus Christ, and the End of the World," appeared on page 28 in *The Western Kentucky Catholic*, dated February 1998. The article was co-authored by Fathers Phil Riney and Dan Kreutzer. In it, the priests provide, among other things, comparative views of "fundamentalists" teaching on end times, versus those of the Roman Catholic Church. The following quotes are from that article. Only those portions relevant to the current discussion are presented. According to Fathers Riney and Kreutzer:

In total reliance on the Scriptures and the Official Teachings of the Roman
Catholic Church, the authentic Revelation of Jesus Christ, we want to
reassert what the Church teaches about prophecy, the Second Coming of
Jesus Christ and the end of the world.

What Catholics believe and teach sharply differs from the understandings
of American fundamentalist denominations. That point of view character-
izes the end of the world in doomsday language. There is an undue and
dangerous preoccupation with Satan, the Antichrist, and a cosmic battle
between good and evil. Catholics, on the other hand, focus on God in Jesus
Christ and the victory of Christ over death and evil at His resurrection
and ascension.

The fundamentalists cling to a pessimistic view of the end of the world. It
will be a terrible and horrific ending in which God, for a time, abdicates
control of the world and hands it over to Satan. Catholics hold an
optimistic view of the end of the world. We look to the end of the world
as a time of new birth, which like any birth may be somewhat frightening
but not catastrophic. We believe the end of the world and the fullness of
our life in God will be a beautiful experience.

One of the hallmarks of fundamentalism is private revelation. Any
fundamentalist believer can become a medium of divine expression.

It should be noted, as discussed in chapter two, that many fringe groups
refer to themselves as fundamentalists. Some handle poisonous snakes
during worship services while others stockpile weapons in anticipation
of overthrowing the government (discussed in Appendix A). However, if
Fathers Riney and Kreutzer are talking about independent, Bible-believing,
Bible-preaching New Testament churches, as described in this book, then
their observations are about right. However, some of their characterizations
are not. For example, believers do not have "... an undue and dangerous
preoccupation with Satan, the Antichrist, and the cosmic battle between
good and evil." It was explained in chapter five that anyone who mistakes
the real person of Satan for an evil force in the universe does so at his
peril. Also, as discussed in chapter five, Satan has a plan for your personal
destruction. To underestimate him and his capabilities is not to "not be
preoccupied with him" but to invite him and his demons to destroy you,
your life, and those you love. St. Peter warns believers:

Be sober, be watchful! For your adversary the devil, as a roaring lion, goes
about seeking someone to devour.

—1 St. Peter 5:8

The article also accuses believers as characterizing the end of the world in "doomsday language." This characterization is partly correct. On the brighter side, however, and as discussed in Appendix A, the seven-year Tribulation will produce the largest soul harvest ever [Apocalypse 7:9]. This is accomplished by God when He pours out what the Roman Catholic Bible calls the seven seal judgments [Apocalypse 6-8:1], followed by seven trumpet judgments [Apocalypse 8:2-11], and culminating in seven bowl judgments [Apocalypse 16]. As can be understood from the descriptions, each succeeding judgment is worse than the former. As the Scripture makes clear, God is bringing these disasters on people of the earth as a result of His fierce wrath:

> ... the cities of the nations (*Gentile nations*) fell. And Babylon the great was remembered before God, to give her the cup of the wine of his fierce wrath... And great hail, heavy as a talent (*80-120 pounds*), came down from heaven upon men; and men blasphemed God....
> —Apocalypse 16:19-21

People will understand that these judgments are the result of God's wrath upon unrepentant men and women:

> And they said to the mountains and to the rocks, "Fall upon us, and hide us from the face of him who sits upon the throne, and from the wrath of the Lamb; for the great day of their wrath has come, and who is able to stand?"
> —Apocalypse 6:16-17

In response to these judgments, some will repent and accept the gospel [Apocalypse 14:6]. However, even as the judgments grow in intensity, many will continue to refuse the truth [see Apocalypse 9:20; 9:21; 16:9; and 16:11]:

> And the fifth poured out his bowl upon the throne of the beast (*the one world government*); and its kingdom became dark, and they (*men*) gnawed their tongues for pain.
> —Apocalypse 16:10

Their judgment is so painful that these unrepentant ones chew their tongues to take their minds off the pain associated with the previous judgments, which included bodily sores and scorched skin [Apocalypse 16:2 and 8-9]. Some are so frightened by cosmic events that they try to kill themselves but cannot [Apocalypse 9:6].

As can be seen by checking these citations, this is "Roman Catholic Bible language" on end times. Is it also "doomsday language," as the Fathers suggest? Doomsday is an Old English word and is defined as "Judgment Day." And that is exactly what has been described above, as quoted from the Roman Catholic Bible. Thus, fundamentalists characterize end times in exactly the same manner as the Roman Catholic Bible! Moreover, while the Catholic Church erroneously teaches that the Roman Catholic Church wrote the New Testament, it is the Catholic Church that denies its veracity, not fundamentalists. God escalates His judgments. At each step up in intensity, some will repent and accept the gospel. However, as incredible as it seems, some will not. For those who fail to repent, it literally is doomsday.

With regard to the charge that, according to fundamentalists thinking, "... God, for a time, abdicates control of the world and hands it over to Satan," this is not a correct characterization. In fact, the Roman Catholic Bible reveals the opposite of what the priests suggest is true. First, Satan is in control of the world now [see Ephesians 2:2 and 2 Corinthians 4:3-4]. Moreover, he also has access to heaven [see Job 1:6 and 2:1]. As discussed in chapter two, when Satan offered Jesus the kingdoms of this world, Jesus did not tell Satan that they were not his to give [St. Matthew 4:8-9]. They were. Second, it is during the Tribulation period that God sends devastation on Satan's one-world government and one-world leader, the Antichrist. Moreover, at the midpoint of the Tribulation, Satan is cast out of heaven and down to earth [Apocalypse 12:12]. Finally, as was discussed in chapter five, Satan has done everything he can to destroy the Jews, God's chosen people, and thwart the greatest soul harvest ever. The operative phrase here is *everything he can*. Satan can only do that which God, in His providential sovereignty, allows. Thus, at no time does God hand over His providential authority to Satan. At the end of the Tribulation, Satan will be bound:

> And I saw an angel coming down from heaven, having the key to the abyss and a great chain in his hand. And he laid hold on the dragon, the ancient serpent, who is the devil and Satan, and bound him for a thousand years. And he cast him into the abyss, and closed and sealed it over him, that he should deceive the nations no more, until the thousand years should be finished. And after that, he must be let loose for a little while.
>
> —Apocalypse 20:1-3

The prophet described how Satan will spend the millennium, the last one thousand years of time before the start of eternity:

> They that shall see thee shall turn toward thee and behold thee. Is this the man that troubled the earth, that shook kingdoms, that made the world

a wilderness and destroyed the cities thereof, that opened not the prison
to his prisoners... and art gone down to the bottom of the pit (*abyss*), as
a rotten carcass.

—Isaias 14:16-19

As the millennium concludes, Satan will be released from the pit for
a little while to gather and lead a last rebellion against God Almighty
[Apocalypse 20:7-8]. Satan's end on this earth and his eternity are recorded
by St. John:

... And the devil who deceived them (*the rebels of the millennium*) was cast
into the pool of fire and brimstone... and... will be tormented day and
night forever and ever.

—Apocalypse 20:9-10

Another false characterization is the allegation that "... the hallmark of
fundamentalism is private revelation." This is not true. Believers halt the
line on revelation at the end of chapter 22 of the book of the Apocalypse
(Revelation), the last chapter in the Roman Catholic, Orthodox, and
King James Bibles. New Testament churches do not go outside Scripture.
Neither do these churches expect additional revelation through Marian
or other apparitions. Moreover, as discussed in earlier chapters, believers
interpret non-scriptural revelation, such as associated with Constantine,
Muhammed, Joseph Smith, and the many Marian appearances, to be not
only anti-scriptural, but demonic in origin and message.

Finally, with regard to Fathers Riney and Kreutzer's claim that, "Any
fundamentalist believer can become a medium of divine expression," such
is not true. First, such expressions are not divine in nature, but demonic,
as explained in chapter two. Second, God's Word forbids such practices, as
already discussed. Third, believers are not interested in divination. When
you know and are known by the One who holds your future in His hands,
you don't need to discern the future!

An excellent book explaining end times prophecy is *Jerusalem
Countdown–A Warning to the World*, authored by pastor John Hagee, 2006,
published by Front Line.

The Rotten Fruit of Replacement Theology

The key to understanding why the Church's teaching on end times
prophecy and events is so skewed is provided in the article. Again, the
Catholic Church does not believe in the Jesus of the New Testament. Like
the Latter-Day Saints, Orthodox Churches, state Churches, and other cults,

they have added non-scriptural sources to their teachings. Many apostate
Churches maintain that they believe in the infallibility of the New Testament.
However, they do not believe in its *sufficiency*. Thus, their teachings belie
their words. As the Fathers note:

> In total reliance on the Scriptures **and** the Official Teachings of the Roman
> Catholic Church, the **authentic** Revelation of Jesus Christ....

According to the Fathers, additional revelations about Jesus Christ
were made known to the Catholic Church, which, as noted in chapter
one, didn't come into existence until the middle of the 5th century. Even if
one erroneously credits Constantine with establishing the Roman Catholic
Church, this means that Jesus revealed additional information about end
times nearly three-hundred years after His ascension! This is in concert
with Latter-Day Saints teaching.

The beauty of replacement theology to the non-scriptural advocates
lies in its support for the notion that God changes His mind. Replacement
theology teaches that God chose the Jews and made a covenant with them
based on their "goodness." However, because over time they became "bad,"
God *changed His mind*. Moreover, because the Church views itself as good
and Jesus promised never to leave it, Church leaders believe that the Church
has replaced Israel and God's promises to Israel transfer over to the Church.
The utility of such a theory to these churchmen is that they can justify
changing and supplanting Jesus' and His apostles' teachings; negating His
promises of eternal life; and placing additional, non-scriptural requirements
on the faithful such as a sacramental salvation system.

However, no Church or church replaced Israel in God's heart, promises,
or prophetic plan. Moreover, God assures us:

> For I am the LORD and I change not; and you the sons of Jacob (*Israel*)
> are not consumed.
>
> —Malachias 3:6

Moreover, God's Word assures us further:

> Your word, O LORD, *endures forever*; it is as firm as the heavens.
> —Psalms 118 (119):89

While God's Word is settled in heaven forever, it is still being changed
today by wicked men on earth!

God changed Jacob's name to Israel and it was he who gave birth to the
heads of the twelve tribes [Genesis 32:29]. Jesus was a descendant of the

tribe of Judah. The body of believers, the *autos*, was *added to the Abrahamic covenant* and God's Word confirms that this body of believers does not supplant Israel. This is how St. Paul described the relationship:

> For you are all the children of God through faith in Christ Jesus. For all you who have been baptized into Christ, have put on Christ. There is neither Jew nor Greek (*Gentile*); there is neither slave nor freeman; there is neither male nor female. For you are all one in Christ Jesus. And if you are Christ's, then you are the offspring of Abraham, heirs according to promise.
> —Galatians 3:26-29

St. Paul does not say that those who are Christ's (believers) receive the promises forfeited by Israel. Nor does he mention forfeiture by Abraham. Quite the contrary, he reveals something startling: Believers are added to the covenant of promise God made with Abraham!

Churches that teach replacement theology do so for a variety of interests. This, in turn, requires them to teach that the prophecies in the book of Apocalypse have already taken place. For example, they refer to Nero as the Antichrist. This is called the "preterit view." Of course, this presents even more problems. For example, the book of Apocalypse reveals catastrophes in the heavens and the earth that, had they already occurred, surely would have been recorded by historians. Also, Jesus returns at the end of the seven-year Tribulation and, according to the Catholic Bible, "Behold, he comes with the clouds, and every eye shall see him, and they also who pierced him. And all the tribes of the earth shall wail over him. Amen" [Apocalypse 1:7]. These Churches are left with a patchwork eschatology (end times teaching) that, like their soteriology, has patch upon patch upon patch until there is no substance left, only patches.

Having eliminated the teachings in the book of Apocalypse and other end times Old Testament prophecies, the Roman Catholic Church has substituted the mistaken teaching that Jesus will return to earth only after the earth has become worthy of receiving her King. Fathers Riney and Kreutzer describe this in their article:

> The Roman Catholic Church eagerly, hopefully, and joyfully anticipates... the Second Advent of Jesus Christ at the end of the age. Many other Christian denominations and world religions do not share the Catholic Church's optimistic view of these future events.

Jesus described what it would be like at the time of His return, as recorded in the Roman Catholic Bible:

But as it was in the days of Noe, even so will be the coming of the Son
of Man.

—St. Matthew 24:37

And how was it in the days of Noe? According to the Catholic Bible:

And when the LORD saw that the wickedness of man on the earth was
great, and that man's every thought and all inclination of his heart were
only evil, he regretted that he had made man on the earth and was grieved
to the heart. Then the LORD said, 'I will wipe from the earth man whom
I have created....

—Genesis 6:5-7

It seems that the Jesus of the New Testament, the Jesus presented so
clearly in the Roman Catholic Bible, does not share the Catholic Church's
optimism that man will get better as time goes by. Neither does St. Paul:

But the wicked and imposters will go from bad to worse, erring and
leading into error.

—2 Timothy 3:13

The Roman Catholic Bible confirms that man will get progressively
worse and Jesus tells us that by the time of His Second Coming man will be
as wicked as he was during the time of Noe. The only optimism believers
can find in this is that they will have been raptured prior to these events,
as taught in the Catholic Bible.

The role replacement theology played in the persecution of the Jews
during the Inquisition was critical. According to Roman Catholic tradition,
then and today, the Christ will return to earth only after the world had been
made Catholic. Replacement theology, taught by the Catholic and Lutheran
Churches in Germany, played a critical role in the people's acceptance of
Hitler's "final solution to the Jewish problem." Replacement theology is
a doctrine of demons [1 Timothy 4:1]. More will be said about Hitler's
demonic ties in Appendix A.

There Is Only One True Jesus

There is only one Christ. However, there are as many "Jesuses" as there
are cults. There is the Jesus in Constantine's vision who placed himself
on the same level as the sun god, thus breaking the first commandment
of Jehovah God—You shall have no other gods beside Me. Some may be
inclined to ask, "If God can and does use evil men for His good purposes,

then how do you know God wasn't using the evil Constantine to spread Christianity when he established his universal Church?" As discussed in chapter four, God does sometimes use evil men to accomplish His good pleasure. However, in each and every instance, God is using the evil ones to spread *His Truth*, not lies! Constantine was not spreading Christ's truth, but Satan's lies as documented in chapter five. The Roman Catholic Church would argue that when Constantine brought the pagan statues into the Christian churches, the people were kneeling before statues of Christians, not pagans. However, this is not true, as demonstrated in chapter five. The pagans that "converted" at Constantine's urging continued to look upon the statues of Semiramis and Tammuz but now called Mary and Jesus. Constantine, with his introduced rituals, icons, and pagan prelates, did not conform the world (pagans) to Christianity, which was Christ's directive. Neither did he follow our Lord's command to "come out of her" (the world). Rather, he created an apostate Christianity in the image of the world. Kneeling in front of icons was and is a pagan practice condemned in the Roman Catholic and all other Bibles.

There is also the Jesus of the Latter-Day Saints who is a created being and the half-brother of Lucifer. There is the Jesus of the Christian Scientists who swooned on the cross but didn't die and rise. There is the Jesus of the sacramental sects who died, was buried, and rose again. However, according to Church teaching, he surrendered his power and authority to Church leaders and councils who voided his word with their "sacred traditions" and made him a liar.

Lastly, there is the Jesus prophesied in the Old Testament and fulfilled in the New. This Jesus is the Son of God who, as our kinsman redeemer, bore our sins on the tree to *pay our debt*. This is the same Jesus who cried out from the cross, "*It is finished.*" This is the all-powerful Shepherd who still gives His sheep eternal life, promises them they will never perish, and holds them securely in His loving hand [St. John 10]. This is the One who pours the cup and sets it before us. This is the Bridegroom who will soon leave His position at the right hand of the Father and return to catch away His bride (the *autos*). This is the Jesus God's Word refers to as the Lamb slain before the foundation of the world, the only One who is worthy to open the scroll, the title deed to the earth, and pour out God's wrath on unrepentant sinners [see Apocalypse 5]. This Jesus is the Judge of the universe, the Judge in front of whom each of us will one day stand. This is the same Jesus *all men* will confess is Lord either in this life or at the Great White Throne judgment of the damned. This Jesus is the Alpha and the Omega, the author and finisher of our faith! Which Jesus will you follow?

APPENDIX A:
CHARACTERISTICS OF A
NEW TESTAMENT CHURCH

MANY UNBELIEVERS LOOK at what the world and the media label "Christian" and conclude, "What hypocrites!" And rightly so. Too often on the nightly news we see some group—identified by the media as "Christian"—carrying signs with hateful expressions such as "God hates fags." Quite the contrary. God loves *everyone*. That is why He sent His Son into this sinful world, to pay for the sins of *all men*, including homosexuals and lesbians [St. John 3:16]. When John the Baptist saw Jesus coming toward him, he identified Jesus as "the Lamb of God who takes away the sin of the world!" [St. John 1:29] As recorded in St. Matthew 9:35-36:

> And Jesus was going about all the towns and villages, teaching in their synagogues, and preaching the gospel of the kingdom, and curing every kind of disease and infirmity. But seeing the crowds, he was moved with compassion for them, because they were bewildered and dejected, *like sheep without a shepherd.*

These were the lost of Jesus' day. He had compassion for them. It is no different today. As His ambassadors, we are to approach these lost sheep as He did, with compassion and love, not with hate-filled hearts or carrying signs of condemnation [2 Corinthians 5:20].

Not all will accept God's free offer of salvation. However, if the sinner repents, that is, agrees with God that he is a sinner in need of a Savior and asks Jesus to come into his life that he might live for Him, then Christ will free him from the bondage of his sin and condemnation [see St. John 8:34-36 and 1 Corinthians 6:9-11]. His sin is already under Christ's blood at Calvary [see Colossians 2:14]. But the sinner must claim Christ's payment for his sin debt to effect his salvation.

Apostate Christianity Today

Before describing the characteristics of a New Testament church, a general background is provided by way of contrast between those who call themselves "Christian" and believers who, by definition, believe in the Jesus of the New Testament and restrict their beliefs only to those revealed in Scripture. If asked, "Do you know what Christian churches teach?" most would reply in the affirmative. However, not only do different churches teach different things, there is broad misunderstanding today on what constitutes Christian beliefs and teaching. We first look at what the *world* calls Christian churches and practices.

Apostate Christianity Encourages Hate

God hates sin but loves the sinner. Those who carry signs expressing hate for anyone are not children of God, but sons of disobedience. Jesus said His followers would be known by their love for one another [St. John 13:35]. Believers have been labeled "homophobic" by the "gay" community and media because they refuse to condone what God's Word calls "an abomination." In an ABC *20/20* interview the evening of July 27, 2000, just several days before the start of the Republican party convention in Philadelphia, Ms. Barbara Walters asked Governor George W. Bush if homosexuality was a sin. The Governor sidestepped the issue by asking rhetorically, "Who am I to say? I'm a sinner, too." Ms. Walters smiled approvingly.

The root meaning of the word homophobia is "fear of mankind." However, believers are not afraid of mankind, homosexual, bisexual, lesbian, or otherwise. What believers *are afraid of* is the eternal destiny that lies ahead for homosexual men and women who fail to repent and invite Jesus to come into their lives and free them. No believer thinks his job is to deride, harm or kill the sinner, no matter what the sin. Those advocating violence against members of the homosexual community are not believers. However, there is no law against them calling themselves Christian, and the media willingly oblige them. As with all aspects of life, Satan is working his plan for men's destruction and eternal separation from God. While Hollywood, the media, and schools push for diversity and acceptance of all lifestyles, true purveyors of hate against homosexuals seldom come under criticism by the media. Modern "heavy metal" and "rap" songs contain lyrics vomiting violence against just about everyone and everything, from virgins to homosexuals. One rapper's lyrics suggests he will "stab them in the head" if they are a "fag" or "lesbian."[1] There has been little condemnation by the media. When believers witness to homosexuals, the media label their words "hate speech." The reasons believers cannot condone homosexual acts, lifestyle, or marriage are obvious from the Scriptures:

> You shall not lie with a male as with a woman; such a thing is an abomination.
> —Leviticus 18:22

Moreover, God's Word tells us:

> If a man lies with a male as with a woman, both of them shall be put to death for their abominable deed; they have forfeited their lives.
> —Leviticus 20:13

Lest you think God changed His attitude on this matter between Old Testament and New Testament, let God's Word assure you He hasn't:

> For this cause God has given them up to shameful lusts; for their women have exchanged the natural use for that which is against nature, and in like manner the men also, having abandoned the natural use of the woman, have burned in their lusts one towards another, men with men doing shameless (*brazen*) things and receiving in themselves the fitting recompense of their perversity (*physical ailments*). And as they have resolved against possessing the knowledge of God, God has given them up to reprobate (*morally unprincipled*) sense, so that they do not know what is fitting… Although they have known the ordinance (*laws*) of God, they have not understood that those who practice such things are deserving of death. And not only do they do these things, but they *applaud others doing them.*
> —Romans 1:26-32

Moreover, verse 24 verifies that they "… dishonor their own bodies among themselves." God's Word couldn't be clearer. St. Paul warns:

> Do not err (*fool yourselves*); neither fornicators, nor idolaters, nor adulterers, nor the effeminate (*male prostitutes*), nor sodomites… will possess the kingdom of God.
> —1 Corinthians 6:9-10

The two above citations from the New Testament make clear that the homosexual lifestyle is counter to God's Word. Therefore, no believer can ever condone the "gay" lifestyle. What believers can and should do and, in fact, are commanded to do by our Lord, is to minister to the lost, whether they be homosexuals, lesbians, bisexuals, fornicators, adulterers, or whatever. While homosexuals may claim their lifestyle is "gay," even most nonbelievers know this to be a lie. God's Word tells us that their lives will be anything but "gay" in the next life. As long as believers continue to follow Jesus' command to love homosexuals, they will continue to speak God's truth in love and encourage those engaged in such lifestyles to repent and admit their need for a Savior and invite Christ to come into their lives and make them free [see St. John 8:30-36]. Believers pray that the minds of all sinners will be opened to the truth of God's Word [2 Corinthians 4:4]. Believers also pray that those carrying signs with hate-filled messages will turn from their sin and invite the Jesus of the New Testament into their lives as Lord and Savior.

Apostate Christianity Encourages Violence

We read about so-called Christian groups that have carried out violence against those seeking abortions. Clinics and personnel have been attacked and killed. Some posit that it is morally superior to kill an abortionist and thereby save thousands of innocent babies from the butcher's knife. The failed logic behind this reasoning is obvious even to most nonbelievers. The Federal Drug Administration approved the production and distribution of the "abortion pill," RU-486 in September 2000. However, the government refused to reveal where the pill would be manufactured due to fear of violence.

Apostate Christianity Encourages Racial Division and Anti-Semitism

Some brand of brave "Christian soldiers" prowl around under cover of darkness and starched white sheets and burn crosses in some people's front yards or write anti-Semitic graffiti on the walls of synagogues to terrorize women and children. Still others wear brown shirts with arm patches boasting a cross on one arm and a swastika on the other. They speak evil of the people God chose to be *His people* [Deuteronomy 7:6-8]. They persecute those of whom God said: "I will bless them that bless you (*the Jews*), and curse them who curse you. In you shall *all* the nations of the earth be blessed" [Genesis 12:3]. The word "nations" in the Old Testament generally refers to Gentiles. This, of course, was a future-truth prophecy of the birth of Jesus through the Davidic line, through the tribe of Judah [Apocalypse 5:5]. This prophecy also included many other contributions that world Jewry has made, particularly in the field of medicine. Despite the fact that the Jews make up less than one-half of one percent of the population, some twenty percent of those awarded Nobel prizes have been Jewish.

The swastika-boasting rebels justify their hateful words and evil actions by twisting God's words [Psalms 56:5 NKJV; 2 St. Peter 3:16] and thereby draw all "after their kind" to a ministry of death [2 Corinthians 4:1-4]. "Skinheads," as they refer to themselves, do not appreciate the fact that many of their fathers and grandfathers went to war to ensure that the horror the swastika represented would never become a national symbol in America. Our nation has been blessed for freeing European Jews who otherwise would have been exterminated in Nazi death camps. Neither do these present-day, would-be goose steppers recognize the occult roots of that demonic symbol. Today, it is associated with witchcraft and symbolizes "Mother Goddess."[2] The swastika has been a symbol of evil since ancient times. It is a symbol associated with Buddhists and Jains (India). To the Hindus, it symbolizes magic and the destructive goddess Kali.[3]

Hitler chose the swastika as the symbol for his Third Reich. The Reich was supposed to last for one thousand years, an imitation of Christ's millennial kingdom [see 1 St. John 2:18]. Hitler knew the demonic significance of the broken cross and chose it for that very reason. The U.S. government didn't admit until well after the conclusion of World War II that Hitler and his henchmen were practitioners of the occult. Hitler set about to exterminate the entire Jewish race, just as the Egyptian Pharao tried to do earlier when he ordered the midwives to kill all newborn Hebrew males [Exodus 1:15-16]. Satan had a plan to kill the promised Messiah who would come through the Hebrew line to reconcile sinful men to God. He worked his first plan through Cain who slew the righteous Abel and later through Herod the Great, as was discussed in chapter five.

Not long after Israel's exodus from Egypt, the Moabite king, Balac, saw the horde coming toward his land. He had seen what Israel had done to his neighbors, the Amorites. Balac sent his servants to fetch the false prophet Balaam to speak against God's chosen people. But every time Balaam opened his mouth to speak a curse, by the power of Jehovah, out came a blessing. Balaam finally suggested that the king send out his most beautiful women to seduce the Israelites, intermarry with them, and thereby avoid a war. Balac followed Balaam's advice. Before long, some of God's chosen ones not only had intermarried, but also had begun to worship Balac's god, Baal. This angered the LORD and He directed Moses to remedy the situation. After application of the remedy, some twenty-four thousand of God's chosen lay dead. God stopped the dilution of the Jewish race through intermarriage, because the Jews figure prominently in His plan for man's redemption [see Numbers 22-25]. Through this preserved race came the prophets and the Messiah.

God is not through using His chosen people to bring men to Himself [see Deuteronomy 28:10]. According to God's plan, 144,000 Jews, 12,000 from each of the twelve tribes, will become witnesses for Christ in the Tribulation period [Apocalypse 7:3-8]. God is calling His chosen people out of the Diaspora and bringing them back to Israel even now in preparation for His purpose [see Ezechiel 37:12]. Today, they are returning in unbelief. However, after God breaths His spirit into them [Ezechiel 37:14], they will produce so great a soul harvest that "no man can number them" [Apocalypse 7:9-14]. Satan had a plan to eliminate these witnesses which, in turn, would have prevented the largest soul harvest ever [see 2 Corinthians 2:11]. In return for exterminating the Jews, Satan promised Hitler great things, including a world dictatorship and possibly even immortality. Thus, elimination of European Jewry was just the first step. After conquering the Allies, Hitler would have eliminated the remaining Jews from *all* the earth. This is why Hitler and his Generals were sure they would win the war. This was Satan's plan and Satan's war. But God had His own plan. He revealed it to the prophet Ezechiel more than 2,500 years before World War II began. God took Ezechiel in spirit and showed him what is known as "the valley of dry bones," and asked him if the bones could come to life [see Ezechiel 37:1-14]. Could Ezechiel's vision have been one of a trench filled with the emaciated and naked bodies of victims of the death camps? Hitler, like Herod the Great, Balac, and Pharao tried to carry out Satan's plans to maintain the wedge between God and man by destroying the Jews. Satan, a liar and the father of lies and a murderer (Cain) from the beginning [St. John 8:44], was long on promise to the Austrian paper hanger and would-be architect, but short on delivery.

No one has given a reason why Hitler spent more time and energy trying to exterminate a defenseless and humble people than win a war. Certainly the pacifistic Jews were no threat to an armed nation. Only rationalizations have been suggested. The real reason lies not in the physical realm but in the spiritual—in this case, the demonic. Hitler eliminated some six million of Europe's eight million Jews and more than half of world Jewry! The reason he was not successful is also spiritual. The prophet Zacharias recorded God's feelings toward Israel this way: "... for he that toucheth you toucheth the apple of my eye" [Zacharias 2:8]. The apple of the eye is generally considered to be the pupil, the most sensitive part. To take on the Jews is to take on God Almighty.

It is worse than a sad commentary that many *who called themselves Christian* were supporters of Hitler's "final solution to the Jewish problem." Have you ever wondered why Hitler called his program the "final" solution? This is a reference to previous attempts by Satan to end the Jewish line through Pharao, Balac, and others. And what exactly is meant by "the Jewish problem"? St. John gives the answer in St. John 4:22: "... salvation is from the Jews." The only one to whom the Jews present a "problem" is Satan and his followers. If he can eliminate the Jews, he can still eliminate salvation for believers in the Tribulation period.

Hitler's top generals, like Hitler himself, were practitioners of the occult. However, the vast majority of his military, their wives, and ordinary citizens were not. Why did practicing Catholics, Lutherans, and other Protestants, claiming to be followers of the Jewish Messiah, support Hitler and his henchmen? Because they had been fed a steady diet of replacement theology, a doctrine of demons, year after year from the pulpits of apostate Churches. The people had been taught that God had forsaken the Jews and that Jesus would return only after the world became "Christian." History had taught that centuries of the Inquisition carried out by the Roman Catholic Church had failed to *convert* the Jews. Now Hitler was being viewed as a hero who would hasten Jesus' return by *eliminating* the greatest obstacle to His Second Coming: unbelieving Jews.

For believers, there are no distinctions among races or ethnicities [Romans 10:12]. The only distinctions are between right and wrong, good and evil, light and darkness. Believers pray that the eyes of those blinded by racism will be opened by the One who gave sight to the blind [St. Luke 4:18-19]. As Doctor John Hagee, pastor of Cornerstone Church in San Antonio notes in his book, " what you do to the Jewish people, God will do to you."[4] Pharaoh tried to have all Hebrew male babies drowned. Jehovah drowned Pharaoh. Haman planned to hang all the Jews in the Persian Empire. Instead, it was Haman who was hanged [see Esther]. Hitler segregated the Jews into ghettos, imprisoned them, killed them, and then burned their bodies. As the war drew to an end, Hitler segregated himself and his top thugs in an underground bunker in Berlin. Prior to taking his own life, Hitler directed his generals to burn his body until nothing but ash remained. What Hitler did to the apple of God's eye, God did to Hitler. As Doctor Hagee notes so succinctly:

> Hitler closed his eyes in death and stepped into eternity to meet a Rabbi named Jesus of Nazareth as his final judge. "I will curse him who curses you...."

Apostate Christianity Encourages Cult-Like Behavior

Cable television broadcasts numerous documentaries on every sort of "Christian" group and "church" that makes those walking in the world look rational by comparison. Some, like snake handlers, are a curiosity. After commanding His disciples to go into the whole world and preach the gospel and to baptize those who believe, Jesus assured them:

> "And these signs shall attend those who believe... they shall take up serpents...."
>
> —St. Mark 16:17-18

Some cults have misunderstood this verse to mean that Christians should pick up serpents in their worship services. However, if one examines the context, it is clear that Jesus was saying that He would protect them even if they were bitten by a serpent. The end of verse 18 goes on to say:

> "And if they drink a deadly thing, it shall not hurt them...."
>
> —St. Mark 16:18

Jesus was assuring His disciples that if someone tried to poison them, He would not allow the poison to work. Poisoning was a common way of eliminating enemies in that day. To "take the cup" was a metaphor for death. In the garden, Jesus prayed: "Father, if it is possible, let this cup pass away from me..." [St. Matthew 26:39]. St. Luke records that prior to visiting certain towns, Jesus commissioned seventy-two disciples to go before Him. To these He gave great powers. When they returned, they were excited about their success. Jesus cautioned them:

> "Behold, I have given you power to tread upon serpents and scorpions, and over all the might of the enemy (*Satan*); and nothing shall hurt you. But do not rejoice in this, that the spirits (*demons*) are subject to you; rejoice rather in this, that your names are written in heaven."
>
> —St. Luke 10:19-20

Notice that it was the demon spirits the disciples treaded upon, not the flesh of men. Moreover, there is no command to handle snakes or drink poison. Notice, too, that Jesus told them not to rejoice in the fact that snakes and scorpions could not harm them. Yet "rejoice" is exactly what snake handlers do. As made clear in the book of Acts, the ability of the one bitten to survive was a sign to *nonbelievers* that his preaching was true. It was not a sign to fellow believers in worship services. St. Paul survived many things on his journeys, including storms at sea and being shipwrecked. He was tended to by some proverbial friendly natives on Malta:

> Now Paul gathered a bundle of sticks and laid them on the fire, when a viper came out because of the heat and fastened on his hand. When

the natives saw the creature hanging from his hand, they said to one another, "Surely this man is a murderer, for though he has escaped the sea, Justice does not let him live." But he shook off the creature into the fire and suffered no harm. Now they were expecting that he would swell up and suddenly fall down and die; but after waiting a long time and seeing no harm come to him, they changed their minds and said that he was a god.

—Acts 28:3-6

This is what St. Mark 16:18 is referring to, confirmation of the message, not using snakes in worship services. Moreover, this special power was given to the disciples for a specific mission at a specific time: preaching the nearness of the kingdom of heaven. But the Jews rejected the offer. These protections do not extend to the present age. No believer should take up snakes or drink poison expecting supernatural protection from God. However, in His graciousness, God may extend such protection.

Apostate Christianity Encourages Rebellion Against Government

Some wearing army fatigues and conducting war games in the back woods tell media interviewers that they are arming for battle with the U.S. government. These are not walking in submission. Jesus never directed anyone to take up the sword. Rather, He condemned the actions of those who did so [St. Matthew 26:52]. Moreover, Jesus never suggested rebellion against the government [St. Matthew 22:17-21]. God's Word reminds us:

Let everyone be subject to the higher authorities, for there exists no authority except from God, and those who exist have been appointed by God. Therefore, he who resists the authority resists the ordinance of God; and they that resist bring on themselves condemnation. For rulers are a terror not to the good work but to the evil. Dost thou wish, then, not to fear the authority? Do what is good and thou wilt have praise from it. For it is God's minister to thee for good. But if thou dost what is evil, fear, for not without reason does it carry the sword. For it is God's minister, an avenger to execute wrath on him who does evil.

—Romans 13:1-4

Not only do these verses make clear that believers are to be subject to civil rule, this citation makes God's view on capital punishment clear. It is God Himself who gives the state the sword to avenge evil upon this earth. This is one way God implements Romans 12:19:

> Do not avenge yourselves, beloved… for it is written, "Vengeance is mine;
> I will repay, says the Lord."

These verses also confirm that God put that individual in the White House, state house, mayor's office, etc. [see Daniel 2:37-38]. These represent His *authority*, but not necessarily His righteousness. In fact, not one word in Romans 13:1-4 implies that the "rulers" run their governments in concert with God's will. Nevertheless, believers are to submit to their rule. While we may be critical of their policies, we are not to *speak evil* against them [see 2 St. Peter 2:10 KJV; St. Jude 8]. St. Peter exhorts believers:

> … submit yourselves to every ordinance of man *for the Lord's sake*, whether
> to the king as supreme, or to governors, as to those who are sent by him
> for the punishment of evildoers and for the praise of those who do good.
> For this is the will of God, that by doing good you may put to silence
> the ignorance of foolish men—as free, yet not using liberty for a cloak of
> vice, but as bondservants of God. Honor all people. Love the brotherhood.
> Fear God. Honor the king.
>
> —1 St. Peter 2:13-17 NKJV

Finally, we are told to *pray* for those in authority that we may lead quiet and peaceful lives [1 Timothy 2:1-3]. Nowhere do the Scriptures tell believers to take up arms against the government, not even in the book of Apocalypse which prophesies a time when the most evil and oppressive of all governments, run by Satan himself, will rule the world. Those whose mouths spew hatred toward sinners and hurl racial epithets at their brothers and sisters in Adam are not Christian, no matter that the media label them so. Those who play army to be prepared to overthrow the government are marching to the beat of a different Commander-in-chief than the One described in Scripture who requires that Christian Soldiers (believers) not only be in submission to government authorities, but also pray for them and refrain from speaking evil against them.

Apostate Christianity Encourages Rebellion Against God's Word

Some church attendees hear a sociological message rather than the gospel. Man is edified by his own works. Recognition and condemnation of sin is not the message from these pulpits. Others are told, "If we just love one another, we will go to heaven." There is not one verse of Scripture that endorses this demonic lie. Yet it is a widely held teaching in many Churches. Self-justification and celebration of the diversity of paths is their doxology. There is no preaching that man is a sinner, deserving of hell, and that he can be washed clean only by the redeeming blood of Jesus. Their choirs do not sing, "O precious is the flow, that makes me white as snow; No other fount I know, *Nothing* but the blood of Jesus." These Churches are singing a different tune. Believers pray that their eyes and minds will be opened to the one and only true gospel presented in the New Testament, the gospel that saves rather than condemns.

Normally, the more vociferous elements leading the women's movement pay little attention to what the Churches do. However, there was an exception in July 2000 when a woman pastor in Baltimore, Maryland was promoted to the position of bishop. She became the first female bishop in the Black African Episcopal Church. The bishop was interviewed on the CBS evening news on July 16, 2000. Nary a word did the bishop say about Jesus. Rather, she expressed her glee at breaking through what she and her female interviewer slyly referred to as the "stained glass ceiling." The good bishop did remark that the world needs care, tenderness, and nurturing. One can't help but wonder what the bishop's message on 1 Timothy 2:12 would be:

> For I do not allow a woman to teach, or to exercise authority (*spiritual authority*) over men....

Practicing homosexual men and lesbians with "life partners" have been ordained to the pulpits of several Churches considered by most to be mainstream.[5] Godly submission of the wife to a godly husband who is walking in submission to Christ is not a topic for the sheep of these shepherds who have entered not by the door into the sheepfold, but have climbed up another way [see St. John 10:1]. Neither is the biblical proscription against women exercising spiritual authority over men—no women preachers, lesbian or not, life-partnered or not—discussed from these pulpits [see 1 Timothy 2:12 above]. Ephesians chapter 5 is not a topic for their Sunday sermons. St. Paul warned:

> For know this and understand, that no fornicator, or unclean person... has *any* inheritance in the kingdom of Christ and God. Let no one lead you astray with empty words; for because of these things the wrath of God comes upon the children of disobedience (*Sodom and Gomorrah may be what is spoken of here*). Do not then be partakers with them... and have no fellowship with the unfruitful works of darkness, but rather expose them.
>
> —Ephesians 5:5-11

God knew some "just wouldn't get it," so he warned again:

> ... Do not err; neither fornicators, nor idolaters, nor adulterers, nor the
> effeminate, nor *sodomites*... will possess the kingdom of God.
> —1 Corinthians 6:9-10

It is interesting to note that the ordination of homosexuals and lesbians has been performed only by Churches that subscribe to replacement theology. As discussed in previous chapters, such Churches teach that they have been given the authority to change God's Laws. This, of course, is precisely the same erroneous thinking the Pharisees demonstrated which brought Jesus' condemnation. Nevertheless, this is why some Churches have broken God's law and ordained openly practicing homosexuals and lesbians. This is why so many in the "gay" community want local congregations to welcome homosexuals and even perform in-church, same-sex marriage ceremonies. They mistakenly believe that if enough Churches and members say that homosexuality is no longer a sin, then God will be more or less forced to go along with their "enlightened" decision because Jesus gave the Church the power to change God's Laws, the "keys" to the kingdom. This is exactly the thinking of Churches that subscribe to replacement theology! They have stripped the all-powerful Christ of the New Testament of His power to *give* eternal life as a gift and preserve His sheep, and substituted in His place an impotent antichrist whose death on the cross did not atone for all the sins of all the world for all time and who is such a bad shepherd that he cannot keep his sheep in the sheepfold. Moreover, neither can this imposter hold the sheep securely in his hand, for they are snatched frequently by Satan. Moreover, this pretender ignored the Father's will, discarded salvation by grace, and established a sacramental salvation system in place of the cross. But man cannot change God's Laws. God tells us clearly that He does not change His mind. "For I am the LORD and I change not..." [Malachias 3:6]. Moreover, God's Word reveals: "Forever, O LORD, Your word is settled in heaven" [Psalms 119:89 NKJV]. Therefore, believers pray for these sheep, as well as their wandering shepherds, that their eyes will be opened to the Word and will of God and that they will come to know the Good Shepherd and follow Him.

Apostate Christianity Encourages Belief in a Jesus Not Found in the New Testament

Many Churches and churches teach a path to salvation that requires things contrary to Scripture. As made clear in this and previous chapters, these reveal a Jesus different from the Jesus of the New Testament. Some

teach that His atoning death on the cross was not sufficient to purchase
your soul, preserve your sanctification, and rescue your body from the
fires and torments of hell. Such a "Jesus" is not the Christ described in
the Scriptures. This antichrist is an imposter, and is every bit as false as
the Latter-Day Saints' Jesus who is a created being and the half-brother of
Lucifer. Apostate Churches teach that the individual must ante up, because
Jesus' atonement was insufficient. These Churches go outside the inspired
Word of God to justify their teachings. Like all cults, they rely on additional,
non-biblical revelations and manmade traditions to support their claims.
One such example was discussed in the Conclusion. According to the
Roman Catholic Church, as confirmed in an article by Fathers Phil Riney
and Dan Kreutzer (discussed in the Conclusion), the book of the Apocalypse
does not contain the complete revelation of the Second Coming of Christ.
Rather, according to Fathers Riney and Kreutzer, the Church relies on "...
the Scriptures *and the Official Teachings of the Roman Catholic Church, the
Authentic Revelation of Jesus Christ.*" If this is the authentic revelation of
Jesus Christ, then the Catholic Bible must present an inauthentic revelation,
since its teachings are at odds with the Church's "authentic revelation of
Jesus Christ"! One must wonder what other teachings contained in the
Roman Catholic Bible's New Testament are viewed as inauthentic by the
Catholic Church which claims that Catholics wrote the New Testament.
These fallacious teachings generally present a problem only for those who
read their Bibles. Many denominations have sown up the tear in the veil to
the Holy of Holies and introduced ceremonials, rituals, repeated sacrifices,
priests, and a religious hierarchy between God and man. All these are
contrary to the Word of God:

> "And every priest, indeed stands daily ministering and often offering the
> same sacrifices, *which can never take away sins*; but Jesus, *having offered one
> sacrifice for sins*, has taken his seat forever at the right hand of God...."
> —Hebrews 10:11-12

The sacrifice that Jesus, our high priest [see Hebrews 4:14], made was
once and for all and does not need to be repeated [see Hebrews 7:27; 9:12;
10:10]. The priests in the Temple offering daily one sacrifice, after another
did not remove sins. Jesus made one perfect sacrifice, which took away
all sins for all time [see 1 St. John 1:7]. He subsequently sat down at the
right hand of the Father, the work of salvation having been completed,
the debt to the Father having been "paid in full." Believers pray for the
sheep and the shepherds of such Churches, for they place their faith in
human institutions, high priests, and Churches—all claiming to be *The*

Church—rather than in the Word of God and the atoning death of the Jesus of the New Testament, the Christ.

Apostate Christianity Encourages Doctrinal Segmentation and Deviation from God's Word

There are "cafeteria Christians." While the alliterative aspects of this appellation are quite satisfying, the phenomenon of picking and choosing which doctrines to accept and which to reject is not limited to any one denomination. There are "cafeteria Catholics" and "persnickety Protestants." Some Orthodox say they trust their Church for administering a sacramental salvation system and baptizing infants by immersion, but they don't "buy" the need for auricular confession of sins to a priest. A Catholic friend of mine who shares this view said he used to feel like a hypocrite when he would confess to his priest that he had spent the weekend at his girlfriends place, promise not to do it again, all the while knowing they had a reservation at a ski lodge the next month. He came to the conclusion that, under such circumstances, one cannot make a "good" act of contrition. He said he finally just quit going to confession.

Some believe that Jesus established the practice of confessing one's sins to a priest. However, this is incorrect, as was shown in chapter four. God's Word tells us to confess (admit) our sins not to a priest, but *one to another* and to pray for each other [St. James 5:16]. St. James is simply reaffirming Jesus' teaching to reconcile yourself to your Christian brother if you have offended him [see St. Matthew 5:24]. There is not a single word in Scripture supporting the notion of confessing one's sins to anyone other than God and, if applicable, the offended party. God's Word commands the believer to admit his sin when a fellow believer says he has been wronged. A believer is to admit his sin, not defend it or rationalize it. Specifically, auricular confession of sins to a priest is not biblical and is antithetical to God's Holy Word. The requirement for confession of one's sins to a priest was instituted by Pope Innocent III (1198-1216) and was one of seventy decrees at the Fourth Lateran Council in 1215. God's Word assures:

> If we acknowledge (*confess*) our sins, he is faithful and just to forgive us
> our sins and to cleanse us from all iniquity (*unrighteousness*).
> —1 St. John 1:9

However, this assurance is only for believers. The *He* in the above citation is God, for only God can cleanse us. The man against whom we sin can forgive us, but neither he nor a priest can cleanse us from our sins.

The life of a believer is markedly different from that of a nonbeliever.
St. Paul tells us:

> For know this and understand, that no fornicator… has any inheritance
> in the kingdom of Christ and God.
>
> —Ephesians 5:5

Do St. John's and St. Paul's teachings above contradict one other? No.
They are talking about two different subjects. St. John is saying that when
the believer turns his back on Christ, rejects the power of the Holy Spirit,
and sins, he is to confess his sin and God will forgive and cleanse him.
Thus, he retains his inheritance in the kingdom [St. Matthew 25:34]. St.
Paul is saying that one who lives a lifestyle marked by fornication (or any
other sin) is not a follower of Christ, and is not a believer. Therefore, he
will have no inheritance in the kingdom. The inheritance of this child of
disobedience will be that which was prepared for the devil and his angels
[St. Matthew 25:41]. One cannot live a sinful lifestyle and then confess it
to a priest or minister and expect God to forgive him. This is legalism, and
Jesus condemned the Judaizers for its practice. Jesus said of the legalists
of His day:

> "… So you have made void the commandments of God by your traditions.
> Hypocrites, well did Isaias prophesy of you, saying, 'This people honors
> me with their lips, but their heart is far from me; and in vain do they
> worship me, teaching as doctrines the precepts of men.'"
>
> —St. Matthew 15:6-9

How then can one ever get control over a lifestyle of sin? He cannot.
One must repent (admit he is a sinner in need of a Savior) and ask Jesus to
come into his life and turn it around. It is only through the power of His
might that the Holy Spirit of God living within the sinner *changes the sinner's
attitude toward sin, renews his mind, and gives him the strength necessary to
withstand the wiles of the devil.* Thus, it is the power of God that changes
lifestyles, not the will of man. God's Word assures believers:

> … Walk in the Spirit, and you will not fulfill the lusts of the flesh.
>
> —Galatians 5:16

Note that believers are assured they will not *fulfill* the lusts of the
flesh. New believers are sometimes surprised that they are still tempted
and sometimes give in to sin. What God's Word promises is that we can,
through the indwelling power of the Holy Spirit, resist the temptation if we

choose. By so choosing, we would not fulfill the lusts of the flesh. When the believer gives in to temptation, he is to confess his sins to God, who will not only forgive him, but also cleanse him.

Apostate Christianity Encourages Reliance Upon Men Rather than God

Some Catholics trust their Church to give them correct information on Church traditions and which saints to pray to, but they "don't buy" the existence of purgatory or the pope's position on birth control. It is only human nature to pick and choose. Like most Catholics, most Protestants mistakenly believe that baptism removes original sin and regenerates a dead spirit. Others teach it is possible to lose one's salvation but gain it back through "good works." These are placing their trust in a ritual rather than Jesus. Others believe singing in the choir, teaching Sunday school, or tithing are paths to heaven. We tend to pick the things we like and reject those we don't. What one accepts, another rejects. The Catholic Church would argue that it is precisely for this reason that we need an earthly "head" of The Church, a pope. However, popes have often disagreed with one another. Joan of Arc's sainthood, the eternal destiny of unbaptized/ uncommunioned babies, and the morality of abortion are but three of several examples already discussed. Therefore, having an earthly "head" of a Church does not solve the problem. However, this is one reason why God gave us His Word in which He tells us to test all things and to hold fast to what is good [1 Thessalonians 5:21]. His Holy Word tells us what to accept. God's Word commands believers to compare what our teachers tell us with His Word [Acts 17:11]. Those who do not know His Word often follow false teachers, as was proved in chapter two.

The world walked in sin during Jesus' day just as it does in ours. In response, Jesus did not round up His disciples to make signs, shout hateful slogans, or picket in front of pagan temples. Rather, Jesus looked with compassion upon those who practiced such abominations as sheep without a shepherd [see St. Mark 6:34]. The only ones at whom Jesus directed His ire were some in the religious establishment. These refused to believe the sanctifying (setting apart) works of the Holy Spirit being done through Him before their eyes. Rather, they ascribed His miracles to a devil [see St. Matthew 12:22-37]. Many of the Jews, like many of today's cafeteria folk, accepted what they liked about Jesus—that he changed water into wine, fed five thousand with a few loaves and fishes, and raised Lazarus from the dead—but rejected His claim that He could forgive sins. Today, some accept that Jesus is the only-begotten Son of God and that He died on the cross for the sins of the world and was buried and rose bodily on the third day. However, they deny the sufficiency of His payment. It seems strange to trust a Church or church for salvation that teaches some Bible truths while it denies others.

Apostate Christianity Is Not Christianity

As God's obedient children and Jesus' faithful followers, believers are His witnesses, and we preach the gospel to every creature [St. Mark 16:15; Acts 1:8]. This we do in a manner that is not condemning, hateful, or self-righteous. Rather, we share the truth with unbelievers—that Jesus is the way, and the truth, and the life, and that no one comes to the Father but through Him [St. John 14:6]—in love and humility, realizing, as it is said, "There but for the grace of God go I" [see Ephesians 4:15; Titus 3:1-7].

Believers are to be living examples to nonbelievers. One of the greatest reasons nonbelievers fail to heed the message to come to Jesus is because they see the way some *calling themselves* Christians live. Moreover, they also see the way *some believers live*, in a carnal manner [1 Corinthians 3:3]. Several television evangelists have run into problems in this area. Satan would rather bring down a nationally recognized preacher lifted up with pride than an ordinary saved sinner. Why? Because the famous are known, and when they stumble, that too is made known by the prince of the power of the air, Satan [Ephesians 2:2]. And when they trip, those in the world look to believers and say with some degree of self-satisfaction, "They're all hypocrites!"

The sheep will not respond to the voice of a shepherd who is a profligate or one whose very presence at the pulpit is in violation of God's Word. Moreover, there can be no spiritual growth for individuals in Churches or churches that teach errant messages and things counter to God's Word.

Characteristics of a New Testament Church

The eleven characteristics of a New Testament church are discussed below.[6]

(1) Its Head and Founder—the Jesus of the New Testament, the Christ

Jesus is the lawgiver, the only legislator, and the session is closed. That is, He made the laws. They are contained in the Scriptures. His church (*ekklesia*) executes and teaches His laws but does not negate His laws or create new ones. This point is also addressed under the next characteristic.

> "... upon this rock I (*Jesus*) will build my church (*ekklesia*), and the gates of hell shall not prevail against it."
>
> —St. Matthew 16:18

> Again, he (*Jesus*) is the head of his body, the church (*ekklesia*); he, who is the beginning, the firstborn from the dead, that in all things he may have the first place.
>
> —Colossians 1:18

Many Churches claiming to be Christian mistakenly believe they have the authority to change God's Law. Some ordain women and homosexuals to the pulpit. Others make God's Word void by their ungodly traditions. However, Jesus said, "... till heaven and earth pass away, not one jot or one tittle shall be lost from the Law till all things have been accomplished" [St. Matthew 5:18]. Some denominational apologists who subscribe to replacement theology justify their anti-scriptural positions on one verse out of context: "my ways are not your ways" [Isaias 55:9]. However, if this verse is put in context, its meaning becomes clear and it is equally clear that it is not a verse that can be used to justify changing God's Law. God is telling the sinner to seek the Lord while He may be found (while He is near), to forsake his wicked ways and unjust thoughts and, if he does, the Lord will have mercy on him. The lesson here is that we are to forgive one another, showing mercy to one who sins against us. However, most demand justice. Rather, He tells us He forgives sinful men—through the shed blood of Jesus—because His thoughts are higher than men's thoughts (which are for justice), just as the heavens are exalted above the earth. The key is found in Isaias 55: 9-10. Never ask God for justice. Rather, plead for mercy [see St. Luke 18:13] and show mercy to others [St. Luke 12:48]. In His righteousness, God gave the Law. In His mercy, He gave us His Son.

The head of the church is not a priest or minister or pope or patriarch but the Jesus of the New Testament, the Christ. If your church teaches that anyone other than this Jesus is its head, get out. You are in an apostate church.

(2) Its Only Rule of Faith and Practice—the Scriptures

When Jesus came to Genesareth, He was met by a group of Scribes and Pharisees from Jerusalem. They asked Him why His disciples ate bread with defiled (unwashed) hands, rather than following the traditions handed down by the ancients. Jesus replied:

> "Well did Isaias prophesy of you hypocrites, as it is written, 'This people honors me with their lips, but their heart is far from me; and in vain do they worship me, teaching as doctrine the precepts (*traditions*) of men.' For, letting go the commandment of God, you hold fast the tradition of men, the washing of pots and of cups; and many other things you do like these... Well do you nullify the commandment of God, that you may keep your own tradition!"
>
> —St. Mark 7:6-9

As He does throughout the Gospels, Jesus again refers to the written Word, a prophecy of Isaias. Jesus accused them of laying down the Law of God and picking up manmade traditions in its place. Jesus often accused the Pharisees of not knowing the Scripture. St. Paul and the other disciples taught:

> For from thy infancy thou hast known the Sacred Writings, which are able to instruct thee unto salvation by the faith which is in Christ Jesus. All Scripture is inspired by God and useful for teaching, for reproving, for correcting, for instructing in justice; that the man of God may be perfect (*complete*), equipped for every good work.
>
> —2 Timothy 3:15-17

The only traditions that play a role in a New Testament church are those that were in effect at the time of the writing of the books of the New Testament and endorsed in them:

> Be imitators of me as I am of Christ. Now I praise you, brethren, because in all things you are mindful of me and hold fast my precepts (*traditions*) as I gave them to you.
>
> —1 Corinthians 11:1-2

> So then, brethren, stand firm, and hold to the teachings that you have learned, whether by word or by letter of ours.
>
> —2 Thessalonians 2:15

The Churches claim that Church traditions were in effect long before we had the New Testament. Therefore, they argue, one must rely on both the New Testament and Church traditions. However, this claim is misleading. While the writings of the New Testament were not assembled into a single work until around 397 A.D., the books that make up the New Testament

were all in existence and widely circulated among the early churches by 95
A.D., as was documented in chapter one. Moreover, history records that the
canon of Scripture was recognized by 266 A.D., as was also documented in
chapter one. Furthermore, as documented in chapter five, only six "Church
traditions" were in existence by 397 A.D. when the New Testament was
assembled into a single work:

- Baptism of infants (220)
- Spiritual regeneration by baptism (220)
- Prayers for the dead (300)
- Making the sign of the cross (300)
- Worship of saints and angels (375)
- Mass as a daily ritual (394)

It is interesting to note that not even one of these traditions is endorsed
in any Gospel, epistle, or any other book of the New Testament. If St. Peter,
or St. Paul, or St. John, or St. Jude, or St. James, or St. Luke, or St. Matthew,
or St. Mark believed in the efficacy of prayers for the dead, then why didn't
a single one of these saints record the importance of same in any of his
writings? Why didn't a single one of them invite the living to seek his
assistance after his departure from this earth? Moreover, why did Jesus not
reveal the importance of prayers to the dead? When asked to teach them to
pray, He began with "Our Father...." Jesus never said a single "Hail Mary,"
nor did He suggest anyone else do so. Neither did He instruct His disciples
to seek the help of His deceased cousin, John the Baptist. Moreover, Jesus
did not begin His prayer to the Father with the sign of the cross, nor did He
instruct others to do so. He condemned superstitions and rituals. In fact,
most of St. Matthew's Gospel, written for the Jews, explains the futility of
the Law and rituals to save.

The Pharasetic system of salvation was based on following the Law and
performing rituals. Jesus dismissed the ability of this impotent approach.
He promised salvation as a free gift to those who believed in Him and He
performed sign miracles (healings, etc.) to authenticate His teaching. When
a paralytic was brought to Him, Jesus told Him his sins were forgiven. When
the Pharisees accused Him of blasphemy, since only God could forgive
sins, Jesus asked them which it was easier to say, "Your sins are forgiven or
arise and walk" [free translation]. The doctors knew they could not cure
the fellow and the Pharisees, the holy ones of Israel, knew they were not
empowered to forgive sins. Jesus was demonstrating that He had the power
and authority to do both and that *saying* one was no more difficult *for Him*
than saying the other. He had the power and authority to cure the body

and give life to the dead spirit! This is one reason why the Pharisees hated Him. They could sell Law and ritual in the form of animal sacrifices and incense. They could not sell the free gift He was offering. Neither could they match it. Jesus was asked why His disciples did not follow the Law and fast like the Pharisees:

> "Can the wedding guests mourn as long as the bridegroom (*Jesus*) is with them? But the days will come when the bridegroom shall be taken away from them, and then they will fast. And no one puts a patch of raw (*new*) cloth on an old garment, for the patch tears away from the garment, and a worse rent is made. Nor do people pour new wine into old wineskins, else the skins burst, the wine is spilt, and the skins are ruined. But they put new wine into fresh skins, and both are saved."
> —St. Matthew 9:15-17

The old garment and old wine skins represent the errant Pharasetic belief in a system of salvation through keeping the Law and performing rituals. The new cloth and the new wine represent the free gift of salvation. Jesus explained that you pick one or the other. The two cannot be mixed. If the new wine is placed into old skins, it will rupture the skins and both the skins and the wine will be lost. The Holy Spirit (new wine) cannot enter into one who holds to the Law and rituals for salvation. He (the old skin) would rupture, split. On the other hand, if the new wine (Holy Spirit) is placed into new skins (those who have been reborn, new creations in Christ), both will be saved.

Additional "Church traditions" that came long after 397 A.D. and compilation of the New Testament as a single work include:

- Worship of Mary (431)
- Introduction of purgatory (593)
- Prayers directed to Mary (600)
- Worship of images and relics (786)
- Use of holy water (850)
- Canonization of dead saints (993)
- Fasting during the season of Lent (998)
- Celibacy for the priesthood (1079)
- Use of prayer beads (1090)
- Seven sacraments suggested by Peter Lombard, bishop of Paris (circa 1150)
- Sale of Indulgences (1190)
- Transubstantiation defined by Pope Innocent III (1215)

- Confession of sins to a priest instituted by Pope Innocent III (1215)
- Bible added to Index of Forbidden Books (1229)
- Cup forbidden to laity at communion by Council of Constance (1414)
- Doctrine of seven sacraments affirmed (1439)
- Doctrine of purgatory (1439)
- Scripture to be interpreted only within context of Catholic tradition (1545)
- Apocryphal books declared to be inspired (1545)
- Immaculate conception of Mary revealed by Pope Pius IX (1854)
- Doctrine of infallibility of pope by Vatican Council (1870)
- Bodily assumption of Mary into heaven revealed by Pope Pius XII (1950)
- Mary proclaimed the Mother of the Church by Pope Paul VI (1965)

Now you can answer the question, "Which came first, Church traditions or the writings of the New Testament?" The first six traditions were introduced into some of the early churches by pagan converts. In the pre-Constantine era, that is prior to 315 A.D., the churches were autonomous. The injection of paganism accelerated under Constantine and was widespread in his universal Church. By the end of the 4th century, the Church Constantine had established was thoroughly Romanized. Prior to Constantine's Edict of Toleration early in the 4th century, Rome was thoroughly paganized. The Roman Catholic Church incorporated many of these pagan practices into its doctrines beginning in the middle of the 5th century when the term "catholic" was first applied to what had grown out of Constantine's universal Church. As discussed in chapter one, St. Vincent of Lérins defined "catholic" as "that which has been believed everywhere, always, and by all." As can be understood by examining the above list of continually evolving Catholic traditions, a strong argument could be made that the Roman Catholic Church is still not catholic because what the Church teaches is still evolving and could therefore not have been believed with regard to "... always, and by all"! Those who died as late as 450 A.D. did not know about the twenty-two traditions adopted by the Church after that year. St. Vincent certainly never believed in papal infallibility (1870) or Mary's bodily assumption into heaven (1950) or that she was the Mother of the Church (1965). Moreover, a segment of the Roman Catholic Church departed (schism) in 1871 shortly after papal infallibility was adopted by the First Vatican Council in 1870. These "latter-day protestants" wanted the "Old" Catholic Church they believed in preserved. Thus, it is clear that papal infallibility was not a doctrine earlier than 1870, or they would have bolted earlier. This sect of Catholicism calls itself Old Catholics because they accept all Church teachings up to papal infallibility, which they deny. Thus, the traditions of men must be rejected:

> See to it that no one deceives you by philosophy and vain deceit, according to human traditions, according to the elements of the world and not according to Christ.
>
> —Colossians 2:8

Jesus said:

> "Heaven and earth will pass away, but my words will not pass away."
>
> —St. Luke 21:33

(3) Its Name—Church or Churches

The meaning of church, *ekklesia*, a called out assembly of believers for God's special purposes, was discussed in the Introduction.

> "I, Jesus, have sent my angel to testify to you these things concerning the churches...."
>
> —Apocalypse 22:16

(4) Its Polity (form of organization)—Congregational

All members are equal. There is no hierarchy [St. Matthew 20:24-28; 23:5-12]. There was no distinction in the early churches between clergy and laity, not in dress or manner. This differed from the pagan religions where the priests wore vestments and headdresses to distinguish themselves from the laity. There was no special class of members who alone, metaphorically speaking, could enter into the Holy of Holies. All believers were priests in that all were able, again speaking metaphorically, to enter into the Holy of Holies to make sacrifices [Apocalypse 1:6].

(5) Its Members—Only the Saved

Visitors are welcome to come and hear the gospel of Christ Jesus and have their lives and eternal destinies changed. However, in order to be a *member* and participate in the Lord's Supper, one *must* be saved. Salvation precedes church membership and is a requirement for same.

> ... you are now... members of God's household: you are built upon the foundation of the apostles and prophets with Christ Jesus himself as the chief corner stone. In him the whole structure is closely fitted together and grows into a temple holy in the Lord.
>
> —Ephesians 2:19-21

> Be you yourselves as living stones, built thereon into a spiritual house, a holy priesthood, to offer spiritual sacrifices acceptable to God through Jesus Christ.
>
> —1 St. Peter 2:5

Jesus' sacrifice opened up the Holy of Holies to all believers. Thus, all believers are now priests in the sense that each can approach God directly. Through Jesus' atoning death on the cross, believers can now make their bodies a *living* sacrifice acceptable to God. How? St. Paul gives us the answer:

> I exhort you therefore, brethren, by the mercy of God, to present your bodies as a sacrifice, living, holy, pleasing to God-your spiritual service. And be not conformed to this world, but be transformed in the newness of your mind (*as a result of your spiritual rebirth*), that you may discern what is the good and acceptable and perfect (*complete*) will of God.
>
> —Romans 12:1-2

The believer is to reflect God's glory by walking in a different manner from those walking in an evil world. Those walking in the world seek constantly to satisfy the needs of the flesh. Many of the things they do are sin. The believer, on the other hand, is a temple of the Holy Spirit. Just as God has sanctified the believer's soul, that is, set it apart for a special purpose, so the believer should sanctify his flesh. This can be accomplished only by the indwelling power of the Holy Spirit [see Ephesians 6:10]. If we sacrifice the things of the flesh, we can better discern God's will for us, accept it, and understand that it is a better will than we have for ourselves. However, the Scriptures do not teach that such sacrifice contributes to the believer's salvation.

(6) Its Ordinances—Believer's Baptism and the Lord's Supper

In accordance with Scriptures, members *do not* confess one baptism "for the forgiveness of sins" in a New Testament church. Baptism removes

no sins, not even one. It is only the precious blood of Jesus that washes
away sin.

> "Go, therefore, and make disciples of all nations, baptizing them in the
> name of the Father, and of the Son, and of the Holy Spirit, teaching them
> to observe all that I have commanded you...."
> —St. Matthew 28:19-20

> "... This cup is the new covenant in my blood; do this as often as you drink
> it in remembrance of me. For as often as you shall eat this bread and drink
> the cup, you proclaim the death of the Lord, until he comes."
> —1 Corinthians 11:25-26

Neither is a New Testament church a legislating church. Jesus addressed
those who legislate new rules:

> The scribes and the Pharisees sit in Moses' seat (*they have stolen his
> authority*). Therefore whatever they tell you to observe, that observe and
> do, but do not do according to their works; for they say, and do not do. For
> they bind heavy burdens, hard to bear, and lay them on men's shoulders
> (*new laws*); but they themselves will not move them with one of their
> fingers. But all of their works they do to be seen by men. They... enlarge
> the borders (*hems*) of their garments.
> —St. Matthew 23:1-5 NKJV

Jesus accused the Pharisees of usurping Moses' authority as the
transmitter of the Law. He indicted them further for saying one thing but
doing another. They created precept upon precept (new law upon new
law), bound them together, and placed these burdensome requirements
upon men's shoulders. Jesus had invited the people to:

> "Take my yoke upon you, and learn from me, for I am meek and humble
> of heart; and you will find rest for your souls. For my yoke is easy, and
> my burden light."
> —St. Matthew 11:29-30

Thus, Jesus drew a clear distinction between the burden the Pharisees
placed upon a man and the light burden He exerted. On the hems (borders)
of the garments worn by the Pharisees was a little loop for every precept.
As they made up more and more laws, the hems of their garments had to
be enlarged to accommodate the additional loops. Jesus' reference to their
apparel was actually a reference to their wicked desire to usurp God's
authority by making new Laws.

(7) Its Officers—Pastors (also Called Bishops) and Deacons

This saying is true: If anyone is eager for the office of bishop, he desires a good work. A bishop then, must be blameless, married but once (*to only one woman*), reserved, prudent, of good conduct, hospitable, a teacher, not a drinker or a brawler, but moderate, not quarrelsome, not avaricious. He should rule well his own household, keeping his children under control and perfectly respectable. For if a man cannot rule his own household, how is he to take care of the church of God? He must not be a new convert, lest he be puffed up with pride and incur the condemnation passed on the devil. Besides this he must have a good reputation with those who are outside (*nonbelievers*), that he may not fall into disgrace and into a snare of the devil. Deacons also must be honorable, not double-tongued, not given to much wine, not greedy for base gain, but holding the mystery of faith in pure conscience. And let them first be tried, and if found without reproach let them be allowed to serve. In like manner let the women (*their wives*) be honorable, not slanderers, but reserved, faithful in all things. Deacons should be men who have been married but once, ruling well their children and their own households. And those who have fulfilled well this office will acquire a good position and great confidence in the faith that is in Christ Jesus.

—1 Timothy 3:1-13

While women have important roles to play in their churches, God has chosen to limit the role of pastor, that is, head servant of the church and shepherd of the flock, to certain men, but certainly not to just any men as the above citation makes clear. The role of deacon is also limited to men. Older women are to teach younger women [see Titus 2:3-5]. Women may teach other women and children. They are also usually intimately involved in the day-to-day running of the church.

A woman may instruct a man in business, math, or rocket science. However, God's Word teaches that women are not to have spiritual authority over men. Thus, God's Word does not allow for women pastors who are over the whole flock, men and women [see 1 Timothy 2:12]. By the same Word, a pastor cannot counsel women on certain matters, as made clear in Titus 2:3-5. This is not an issue of equality, intelligence, or capabilities but of divine order. A divine order is seen in the roles of the Father, the Son, and the Holy Spirit. One gender is not inferior to the other, just as one person in the Trinity is not inferior to the other two. However, in the spiritual realm, men and women have different roles, as revealed in God's Holy Word. However, the most important responsibility a believer has is shared equally by men and women, namely, to spread the gospel to a lost world. Women can certainly serve as missionaries and can lead men, as well as women, to Christ. It should be understood that this divine ordinance in no way sanctions unfairness in business practices. Moreover, godly men should support the idea of equal pay for equal work, equal opportunities for women, and a harassment-free work environment.

The above citation on pastors and deacons from 1 Timothy contains some of the clearest truths about churches and the ministry. Verse 5 states, "For if a man cannot rule his own household, how is he to take care of the church of God?" Obviously the "church" referred to in this verse cannot be the Church, the Roman Catholic Church, the Greek Orthodox Church, the Russian Orthodox Church, the Anglican Church, or any other universal Church! In fact, this is an excellent example of the Greek *ekklesia*.

(8) Its Work—Feed the Flock and Spread the Gospel

The work of the church includes bringing people to Christ through the preaching of the gospel, baptizing them, and teaching them so they can become witnesses for Christ. The New Testament church is quick, that is, alive. It is not a stagnant organization but a living, growing organism. It is active in seeking conversions of unbelievers, rather than dead through repeated rituals.

> "All power in heaven and on earth has been given to me. Go, therefore, and make disciples of all nations, baptizing them in the name of the Father, and of the Son, and of the Holy Spirit, teaching them to observe all that I have commanded you; and behold, I am with you all days, even unto the consummation of the world."
>
> —St. Matthew 28:16-20

St. Paul exhorts believers:

> I charge thee, in the sight of God and Christ Jesus, who will judge the living and the dead by his coming and by his kingdom, preach the word, be urgent in season, (and) out of season; reprove (*be a living example to others*); entreat (*plead*); rebuke (*correct*) with all *patience* and teaching.
>
> —2 Timothy 4:1-2

The word *patience* cannot be stressed enough. A believer can get frustrated with someone when he or she continues to reject the truth of the gospel time after time after time. Sometimes it is hard to remember that he has been blinded by the god of this world and it's not that he is stubborn. He really just can't see the truth [see 2 Corinthians 4:3-4].

It is important for believers to attend a Bible-believing, Bible-teaching church. St. Paul warns:

> ... there will come a time when they will not endure sound doctrine; but having itching ears, will heap up to themselves (*draw close to*) teachers according to their own lusts, and they will turn away their own hearing from the truth and turn aside rather to fables.
>
> —2 Timothy 4:3-4

God speaks to His children through His Word. Unfortunately, some preachers don't. The above citation prophesies a time when people will reject the truth and turn to preachers who preach fables. Therefore, the believer is commanded to be on guard and to compare the veracity of what the preacher teaches with the Word of God [Acts 17:11]. When one attends a New Testament church, God's Word is not only read, but verses are corroborated and explanations given. The Word of God comes to life. God's Word is taught in Sunday school, in the Sunday morning and evening services, and in the weeknight service. It is reinforced through periodic revival services. New Testament church services include no rituals.

(9) Its Financial Plan—Tithes and Offerings

> "Bring all the tithes into the storehouse that there may be meat in my house, and *try me in this*," saith the LORD: "if I open not unto you the flood-gates of heaven, and pour you out a blessing even to abundance."
>
> —Malachias 3:10

God is speaking in the above citation. While Deuteronomy 6:16 tells us: "You shall not put the LORD, your God, to the test," God makes an exception in Malachias and tells us to do just that, to put Him to the test! The New Testament teaches that in whatever manner we sow, so shall we reap. St. Luke assures believers:

> ... give and it shall be given to you; good measure, pressed down, shaken together, running over, shall they pour into your lap....
>
> —St. Luke 6:38

In Jesus' day, women carried groceries home from market using their aprons. Aprons had hand loops similar to what we see attached to cameras and other articles today. The woman would take hold of the hand loops, which were located a bit below hip level, and pull up. Then she would sit down. This created a type of basket or pouch in her lap. After her lap had been filled, she would continue to grasp the loops, stand up, and journey home with her purchases.

God's Word tells us that those who preach the gospel should earn their living from doing same.

> So also the Lord directed that those who preach the gospel should have their living from the gospel.
>
> —1 Corinthians 9:14

(10) Its Weapons of Warfare—Spiritual, Not Carnal

The greatest weapon the believer has is prayer. Sometimes a nonbeliever will say, "Well, the least I can do is say a prayer for him." No, that's actually the most powerful thing a believer can do for himself or anyone else. No less than St. James, Jesus' brother [see chapter five], tells us:

> Confess your trespasses to one another, and pray for one another, that you may be healed. The effective, fervent prayer of a righteous man avails much.
>
> —St. James 5:16 NKJV

Entire books have been written on prayer. The word is used over 150 times in the Old Testament and more than 160 times in the New. The word pray means to "ask." It is different from praising or adoring God. It is different from meditating on the Scriptures, confessing sins, humbling oneself, and giving thanks. The Koran tells the faithful to pray five times a day. St. Paul tells us to "… pray at all times…" in Ephesians 6:18 and to "Pray without ceasing…" in 1 Thessalonians 5:16.

Sometimes people's prayers are not answered. St. James tells us "… you do not have because you do not ask. You ask and do not receive, because you ask amiss, that you may spend it upon your passions" [St. James 4:2-3]. Many believers simply do not ask. They mistakenly believe God is too busy keeping the planets in their orbits to listen to their little requests. Others ask for things they shouldn't. The Scriptures tell us also that our prayers should be in accordance with the will of God. If it's OK to have it, then it's OK to pray for it.

Jesus tells us how to pray. We should not pray to be seen by men. Rather, we should go behind closed doors. This should not be misinterpreted to mean that believers should not pray as a body, a church, an *ekklesia*. It simply means do not pray to be seen by men, lest their admiration is your reward. He also tells us not to use repetitious prayers, multiplying our words, because this is the way of the heathen [see St. Matthew 6:57].

To most of us there is nothing more annoying than being asked the same favor over and over and over again. It's not just a cliché. Children really do ask, "Can I? Huh? Please? Can I please? Pretty please?" Sooner or later, more often sooner than later, parents give in and give out and say in frustration, "Yes! A thousand times yes! Just quit asking." Do you think God likes our constant asking, particularly for the same thing, over and over and over again, any more than we like to hear it from our kids? That's *exactly* what God wants His children to do! Ask and ask and ask again. God wants His children to be dependent on Him and He wants to pour out blessings on them. After instructing His disciples how to pray, Jesus gave them and us an example:

> And he said to them, "Which of you shall have a friend and shall go to him in the middle of the night and say to him, 'Friend, lend me three loaves, for a friend of mine has just come to me from a journey, and I have nothing to set before him'; and he from within should answer and say, 'Do not disturb me; the door is now shut, and my children and I are in bed; I cannot get up and give to thee'? I say to you, although he will not get up and give to him because he is his friend, yet *because of his persistence* he will get up and give him all he needs. And I say to you, "ask, and it shall be given to you; seek, and you shall find; knock, and it shall be opened to you."
>
> —St. Luke 11:5-9

In this analogy, the one already in bed is God. The one asking for bread is not asking for it to satisfy *his* passions, *his* flesh. Rather, he is asking for bread to feed his friend, who has come unexpectedly. This example fits exactly with what the Scriptures teach concerning prayer. If one is praying for a new car so he can continue to get to work and earn a living to support his family, he is not praying selfishly. On the other hand, someone who prays for a new car so his friends will be envious is praying selfishly. His request is for something he can spend on his passions [see St. James 4:2-3 above].

As was made clear in chapter five, Jesus never told His followers to take up the sword. Yet, many who refer to themselves as "The Church" did exactly that. Jesus condemned such actions. When they were in the garden and St. Peter drew his sword and cut off the ear of the servant of the high priest, Jesus rebuked him:

> "Put back thy sword into its place; for all those who take the sword will perish by the sword."
>
> —St. Matthew 26:52

Our battle is in the spiritual realm, not the earthly. Jesus went on to tell St. Peter:

> "'... dost thou suppose that I cannot entreat my Father, and he will even now furnish me with more than twelve legions of angels?'"
> —St. Matthew 26:53

In the above citation, Jesus makes the point that it is not a matter of muscle, or manpower. While we do not know how many sinners came to Gethsemane to take Jesus away that night, we do know that a Roman legion consisted of 6,000 fighting men. Thus, Jesus told St. Peter that He could call more than 72,000 angels to protect Him. Sheer numbers do not determine the outcome in a spiritual battle. It is recorded in Isaias 37:36 that a single angel killed 185,000 Assyrian soldiers in one night!

On a previous occasion, Jesus and His disciples had been traveling to Jerusalem. A messenger had been sent ahead to secure a place for a night's lodging in a Samaritan village. The Samaritans hated the Jews, and the Jews reciprocated. Assyrian and Babylonian armies used the area of Samaria as a re-colonizing territory for conquered peoples. Foreigners had entered into mixed marriages with the local Jewish denizens. Therefore, Samaria had a religion consisting of Judaism mixed with paganism. The Samaritans tolerated Jews passing through if they were spending money, but only if they were headed *away from* Jerusalem. When the lodge keeper learned that the group was traveling to Jerusalem, he informed the messenger that there was no lodging available. When word came back to Jesus, James and John, the "sons of thunder," as He had nicknamed them, asked if He would like them to call down fire from heaven to destroy the city. Jesus replied:

> "You do not know of what manner of spirit you are; for the Son of Man did not come to destroy men's lives, but to save them." And they went to another village.
> —St. Luke 9:56

When the people rejected Jesus, He did not retaliate. Neither did He allow His disciples to do so. Moreover, it is revealed that:

> ... our wrestling is not against flesh and blood, but against the Principalities and the Powers, against the world rulers of this darkness, against the spiritual forces of wickedness on high.
> —Ephesians 6:12

If our fight is not with flesh and blood, then the sword is of no avail:

> For though we walk in (*but not according to*) the flesh, we do not make war according to the flesh; for the weapons of our warfare are not carnal, but powerful before God to the demolishing of strongholds....
> —2 Corinthians 10:3-4

Clearly, those state Churches that tortured unbelievers and put them to the sword or stake were not carrying out *God's* will. Pope John Paul II apologized to the Jews from the Vatican on March 12, 2000 for violence and other sins committed against them over the ages by the Roman Catholic Church. Thus, contrary to earlier Church claims, the Holy Spirit could not have been leading the Roman Catholic Church to convert Jews under pain of death. This brings us to the last characteristic of a New Testament church.

(11) Its Independence—Separation of Church and State

As was discussed in chapter five, a number of Churches in various countries rose to prominence after the Protestant Reformation to become state Churches. After arriving at such powerful positions, each one, without exception, began to persecute non-state churches, as well as individuals who would not join "The Church." Among the first waves of persecutions were economic sanctions. These were followed by physical persecutions and, in many instances, death. Do you think this is what God wanted? If He wanted it then, He must want it now also, because He tells us, "For I am the Lord and I change not..." [Malachias 3:6]. Do you think this is what Jesus went to the cross to achieve? I can only hope that you don't. Remember, to be a Christian is to be a "little Christ." That's what the word Christian means. Can you picture Jesus telling His disciples to preach the gospel to all creatures and to torture and kill those who refuse to believe? I don't think so. Jesus wouldn't even let James and John call down fire to destroy the inhabitants of a single city. Jesus told His disciples: "And whoever does not receive you—go forth from that town, and shake off even the dust from your feet for a witness against them" [St. Luke 9:5]. He never directed them to put anyone to the sword!

Some will point out what they believe to be analogous instances in the Old Testament where God told the Israelites to invade a country and kill all its inhabitants. And He certainly did tell them to do exactly that. However, the problem with this analogy is that it is inappropriate. God never told the Israelites to go into a country and *convert* the inhabitants and, if they refused, kill them. But this is exactly what many of the Churches did! "Believe or die in the name of Jesus," was their cry.

The Old Testament reveals that in choosing a people for His own, the Jews, God's purpose was to pour out blessings on an obedient Israel so that the surrounding heathen nations would notice the God of the Israelites blessing them for their obedience and would want those same blessings for themselves and be drawn to the God of Israel [see Deuteronomy 28:7-14]. This is the appropriate analogy. The believer is to draw the unbeliever to Jesus by the way the unbeliever sees the believer living his life and being blessed by God. The unbelieving neighbor is to look across the fence to the believer and see something the believer has that he would like to have also. It might be the believer's joy, or his certainty of salvation. However, if the unbeliever does not respond, the believer is not scripturally authorized to jump the fence and beat the blue blazes out of his neighbor until he converts. This is the way state-run Churches were gaining "converts"—through intimidation and physical violence.

How to Locate A New Testament Church

New Testament churches are located throughout the U.S. A partial listing of New Testament churches can be found on the Internet at: www.BBFI.Org. A complete listing is maintained by Baptist Bible Fellowship International, P.O. Box 191, Springfield, Missouri, 65801-0191. The organization may be contacted at (417) 862-5001. If you are in doubt about what a church teaches, ask the pastor three questions. Do you baptize infants? Can one lose his salvation? Has the Church replaced Israel? If the answer to any of these is "yes," then it is not a New Testament church.

My prayer is that God will continue to bless you and keep you near to His heart. I'll see you "When the Roll Is Called Up Yonder." If we haven't met already, come over and introduce yourself. I'd love to get to know you.

NOTES

Introduction

1. *Catholicism & Reason, Creed and Apologetics*, Rev. E. Hayes, et.al., C.R. Publications, Norwood, Massachusetts, 1996, p. 141.
2. *Catechism of the Catholic Church*, Libreria Editrice Vaticana, Liguori Publications, 1994, paras.105 and 107.
3. "Old Catholics," *Microsoft® Encarta® 97 Encyclopedia.* © 1993-1996 Microsoft Corporation. All rights reserved.
4. All biblical quotes are from the "Holy Bible," Imprimatur, Rt. Rev. MSGR. Francis W. Byrne, Vicar General, Archdiocese of Chicago, May 6, 1969, 1969 edition (Douay-Challoner text), Catholic Bible Publishers, Chicago, Illinois, unless indicated otherwise. Words in italics enclosed within parenthesis within quotes are not part of the Bible text but are added for clarity. Words in italics not in parenthesis are for emphasis. In a relatively few instances, the King James Version (KJV) of the Holy Bible is cited because in those instances it is clearer in its translation than the Catholic Bible. Such citations are clearly identified as such by the letters KJV. In some instances, the New King James Version is cited for clarity, NKJV.

Chapter One

1. *The Bible, Embracing God's Truth*, M. Anders, Thomas Nelson Publishers, Nashville, Tennessee, 1995, p. 39.
2. "Catholic Church" and "Vincent of Lérins, Saint," *Microsoft® Encarta® 97 Encyclopedia.* © 1993-1996 Microsoft Corporation. All rights reserved.

3. *Catholicism & Reason, Creed and Apologetics*, Rev. E. Hayes, et.al., C.R. Publications, Norwood, Massachusetts, 1996, p. 141.
4. Rev. E. Hayes, op. cit., p. 142.
5. *Christianity*, Roland H. Bainton, Houghton Mifflin Company, Boston, Massachusetts, 1964, p. 277.
6. *Vicars of Christ, The Dark Side of the Papacy*, Peter De Rosa, Crown Publishers, Inc., New York, New York, 1988, pp. 217-218.
7. *Protestants & Catholics, Do They Now Agree?* J. Ankerberg, Harvest House Publishers, Eugene, Oregon, 1995, pp. 259-260.
8. Peter De Rosa, op., cit., p. 219.
9. R. H. Bainton, op. cit., p. 296.
10. *Holman Bible Dictionary*, Holman Bible Publications, Nashville, Tennessee, 1991, p. 185.
11. *A History of the Jews*, P. Johnson, Harper & Row Publishers, New York, New York, 1987, p. 91.
12. *The Glorious Journey*, C. Stanley, Thomas Nelson Publishers, Nashville, Tennessee, 1996, p. 158.
13. *Catechism of the Catholic Church*, Libreria Editrice Vaticana, Liguori Publications, 1994, paragraph 846.

Chapter Two

1. *The Handwriting of God*, G. Jeffrey, Frontier Research Publications, Inc., Toronto, Ontario, 1997, p. 254.
2. *Catholicism & Reason, Creed and Apologetics*, Rev. E. Hayes, et.al., C.R. Publications, Norwood, Massachusetts, 1996, p. 147
3. *Invasion of Other Gods*, D. Jeremiah, Word Publishing, Dallas, Texas, 1995, p. 108.
4. *Fast Facts on False Teachings*, R. Carlson et. al., Harvest House Publishers, Eugene, Oregon, 1994, p. 136.
5. *UFOs and the Alien Agenda*, Bob Larson, Thomas Nelson Publishers, Nashville, Tennessee, 1997, pp. 1-11.
6. *Fourteen Things Witches Hope Parents Never Find Out*, D. Benoit, Hearthstone Publishing, Ltd., Oklahoma City, Oklahoma, 1994, p. 22.
7. R. Carlson, op. cit., p. 138.
8. *Embraced by the Darkness*, B. Scott, Crossway Books, Wheaton, Illinois, 1996, p. 15.
9. D. Jeremiah, op. cit., p. 68.
10. D. Jeremiah, op. cit., p. 107.

Chapter Four

1. Christianity, Roland H. Bainton, Houghton Mifflin Company, Boston, Massachusetts, 1964, p. 61.

Chapter Five

1. "Constantine the Great," *Microsoft(R) 97 Encyclopedia.* (c) 1993-1996 Microsoft Corporation.
2. *Catholicism & Life, Commandments and Sacraments*, Rev. E. Hayes, et.al., C.R. Publications, Norwood, Massachusetts, 1996, p. 54.
3. *Holy Bible, Catholic Doctrinal Guide*, Imprimatur, Rt. Rev. MSGR. Francis W. Byrne, Vicar General, Archdiocese of Chicago, May 6, 1969, 1969 edition, Catholic Bible Publishers, Chicago, Illinois.
4. *Vicars of Christ, The Dark Side of the Papacy*, Peter De Rosa, Crown Publishers, Inc., New York, New York, 1988, p. 405.
5. "Canonization," *Microsoft® Encarta® 97 Encyclopedia.* © 1993-1996 Microsoft Corporation. All rights reserved.
6. Rev. E. Hayes, op. cit., p. 55.
7. "Rosary," *Microsoft® Encarta® 97 Encyclopedia.* © 1993-1996 Microsoft Corporation. All rights reserved.
8. *The Gates of Hell Shall Not Prevail*, D. J. Kennedy, Thomas Nelson Publishers, Nashville, Tennessee, 1996, p. 171.
9. *Revelation*, T. LaHaye, Zondervan Publishing House, Grand Rapids, Michigan, 1975, p. 30.
10. *The Secret of the Rosary*, St. Louis De Montfort, Montfort Publications, Bay Shore, NY, Imprimatur, Thomas Malloy, S.T.D., Brooklyn, 1954, pp. 78-79
11. "Constantine," The Encyclopedia Americana, International Edition, Volume 7, Grolier Incorporated, Danbury, Connecticut, 1996, p. 648.
12. Ibid., p. 649.
13. *The Trail of Blood*, J. M. Carroll, Ashland Avenue Baptist Church, Lexington, Kentucky, 1995, p 14.
14. Ibid., p. 18.
15. *A Woman Rides the Beast*, D. Hunt, Harvest House Publishers, Eugene, Oregon, 1994, p. 262
16. Peter De Rosa, op., cit., p. 207.
17. J. M. Carroll, op., cit., p. 3.
18. *The Story of Civilization, Part III* W. Durant, Simon&Shuster, New York, New York, 1950, p. 656.
19. D. Hunt, op., cit., p. 46.

20. "Gratian (359-383)," *Microsoft® Encarta® 97 Encyclopedia.* © 1993-1996 Microsoft Corporation. All rights reserved.

21. St. Matthew 22:21; Romans 12:2; and Apocalypse 18:4.

22. D. Hunt, op. cit., p. 158.

23. "Tammuz," *Microsoft® Encarta® 97 Encyclopedia.* © 1993-1996 Microsoft Corporation. All rights reserved.

24. "Ishtar," *Microsoft® Encarta® 97 Encyclopedia.* © 1993-1996 Microsoft Corporation. All rights reserved.

25. *Christianity*, Roland H. Bainton, Houghton Mifflin Company, Boston, Massachusetts, 1964, p. 76.

26. T. LaHaye, op. cit., pp. 37 and 231

27. Peter De Rosa, op., cit., p. 38.

28. H. Bainton, op. cit., pp. 76-77.

29. Ibid., pp. 104-106.

30. Peter De Rosa, op., cit., p. 401.

31. D. Hunt, op. cit., p. 184.

32. Ibid., p. 479.

33. Peter De Rosa, op., cit., p. 101.

34. H. Bainton, op. cit., p. 190.

35. "Schism, Great," *Microsoft® Encarta® 97 Encyclopedia.* © 1993-1996 Microsoft Corporation. All rights reserved.

36. Peter De Rosa, op., cit., pp. 89-93.

37. H. Bainton, op. cit., p. 233.

38. Ibid., pp. 241-242.

39. Peter De Rosa, op., cit., p. 113 (Benedict IX), and 51-52 (John XII).

40. Ibid., p. 122.

41. "Trent, Council of," *Microsoft® Encarta® 97 Encyclopedia.* © 1993-1996 Microsoft Corporation. All rights reserved.

42. *Way of Life Encyclopedia of the Bible & Christianity*, D. W. Cloud, Way of Life Literature, Oak Harbor, Washington, 1997, p. 401.

43. Peter De Rosa, op., cit., pp. 374-376.

44. Rev. E. Hayes, op. cit., p. 139.

45. *The Catholic Church and the Bible*, Rev. P. Stravinskas, Ignatius Press, San Francisco, California, 1987, pp. 107-108.

46. Ibid., p. 13.

47. D. W. Cloud, op., cit., pp. 523-524.

48. Peter De Rosa, op., cit., p., 24.

49. D. W. Cloud, op., cit., p. 399

50. «Vatican Council, First,» *Microsoft® Encarta® 97 Encyclopedia.* © 1993-1996 Microsoft Corporation. All rights reserved.

51. P. Stravinskas, op., cit., p. 121.

52. *Protestants & Catholics, Do They Now Agree?* J. Ankerberg, Harvest House Publishers, Eugene, Oregon, 1995, p. 246.
53. *Catechism of the Catholic Church*, Libreria Editrice Vaticana, Liguori Publications, 1994, paragraphs. 846 and 847.
54. P. Stravinskas, op., cit., p. 117.
55. *Catechism of the Catholic Church*, Libreria Editrice Vaticana, Liguori Publications, 1994, paragraph 964.

Chapter Six

1. "San Fernando (Philippines)," *Microsoft® Encarta® 97 Encyclopedia.* © 1993-1996 Microsoft Corporation. All rights reserved.
2. "Stigmata," *Microsoft® Encarta® 97 Encyclopedia.* © 1993-1996 Microsoft Corporation. All rights reserved.
3. "Francis of Assisi, Saint," *Microsoft® Encarta® 97 Encyclopedia.* © 1993-1996 Microsoft Corporation. All rights reserved.
4. *The Catholic Church and the Bible*, Rev. P. Stravinskas, Ignatius Press, San Francisco, California, 1987, p. 129.
5. *Way of Life Encyclopedia of the Bible & Christianity*, D. W. Cloud, Way of Life Literature, Oak Harbor, Washington, 1997, p. 107.

Appendix A

1. *USA Today*, July 27, 2000, "Rapper's hate-filled lyrics anger some, while others say it's just a clever act," p. 1 D.
2. *Who's Watching the Playpen?* David Benoit, Hearthstone Publishing, Ltd., Oklahoma City, Oklahoma, 1995, p. 141.
3. "Cross," *Microsoft® Encarta® 97 Encyclopedia.* © 1993-1996 Microsoft Corporation. All rights reserved.
4. *Final Dawn Over Jerusalem*, Rev. J. C. Hagee, Thomas Nelson Publishers, Nashville, Tennessee, 1998, pp. 34-38.
5. *Time*, July 3, 2000, p. 48.
6. *The Trail of Blood*, J. M. Carroll, Ashland Avenue Baptist Church, Lexington, Kentucky, 1995, 'Marks of the New Testament Church,' pp. 4-5.

Printed in the United States
106183LV00002B/94-330/P